Back to the Land

Back to the Land

The Enduring Dream
of Self-Sufficiency
in Modern America

Dona Brown

THE UNIVERSITY OF WISCONSIN PRESS

The University of Wisconsin Press
1930 Monroe Street, 3rd Floor
Madison, Wisconsin 53711-2059
uwpress.wisc.edu

3 Henrietta Street
London WC2E 8LU, England
eurospanbookstore.com

Printed in the United States of America

Library of Congress Cataloging-in-Publication Data
Brown, Dona.
Back to the land: the enduring dream of self-sufficiency
in modern America / Dona Brown.
p.   cm. — (Studies in American thought and culture)
Includes bibliographical references and index.
ISBN 978-0-299-25074-4 (pbk.: alk. paper)
ISBN 978-0-299-25073-7 (e-book)
1. Urban-rural migration — United States — History.
2. Self-reliant living — United States — History.
I. Title.   II. Series: Studies in American thought and culture.
HT381.B76   2011
307.2´60973 — dc22
2010038899

Contents

Illustrations

Acknowledgments

For me this book has been a venture into unknown historical terrain, so I have incurred even more scholarly obligations than usual. At a New England American Studies Association conference back in 2001, just as I was getting started, David Watters offered a number of useful suggestions. At the Agricultural History Society's 2008 conference, Katherine Jellison, Sally McMurry, and Jane Pederson were especially kind and helpful to a newcomer to the field of agricultural history. Alan Lessoff gave me much-needed encouragement at a key moment. My colleagues at the Center for Research on Vermont provided enthusiastic interest combined with solid advice and astute criticism. At a symposium celebrating their twentieth anniversary, the University of Southern Maine's American and New England Studies Program made the perfect audience: sympathetic, skeptical, extremely well informed. Robert Gross worked his usual magic, responding to my few idle remarks during a New Year's Eve dinner with comments that were so insightful and stimulating that they reshaped whole lines of argument.

Many librarians and archivists have assisted me; some of them, in these hyperconnected days, I have never met. My thanks go to Marlene Hitt at the Bolton Hall Museum in Tujunga; Robert G. Marshall at the Urban Archives Center at California State University, Northridge; Anne Prichard at the University of Arkansas Special Collections; Julia Cagle and Jane Kanealy at the San Diego Historical Society; Tevis Kimball at the Jones Library in Amherst, Massachusetts; and the staff at the New York Public Library's Manuscripts and Archives Division. At my own institution, Peggy Powell and Sylvia Bugbee helped me to negotiate the far-away collections of the Annex; working with Prudence Doherty and Chris Burns in Special Collections was an education in itself.

My colleagues in the history department at the University of Vermont have been unfailingly supportive, through good times and bad. No one could wish for a better scholarly home. In particular, I thank Amani Whitfield for taking the time to read an early draft and for his perceptive comments, and Melanie Gustafson for her generous attention to my project. Both made important contributions to the conceptualization of this book. At the University of Wisconsin Press, Paul Boyer listened to my ideas and heard something promising in my vague remarks. Gwen Walker made a number of thoughtful and imaginative suggestions. Both have been exemplary editors. Jeffrey Jacob was a most generous and helpful manuscript reader, and copy editor MJ Devaney went beyond the standards even of her exacting profession.

There are several people I had always in mind as I wrote this book. Every day, I see more clearly how fortunate I have been in my family. My father was my first teacher. There was never a book he thought was too hard for me to understand; no aspiration seemed too high for me in his eyes. My mother taught me that good work well done is one of the greatest pleasures in life. Her clear-eyed intelligence and thirst for knowledge set such a high standard that until the last days of her life I had to work hard to keep up with her. Somewhere along the way, my brother David grew from the stubborn, reckless kid I remember from childhood into a man of great patience, kindness, and courage. These past few years have been difficult ones for our family, but without his strength to lean on they would have been much harder.

Sarah Darling was my reality check throughout the writing of this book. I counted on her memories of the days when we first read back-to-the-land books, and more than that, I counted on her moral compass. She always brought my attention back to the questions that matter most. My dear companion Steve Nissenbaum was so much a part of it all that I do not know how to thank him. He sacrificed his own projects; took over too many of my obligations, and sat through endless reports of every minor detail of each day's writing process. I owe this book in part to his scholarly imagination, keen eye, and relentless perfectionism. The rest I owe to his love and his confidence in me.

Back to the Land

Introduction

For many of us today, the phrase "going back to the land" brings to mind a vision of the 1960s and 1970s: of yurts and teepees and domes, of communes in New Mexico or Vermont. "Got to get back to the land, and set my soul free," proclaimed Joni Mitchell's Woodstock anthem. But although the eruption of creative energy that has come to be called simply "the sixties" looms large in collective memory, the back-to-the-landers of that era were just a small part of a much larger story. Americans have been dreaming of going back to the land for a hundred years or more. At the very moment when the population of the United States was turning decisively urban, some people were already beginning to calculate what they were losing. From that time on, the back-to-the-land impulse would be an enduring feature of American life, fading in and out of view, but never completely disappearing. At key historical moments, it would return in force. This book explores how some Americans at those key moments turned away from the promise of the city and looked back toward the land.

The story begins long before the Summer of Love. As early as the late nineteenth century, books with back-to-the-land themes were appearing sporadically; at the beginning of the twentieth, the trickle became a flood. The writers responsible for this outpouring came from a wide variety of ideological backgrounds: they were anarchists, socialists, and progressives; promoters of the arts and crafts, the "simple life," or the single tax. Yet they were responding to a common set of pressing social concerns. The immediate trigger was a series of financial crises: a panic in 1893 had brought on a severe depression that lasted years. A short period of recovery was interrupted by another panic in 1907. Bolton Hall, a key figure in this first back-to-the-land generation, spoke

3

for many back-to-the-land reformers when he urged city dwellers to find some way to protect themselves from these cyclical crashes, panics, and depressions. Only the "green earth," Hall wrote, could provide a "sure refuge from blue envelopes [we call them pink slips now], black Fridays, and red ruin."[1]

In the background of these recurring economic crises were other long-standing problems. Most visible, of course, were the mushrooming industrial cities and the social disequilibrium they generated: the slums, the labor struggles, the workshops filled with immigrants arriving daily from the most unfamiliar parts of Europe. Along with those Europeans, moreover, an unprecedented number of native-born rural Americans were flooding into the same cities, leaving the refuge of the "green earth" behind. They too were part of the problem. Often bringing with them the education and skills to command a white-collar job, these native-born migrants were mostly one step ahead of recent European arrivals. Nevertheless, they, too, were vulnerable to the boom-bust cycle.

Few leaders of the movement were so naïve as to believe that "going back to the land" would provide a definitive solution to the problems generated by the historic forces at work in industrial America. Most believed that real change would depend on a fundamental realignment of power: socialist revolution, perhaps, or the adoption of the single tax, or perhaps just tinkering with the existing structure by trust busting, securing the vote for women, and passing child labor laws. Bolton Hall, for one, predicted that things would get worse before they got better: "Day by day the cost of living advances[;] . . . week by week more wealth passes away from the wage-earners to the wage-getters; month by month monopoly of the necessities of life draws closer." Hall, a single-tax reformer, believed there could be no real public solution "short of the abolition of special privilege."[2] In the meantime, though, returning to the land might offer a private remedy. Back-to-the-land advocates called it "one way out."

Some reformers thought of it chiefly as a "way out" for the poorest city dwellers. They aimed to move working people, and especially recent immigrants, out of the crowded slums and onto self-supporting farms, to perform the kind of social engineering that would make "adequate farmers" out of "young city Hebrews" or "outcast Irish Roman Catholic street boys," as Lyman Beecher Stowe put it in the progressive *Outlook* magazine.[3] This wing of the back-to-the-land movement included both native-born progressives like Stowe and leaders of immigrant communities like Joseph Krauskopf, head of Philadelphia's most advanced Reform Jewish congregation. These reformers founded agricultural schools, arranged for the distribution of tiny garden plots on vacant city lots, and helped to organize large-scale colonies in remote areas.

More often, however, this first generation of back-to-the-land enthusiasts aimed their advocacy elsewhere: at that very large pool of recent migrants who had come not from Russian shtetls or Italian villages but from American hinterland towns. The writers who targeted this audience were influenced by their reading of Leo Tolstoy, Peter Kropotkin, and Henry George. Mostly, though, they shared a broad commitment to the homegrown, non-Marxist, radical tradition historians have termed "producerism."[4] They envisioned a return to the land as a means of preserving artisanal skill, personal autonomy, and household self-sufficiency in the face of a rising tide of mechanization, monopoly, and consumerism.

They targeted workers in the middle ranks for good reasons. In the early years of the twentieth century such workers were feeling the full impact of the rapid transformation of their shops and offices. Rural Americans who migrated to cities found work in settings that were changing as quickly as the factories and sweatshops that employed many European immigrants. Big businesses were squeezing out small-scale independent proprietors everywhere, opening up a host of low-wage white-collar positions just in time for the new arrivals to enter them. The evidence suggests that back-to-the-land ideas found the most support among the rapidly growing ranks of clerical workers, sales workers, and high-status (but poorly paid) professionals, along with the skilled crafts workers who occupied the jobs just the other side of the blue-collar/white-collar divide. Like those at the bottom of the job hierarchy, such "middling" workers might consider a return to the land because they hoped it would guarantee them basic food and shelter. But they were also motivated by "producerist" values. Some distrusted the new consumer temptations they and their children faced in the cities. Others feared a loss of autonomy, sensing that the power of giant corporations was rendering them increasingly dependent and helpless, making them "cogs in a wheel" that turned relentlessly and without their consent. Most advocates of a return to the land for these "middling" workers did not advise them to take up commercial farming on a large scale but to acquire a few acres outside the city, where they could reduce their expenses by growing their own food.

Ebb and Flood

The first back-to-the-land movement peaked during the years just before World War I. (Each of the first three chapters of this book explores that first movement from a different angle.) After the war, it faded from public view. As Bolton Hall acknowledged in 1926, in the new political climate, all radical and progressive causes were forced to become "less conspicuous." They did become less conspicuous, but they did not disappear. In southern California, for example, the back-to-the-land idea moved onto new ground, losing some of its associations with radical social agitation as commercial real estate developers joined back-to-the-land promoters to foster a common landscape of "little lands." (Chapter 4 explores this transformation.)

Bolton Hall predicted in 1926 that the radicals would reemerge when "winter comes to booming 'prosperity'"—and he was right, of course.[5] Economic "winter" arrived in the 1930s in the form of the Great Depression, creating many new opportunities for back-to-the-landers. Like other progressive reformers who found themselves propelled into positions of power by the mobilization of the New Deal, progressive back-to-the-landers were handed a chance to put their plans into practice during the thirties, this time with more credibility than ever before and with federal funds. The projects they implemented were the culmination of struggles begun a generation earlier, designed to address social problems that had been on the lists of progressives for years: slum tenements, farm tenancy, and the assimilation of immigrants. (The story of these projects is told in chapter 5.)

New Deal programs marked the culmination of the progressive back-to-the-land vision in another way, too. Although it may seem natural today to assume that the idea of going back to the land was rooted in nostalgia, many early back-to-the-landers would have found that notion absurd. They were fond of arguing that their movement led not "back" but "forward" to the land—"*Forward* to better things than man has ever known in the past."[6] Future-oriented, often technocratic, they were convinced that the forces of history were on their side. New technologies, they believed, were luring people irresistibly to the suburbs and making household self-sufficiency easier. One 1916 magazine article laid out the promise in its title: "Electricity Will Do the Drudgery in Densely-Peopled Garden Cities."[7]

Many New Dealers shared this faith in a rural future made easier by technological advances. Opponents of their back-to-the-land projects accused them of nostalgia: one socialist critic dismissed the projects as "little modern Arcadias."[8] But to supporters, the plan to move factories and their employees from deteriorating city centers to cleaner, less crowded rural areas seemed not retrograde but preeminently scientific and modern. This was the position endorsed by Frank Lloyd Wright, for example, who dressed it in fittingly modernist architectural forms in the prototype of Broadacre City that he set out in 1932. Reformers with this attitude typically rejected as too romantic the very phrase "back to the land." Ralph Borsodi used the term "homestead" in his 1929 *This*

Ugly Civilization, and New Deal advocates coined the phrase "subsistence home-stead" for their projects.

By the time the New Deal and the Second World War were over, this progressive wing of the back-to-the-land movement had played its last hand. Postwar liberals would still attempt to ensure security, independence, and autonomy for citizens—but they would use Social Security programs, worker's compensation, and a full employment economy, not self-sufficient homesteads. Government analysts Russell Lord and Paul Johnstone delivered the consensus judgment of New Deal experts when they concluded in their 1942 study of subsistence homesteads that Americans did not really want to live in Arcadian simplicity or even to become pioneering "homesteaders." They wanted more cash and more consumer goods: "Good housing with earth to dig in, a chance to garden, elbow room, a wholesome and beautiful place in which to rear children—such things are good and widely desired. But they do not function as a substitute for an adequate cash income and security of employment."[9]

Other back-to-the-landers—those with a more "producerist" sensibility—traveled in a different direction. (Chapter 6 explores their story.) Increasingly wary of the power of the federal government as well as of the pervasive control of monopoly capital, they found allies among those who were rediscovering American regional identity as a counterweight to the centralizing tendencies of both government and business. Among those allies were the Southern Agrarians, whose 1930 manifesto *I'll Take My Stand* opened the Depression-era debate by linking regional distinctiveness with the survival of the self-sufficient farm. This wing of the back-to-the-land movement turned against an uncritical faith in progress. The editors of the decentralist magazine *Free America*, for example, condemned the policies of Secretary of Agriculture Henry Wallace, who main-tained in 1939 that "decommercializing" agriculture would be a "backward step." The editors argued that it was precisely the continued adherence to "backward" self-sufficiency that had kept some farmers solvent while others had been forced off their land. "Mightn't this wholesale misery"—dispossessed tenants, farm bankruptcies, even the Dust Bowl—"have been averted by de-commercialized, more self-sufficient agriculture?" They concluded defiantly: "We prefer the 'backward' method."[10]

This wing of the movement—decentralist, regionalist, sometimes nostalgic—did not disappear after World War II. Its ideas were kept alive through the 1940s and 1950s by small groups of pacifists and other marginalized dissidents. Borsodi's School of Living continued to publish a decentralist journal, and up in Vermont, a small group of radicals settled around Pikes Falls, where Helen and Scott Nearing lived until 1950. Even in the wake of the postwar economic boom—even after New Deal and Great Society programs had created a very different type of "social security" for many Americans—the old dreams did not completely disappear.

In the 1970s, a new generation of back-to-the-landers once again embraced the old vision of self-sufficiency (chapter 7's subject). But some elements of the vision were changing once again. In this generation, the nostalgia could be unabashed. In 1979, John Shuttleworth, the founder of *Mother Earth News*, offered his own childhood memories of the 1930s as a model for what he wanted his pioneering back-to-the-land magazine to accomplish. In those days, Shuttleworth recalled, "people still controlled their food supplies and their housing and their transportation and their work and their entertainment and all the other aspects of their lives on a very direct and a very personal basis." They were "free men and women" whom government and corporations "left alone."[11]

This passage, with its homage to family and community independence, was characteristic of Shuttleworth's increasing identification with 1930s-style decentralism. But Shuttleworth also added something entirely new to that inherited vision. In the second issue of *Mother Earth News* in 1970, he invoked the old motive for a return to the land—"This magazine is about . . . giving people back their lives"—alongside a new one: "stopping the rape of the planet."[12] In adopting an environmentalist perspective, Shuttleworth was typical of his generation of back-to-the-landers, who had a profound sense of the vulnerability of the natural world and of the planet itself—"Mother Earth." In the 1910s, back-to-the-landers had feared nationwide economic crisis: "black Friday and red ruin," to reprise Bolton Hall's phrase. Those who came of age during the Depression faced that "black Friday" and were prepared for worse: chaos, violence, the end of capitalism or of democracy.[13] In the 1970s, back-to-the-landers added entirely new concerns to the old list: pollution, scarcity, and an overcrowded planet.

Doers and Dreamers

This book is in part a history of the "official" back-to-the-land movement—its ideas and its projects. (That history begins with chapter 1.) But writers and activists were not the only ones to pursue a back-to-the-land dream. On one hand, there were individuals who joined up, made good, stuck it out, or deserted the cause—but never published their stories. On the other hand were people who never did find their "one way out." Perhaps they hoped one day to go back to the land, but in the end they simply went back to work. These were the "consumers" of the back-to-the-land dream: the people who bought the books and read the magazines. One author caught their mood in 1921: "They send for seed catalogues—and dream; attend poultry shows—and dream; . . . make furtive sketches in idle moments of unbuilt cottages and unplanted gardens—and dream."[14]

Dreaming was part of the back-to-the-land impulse from the beginning. But dreaming leaves few historical records. (Chapter 2 explores some of the records that do exist.) Nor is it easy to find evidence of individuals who really did go back to the land but never published accounts of their experiences. (Chapter 3 examines that evidence.) It is difficult at times to define just what "going back to the land" meant in some settings; it can be hard to determine whether a person moved to the suburbs to raise chickens or to play golf. So it is not surprising that some historians have perceived the back-to-the-land impulse as "nebulous, romantic, or escapist," in the phrase of historian Paul Conkin, who has written extensively on back-to-the-landers and their allies.[15]

Judged by the standards of the great political struggles of the twentieth century, the back-to-the-land movement does appear "nebulous." Its advocates can point to no accomplishments so concrete as the prohibition movement's Eighteenth Amendment or the civil rights movement's role in ending segregation. Some scholars have even denied that it was a "movement" at all, arguing that back-to-the-landers lacked both sufficiently famous leaders and sufficiently articulate ideologies to qualify for that designation.[16] One historian writes that the turn-of-the-century movement had "no perceptible intellectual base, no patron saint." Another characterizes the ideology of the 1970s as "variety co-existing with vagueness."[17]

To understand the back-to-the-land impulse as a historical phenomenon, we must come to grips with both its "variety" and its "vagueness." A back-to-the-land inclination may lead a person to support a political program, to look for a private retreat, or, indeed, to escape into a daydream. At one end of the spectrum, the back-to-the-land impulse generated a political agenda embraced by ideologically committed activists. New Deal liberals attempted to rebuild a collapsed economy; single-tax advocates committed themselves to an equitable redistribution of land; and Jewish radicals hoped to build a new cultural identity to replace the life they fled in the Pale. Sometimes, though, the vision was more like a millennial faith. In John Steinbeck's epic *Grapes of Wrath* (1939), for example, the dream is born from the desperate struggle of Oklahoma farmers driven from their homes to the migrant labor camps of California. In his final soliloquy, everyman Tom Joad promises his mother that though he may die, his spirit will live on: he will be there on that day "when our folks eat the stuff they raise and live in the houses they build."[18] At other times, the dreamer looked not forward but back, longing for the days when "we didn't punch anybody's time clock and we didn't conform to anyone's production standards," as John Shuttleworth wrote in *Mother Earth News*.[19]

Sometimes it was simply a private dream. Lena Walters was a real-life sales clerk. She wrote to one of her favorite back-to-the-land authors in 1906: "I stand all day behind a counter. . . . When I look out at all, I see a narrow, dusty street . . . and oh! How tired I am of it." For Walters, the back-to-the-land book she read offered an escape fantasy in the most literal sense. She asked for help finding a farm of her own: "Can you tell me *where* I can find such a place, and *how* I can keep it?" but she concluded, "I know you can't."[20]

Between the daydream of Lena Walters and the programs of professional reformers were many different versions of the dream, and many different degrees of commitment. Freelance journalists spun back-to-the-land stories for pay, but they might also be tempted to try it themselves. Families cultivated their one-acre plots—perhaps in the organized back-to-the-land communities of southern California, perhaps in the suburban communities next door to them. Everywhere along the spectrum are visible the powerful motives that drove ordinary people to think about staking all they had on a return to the land: the desire for autonomous and fulfilling work, for independent proprietorship, for a buffer against the ups and downs of the economy, and for a modicum of security in old age.

Sometimes the "producers" of the back-to-the-land dream did not quite see eye to eye with its "consumers." Some reformers hoped, for example, that returning people to farms would shore up the crumbling edifice of the traditional household, evidently threatened by the wholesale exodus from farms to cities. As reformer William Ellsworth Smythe explained in 1921, rural life was "far more favorable to domestic felicity" than life in city apartments. It taught husbands and wives to work together on common projects and encouraged them to produce more children.[21] Moreover, early back-to-the-land advocates frequently framed their producerist arguments in gendered terms: access to land was essential to personal independence, autonomy, and freedom of conscience—characteristics they commonly labeled "manhood."

Yet, facts on the ground in those early years suggest a rather different story. Among those who left traces in the historical record, a disproportionate number of unmarried working women expressed interest in returning to the land. It is ironic but intriguing that the most enthusiastic audiences for back-to-the-land ideas included not only traditional male heads of households but "spinsters": "oh lots and lots of spinsters," as one participant later recalled, "who had been stenographers and book-keepers and file clerks and teachers for more years than they wanted to remember."[22] For single women, too, an acre or two of land might offer a modest degree of that very independence and self-sufficiency—the "manhood"—reformers thought they were safeguarding for men.

But What about Thoreau?

In popular perception as well as in scholarly accounts, back-to-the-land ideas have generally been viewed as part of a larger romantic impulse—one variant of the kind of "back-to-nature" enthusiasm that also generated interest in wilderness vacations or the nature writing of John Burroughs and Gene Stratton Porter. Agricultural historian David Danbom, for example, characterizes the back-to-the-landers of the early twentieth century as "romantic agrarians" who combined an older tradition of American republican agrarianism with a romantic longing for a rural life in close contact with nature.[23] In a related vein, David Shi claims some back-to-the-land writers as part of a recurrent impulse toward the "simple life" in their rejection of materialism in favor of a life closer to nature.[24] And Rebecca Gould's *At Home in Nature: Modern Homesteading and Spiritual Practice in America* situates the contemporary back-to-the-land movement in a persistent philosophical and religious outlook rooted in transcendentalist and romantic conceptions of a "sacralized" natural world.[25]

All these interpretations have merit, but my own findings have led me in a rather different direction. To begin with, though it is natural to view earlier back-to-the-landers through the lens of the 1970s, I have found that it can be misleading. Ever since the 1970s, to be sure, back-to-the-landers have expressed a profound attachment to the natural world, along with a commitment to environmentalism. (Jeffrey Jacob argues, indeed, that late twentieth-century back-to-the-landers are best understood *primarily* as environmentalists. His informants testified that they were more committed to environmentalist politics than they were even to food self-sufficiency.)[26] Earlier back-to-the-landers, however, generally articulated different priorities. They might express their appreciation of the beauties of nature and the pleasures of rural life, but those expressions are not in themselves very revealing: countless people who never considered uprooting themselves from their jobs and returning to a farm expressed similar attitudes. In fact, the earlier literature dwelt comparatively little on the joys of rural life and a great deal more on the rising cost of food, job insecurity, and the desire for independent work.[27] As one back-to-the-land writer put it in 1913, the "impelling motive" of the movement was "not so much a love of Nature as a recognition of economic needs."[28]

The case of Henry David Thoreau offers an instructive example. The impact of his 1855 *Walden* on back-to-the-landers in the 1970s was unquestionably great, attested to by dozens of personal accounts. *Mother Earth News* authors used *Walden* virtually as a sacred text, citing Thoreau's authority for trying a new career, resisting the use of DDT, even for borrowing tools.[29] Helen and Scott Nearing, the most famous homesteaders of that decade, regarded Thoreau as their single most important role model.[30] But the first back-to-the-land writers rarely made any use of Thoreau at all: one can search in vain among those texts for even a mention of his name. Perhaps that was because at the beginning of the century Thoreau was still perceived primarily as a nature writer. (One Thoreau scholar argues that it was not until the Great Depression that readers began to see *Walden* as an argument for the "simple life.")[31] Intriguingly, the one early back-to-the-land author who *did* write extensively about Thoreau was the culturally avant-garde Philip G. Hubert, a music critic by trade, who found in *Walden* a defense of his own particular brand of "simple life" devoted to books, conversation, and a great deal of cultivated idleness.[32] Rebecca Gould points out that this enthusiasm for idleness was precisely the aspect of Thoreau that Helen and Scott Nearing disliked most. As Gould puts it, "all readers of *Walden* have their *own* Thoreau."[33]

Dreamers and Readers

My own work on this project did begin with books, though not Thoreau's. On the twenty-fifth floor of the library at the University of Massachusetts, I discovered shelves and shelves of volumes that were far less well known than *Walden* and now much less frequently read. It was a sizeable collection: once a land grant university's pride and joy but now placed off in a corner with the outdated textbooks. As Rebecca Gould notes in *At Home in Nature*, back-to-the-landers seem always to have generated "as many texts as vegetables."[34] (Back-to-the-land writers have been aware of the irony from the beginning. In 1913 one author joked that it was all the fault of the magazine editors, who said to the writers, "This is good stuff for five dollars a page; write us some more.")[35] But most back-to-the-land writing did not aspire to the literary heights on which *Walden* is now established. Much of it did not pretend even to the polish of the nature books of Gene Stratton Porter or Ernest Thompson Seton. It appeared in popular, even ephemeral forms and was subject to the marketplace constraints of mass publications: "five dollars a page" would not usually buy another *Walden*.

The prototype for these popular back-to-the-land books bore the title *Ten Acres Enough*.[36] First published in 1864, *Ten Acres Enough* was extraordinarily long lived: it had gone through twenty-five editions by the 1880s and was reprinted thereafter in 1890, 1905, 1912, 1916, and 1928.[37] Nearly a century after it first appeared, Helen and Scott Nearing included passages from *Ten Acres Enough* in their 1950 *Maple Sugar Book*. In 1976, *Mother Earth News* printed excerpts from it, too. Even then, its story was not over. The book was reintroduced in 1996 as *Ten Acres Enough: The Small Farm Dream Is Possible* and in 2004 as *Ten Acres Enough: The Classic 1864 Guide to Independent Farming*. It remains in print today in a "revived" 2008 edition, a century and a half after it was written.[38] Lest we assume that its value is now purely antiquarian, one 2007 reader-reviewer on the Amazon.com website gave the book the highest possible five-star rating. Having feared that *Ten Acres Enough* would be "irrelevant and dated," this reviewer was pleased to report that it was both inspiring and useful, even if its "writing style is perhaps a bit different from what we are used to nowadays."

The surprising durability of this text tells us a great deal about the back-to-the-land impulse as well as about the books that have given it expression. In 1864, it certainly did not look as if *Ten Acres Enough* would survive the year, much less a century and a half. A review in the influential *American Agriculturist* accused the anonymous author of all kinds of misrepresentations. The book appeared to be a front for "some New Jersey Land Company" whose advertisements, indeed, appeared on its last pages. Worse, one chapter was plagiarized from an article written by Donald Grant Mitchell in the *New Englander*: "A more out and out specimen of literary robbery we have seldom seen." The next month, however, the *American Agriculturist* dispensed its pardon. The author of *Ten Acres* had apologized for neglecting to attribute the Mitchell excerpts properly and removed the real estate advertisement at the back of his book. The reviewer, in the meantime, had visited the author's farm and could vouch for the legitimacy of the story, although, as he put it (in a judgment that might apply to almost any popular back-to-the-land book for generations to come), "a spice of romance runs through the book, and what *actually was*, is curiously mingled with what *might have been*."[39]

The anonymous author of *Ten Acres Enough* was Edmund Morris, a journalist who resigned from the editorship of a Trenton newspaper in 1856 and returned to his childhood home in nearby Burlington, New Jersey.[40] The suspicions of the *American Agriculturist*'s editor were partly correct: Morris *was* selling real estate for a living, but he was also writing books. In addition to *Ten Acres Enough*, Morris wrote *How to Get a Farm, and Where to Find One* (1864) and *Farming for Boys* (1868), books that offered straightforward advice about contemporary farm practices. But *Ten Acres Enough* was not a standard farm advice manual. Nor was it much like the books of Donald Grant Mitchell, the writer whose work Morris was accused of plagiarizing. Mitchell was a pioneer in the genre of "country life" stories, the kind that recounted tales of well-to-do businessmen and professionals who had "grown tired of thumping over the city pavements," as he put it.[41] Books like Mitchell's *My Farm at Edgewood* (1863) might occasionally offer agricultural advice, but their focus was on genteel leisure occupations and the aesthetic appreciation of the rural environment. (The chapter Morris was accused of plagiarizing was called "Gentleman Farming.") Avoiding both practical advice and social commentary, such works were designed not to solve the problems of readers but to provide what one later reviewer called the "curious and agreeable melancholy which comes from feeling that it would be nice to get back to nature" while simultaneously "realizing . . . that you have no intention of doing so." The reviewer called such works "garden goozle."[42]

In contrast, *Ten Acres Enough* devoted little space to rural leisure activities. Instead, it offered detailed information about deep plowing, how best to save manure, and the treatment of worms on peach trees. It was more like one of the new guides to market gardening (perhaps like Charles Barnard's 1869 series *My Ten Rod Farm, The Strawberry Garden,* and *Farming by Inches*) promoting the cultivation of crops that catered to gourmet urban markets.[43] But *Ten Acres Enough* was not quite that kind of book, either.[44] Standing out clearly from the advice about weeds and manure was its central premise: city workers tied to the "desk, the counter, or the workshop" would be happier and more secure if they left those jobs for the farm.

Ten Acres Enough tells the tale of a businessman who weathered the panic of 1837 as a young man, only to face another downturn in 1854. By a timely decision to sell his business and buy a small farm, the man avoided the greater catastrophe looming ahead: the "tremendous crash of 1857."[45] Others, Morris argued, should do the same. Farming a few acres close to town, "a man of ordinary industry and intelligence" could avoid such economic calamities and "insure a maintenance for his family, free from the ruinous vibrations of trade or commerce in the metropolis." The author's particular enthusiasm was for intensive cultivation of summer fruit—a high-profit, very labor-intensive product with almost unlimited market appeal—but the specific crop was not the important thing. What Morris promised was security—"a safe and quiet harbor"—and a competency—"a moderate income, so that it be a sure one."[46]

In 1889, when Philip G. Hubert published his own back-to-the-land account, he credited *Ten Acres Enough* with converting him to the cause. Hubert, the music critic who took *Walden* as a model, at first glance appears to have nothing whatever in common with Edmund Morris. While Morris extolled the efficacy of weeding, pruning, and spreading manure, Hubert chronicled his efforts to find time for his cherished books and music. Hubert had no intention of caring for ten acres of intensively planted crops: "I should no more think of ordinary farm life for myself than I should undertake to compete with an Irish laborer in the raising of potatoes for market." In defense of his position, Hubert placed Thoreau's words "I can see nothing so holy as unrelaxed play and frolic in this bower God has built for us" on the title page of *Liberty and a Living*.[47]

Nevertheless, *Ten Acres Enough* had moved him. At the time he came across it, Hubert explained, he had been "very tired of city life, of late hours and long hours, of nervous strain, of incessant work with few breathing spells." Reading *Ten Acres Enough* had caused Hubert to ask himself a fundamental question: "Why is it not possible for a healthy man . . . to make bread and butter for his little ones and himself without chaining himself down to a life of drudgery?"[48] Hubert did not pay much heed to the details of Morris's plan, yet he embraced what he perceived to be Morris's answer to his question. More than any specific "way out" proposed by an author, it was the basic formula of the back-to-the-land book that spoke most clearly to its readers. In nearly every detail, *Ten Acres Enough* laid out that formula.

Like many a future back-to-the-land book, Morris's book was first published anonymously, and like many, it met with accusations that it was plagiarized or simply untrue. By its nature, the genre invited such scrutiny: it required the appearance of strict conformity with literal truth. Readers of back-to-the-land literature looked first to the bona fides of authors. How could they know whether to follow the author's suggestions about the peach worms, the manure, and everything else, if they could not be sure the author was who he said he was? Often the full title of the book would stake that claim to honesty: in this case it was *Ten Acres Enough: A Practical Experience, Showing How a Very Small Farm May Be Made to Keep a Very Large Family*. Then there would be charts of vegetables, lists of expenses, descriptions of techniques—signifiers that pointed to the credibility of the author. First-person narratives, too, underwrote the claim to truthfulness. "Like thousands of others before me," Morris wrote, "I began the world without a dollar."[49]

Ironically, if back-to-the-land readers had perused *Walden* carefully, they would have found a text that seemed, at first glance at least, to fulfill their requirements. In a chapter called "The Bean Field," Thoreau describes his experience cultivating a plot of beans. He supplies many pertinent details about the experiment: how many hours he labored; how much he spent on seeds; what kind of fertilizer (or lack of fertilizer) he used on the soil. (At least one later reader did peruse those details carefully. The author of a 1971 article published in *Mother Earth News* hoped that he might be able to cite Thoreau's authority on behalf of a favorite cause: he wanted to encourage more consumption of that quintessential New Age delicacy, bean sprouts. Had Thoreau perhaps sprouted some of those beans? Apparently not, however: "A check of *Walden* and some of Thoreau's other writings produced no such record.")[50] In fact, as historian Robert Gross has made clear in his essay "The Great Bean Field Hoax," Thoreau was really not the proper authority to consult: every bit of the bean story was part of an elaborate joke.

Thoreau's "conscientiously itemizing his 'income' and his 'out-goes' down to the last half-penny," as Gross describes it, made *Walden* look a bit like a back-to-the-land book.[51] But the bean story was not a faithful record of Thoreau's efforts to learn self-sufficiency; instead, as Gross demonstrates, it was an elaborate parody of mid-nineteenth-century agricultural treatises. Thoreau's agenda was to skewer the materialism and competitiveness of modern agriculture, not to help people get back to the land. He flouted standard agricultural practices, growing his beans without fertilizer, hoeing them in the morning when the dew is most likely to spread disease, putting up only a fitful resistance to the woodchucks. Not surprisingly, in the end Thoreau reports harvesting only a meager crop. Early back-to-the-land readers might have appreciated his joke, but they could not follow his example.

One More Time

When I set out to write a history of American back-to-the-land movements over a decade ago, I feared there would be little general interest in a subject so unrelated to the pressing questions of the rapidly globalizing, hyperconnected world of the late twentieth century. Nowadays, those worries appear groundless. Even before the great economic meltdown of 2008, there were signs that a new wave of back-to-the-land enthusiasm was on the horizon. Cultural critics from both the right and the left were voicing discomfort with the greed, the luxury, and the debt they feared were becoming characteristic of fin de siècle culture. The global industrial system appeared increasingly fragile: many people now distrusted their food sources, and many more anticipated an end to the cheap oil on which the whole system was founded. With the onset of a financial and economic crisis some were calling the "Great Recession," record numbers of Americans responded by taking a step that might at first glance seem pitiably inadequate: they planted gardens. Veteran *New York Times* columnist

Verlyn Klinkenborg explained why: "Growing a vegetable garden isn't going to balance the budget or replace lost benefits or even begin to make up for the shock of a lost job," he explained, "but part of the crisis we face is a sense of alienation and powerlessness."[52] Back-to-the-landers all the way back to the turn of the previous century would have been quick to catch the connection.

Part I

The First American Back-to-the-Land Movement

1

The Back-to-the-Land Project

In the spring of 1907, an anonymous writer for the *Nation* reviewed a new book called *Three Acres and Liberty*. As the reviewer noted wryly, the book was one of many: "In this country and pretty nearly all over Europe, a cry of 'The People Back to the Land,' or 'The Land Back to the People,' is being sounded mightily at the present time." The reviewer was more than a little patronizing about this development, noting that such a demand for a return to the "poor, old, hackneyed 'simple life'" appeared every time the economy went sour: "Whenever the flood-tide of prosperity subsides . . . we . . . become convinced that we are well on the way to ruin, and that the city is responsible for it all."[1] The reviewer was right about one thing: the "flood tide of prosperity" was indeed about to subside. Within a few months of the publication of *Three Acres and Liberty*, a bank panic and a stock market crash would bring about a general economic crisis.

As the *Nation* reviewer pointed out, there was indeed a great deal of back-to-the-land talk at the turn of the twentieth century. Books with back-to-the-land themes had begun to appear in the last decades of the nineteenth century. By the 1910s there was a veritable publishing boom underway. Back-to-the-land articles appeared everywhere in the magazines—not only in specialized publications like *Country Life in America* but also on the sober fact-filled pages of the *World's Work*, in Gustav Stickley's handsome arts and crafts journal the *Craftsman*, amid the muckraking articles of *Collier's* and the genteel fiction of the *Atlantic Monthly*. In styles ranging from the humorous to the earnest, from the statistical to the confessional, these texts encouraged Americans to escape from the city to the farm.

Back-to-the-land writing could take the form of dry facts or cliff-hanging fiction, it could be technical or folksy, but a contemporary reader would have had little trouble identifying the genre. The titles were easy to recognize, often referring playfully to previous books. Bolton Hall, the author of *Three Acres and Liberty*, had crafted his title to echo Philip G. Hubert's *Liberty and a Living*. (Hall also used a part of Hubert's title for his second book, *A Little Land and a Living*, published in 1908.) In fact, Hall's title reverberated all the way back to the grandfather of back-to-the-land books, the 1864 *Ten Acres Enough*, and to its 1869 parody, *Five Acres Too Many*.

The "acres" formula was equally familiar to readers across the Atlantic. A British author named Frederick A. Morton brought out *The Simple Life on Four Acres* in 1907, followed by *Winning a Living on Four Acres* in 1909. The phrase reached far back into the nineteenth century in Britain as well, to the frequently reprinted *Our Farm of Four Acres, and the Money We Made by It* (1859). By the early years of the new century, such phrases may have recalled for Americans a faint memory of the lost promise to newly freed slaves of "Forty Acres and a Mule." In Britain, they echoed an 1885 land reform campaign whose rallying cry had been "Three Acres and a Cow." The *Nation* reviewer caught that particular reference. He believed that wealthy American city dwellers would be far more tempted by "Mr. Hall's Three Acres and—Liberty" than by those same three acres "and a Cow."[2] By the 1910s, writers were already using the formula as a joke, as in Walter Dyer's 1913 lament, "Eighty Acres and Bondage," in the *Craftsman*: "We have the eighty acres, but not yet the liberty."[3] Other writers skipped the "acres" formula but signaled their meaning with subtitles: *The Key to the Land: What a City Man Did With a Small Farm*; *The Bend in the Road, and How a Man of the City Found It*; *Second Wind: The Plain Truth about Going Back to the Land*.

Such titles, with their joking references to one another, promised a shared theme, and *Three Acres and Liberty* began with a little parable that neatly expressed it. As Bolton Hall explained, his readers were like a horse that had been "hobbled" (his front feet strapped together) every night, to keep him from wandering off. With the hobbles on, the horse could not walk but only hop. But when the hobbles were removed in the morning, the horse continued to hop, still believing he was tied—"until," as Hall explained, "he saw his mate trotting off" and finally realized he was free. The moral: "We are not tied to a desk or to a bench: we stay there only because we think we are tied." *Three Acres and Liberty*, Hall concluded, "is intended to show how anyone can trot off if he will."[4] (The *Nation* reviewer was thus playing his own game with Hall's image when he titled his review "Hobbling Back to Nature.")

To bolster the argument that "anyone can trot off if he will," back-to-the-land writers offered a parade of statistics, case studies, and personal examples. In *Three Acres and Liberty*, Hall assembled a grab bag of material, from a report of a Sacramento farmer's blackberry yield to instructions for building a cold frame. Scattered throughout the text were tales of elderly, disabled, and teen-aged city dwellers who had increased their security by cultivating small plots of land. After all, if a man "so weak and emaciated that the doctor was afraid [he] would be unable to get out of his office without assistance" could become a self-supporting gardener, then indeed, anyone could "trot off."[5]

Hall's rather manic enthusiasm for such anecdotes was inimitable; he delighted in accumulating masses of examples gleaned from his wide-ranging correspondence with reformers and charitable organizations across the United States and Europe. But most back-to-the-land writers offered similar kinds of encouragement. In 1910, for example, a series called "Cutting Loose from City Life" began to appear in *Country Life in America*, an elegant and lavishly illustrated new magazine whose focus was the genteel rural life. Each title told its whole story: "How Two Young People—One an Invalid—Found Health and a Competence by Exchanging City Life for a Little One-Acre Home in the Country" or "How a Middle-Aged Professional Man, Broken in Health and With Small Capital, Found Physical and Financial Cure and Provision for Old Age, on an Ozark Farm."[6]

Novelists concocted similar tales. In *The Heron Nest* (1909), W. Bert Foster, a writer who specialized in children's books, described the plight of a family facing an almost comical series of catastrophes: the father and primary bread-winner has lost his sanity as a result of a financial disappointment, bringing the family to the brink of poverty. As this story opens, all three children lose *their* jobs. Forced into action, the family moves to the country and begins to grow onions.[7] A remarkably similar set of problems drives Grace Richmond's fictional family to the country in *Strawberry Acres* (1911). Three brothers and a sister, left in poverty by their father's death, inherit a farm outside town and proceed to transform their lives by growing and marketing premium strawberries.[8] From *The Key to the Land* to *The Bend in the Road*, authors told similar tales of urban loss and rural recovery.

Why Back to the Farm?

What accounts for this outpouring of words? At first glance, the answer may appear simple enough. Americans in these years were experiencing a profound demographic change, as the United States reached the tipping point in its transformation from a rural to an urban society. While two-thirds of the nation still lived in rural areas in 1890, just over half did so by 1910. Clearer still was the shift away from farming as an occupation. By 1890, 43 percent of American workers were farmers; by 1910, the figure had declined to less than a third.[9] These statistics make it clear that for millions of first-generation city dwellers, going back to the land would not be a very long journey.

At the same time, and in spite of the decisive demographic shift toward the city, most Americans at the turn of the century still took it for granted that rural life was intrinsically superior to urban life. They were accustomed to hearing from politicians, journalists, and clergymen that the best life for the individual was in the countryside and that the republic depended for its survival on the sturdy independent landowner, secure on his own domain. This agrarian rhetoric—so deeply rooted in American politics and culture—had reached its apotheosis only a few years earlier, in William Jennings Bryan's 1896 "Cross of Gold" speech: "Burn down your cities and leave our farms, and your cities will spring up again as if by magic. But destroy our farms and the grass will grow in the streets of every city in the country."

Such rhetoric might have begun to ring a little hollow by the early twentieth century, but expressions of agrarian sentiment were still ubiquitous. Theodore Roosevelt regarded as a "mere truism" the assumption in his 1906 state of the union message that "no growth of cities, no growth of wealth, no industrial development can atone for any falling off in the character and standing of the farming population."[10] Indeed, those ideas would still play a role in the *second* President Roosevelt's presidency thirty years later. In a 1936 campaign speech, Franklin Roosevelt would defend his administration's policies by invoking "the American farmer, living on his own land," as "our ideal of self-reliance and of spiritual balance—the source from which the reservoirs of the Nation's strength are constantly renewed."[11]

Most early back-to-the-land advocates did share these agrarian beliefs, and they expected their readers to share them.[12] Truman DeWeese certainly anticipated no argument when he wrote in *The Bend in the Road, and How a Man of the City Found It* (1913) that "the life that doesn't keep one in close communion with growing things . . . is empty, artificial, and unsatisfying."[13] David Grayson expressed a well-worn sentiment with an equally well-worn metaphor when he exclaimed in *Adventures in Contentment* (1907) that the cities depended on recruiting "the fresh, clean blood of the country, with boys who still retain some of the power and the vision drawn from the soil."[14] The *Nation* reviewer must have had such a belief in mind when he accused *Three Acres and Liberty* of "antiquated

Rousseauism," but back-to-the-land writers were hardly its only defenders. Like most Americans for generations, they believed that rural America was the real America.

Still, that agrarianism—however pervasive and long-standing—does not go very far toward explaining the explosion of interest in back-to-the-land ideas at the turn of the century. More to the point in these postpopulist years was a growing perception that the old rural values were under a new kind of attack. Mass migration of rural people to cities was widely perceived as a grave problem; the official disappearance of the frontier in 1890 contributed to an anxious reassessment of American rural life and American character itself. One product of those concerns was the birth of the country life movement, called into official being by President Theodore Roosevelt in 1908 with the creation of the Country Life Commission, whose job was to explore the problems of rural America.

The country life movement encompassed a variety of responses to a perceived crisis—or set of crises—in the countryside. Rural sons and daughters were leaving the farm. Rural families seemed isolated from modern America. One group of country life writers viewed the basic problem as economic: inefficient, unproductive, and outdated farming practices, they theorized, were responsible for the relative "backwardness" and poverty of rural life. For another group, the crisis in the countryside was fundamentally cultural, resulting from the social isolation of rural families. To address these multiple challenges, country lifers advocated an array of programs, ranging from school centralization to road building, from church consolidation to farmers' institutes.[15]

Some back-to-the-land advocates had a foot in the country life camp. Noted progressive writer and editor Walter Hines Page was appointed one of the seven members of Theodore Roosevelt's Country Life Commission when it was created in 1908, in recognition of his efforts to modernize the production methods of southern farmers. Page never wrote his own back-to-the-land book, but for several key years he turned his magazine, the *World's Work*, into a clearinghouse for people who wanted to get back to the land. (More about that in chapters 2 and 3.)

Many back-to-the-land advocates also shared some of the basic attitudes of country lifers, notably a preference for a "scientific" approach to agriculture and a confidence in the expert advice available at the land grant colleges and their experiment stations. In *Happy Hollow Farm* (1914), his account of his family's journey back to the land in the Ozarks, William R. Lighton reported proudly that they had embraced a modern approach to farming. "We talked with the chemists, and the horticulturists, and the agronomists, and the animal husbandry men, and every other man [at the University of Arkansas] who looked or acted like an expert in anything."[16] This laundry list of experts echoed country life leader Liberty Hyde Bailey's call for "soil experts, health experts, pruning and spraying experts, forest experts, farm machinery experts, drainage and irrigation experts, recreation experts, market experts . . . [and] housekeeping experts" to revitalize rural communities.[17]

In spite of this common ground, however, back-to-the-land ideas never fit comfortably within the country life movement.[18] The more hard-core "scientific" wing of that movement, as historian William L. Bowers has classified it, was inclined to scoff at any effort to bring people back to the land, believing that the depopulation of the countryside was essentially the product of a healthy Darwinian elimination of the "unfit."[19] The more "romantic" country life leaders, using Bowers's designation, did adhere to the traditional agrarian view that the farm was the moral repository of the nation and sought to protect the status of farming as a unique way of life. Among those reformers, there was at least a shared belief that the flow of population toward the cities was a misfortune. From such a position, it would have been possible to make a case for a wholesale return to the land—but country life advocates did not typically make that case.

Liberty Hyde Bailey, perhaps the foremost spokesman for that "romantic" wing of the country life movement, once came close to endorsing the back-to-the-land idea. In a 1901 essay in the *World's Work*, Bailey posed an important question for would-be back-to-the-landers: "Can I Make a Farm Pay?" His answer was a qualified affirmative: "Yes, If You Like It—A Cog in the Wheel of Town Life or an Independent Proprietor—It Depends on Yourself."[20] But Bailey did not usually offer even this sort of cautious encouragement. In *The Country-Life Movement in America* (1911), he clarified his position on the very first page: the country life movement, Bailey declared emphatically, "is not a back-to-the-land movement." The country life effort would not benefit from a return of city people to the soil; in fact, the "country-life and back-to-the-land movements" are "in many ways . . . distinctly antagonistic."[21] Taking up the issue again several pages later, Bailey pointed out what was for him a fundamental distinction: "Some persons seem to think that the movement of city men out to the country offers a solution of country problems." On the contrary, he explained, "it usually offers only a solution of a city problem."[22]

Bailey meant to dismiss the whole idea with that assessment, but his observation was right on target. Back-to-the-land advocates *were* in fact responding "only" to urban problems, targeting "only" urban audiences. As Bailey recognized, back-to-the-land ideas developed as a response to problems beyond the scope of the country life movement.

Black Fridays and Red Ruin

Most back-to-the-land advocates did not propose a return to the soil as a solution to the problems of farmers or to the nation's perceived need for rural roots. Nor is there much explanatory force in characterizing this first generation of back-to-the-landers as romantic exponents of a return to nature, although their critics sometimes portrayed them that way. Indeed, although their work appeared at a time of widespread fascination with wilderness experiences of all kinds, the authors of these books and articles did not embrace the cult of wilderness or express a great deal of enthusiasm for "roughing it."

It was not that they never mentioned any of these matters; they certainly shared a general conviction that rural life was more pleasant than city life and assumed that everyone else believed that, too. Just as they shared the old agrarian assumptions of their generation, they usually shared contemporary opinions that open space was good for children, fresh air was rejuvenating, and close contact with the natural world was good for the soul. But the one crucial stimulus for back-to-the-land enthusiasm at the turn of the century was neither romantic nor agrarian; it was the boom-bust cycle of industrial capitalism. In this generation, back-to-the-land agitation was born from Wall Street crashes, bank panics, and depression—"blue envelopes, black Fridays, and red ruin," as Bolton Hall phrased it. In 1893, a seismic panic and stock market crash had sent waves of shock throughout the economy and ushered in years of depression.[23] During the winters of 1893–94 and 1894–95, nearly 20 percent of the urban workforce was out of work. Average earnings were down nearly a quarter. Years went by before employment and wages reached their earlier levels. A brief period of recovery was followed in 1907 by a new series of financial crises: another Wall Street crash, a bank panic, and a recession.

The downturns of 1893 and 1907 were not the first of their kind, of course. The very first back-to-the-land book, *Ten Acres Enough*, had been a response to a major financial crisis in 1857. By the turn of the century, however, there were millions of new city dwellers poised to discover for themselves just how dependent they were on wages and salaries and just how much of their income was eaten up by high rents in crowded urban centers and high prices for food obtained at the end of a long supply chain. One lost job, one illness in the family could move such a worker into the ranks of the desperate poor. Those were precisely the sorts of stories back-to-the-land writers told.

Back-to-the-land authors of this generation repeated in unison that the chief reason for returning to the land was that it would enable one to defend oneself against depressions, panics, joblessness, high prices, and low wages. As

SHE STARED IN FASCINATION AT THE ENVELOPE—FOR IT
WAS BLUE!

A middle-aged newspaper reporter brings home to his wife the dreaded "blue envelope"—official notice that he has been fired. From the anonymous *A Living Without a Boss* (1911).

one author explained, the "very primitive" search for security topped his list of reasons for going back to the land. The "nightmares of war, of strikes, of bankwrecking, of political strife" need not haunt those who can provide their own food and shelter. "This," he judged, "is elementary."[24] Because they focused resolutely on these compelling and "elementary" matters, back-to-the-land writers rarely maintained a romantic or bucolic strain for very long.

In fact, it was not so much their romanticism as this relentless focus on concrete agricultural advice that put back-to-the-landers at odds with country life reformers. The hallmark of the back-to-the-land book was the detailed information displayed in charts of vegetable planting dates, sketches of garden plans, and tables of expenditures. Even fictional back-to-the-land works often provided exhaustive discussions of crops, soils, and markets. One reviewer praised Bolton Hall's *Three Acres and Liberty* for just such down-to-earth details. In contrast to the romantic "garden goozle" of so much writing about rural life, *Three Acres* was a "Baedeker's [travel guidebook] for those who actually proposed to take the trip" back to the land.[25]

With one voice, moreover, back-to-the-land writers endorsed household self-sufficiency. While many of them encouraged readers to develop a cash crop from their new farm or garden, nearly all insisted that market production should be subordinated to the greater goal of an independent subsistence. In *Three Acres and Liberty*, for example, Hall proposed the cultivation of a wide variety of unusual market crops, from mushrooms to frogs. ("Near San Francisco," he noted hopefully, "there are a number of frog ranches.") Nevertheless, "the kitchen garden is the first indispensable and should first be given attention."[26] Hubert offered the same advice in *Liberty and a Living*: "No matter what the profits of the farm are to come from, the home garden should have first attention: that is what men live by, regardless of prices or hard times."[27]

Food self-sufficiency was the central preoccupation of back-to-the-land advocates. There was a reason for that: the price of food placed a heavy burden on households at the turn of the century. In 1901, the average family spent 40 percent of its budget on food—up from 30 percent in the years before the 1893 depression.[28] (In the first decade of the twenty-first century, in comparison, the average American family spent just under 10 percent of its income on food.) As one fictional character explained, "A family can't starve, at least, if the members are energetic and cultivate a piece of ground of respectable size."[29] Even stories that featured well-to-do protagonists emphasized subsistence; thus Harrison Whittingham's *That Farm*—an account of a wealthy merchant's experiments with a variety of commercial crops—concluded with a similar meditation: "Though all the cows and hogs may die, and the corn wither in my fields, there is still a roof for our heads, and enough will always grow to feed us."[30]

That argument may have made sense to many city dwellers, but it placed back-to-the-land advocates squarely at odds with most country life reformers and indeed with most agricultural experts of all kinds, who were actively engaged in steering farmers toward greater dependence on the market. William Lighton, who told the story of his family's return to the land in *Happy Hollow*

Farm, was generally an enthusiastic supporter of "scientific" agriculture. (Lighton was the one who boasted that he had spoken with all the agricultural experts at the University of Arkansas.) Nevertheless, although his banker thought his plans for food self-sufficiency were nothing more than "silly trifling," Lighton himself insisted that his family's ability to provide its own food was the project's greatest strength.[31] On this one critical point, he was prepared to reject expert advice. At a time when many rural people were working hard to gain greater access to industrially produced consumer goods, food self-sufficiency must surely have seemed naïve, sentimental, or out of touch to those who were shaping rural policy. The matter looked altogether different to city dwellers who embraced it.

Most back-to-the-land advocates understood that their program of self-sufficiency would not right all the world's wrongs. It would not end depressions and panics, make jobs secure, or build a safety net for old age. Certainly, it would do little to equalize distribution of wealth or access to opportunity. As Bolton Hall put it, "short of the abolition of special privilege" there was no real solution to the problems afflicting the nation and its economy. Still, he insisted, when prices rise or banks fail, "each of us can achieve a certain individual independence by producing for ourselves the most of what we and our neighbors must have in order to live at all."[32] Self-sufficiency was not justice, but it was "one way out."

One Way Out

Back-to-the-land advocates shared a commitment to self-sufficiency as "one way out," but they arrived at it through a bewildering array of political and social routes, from the center of contemporary American political discourse all the way out to its radical fringes. Some back-to-the-land advocates were socialists or anarchists; others were capitalists inclined toward charity. Some were progressive reformers with an eye to helping new immigrants; others were immigrants themselves. Some were proponents of the arts and crafts movement; others believed that Henry George's single tax was the chief reform of the age. Some, indeed, embraced no cause more revolutionary than that popular blend of new and old ideas referred to as the "simple life."

A fascination with the "poor, old, hackneyed simple life," as Bolton Hall's *Nation* reviewer referred to it, was perhaps the most mainstream influence on back-to-the-landers. David Shi, the simple life's most important historian, has summed up the diverse threads of its thinking as "an approach to living that self-consciously subordinates the material to the ideal." The more memorable phrase is Wordsworth's "plain living and high thinking."[33] As the *Nation* reviewer made clear, interest in the "poor, old, hackneyed simple life" had come and gone before. Renewed interest in these years seems to have been triggered by a book called *The Simple Life* that appeared in the United States in 1901, written by the Alsatian Protestant minister Charles Wagner, who had gained some renown from his Paris lectern as an advocate of a social-gospel style of Christianity. Wagner's book was widely read in the United States, after an enthusiastic recommendation from Theodore Roosevelt set the stage for a national tour in 1904.

Simple life ideas were already evident in back-to-the-land writing even before Wagner's book appeared.[34] Hubert's *Liberty and a Living* (published in 1889 and 1903) recounted the author's move from Manhattan to a one-acre plot out on rural Long Island, where he provided for his family by gardening and fishing (and by continuing to write). As Hubert saw it, Americans worked too hard in the pursuit of too much money and ended up incapable of enjoying leisure or

HOME

From the frontispiece of Philip G. Hubert's *Liberty and a Living* (1889). A stylishly rustic room testifies to this family's adherence to the "simple life": sparse furnishings and bare floors bear witness to frugality in outward display, while the open grand piano and the violin on the center table demonstrate devotion to culture. The musical inscription over the fireplace is a little joke for those with a taste for the avant-garde music of the day: the invocation of the fire-god Loge from Richard Wagner's opera "Die Walküre."

culture. The "problem to be solved" was the fact that life, "to the average man, means hard, anxious work, with disappointment at the end, whereas it ought to mean pleasant work, with plenty of time for books and talks."[35] The solution Hubert proposed was to reject long hours of work and superfluous luxuries in favor of plainer living in the country where one would have free time to indulge in music, books, and outdoor leisure. The house Hubert built expressed that philosophy: it was "simple" and relatively inexpensive, he reported, but its great room's massive hand-hewn beams reflected the most advanced decorating styles.

Perhaps the best example of the intersection between the "simple life" idiom and back-to-the-land writing was a series of sketches published under the name of David Grayson in the *American Magazine*. *Adventures in Contentment*, the book made from those sketches, was published in the same year as *Three Acres and Liberty*, but the two were miles apart in style and approach. Hall's book chronicled colossal yields from urban garden plots; David Grayson chronicled his own inner moods. Hall told hopeful stories of poor and disabled city dwellers gaining independent livings for themselves; Grayson told the tale of an urban professional forced by exhaustion and illness to retire to a farm. Hall's prose was direct and punchy; Grayson's was dream-like and musing. The contemplative style of *Adventures in Contentment* somewhat resembled Wagner's *Simple Life*, blending commentaries on the natural world, books, and human nature into a self-consciously homespun philosophy.

In fact, *Adventures in Contentment* is hardly a back-to-the-land book at all. Its first reviewers and readers were confident that it advocated a return to the land (more about why in chapter 2), but a modern reader might miss the message altogether. David Grayson regarded fields and barns as objects of philosophical contemplation rather than sites of production. As to the farm, its chief virtue was the opportunity it offered to cultivate the simple life: "If a man is in reality simple, if he love true contentment, it is the place of all places where he can live his life most freely and fully." "The city," he argued, "affords no such opportunity" for contemplation. Instead, as writers since Virgil had been arguing, city living destroyed "the desire for the higher life" through "the seductiveness with which it flaunts its carnal graces."[36] From this perspective, a return to the farm was essentially an aid to the development of a "higher life" rooted in very old—indeed, ancient—beliefs about the wickedness of city existence.

Arts and Crafts

Some back-to-the-land advocates gave the "simple life" tool a somewhat sharper edge than it had in David Grayson's hands. Gustav Stickley, a leading figure in the American Arts and Crafts movement, was an important advocate of a return to the land. Stickley began publishing his magazine the *Craftsman* in 1901 as a showcase for his unified vision of furniture and housing design; it quickly came to promote an entire attitude toward life—what might now be termed the Craftsman "lifestyle." Following in the footsteps of John Ruskin and William Morris in England, Arts and Crafts advocates in the United States searched for a means of restoring the dignity and value of labor by recreating the preindustrial workshops of skilled craftsmen and the self-sufficiency of workers on small plots of land. By 1910, nearly all *Craftsman* issues were carrying articles on back-to-the-land themes, often written by Stickley himself. Each featured a design for a house, and these too sometimes furthered Stickley's rural interests, as did "Craftsman House #108," which lived up to its claim that it was "designed with especial thought for the convenience of the New Farmer" by including designs for a barn and a poultry house.[37]

Stickley's agenda was an aesthetic one that over time became increasingly political: a program of liberating Americans from their dependence on the degenerating effects of industrially produced mass-marketed goods. Stickley made use of the rhetoric of the simple life to attack the new power of advertising and the rise of consumer culture. In 1902, he reviewed at length Charles Wagner's *The Simple Life*; an excerpt from the book appeared later that year. The November 1904 issue of the *Craftsman* featured Wagner's photograph as the frontispiece and included three articles about Wagner and his message.[38] In a defining 1911 editorial, Stickley reproached the American public for doing "exactly as it is ordered or cajoled by advertising picture and pen." Advertisers fooled the public into purchasing adulterated food, mass-produced artworks that "pervert[ed] its intelligence," clothes that made people "ridiculous and miserable," and furniture that was "a degradation to art and a mockery to comfort." All this was done, he concluded, only so that "the factories flourish and increase." He urged Americans not to accept "this monstrous condition of commercial prostitution" but to seek an alternative to the "commercializing" of "our souls." The title of the editorial made that alternative clear: "Why Back to the Farm?" For Stickley, a return to the land was a fundamental part of the rejection of useless and ugly manufactured goods and of the bondage to the marketplace they encouraged.[39]

Historians have often pointed out the dilemma of Arts and Crafts advocates, who found that their efforts to create better conditions for workers could be sustained only by producing very expensive products for the wealthy. In addition, Arts and Crafts enthusiasts often found their efforts co-opted by the very advertisers whose influence they struggled against.[40] Stickley was painfully aware of these internal contradictions. In the pages of the *Craftsman*, he tried to resolve them, arguing that the simple life on the farm and in the workshop (if not the high priced handmade furniture and decorative objects) was within reach of ordinary people. One *Craftsman* article, entitled "A Living from a Three-Acre Farm: Possibilities of Health and Happiness for the Man with Small Means," explained how people from the "intelligent class of city laborers, having families and some capital," who were "dissatisfied with their present life and its limitations," could make a living on a small farm.[41]

Hoping to provide land and training to a broader spectrum of the population, Stickley formed plans for a project called Craftsman Farms. He established a farm in Morris Plains, New Jersey, built cottages, and laid plans for a "school for citizenship," which he hoped would educate "less fortunate youths" in the newest agricultural techniques. The plans came to nothing: overextended financially, Stickley published the last issue of his *Craftsman* in 1916 and was forced to declare bankruptcy.[42]

Stickley's Craftsman movement and its back-to-the-land component had a decidedly trans-Atlantic feel. In its first two issues, as one might expect, the magazine acknowledged British arts and crafts leaders William Morris and John Ruskin, but soon it was branching out, featuring not only the ideas of Charles Wagner, but also those of English socialist Edward Carpenter and Russian anarchist Peter Kropotkin. With such guides, Stickley was journeying along paths decidedly less well-traveled than those of the more conventional simple life. Among British socialists, Edward Carpenter was a tremendously influential and controversial figure. Along with Eleanor Marx and William Morris, he had helped to found the Socialist League in 1884; in 1893, he was a founder of the Independent Labor Party. His radicalism extended in all directions, with a *joie de vivre* best expressed in the title of one of his books: *Civilization, Its Cause and Cure* (1891). In addition to a return to the land, Carpenter espoused vegetarianism, Hindu mysticism, and the free expression of homosexuality— all while living on and working his own small farm with the help of his lifelong partner and the proceeds of a family inheritance. He was perhaps best known in England for his handmade sandals, which became a badge of the left counterculture in the late nineteenth century.[43] Stickley published extracts from several of Carpenter's works in the *Craftsman*, describing him as a "great leader and genius" who was unfortunately little known in the United States: "an English gentleman by class and education" who had "voluntarily elected to earn his daily bread . . . as an artisan."[44]

The anarchist Peter Kropotkin was another matter still. Exiled from Russia as a young man, Kropotkin settled in England in 1886, where he joined an assortment of British socialists and labor union activists looking for ways to bring "the land to the people, or the people to the land." England provided a richly supportive environment for back-to-the-land and redistributive projects in the late nineteenth century.[45] An aristocratic monopoly on land made systemic change nearly impossible, but along the entire spectrum of the left, from anarchists and Marxists to trade union and parliamentary socialists, a commitment to back-to-the-land efforts ran broad and deep. At the turn of the century, in spite of their different circumstances, connections flourished between American and British back-to-the-land advocates. British and American books crossed the Atlantic frequently, and Kropotkin's work was an important part of that trans-Atlantic trade in ideas. The *Craftsman* published excerpts from Kropotkin's works and discussed his ideas at length, helping to introduce them to American readers. True, Stickley acknowledged, Kropotkin was an "Anarchist-Communist," and that was a "term full of terror for the average American reader." Yet it was important for *Craftsman* readers to know that "throughout the civilized world" Kropotkin was "known and honored as a brilliant scientist."[46]

Two of Kropotkin's books were particularly important in popularizing his views in the United States. (Kropotkin visited the United States in 1897, when the *Atlantic Monthly* agreed to publish his memoirs.) The first, *Mutual Aid* (1902), was a challenge to social Darwinism. It argued that neither animals nor human beings were motivated primarily by a struggle for dominance but that they were naturally inclined to help and support one another—that, in fact, evolution rewarded cooperation. As Kropotkin put it, he wanted to combat the general belief that "the struggle for the means of existence . . . of every man against all other men, was 'a law of Nature.'" The erroneous assumption that a "pitiless inner war for life" was a necessary condition of progress was a barrier to the real evolution of human society.[47]

Mutual Aid was widely read among American progressives. (In 1903, the *Craftsman* published its review, followed the next month by a more in-depth study of a single chapter.)[48] The book was particularly popular with those Americans who shared the homegrown mystical faith in a naturally evolving socialism (as opposed to socialism that emerged from class conflict), along the lines described by Edward Bellamy in *Looking Backward*. To those Americans who had followed the spiritual and political evolution of Leo Tolstoy to Christian anarchism, *Mutual Aid* seemed to walk the same path, integrating the new Darwinian vision of a world in endless flux with an older search for the reconciliation of humankind in the kingdom of God.

For most American back-to-the-land writers, however, Kropotkin provided inspiration of a more practical sort, derived from an earlier collection, *Fields, Factories, and Workplaces* (1899). There, Kropotkin argued that progressives should anticipate and welcome a future deglobalization of the economy, when nations and regions would aspire to self-sufficiency in agriculture and industry. He asserted that experts had far underestimated the productive capacities of the land, and that it would be possible in a just system to feed every human being and to do it so efficiently that there would be leisure time to spare. What caught the attention of most American writers, however, was the sheer force of the statistics. Kropotkin was a geographer by training and had traveled throughout Russia and many parts of Europe. He displayed this extensive knowledge with a brilliant array of examples of tremendous crop yields on tiny acreage in those parts of Europe that had been forced by population pressure to develop "intensive" agricultural techniques.

A Little Land Well Tilled

Intensive farming—"a little land well tilled"—was the concept most often linked to Kropotkin's name in these years. (The preface to *How to Live in the Country*, for example, praised its author Edward Payson Powell for "knowing birds as well as [naturalist John] Burroughs, fruit as well as [botanist Luther] Burbank, and intensive farming better than Kropotkin.")[49] In the United States, the progressive agricultural press had been advocating what they considered "intensive farming" since the mid-nineteenth century; the phrase had then referred primarily to raising crop yields by crop rotation and the use of fertilizers. At the turn of the twentieth century, "intensive farming" meant techniques that allowed European peasants to get large yields from small places. It might refer to methods that entailed expending a lot of energy on a small plot: careful weeding, watering, and harvesting to prevent waste. Or the phrase might refer to the techniques pioneered by European market gardeners around cities: gardening under glass, the careful or the lavish use of manure, or intercropping— growing several crops either simultaneously or right after one another on the same ground. Among British gardeners, such techniques were known as "French gardening," because they were used in the suburbs around Paris. As Kropotkin explained, such techniques had been practiced for centuries in the heavily populated parts of northern Europe.

Most American back-to-the-landers probably encountered Kropotkin's ideas first by reading Bolton Hall, who assimilated into his own work both of the arguments for which Kropotkin was famous. Industrial capitalism, in Hall's depiction, had made life just the sort of brutal Darwinian struggle Kropotkin had asserted was neither natural nor inevitable. Intensive farming could help people "who could no longer keep up the rapid pace of our industrial life," people whose physical disabilities "held them back in the race for work," people who had been defeated by "sharp competition in modern business"— people, in short, who had lost that Darwinian struggle.[50]

To Hall and others like him, the idea of intensive farming had a distinct political resonance. Not simply a method of producing high yields, intensive farming seemed to favor the amateur, the small landowner, and the undercapitalized. It implied that one might substitute hand labor and personal care for expensive equipment, hired labor, and borrowed money. Today an advocate might refer to this sort of intensive agriculture as a "soft" or "appropriate" technology—small scale, democratic, easy to comprehend, and widely accessible without expensive inputs or expert knowledge. (Today, however, the phrase "intensive farming" has lost nearly all its positive connotations and is used as a synonym for unsustainable and destructive farm practices: heavy applications of pesticides and herbicides and "intensive" crowding of animals.) For these reasons, the idea of intensive farming and especially the phrases "a little land well tilled" or simply "little lands" came to signify something more than a technique. In the back-to-the-land setting, these phrases were understood to represent opportunities for would-be farmers with little money and not much experience. In the American context, too, Kropotkin's assertions that the land could support a vastly larger population could be read as an argument against nativists who contended that immigration undermined the ability of the nation to feed itself.

Bolton Hall embraced the concept of intensive farming with religious intensity. Friends and colleagues were skeptical, but he maintained his conviction that there was an almost limitless possibility in an acre of land. Later in his life he insisted that there was scientific proof that the entire world's population could be supported from the agricultural products of Texas alone. Herbert Quick, editor of *Farm and Fireside*, wrote to Hall affectionately: "To me, your position on the capacity of land to support population is of all things in the world the most absurd, but I know you believe in it."[51] Hall may have taken his faith in the land's capacity to absurd lengths, but that was because intensive agriculture was inextricably linked with his conviction that in America there was room for the immigrant and hope for the poor.

Not everyone who advocated "intensive farming" at the turn of the century shared Hall's understanding of its meaning. Some agricultural experts in the country life movement promoted intensive techniques as a means for farmers, mired in old-fashioned subsistence practices, to break through to capital accumulation. (This was reading Kropotkin "against the grain," interpreting intensive techniques as "hard" technology, requiring expensive infrastructure and expert intervention.) The idea that Chinese or Belgian or Russian peasants produced prodigious yields from intensive gardens might lead to admiring efforts to imitate their work—but it could also feed nativist fears of being over-whelmed by aliens.

Stickley, for his part, suggested in 1911 that Americans could learn from the example of recent immigrants: while native-born workers were responding to hard times by sitting "with folded hands in dejection, lamenting that there was no profitable employment," Japanese, Chinese, and Italian immigrants were "showing Americans how much better and easier it is to get a living directly from the soil."[52] On the other hand, George H. Maxwell, an advocate for irri-gated homesteads in the West, argued in several books that millions of "home-crofts" were urgently needed in the West in order to stop the movement of Japanese farmers onto American land. In *Our National Defense* (1915), Maxwell based virtually his entire argument for government-sponsored homesteads on his apprehension that Japanese intensive gardeners had made their own small nation unnaturally vital and strong and his belief that their strength, combined with American weakness in this regard, would lead ultimately to war.[53] Max-well, too, believed that Kropotkin's statistics supported his argument.

More often, perhaps, popular writers picked up Kropotkin's promises of the potential in intensive farming and were simply deaf to its political implica-tions. In W. Bert Foster's novel *The Heron Nest*, for example, two brothers in their onion patch converse about intensive farming using the language of race—or perhaps it is race they are discussing in the language of farming: "'Talk about Chinese gardening!' exclaims Jack. 'We beat the Chinks, I do believe. We're going to get a lot of stuff off of this little piece, Billy.'" Jack's brother Billy re-sponds with a little lecture: "Consider the farmer of Brittany. There intensive farming has been carried on for generations." "Billy" surpassed even Bolton Hall in his optimistic assessment of the potential in intensive farming. He as-serted that a family could be "kept in comfort" not on three acres but on a mere *quarter* of an acre of land.[54]

Vacant Lots

Bolton Hall's reading of Kropotkin was influenced by his own political experi-ences. Many years before he wrote *Three Acres and Liberty*, Hall had gotten in-volved with the Vacant Lot Gardening Committee in New York, an effort to make vacant city lots available as gardens for the poor. The New York vacant lot project had been inspired by an experiment in Detroit conducted during the depression years of the 1890s. Nicknamed the "Pingree Potato Patch Plan" for the leadership of the reforming Mayor Hazen Pingree, Detroit's vacant lot project inspired a number of other cities to experiment with similar self-help initiatives.[55] In *Three Acres and Liberty*, Hall described at length how these tiny plots of land could make the difference between health and illness—or even between life and death—for the poor.

In fact, Hall did more than write about it. After the publication of his second book, he conducted his own experimental garden on a third of an acre up in Harlem (137th Street and Lenox Avenue, to be precise). There, as the sensationalist *New York World* had it, the "lawyer, lecturer, author and plutocrat was transformed into a blue jeaned farmer."[56] As this description suggests, Hall's political commitments were a little baffling to some observers. A well-known figure in New York, he was treated by the city press with a combination of patronizing affection and bewilderment.

Bolton Hall was the son of John Hall, the pastor of the Fifth Avenue Presbyterian Church whose congregation was made up of New York's wealthiest and most conservative Christians. In 1898, the *New York World* reported that Hall had been "disinherited for his charities" (at his father's death years earlier) and was now declaring bankruptcy. As the story went, "Rev. John Hall preached to the rich, received their confidences[,] . . . sympathized with their sorrows and was one of them," while his son "preached to the poor, heard their complaints, helped them in every way he could," and finally, by virtue of his bankruptcy, "made himself one of them."[57]

Hall was trained as a lawyer; one newspaper referred to him as a "millionaire lawyer," but he apparently denied the "millionaire" designation. A letter from Elbert Hubbard, the founder of the Roycroft Arts and Crafts workshop, apologized for having passed on rumors about Hall's wealth, adding "I am glad to know that you are not a rich man—it puts you right in my class and brings us very close together."[58] That was not quite an accurate description, either. Hall walked a very fine line; he was both a member of New York's loftiest social circles and a radical reformer. For most of his life, he lived in elegant Manhattan neighborhoods—but in houses he did not own. (First his father-in-law and later his son-in-law owned the properties.) His wife's name often appeared in the society columns along with those of other wealthy ladies who sponsored charitable efforts. Some of Susie Scott Hall's social activities, however, suggest the ambiguity of the couple's position. In 1895, for example, the *New York Times* announced with full society pomp a reception to be held by Mrs. Hall that afternoon, but went on to explain that the great single-tax reformer Henry George would be one of the guests and that "the relation of the land question to the unemployed will be discussed."[59]

Lawyer, socialite, millionaire or not, Hall had exemplary radical connections. He was arrested with Ida Rauh Eastman for distributing birth control pamphlets in 1916. A year later he testified on behalf of defendants Emma Goldman and Alexander Berkman when they were tried for speaking out against conscription. Years before, at a dinner honoring Tolstoy in 1898, Hall intimated something of the role he imagined for himself. "The destruction of our present system of society," he argued, would not be accomplished by "the Goths and the Vandals whom we are raising in the slums of our great cities and in the isolation of our farms and jails" but by "educated and influential" people. It was privileged people like himself, Hall argued, who had the opportunity to "study the keystone of the arch." It would be they, "from their position of advantage," who would "pull it out" and bring the system down.[60]

One journalist mused, "Mr. Hall is a philosophical anarchist and a genial socialist—or he is a genial anarchist and a philosophical socialist—or is he only a land reformer?"[61] Perhaps "only" a land reformer was the best description after all. In fact, Hall was best known in his day as a proponent of Henry George's plan for a single tax.

The Single Tax

Single taxers were a committed and fervent group at the turn of the century. Following the analysis laid out by Henry George in *Progress and Poverty* (1879), they based their arguments on the fundamental premise that no one had a right to own the natural resources—land in particular, so critical to survival—that belonged to all humans collectively. As Joseph Dana Miller explained in the *Single Tax Year Book* (1917), "Men have a right to land because they cannot live without it and because no man made it. It is a free gift of nature, like air, like sunshine . . . It is, if you please, a natural right."[62] Henry George had concluded that the profound injustice he saw everywhere around him had arisen over time from the custom of allowing property in land to accumulate in the hands of a few powerful men. He proposed a radically simple solution: remove land from the open market. It would be just, George argued, to confiscate the landgrabbers' holdings, but it would be simpler to tax away all the profit in holding the land: "We may safely leave them the shell, if we take the kernel."[63]

Taxing the full value of the "unearned increment"—that is, the increase in land value caused by the general growth of the community rather than by improvements made by the owner—would mean that speculating in land would no longer make sense. If the incentive for holding land as a speculative investment disappeared, those who had real uses for land—for farming or mining, shops or housing—would find it readily available. Most important, everyone would have access to enough land to guarantee a basic subsistence. It was a complex argument, but one that made sense to a great many people at the turn of the century. (Because the idea was so difficult to explain, one single-tax advocate invented a game to demonstrate how the status quo inevitably led to the concentration of wealth and resources in the hands of the few: she called her game "The Landlord's Game," but when she sold its patent to Parker Brothers in 1935 they renamed it "Monopoly.")[64]

Bolton Hall was a key figure in the single-tax movement, one of the founders of the New York Tax Reform Association and president of the American Single Tax League. Hall remained a committed single taxer all his life, long after the movement's popularity had waned. (He died in 1938.) Perhaps it was this enduring conviction that allowed Hall to live with the conflicting ideological and personal demands that characterized his life. At any rate it helped him to apply a little humor to the situation. In the 1900 census, Hall, his wife and two children were living with his father-in-law (along with a maid, a cook, a laundress, a nurse, and a children's maid) in a house on East 65th Street. Hall told the census taker that year that his occupation was "land gambler." (The authors of *Who's Who Among North American Authors* seem not to have understood this tongue-in-cheek self-description: they listed Hall as "land speculator" in 1921.)[65]

Hall was not alone in linking his single-tax faith to a back-to-the-land agenda. Henry George himself had argued that if land were removed from the market, independent smallholdings would again be ubiquitous. Workers, now able to provide for their own needs, could be truly independent of the demands of their employers.[66] The wealthy Philadelphia manufacturer Joseph Fels (whose company made the famous Fels-Naptha soap) was an ardent supporter of both single-tax and back-to-the-land programs. Like Hall, Fels began his philanthropic work as a supporter of his city's Vacant Lot Cultivation Association. Fels, too, had been moved by the poverty and suffering he witnessed during the depression years of the 1890s, and he was convinced that land speculation was the root cause of the pervasive injustice he saw around him. Like Hall, Fels became a conduit for trans-Atlantic back-to-the-land communication. In the first decade of the twentieth century, Fels established a second home in England, where he met Kropotkin and other key players, and became active in the British movement. He put his money to work on behalf of many causes, from supporting a campaign to pass single-tax legislation in Denmark to offering financial help to Booker T. Washington to establish self-sufficient towns for African Americans.

Back home in Philadelphia, Fels played a similar role, in a city that was awash in back-to-the-land ideas.[67] His brother Maurice was deeply involved with the colony of Alliance, a nearby Jewish back-to-the-land settlement, operating a demonstration farm and a canning factory nearby. William L. Price, an influential Arts and Crafts–inspired architect, and Frank Stephens, a sculptor, founded several experimental communities around Philadelphia. The most important of these was Arden, in nearby Delaware, bankrolled by Joseph Fels. Founded in 1900, Arden was arguably the most successful single-tax "enclave," as they were dubbed.[68] Fels also gave critical support to the largest of the enclaves, in Fairhope, Alabama, funding its library and telephone system and more than once rescuing the community from financial disaster.

Fiske Warren, a wealthy Massachusetts paper manufacturer, founded two similar single-tax colonies: Tahanto in Massachusetts and Halidon in Maine. And Hall himself established a single-tax enclave of his own on a more modest scale in New Jersey, called Free Acres. These "enclaves" were intended to liberate land from the speculative marketplace so that its inhabitants could use it for self-sufficient gardening, but farming and gardening were not always an important part of the community's agenda. Fairhope, for example, did not become an agricultural community at all but a small resort city, as befitted its location on the shore of the Gulf of Mexico. At Tahanto, Arden, and Free Acres, colonists maintained active gardens, but many members used their leaseholds primarily for summer vacationing.[69]

Still, one never knew where the experience of those summer single taxers might lead. One vacationer at Arden was a young economics professor named Scott Nearing—at the time a "mild liberal," as socialist and fellow Ardenite Upton Sinclair later recalled.[70] From 1906 to 1915, while Nearing taught economics at the Wharton School, he and his wife Nellie Seeds Nearing spent their summers at Arden. It was there that Nearing became a vegetarian, and there, too, that he learned to garden and to build with stone. Although Nearing soon rejected the single-tax agenda in favor of socialism, he maintained a close relationship with Fels. As Nearing later recalled, "My quest for the good life began in a back office in Philadelphia and led on to a Delaware community called Arden."[71]

The skills Nearing acquired at Arden would come in handy when his increasingly radical and idiosyncratic views got him fired from his teaching position at the Wharton School, blacklisted by other academic employers, and later even ejected from the Communist Party. When he left New York for the wilds of Vermont in 1932, Scott Nearing would bring his Arden experiences with him. Years later, he and the woman who became his second wife, Helen Knothe

A SIMPLE MANSION AT FREE ACRES

Bolton Hall poses in front of his "simple mansion" at Free Acres, the single tax "enclave" he founded in New Jersey in 1910. The juxtaposition of the dress shirt and tie with the broom and rudimentary cabin reflects Hall's characteristic sense of humor, as does the sign above the cabin door: "Suepine Hall" is a complex pun, alluding to the "pine" cabin itself and to the promise of relaxation there—a "supine (Bolton) Hall." It is also a slighting reference to his legal practice ("suing"). Perhaps he was even including his wife Susie's name in the joke. From the second edition (1918) of Hall's *Three Acres and Liberty*.

Nearing, wrote their own back-to-the-land story, *Living the Good Life* (1954). Reprinted in 1970, that book would become the bible of a back-to-the-land movement yet another generation in the future—and in it, the building and gardening skills learned at Arden would be passed on.

Little Lands

Single taxers were not the only ones to establish back-to-the-land colonies in the early twentieth century. William Ellsworth Smythe based his colonies on a somewhat different ideological foundation. Born in Massachusetts, Smythe had gone west and became a journalist for the *Expositor* in Kearney, Nebraska, and then the Omaha *Bee*. During the drought of 1890, while he was in Omaha, Smythe began the work of his lifetime. In the course of the depression that followed, his commitment deepened into a vision that became for him "a philosophy, a religion, and a programme of practical statesmanship rolled into one."[72] For Smythe, the answer was not a tax on the unearned increment, although he found the Georgist position compelling. Nor was his answer "simple living" or a rejection of consumerism. Smythe was concerned about people who already had too little to renounce. Socialism he found irresistibly logical: no one who acknowledged "the slightest obligation to God and humanity," he wrote, could be satisfied with a system in which "a few . . . possess far beyond their need while many need far beyond their possessions."[73] Yet socialism was a distant dream. For Smythe, it was irrigation that would provide the "one way out."

During the 1890s, Smythe launched *The Irrigation Age* as the mouthpiece for the campaign to make western lands available to smallholders and to secure the federally funded irrigation projects that would make those lands usable. In *The Conquest of Arid America* (1900), Smythe imbued with messianic intensity the case for federal arid land reclamation. In his view, irrigation was no mere technical fix: it possessed almost magical powers to transform American society. Because the West enjoyed what Smythe called "the inestimable blessing of aridity," settlement there would compel farmers to irrigate, and "irrigation is an endless miracle." Irrigation would call on communities to embody all the ideals of the back-to-the-land vision: it would favor diversified crops on small plots, making farmers independent and self-sufficient. The small size of the farms would allow people to live close to one another, and "the nearer the neighbors, the greater the social advantages." Traditional rural life had been "exceedingly barren on the social side," Smythe explained in a promotional pamphlet. The new irrigated communities would do away with the "hunger of the heart" and "starvation of the soul" that had made the old farm life so hard.[74] Irrigation would require not just conquest but cooperation, encouraging settlers to reject Darwinian competition and to embrace greater mutual dependence.

In 1902 the federal Newlands Act, providing for irrigation projects on government owned land, became law; but by then Smythe had turned toward more direct methods of bringing people back to the land. Already he had helped to establish a back-to-the-land community in New Plymouth, Idaho, under the auspices of the National Irrigation Congress.[75] In 1909, Smythe founded an irrigated farm community called San Ysidro, just south of San Diego. That community received a great deal of press attention; the enthusiasm generated several spin-off communities in California, some actively sponsored by Smythe, others modeled on his vision. (Their story appears in chapters 3 and 4.)

Smythe's California settlements were known as "Little Lands," a shorthand reference to Hall's *A Little Land and a Living*. Smythe enthusiastically acknowledged Hall's influence on his ideas: "Many a smiling garden, and many a humble roof, trace back to the study of this scholarly man and lover of the race."[76] One of Smythe's colonies outside Los Angeles even acknowledged Hall's influence by playfully naming its clubhouse "Bolton Hall." The Little Lands colonies were intended to offer homes to people with very limited resources. Settlers would purchase small plots, build their own modest houses, and raise their own food; there they could provide a living for themselves even when all other options had failed them. Near the end of his life, Smythe summed up his vision: the land, he wrote, was to be "the healing and the saving of the people—of our people and of all the peoples."[77]

Hope for Our Newest Citizens?

Theoretically, most back-to-the-land advocates envisioned a return to the land just that way, as a universal solution to the problems of "all the peoples"—rich, middle class, and poor, native born and immigrant—one that would provide "hope alike for the idle, unhappy rich, for the hopeless, miserable poor, and for those in-between classes who might escape but do not know the way."[78] But they did not usually propose that "all the people" go back to the land together.

To be sure, Hall reported that his Free Acres colony included both native-born and immigrant Americans—"Roumanians, Hungarians, Italians, Jews, Germans, Americans and Irish"—and that "we get along first rate together."[79] But he was very much aware that this mix of people made Free Acres the exception rather than the rule. (He wrote this description in a 1924 letter to Charles F. Weller, who was working to liberalize the new federal immigration restrictions, aimed at a number of the ethnic groups on Hall's list.) Smythe's Little Lands colonies did host substantial numbers of first-generation immigrants, but they were mostly from western and northern Europe, at a time when the great majority of immigrants were coming from eastern and southern Europe. Nor would back-to-the-land communities—even those where immigrants were welcome—risk a challenge to the nation's most fundamental racial institutions. When single-tax leaders decided to found their colony in Alabama, it was with the understanding that if they chose to settle in the South they would be establishing a utopian community for whites only. Charles Weeks, who organized several California colonies, had no qualms about putting the matter plainly. In his colonies, only "high class people" were chosen: "those living as nearly as possible on the same plane, all belonging to the Caucasian race."[80]

Some white native-born reformers did see the back-to-the-land movement as a means of assisting people on the other side of the ethnic and class divides. African Americans were almost never included in back-to-the-land plans, but in 1907 Joseph Fels made an attempt to interest Booker T. Washington in sponsoring all-black single-tax colonies.[81] More typical was Lyman Beecher Stowe's enthusiastic support of special agricultural schools for recently arrived immigrants stranded in urban slums. In the *Outlook*, he praised the Lincoln Agricultural School in Lincolndale, New York, a Catholic school that trained "outcast Irish Roman Catholic street boys" who were "sent there from the New York Catholic Protectory." Stowe also commended the Baron de Hirsch School in Woodbine, New Jersey, for performing what he called "the modern miracle of turning young city Hebrews into adequate farmers."[82]

A 1912 *World's Work* article was similarly enthusiastic about a Little Lands experiment designed for immigrants. The article, "A Safe Way to Get on the Soil," praised the work of Father Bandini in Tontitown, which it described as a "new hope for our newest citizens and for the small seekers for land." (The phrase "small seekers" was a not very artful way of referring to Little Lands.) Tontitown was a farm colony in the Arkansas Ozarks settled by Italian immigrants.[83] By 1912 it was a thriving community of seven hundred inhabitants with "a good Catholic school."[84] The *World's Work* reporter did not describe the Tontitown project as segregated, although she made it clear that it was for Catholics only. She preferred to think of it as uniquely tailored to the special needs of this ethnic group. (Gregarious Italians would have been unhappy on isolated single-family settlements.) Nevertheless, she concluded, Tontitown was a model for everyone: "'a way out' to the man of small means who wants to get back to the land—be he Italian, or German, or just plain American."[85]

That claim of universality might have been appealing, but it did not conceal an important ambiguity in the back-to-the-land argument. In an attempt to cast doubt on the whole effort, one skeptical writer took aim at the unacknowledged incompatibility between back-to-the-land proposals intended for middle-class people and those aimed at helping working-class people and recent immigrants. Going back to the land might be a good thing for the "patched straw-hatted Pole, Czech, or Swede," he wrote, "but for you, the average city worker, there is nothing but loss. You are not used to manual labor; you are not used to loneliness."[86] This passage, with its "you" aimed at (presumably) native-born white-collar readers, reveals a truth that back-to-the-land advocates generally tried not to notice. Many back-to-the-landers embraced not one but at least two distinct back-to-the-land efforts—one for "us" and one for "them."

Even Bolton Hall distinguished between the nameless poor people who were the beneficiaries of his vacant lot programs and the readers he imagined for his books: "You see that these poor ignorant people, women, boys, cripples, old men . . . have all been able to support themselves by their work on the land." But Hall hastened to add, "You can do much better."[87] He was even willing to bend his fundamental rule that to succeed, a person must be willing to do his or her own work in the garden, since the "you" he was speaking to—"those who will read this book"—were clearly distinct from the poor and displaced people who worked the vacant lots. Addressing his readers, Hall conceded, "you can hire Italians or Germans to do it better and cheaper than you can do it yourself."[88]

Like most back-to-the-land writers, Hall assumed that he was writing for an audience who might be inspired by the massive yields Breton peasants were able to acquire from their small plots but would have been horrified at the idea of working or living like those peasants. Such an audience might sympathize with efforts to give immigrants a chance to escape the city or to create independent African American farming communities, but they would perceive those efforts as entirely separate from their own personal concerns. In any case, although progressive back-to-the-landers did support programs for immigrants and slum dwellers, most back-to-the-land projects designed for nonwhite, nonnative, or working-class people would be created and sustained by members of their own communities.

Back to the Land
from the Other Side of the Tracks

Jewish philanthropists in particular gave primary importance to the back-to-the-land project, creating an extraordinary variety of programs to help place

Jewish workers on the land.[89] Jewish experiences in the Russian Pale had fostered widespread back-to-the-land sentiments a generation before the great waves of migration to the United States began. The idea of a return to the land had grown out of a comprehensive political debate over the future of Jews in Russia. Jews who looked for a secular solution to their desperate situation in Russia saw a return to the land as part of a process of reinventing Jewish culture and shaking off the historic burdens of the ghetto. Whether they embraced a Zionist, socialist, or bundist agenda, political organizers and intellectuals nearly all accepted that there was a powerful imperative to create Jewish farmers—in Palestine, perhaps, or, if not there, in South Africa, Argentina, or the United States. As early as 1881, a group called Am Olam (Eternal People) had been founded in Odessa to assist Jews in settling on communal farms in the United States. Am Olam settled four communes in Louisiana, South Dakota, and Oregon. All had difficult and short life spans, but individuals who had lived in Am Olam settlements went on to play important roles in Jewish agricultural communities for years to come.[90]

After the devastating pogroms of 1881 inaugurated a new era of violence in the Pale, Jewish migration out of Russia became a flood. Distressed by the ever-increasing numbers of desperately poor Russian Jews in the crowded tenements of New York—and fearful that their visibility would draw negative attention to Jews in America—Jewish philanthropists had strong incentives for encouraging a return to the land.[91] In 1891, German banker and philanthropist Baron Maurice de Hirsch founded the Jewish Colonization Association, which would fund nearly all Jewish agricultural settlements worldwide between 1890 and 1917. Baron de Hirsch's funds bankrolled the Jewish Agricultural and Industrial Aid Society, founded in 1900 to help Jewish immigrants leave American cities and establish themselves on farms or in rural industrial ventures. By 1908, the Society reported that it had helped to settle well over two thousand Jewish families on the land.[92]

In the long run, only a small minority of Jewish immigrants would try their luck on the land, but providing a network of support for agricultural endeavors engaged the time and resources of many Jewish charitable organizations. One young man's story illustrates how far-flung that network was. Benjamin Brown (formerly Lipshitz), an immigrant from the Pale, took a new surname from the American farmer who gave him his first job on a farm outside Philadelphia. Philadelphia was a center for Jewish back-to-the-land efforts, as it was for those headed by non-Jews. Joseph Krauskopf, the influential leader of the city's most advanced Reform congregation, established the National Farm School there in 1896 to give Jewish farmers the skills they would need to leave the slums and make a life in the country. Brown attended Krauskopf's National Farm School and then applied for and received a loan from the Jewish Agricultural Society to buy a farm in Kentucky. When that project proved unworkable, Brown returned to Philadelphia where he began to organize a colonization effort. With Krauskopf's backing, Brown led two hundred people to Utah, where they settled the largest Jewish back-to-the-land colony in the United States, a community they named Clarion.[93]

Between 1881 and 1915, around forty Jewish agricultural colonies were established in the United States (along with many others in Argentina, Canada, South Africa, and Palestine).[94] Some were collectivist, some were based on private property; many attracted Jews from socialist or labor backgrounds, others were less political. The people of Clarion had better reason to hope than most; they had the support of the influential Krauskopf, the blessings of the local Mormon authorities, and generous financial aid from the Jewish community in Salt Lake City. But the community was not so lucky in gaining the approval of the Baron de Hirsch–funded Jewish Agricultural Society; its leaders were opposed to the collectivist elements of the Clarion organization. The society not only refused to grant the Clarion colony financial support but publicly attacked it and warned others not to fund it, ultimately making the colony's failure inevitable.

Even this rancorous conflict, however, suggests how widespread was the Jewish belief in the value of a return to the land. Capitalists and socialists, labor organizers and business leaders, religious and secular, assimilated Germans and "oriental" Russians—all condemned the harsh necessity that had made European Jews traders and peddlers—"luftmenshn" who lived on air rather than sweated and toiled on the land. The Clarion colony's 1912 promotional pamphlet promised that a "great exodus from the congested cities toward the country" would transform Jewish culture. "New and fresh blood," as they put it in a rather disturbing image, "will begin to circulate through our enfeebled Jewish veins." Farming would prove to the world that Jews had been forced into their occupations as peddlers and tailors by the oppressive circumstances of the ghetto, not by their collective character. As the Clarion pamphlet put it, "Wherever the Jew has an equal opportunity . . . he throws off his peddling pack and yard stick and is off to the infinite bountiful prairies of the West."[95] Krauskopf, too, argued that farming would transform the minds and bodies of Jews and "build up physical and mental and spiritual health instead of ghetto degeneracy and disease."[96]

This perspective, with its distaste, even revulsion, for the "ghetto degeneracy" of life in the Pale, was clearly rooted in the unique circumstances of Jewish life. But it also resonated with American back-to-the-land ideas. Krauskopf had been inspired by an 1894 meeting with Tolstoy; Hall, Stickley, and many other non-Jewish radicals had an equal regard for Tolstoy's words and example. Mainstream Americans had their own agrarian values to draw on: many of them, too, shared with Jewish back-to-the-landers a sense that the farm would return to an "enfeebled" society the "physical and mental and spiritual health" of its people.

These ideas even found an answering echo among some African American leaders, in spite of the uniquely discouraging conditions they confronted. Most African Americans were already "on" the land and often kept there by force, so they were hardly a likely audience for promoters targeting city dwellers. Few of those who had left for cities would be eager to return to the system of near enslavement that characterized rural life for most African Americans. Nevertheless, some of the fundamental beliefs of the back-to-the-land movement resonated here, too. Booker T. Washington, in particular, embedded those beliefs in the cooperative extension work at Tuskegee and the farm training for students there. The Tuskegee Institute assisted local residents in Fort Davis in west Texas, where a number of Buffalo Soldiers had been stationed during the late nineteenth century, in purchasing two thousand acres of land for small farms. Tuskegee also sponsored mobile farmers' institutes that encouraged southern black farmers to embrace key back-to-the-land directives: to diversify their crops, stay out of debt, and produce more of their own food and clothing.[97]

Washington argued that self-sufficient agriculture was a critical means of advancement for African Americans. He spoke lovingly of his own gardens, and he encouraged household self-sufficiency as the best way to escape the trap of sharecropping. Most important, Washington insisted that people who wished to acquire the full dignity of independence and citizenship should be able to feed themselves. One of his informal Sunday evening talks, for example, expressed the essence of the Tuskegee message. Washington argued that African Americans who sought rights in the city had their priorities wrong. "We like to go into a city and discuss what seat we shall sit on in the car, where we will walk on the street . . . where we will drink soda-water"—but these were secondary matters. Instead of agitating for the rights of citizenship, "the man who is wise, goes out into the country, miles from any street car or soda fountain, and makes a kingdom for himself." There, as Washington promised, the black man would be "where he is master of all, and where he can say what shall take place and what shall not take place."[98]

Like nearly every other aspect of early twentieth-century culture, back-to-the-land projects were deeply divided by class and race. But their advocates also shared a vision that was in many ways consistent across the class divide and even across the color line. Older American agrarian attitudes about the vital significance of rural life resonated with Jewish hopes that a new life on the land would create a regenerated people and even with the Tuskegee plan to create an independent black yeomanry. Booker T. Washington promoted self-sufficient farming as a means of defending the honor and dignity of African Americans who had virtually no other means of defending themselves. Still, his prescription was not completely different from the one advocated in the popular mainstream press, presumably aimed at middle-class or at least literate, primarily white and native-born, back-to-the-landers.

In *Collier's*, for example, Julian Burroughs (son of the famous nature writer John Burroughs) articulated the connection between self-sufficiency and independence, explaining that a back-to-the-lander must undergo "a complete revolution in his attitude toward all the real things of life." The "revolution" Burroughs contemplated—spending far less money on clothes, entertainment, and even doctors' bills—entailed a complete rejection of the consumer temptations just beginning to present themselves to many city dwellers in favor of a way of life based on old-fashioned producer values. These readers, too, were enjoined to avoid going to town to buy soda water—and to build instead a "kingdom" in the country.

The common ground that supported all these variations on the back-to-the-land agenda was a "producerist" vision linking self-sufficient households, autonomous work, and personal independence.[99] Edward Payson Powell put it succinctly in *The Country Home* (1904): "In the country our first aim is not to amass, but to produce; not so much to spend, as to create."[100] Nearly all back-to-the-landers shared Booker T. Washington's belief that independence of thought and action was rooted in the ability to feed and shelter oneself. Nor was Washington the only spokesman to refer to that independence as "manhood," a word that had long-standing associations with citizenship and an older artisanal republican tradition. A back-to-the-land advocate might envision an audience of native-born Protestant white-collar workers, Jewish garment workers, or even African American tenant farmers, but the message remained much the same. Self-sufficient households on the land could fulfill the dream of an independent competence, in a time when it seemed increasingly that nothing else could.

2

Adventures in Contentment

Some Back-to-the-Land Writers and Their Readers

After *Three Acres and Liberty*, Bolton Hall wrote several more books, beginning with *A Little Land and a Living* (1908) and *The Garden Yard* (1909). Hall wrote about the single tax and about Tolstoy; he wrote advice books about sleep and about the grieving process. (His *Halo of Grief* was reportedly a favorite of a much later homesteader, Helen Nearing.)[1] He even wrote a simplified version of the King James Bible. Hall was not particularly interested in making a profit from his books. In fact, he was so eager to get his messages out that in 1914 he put a notice in the *Survey* (the journal of record for social workers) offering to *lend* his books to anyone who wanted them. With the exception of *Three Acres and Liberty*, published by Macmillan, Hall brought out his back-to-the-land books under his own imprint, Arcadia Press, which he apparently financed himself. Hall did not depend on book sales for his living, but he was still in some sense a professional author: he wanted his books widely read, and he expended a good deal of effort distributing them.

Macmillan had not been his first choice as publisher for *Three Acres and Liberty*. Hall submitted the manuscript first to the ambitious new publishing house of Doubleday and Page, already well known for its interest in the back-to-the-land question. In an uncharacteristic failure of vision, that press rejected his manuscript. An editor praised the book: "It is a good idea and well carried out—that we admit." The problem was that he thought the back-to-the-land fad was already over: "The same sort of thing has too often been written up before." Still, the editor was not sure: "We may prove to be wrong—for your sake we hope so."[2] His doubt turned out to be well founded, and his own publishing house helped prove him wrong.

Although Doubleday, Page turned down Bolton Hall, it published many back-to-the-land titles, beginning in the first year of its existence with J. P. Mowbray's *A Journey to Nature* (1901). The press brought out back-to-the-land stories penned by several of its established fiction writers, including Walter Prichard Eaton's *Idyl of Twin Fires* (1915), Grace Richmond's *Strawberry Acres* (1911), and Thomas Dixon's *The Life Worth Living* (1905). (Dixon was the author of the infamous *The Leopard's Spots* and *The Klansman*, books that helped to romanticize the restoration of white supremacy in the South at the turn of the century.)

From its founding, Doubleday had a significant stake in back-to-the-land publishing. In 1900, after dissolving his partnership with S. S. McClure, Frank Doubleday formed a partnership with Walter Hines Page, former editor of *Atlantic Monthly*. Doubleday kept a firm hand on the book trade; Page took charge of the periodicals. Their interest in back-to-the-land material was evident on both sides of the house. In the first five years of the new century, the press launched three (or, depending on how they are counted, four) magazines, a gesture of reckless ambition that fueled rumors that Rockefeller was funding the company. All the magazines had back-to-the-land features. *Country Life in America* was a glossy, heavily illustrated magazine that offered advice about rural life to people with the means to gratify their whims. The *Garden Magazine*, along with a short-lived effort called *Farming* which soon merged with it, was devoted to more practical advice about growing things.[3]

Most significant was Page's own mouthpiece, the *World's Work*, a hard-core progressive magazine specializing in the analysis of complex social problems. Even in its first year of publication in 1901, its pages were already filled with articles like "Going Back to the Soil" and "Can I Make a Farm Pay?" In 1912, Page turned the attention of the *World's Work* entirely to the problem of getting people back to the land, operating a clearinghouse for would-be farmers under the title "Does Anybody Want a Farm?"[4]

In fact, Doubleday identified itself with the back-to-the-land movement in the most concrete way possible. In 1910 the press moved its offices and printing plant out of Manhattan to a brand new facility on forty acres in rural Garden City, Long Island, making such a huge impact there that it got its own post office and train depot: the Country Life Press station. Heavily publicized, the Garden City plant offered a model for future decentralized suburban factories; it had space for gardens and tennis courts and had a doctor and dentist on call for employees. Although in later years the suburbs drew all sorts of businesses out of cities, at the time it seemed a daring experiment in new social arrangements—part of a rural renaissance. Doubleday and Page were so proud of their experiment that they published a book to commemorate it, complete with copious illustrations of "The Italian Pool," "The North Court—in Iris Time," and, of course, the state-of-the-art printing press itself.[5] They made a point of rebutting their critics, who had predicted that editors and writers would not be willing to move out of Manhattan.

Frank Doubleday and Walter Hines Page were not the only literary professionals to take note of the growing market for back-to-the-land literature. As one author pointed out, a professional writer would have been very obtuse not to notice that such writing paid. Truman DeWeese's *Bend in the Road* was a jocular book filled with alliterative phrases ("pleasant pastoral pursuits"), really more "garden goozle" than back-to-the-land argument; it reflected the author's expertise in advertising, not agriculture. DeWeese was a pioneer in the professionalization of that field, author of several advertising textbooks, and director of advertising for the Shredded Wheat Company.[6] Perhaps because he was an advertising man, DeWeese understood a critical fact about back-to-the-land writing. As he explained, a lot of nonsense had been written about a return to country life: "The joke-writers [and] . . . paid humorists have amused the shallow public with all sorts of entertaining stuff about the city man who 'left a lucrative practice' to struggle with . . . worm-eaten apple trees." The reason for this outpouring of literature was simple. It paid: "The publisher has read it over and said, 'This is good stuff for five dollars a page; write us some more.'"[7]

For some writers, of course, writing about going back to the land was much more than a response to the market. For Bolton Hall, Gustav Stickley, and William Ellsworth Smythe, writing was part of a lifelong commitment to creating opportunities for people on the land. For other professional reformers, back-to-the-land writing was a secondary interest or perhaps a diversion from their other pursuits. Harvey W. Wiley, the first chief chemist of the U.S. Department of Agriculture, was best known as the author of the 1906 Pure Food and Drug Act. After leaving the federal government, he became the director of the food and health department of the Good Housekeeping Institute, where he established the Good Housekeeping Seal of Approval. Most of his book titles reflected his professional expertise: *Foods and Their Adulteration* and *The Pure Food Cook Book*. Wiley's back-to-the-land story, *The Lure of the Land: Farming after Fifty* (1915), was only tangentially related to his area of expertise.

Some back-to-the-land authors, on the other hand, were simply professional freelance writers who happened on a likely topic for an article or a book. Grace Richmond was an established novelist who turned her attention to the back-to-the-land movement just once, with *Strawberry Acres*. Similarly, W. Bert Foster, who wrote *The Heron Nest*, made his living writing dime novels like *Swept Out to Sea; or, Clint Webb among the Whalers* and more respectable children's books like *With Washington at Valley Forge*. Frederick Rockwell, the author of *The Key to the Land* (1915), was a professional gardening writer: his books included *Gardening Indoors and Under Glass* and the *Gardener's Pocket Manual*. His back-to-the-land story, however, was more of a novel than a guide; it told the tale of an iron manufacturer driven out of business (and back to the land) by a trust. Freeman Tilden (whose name seems improbably apt for a back-to-the-land writer) wrote all sorts of books. His most enduring work was a popular series on the national parks, which earned him iconic status with the National Park Service later in his life. (Tilden's *Interpreting our Heritage* is still in print today, and as one Amazon .com reader put it, "Tilden is to Environmental Interpretation what Muir was to the environmental movement.") In 1917, Tilden wrote *Second Wind*, a back-to-the-land narrative about a professor who loses his job. Walter Prichard Eaton was a similarly eclectic and prolific author. Among many other things, he wrote a series of books about the Boy Scouts and their adventures—from *The Boys Scouts of Berkshire* through *The Boy Scouts in Death Valley*. Eaton's back-to-the-land story, *Idyl of Twin Fires*, tells the story of a journalist who moves to a house and farm in the Berkshires.

Back-to-the-land writers were in most ways no different from the other journalists and authors of their generation. Whether they wrote from ideological commitment, personal ambition, or the desire for a quick profit, most were freelance writers working at a time when the literary marketplace itself was becoming increasingly competitive, masculine, nationalized and industrialized.[8] That context is important to an understanding of what and how they wrote.

William Lighton's
Happy Hollow Farm

Some authors' motives were neither pure commitment nor pure profit. William R. Lighton, for example, actually did go back to the land shortly before he wrote his first story about it. A young journalist living in Omaha, Lighton had tried a number of occupations before he established himself as a writer. In 1899, he published a novel called *Sons of Strength* with Doubleday and McClure. In 1906 he covered the San Francisco earthquake for the Boston *Evening Transcript*. Then in 1908, Lighton and his family moved to Fayetteville, Arkansas. Lighton's published accounts of the move emphasized their desire to build a new Craftsman-style house on land less expensive than what they could find around Omaha. His children later told a different story, remembering that their father had been suffering severe bouts of pneumonia and pleurisy and thought the warmer climate might help him to recover.[9] Two years after their move, Lighton's essay "The Story of an Arkansas Farm" appeared in the *Saturday Evening Post*.

As Lighton explained, that first "little story of our farm" was the result of a visit from "one of the members of the staff of the Saturday Evening Post . . . on a hunt for 'copy.'"[10] The little story grew quickly into a whole series, as Lighton responded to audience demand. "The day that story appeared," Lighton later recalled, "letters began coming to us." He counted thirty-five hundred in the first three months.[11] No record remains of these letters, but looking back in 1968, Lighton's daughter also recalled that the family had been besieged by letters and visitors: "Literally hundreds of people not only wrote Dad about wanting to do something of the same thing, but 'descended' on us at the house to see in person what the place was like."[12]

Lighton was not slow to recognize a good thing when he saw it. Over the next four years, in a truly impressive display of journalistic entrepreneurialism, he parlayed the story of his family's Arkansas experiences into an article for the St. Louis *Post-Dispatch* ("Newspaper Man Finds Peace and Plenty on Ozark Farm") and a series of essays for the *Country Gentleman* ("Happy Hollow Farm"). Lighton also put his story to use as advertising copy. "Story of an Arkansas Farm" became a pamphlet for Frisco Lines, a railroad near Fayetteville, and then for the Missouri Pacific-Iron Mountain-St. Louis Railroad—same text, different pictures. Lighton reused the text again for a third pamphlet. This one advertised land considerably farther away, along the Oregon Electric Railway, with a "Willamette Valley Postscript" added.[13]

During the same years, Lighton tried yet another scheme to capitalize on the popularity of his back-to-the-land material. He founded a magazine titled (fittingly) *Back to the Land: A Magazine of Modern Farming for the Man Who Wants to Make a Profitable, Modern Farm-Home* (in the third number he added "or Woman" to the title after "the Man"). The first issue in September 1910 included the works of several neighbors alongside Lighton's *Saturday Evening Post* article. Most of the articles offered straightforward farming advice about green manures, crop rotation, and breeding stock. But the magazine's message seemed at least as powerful in its advertisements, in which real estate brokers and railroad agencies made some rather extravagant promises. These ads described north-western Arkansas as the "healthiest part of the world," where "failures are un-known" and where one might acquire a "home and independence on twenty acres" for "$25.00 cash." Lighton promised the reader inclined to doubt such claims that the magazine would stand behind its advertisers' promises, essentially offering to play the role of real estate broker. As editor, Lighton acknowledged that "those who are hunting homes are often badly confused in trying to make up their minds amongst the multitude of advertised chances." Just to make it all easier, the magazine vouched for "the trustworthiness of every real estate advertiser in these columns."[14]

Lighton's transformation of his back-to-the-land tale into advertising fodder for railroads and real estate companies garnered some appreciation from businessmen in his new home. As the guest of honor at an Arkansas Board of Trade dinner, he heard the attorney general—seconded by "General Passenger Agent E. W. Le Beaume and Advertising Agent R.E. Bassett of the Cotton Belt Railroad"—assert that he was the best thing that ever happened to Arkansas.[15] In spite of the praise, however, his magazine does not appear to have thrived; it lasted only a little more than a year.

Lighton recycled his back-to-the-land work one more time, generating two full-length books based on his farm experiences: *Letters of an Old Farmer to His Son* (1914) and *Happy Hollow Farm* (1915). But Lighton's commitment to the back-to-the-land experience proved not to be quite as deep as his commitment to the back-to-the-land story. His most popular writing was a series of dialect tales recounting the life and fortunes of a western character named Billy Fortune. That character now led Lighton in a new direction. The family sold their Arkansas farm and moved to Hollywood, where Lighton wrote the screenplay for the 1920 movie *Water, Water Everywhere,* based on his Billy Fortune stories and starring Will Rogers. At the time of the 1920 census the family was once again in Fayetteville, but they were renting a house in town, not back on their farm. Lighton is listed in that census as "author—fiction." He continued to spend most of his time in Hollywood until his death there in 1923.

All of this is not to say that Lighton's interest in rural life and agriculture was a fake. He actually did know a lot about farming, and he clearly loved it. Before the family moved to Arkansas, Lighton's expertise had already gained him a little fame back in Omaha, where the city's *Daily News* had written as early as 1906 that "when W. R. Lighton is not writing he is tending to his chickens." The article linked his two skills as a writer and a farmer: "His fame as a poultry fancier has not become so widespread as his reputation as a novelist and short story writer, but if his pen should unaccountably lose its force and ability to entertain, Mr. Lighton could profitably turn his attention to raising chickens." As if to underline how volatile and unreliable a writing career could be, the paper reiterated that "if financial adversity overtook him, he would have no trouble in making good as a poultryman and a gardener."[16]

In later years, as Lighton's fiction grew more and more popular, his editor at the *Saturday Evening Post* joked that he was foolishly wasting his valuable (and well-paid) time on farming: "We are all delighted with the new Billy Fortune yarn. Our check for one thousand dollars will go to you on Tuesday next. There are times when red hogs are not in it with literature." And again, "Take care of the typewriter and the Duroc Reds [Lighton's favorite breed of pigs] will take care of themselves."[17] In the end, that is what Lighton did. The back-to-the-land movement had been a stroke of luck. For a few years he was able to combine his farming and writing skills. But writing trumped farming in the end.

Truth or Fiction?

William Lighton was no fraud. He did have a farm in the Ozarks, but his real story was not quite the same as the one he told so many times. There was nothing inherently wrong with that, of course. There might be many good reasons for a writer to tell a story that was not his own, even in the guise of a personal narrative. For back-to-the-land stories, however, the issue was a little more complicated. The letters Lighton received after his *Saturday Evening Post* article appeared in print made it clear that what his readers wanted was the literal, unvarnished truth. "Was our story fact or fiction?" Lighton reported they had inquired. "Was it actually possible for a pair of average mortals . . . to find what we had found, to do what we had done? Would there be a fighting chance that the writers might do for themselves such a thing, having a little money and plenty of courage and strong desire?"[18] Lighton printed up a pamphlet to send to all those correspondents. First of all, he protested, his story was "literally true, every word of it, without a scrap of fiction or exaggeration."[19] Lighton found it necessary to answer so categorically because he knew that back-to-the-land authors had to avoid even the appearance of invention. The rest of his pamphlet addressed his readers' practical questions about land prices, the social environment, the labor problem.[20] But if readers were to trust that information, they needed reassurance. They viewed these stories, after all, not as simple entertainment, but as possible models for their own behavior.

Writers who hoped to sell their stories found it necessary to wrap them in a variety of truthful-looking packages. Like Lighton, they typically presented their work as coming from an ordinary man (or less frequently a woman) with a personal story to tell, and they took pains to avoid the impression that the story was carefully wrought by a professional. One 1908 article in the *Century Magazine*, for example, began a fact-laden report on the growth of fruit farming in the Northwest with what had clearly become an almost obligatory touch of personal candor. In this case it was a letter from one family member to another. "Dear Cousin Joe: Cousin Phebe tells me that you are in poor health, and that she thinks you would give up railroading if you could find some better way of earning a living." The narrator, who is described as over sixty and on a government pension, suggests coming to Washington and growing fruit on a "one-acre ranch."[21]

Like Lighton's stories, many back-to-the-land accounts were written in the first person and at least appeared to be autobiographical. Writers offered to reveal all sorts of personal information, ostensibly so that readers could judge the feasibility of their own return to the land. Lighton made it explicit: "I've told you some rather intimate things, for I've wanted you to know the state of mind we were in when we began our life of farming."[22] Some writers revealed personal financial information: "Behold me, then, Harrison Whittingham, head of the Melvin and Whittingham Dry-Goods Company, with an average income of something more than $30,000 a year, and a bit laid by."[23] Other writers began with the confession of a private dream: "In the back of my mind lay the wishful hope, since a minister is, like all men, a son of mother earth, that sometime, somehow, I might get back home to mother again."[24]

Often, the stories began with a personal crisis. Lighton referred to that well-established convention when he wrote that his story was "different from the general run of back to the land stories" (in itself a fairly typical claim!) and proved it by listing a series of disasters that had *not* befallen his family: "I hadn't lost my job in town. I wasn't facing a nervous breakdown after long years of faithful service of an inhuman employer. We hadn't been worn to desperation trying to make both ends meet."[25] Lighton's mockery was apt. Other back-to-the-land tales did typically begin with such a moment of truth—the loss of a job, a mental or physical illness, a child at risk. His claim that there had been no such "harsh and bitter fact in our lives," however, was not quite "literally true." His daughter later recalled that the family had left Omaha precisely because of the "harsh and bitter fact" of her father's chronic and debilitating lung ailments. Perhaps Lighton simply liked the image of himself and his family as sturdy pioneers rather than frail urban refugees: "We weren't driven to it, you see; we didn't go at it in fear and trembling—as a last hard resort. We went at it with fine, strong zest, as to our life's crowning adventure."[26]

Lighton, at least, was writing under his own name. Frederick Orin Bartlett, a moderately successful novelist and playwright, published his stories *One Way Out* (1911) and *New Lives for Old* (1913) under the name Will Carleton. J. P. Mowbray, who wrote *Journey to Nature*, was actually Andrew Carpenter Wheeler, a drama critic and highly paid journalist for the New York *World*. And then there was David Grayson.

The Strange Career of David Grayson

"Dear David Grayson," the woman began her letter. "If you are real, and not only a writer, I want you to help me." The woman's name was Florence Folsom, and she lived in the prosperous suburb of Upper Montclair, New Jersey. She had money troubles, but her real problem was ethical. "My husband is a lawyer, 34 years old. He is 'in wrong,' as the boys say. He came to New York about 13 years ago, a country boy, unshaped, eager, weak, light, frivolous." These character weaknesses had become terrible flaws in her husband's new urban environment. He had become addicted to drugs—"an absinthe user and a cigarette fiend." Worse yet, his work itself was immoral, so corrupt that she would not explain it on paper: "I can't tell you, here, *how* bad it all is; but bad enough." Worst of all, he had passed on his newly learned vices to their nine-year-old son, who had become "lazy, stubborn, a liar and slovenly."

Florence Folsom already knew what she and her family required—"to get out of this pretentious, expensive house" and into the country: "I've had the vision for months, of a wholesome simple out-door life for us all. I don't care how poor we are—I want to be poor."[27] That was why she was writing to David Grayson, the author of a very popular series of sketches for the *American Magazine* about a city man's return to country life. She did not know—although she clearly suspected—that "David Grayson" did not exist. (After all, she began her letter with "If you are real . . .") She knew only one thing for certain about this writer: he would understand her desire to get back to the farm.

Contemporaneous reviewers sometimes characterized David Grayson as a "twentieth-century Thoreau" or placed him in the company of popular nature writers like John Burroughs or Gene Stratton Porter. Others, with an eye to the dreamy, contemplative spirit of Grayson's sketches, drew comparisons with the work of Donald Grant Mitchell, the mid-nineteenth-century author who had written some of the earliest "country life" classics. What his early readers did not know was that the author "David Grayson" was actually Ray Stannard Baker, who by 1907 was well known under his own name as a crusading progressive journalist.

Starting as a reporter for the Chicago *Record*, Baker had built himself a reputation in the 1890s with his coverage of the Pullman strike and Coxey's army's march on Washington. He had joined the staff of *McClure's Magazine* in 1898 and risen to national prominence as the magazine turned to the aggressive style of investigative journalism soon to be known as "muckraking." In 1903, Baker's groundbreaking reports on the labor movement together with Ida Tarbell's exposé of Standard Oil and Lincoln Steffens's "Shame of the Cities" placed the

The muckraking reporter Ray Stannard Baker, gazing fearlessly into the camera, seems to assure viewers he will report only the cold, hard facts. Readers imagined his alter ego David Grayson very differently: not as the unflinching young reporter, but as a gentle older man, "a wee bit gaunt and stooped, more than a little gray," with a "quiet light" in his eyes. (George Grantham Bain Collection, Library of Congress.)

writers of *McClure's* at the forefront of progressive journalism. But in 1906, at a moment of personal crisis, Ray Stannard Baker also began to write under the name of David Grayson. In that same year Baker determined to stake his rising reputation—and his savings—on a joint enterprise with his colleagues at *McClure's*.[28]

The magazine itself was at a point of crisis in 1906. That spring, President Theodore Roosevelt had turned against his journalistic allies, comparing investigative reporters who uncovered corruption in business and government with "the man with the muck rake" in John Bunyan's *Pilgrim's Progress*, who "fixes his eyes . . . only on that which is vile and debasing." For the *McClure's* staff, the attack was a painful blow from a critically important political ally. For Baker, the attack was personal, coming from a president who had previously been lavish with his praise. Since Baker's debut as a crusading journalist in the 1903 issue of *McClure's*, Roosevelt had made conspicuous gestures of support for him, repeatedly seeking out his advice on public policy matters. Now Baker appealed to Roosevelt personally to moderate his criticism and clear the names of legitimate journalists, but to no avail. The president's denunciation opened Baker and his colleagues to attack from other quarters as well, and he found himself lampooned in the press as "Hooray Hooray Raker" and "Ray Under Taker."[29]

In the meantime, a second source of trouble for *McClure's* had unfolded, in the shape of a long and expensive libel suit that grew out of Baker's investigation of railroad trusts. The magazine stood firmly behind Baker throughout the lawsuit, paying a hefty fine when they finally lost the case in 1908. But Baker's next investigative piece, this one on the Armour Company beef trust, was not published, perhaps signaling S. S. McClure's retreat from a commitment to the magazine's "muckraking" style. Because of that prospective retreat, and because of long-standing personal and professional conflicts between McClure and his staff, in May 1906 the inner circle of *McClure's* writers determined to quit, pool their money, and purchase the *American Magazine*. As Baker later told the story in his autobiography, John Phillips, the new editor of the *American*, pleaded with his colleagues for new and different material for the magazine's first issue. Searching for something to contribute, Baker made a crucial decision: he tore up his two half-finished novel manuscripts and submitted instead a piece based on his most intimate notebook writing, never intended for publication. The sketch, titled "The Burden of the Valley of Vision," came out in the *American Magazine's* inaugural issue in 1906 under the pseudonym of David Grayson.

The David Grayson stories were an instant hit, garnering an enthusiastic response from a wide reading public. By the time of their 1907 publication in book form, the sketches had generated a cult following that would last for years: *Adventures in Contentment* was followed by *Adventures in Friendship* (1910), *The Friendly Road* (1913), and *Great Possessions* (1917). As Baker's colleague Walter Hines Page—himself no stranger to the insecurity of life as a freelance journalist—commented appreciatively, "the beauty of the thing is its steadiness."[30] Although Baker's identity was made public in 1916, he continued to write as David Grayson for the rest of his life.[31] By then, he had come to see Grayson as a kind of alter ego, an author with perspectives and experiences significantly different from those of Ray Stannard Baker.

Baker was not always sure he wanted the Grayson sketches to encourage people to go back to the land. In his autobiography, Baker acknowledged that he loved rural life and believed that it was healthy, but he stopped short of recommending it as a general prescription, commenting ruefully that many readers seemed to "think that there is some magic in living on the land."[32] Although *Adventures in Contentment* is indeed the tale of a man who leaves the city for a farm, the cryptic title of its inaugural sketch, "The Burden of the Valley of Vision," does not seem to suggest that Baker intended to write one more version of *Three Acres and Liberty* or *One Way Out*.

At first glance, in fact, *Adventures in Contentment* seems like one of those romantic "garden goozle" books that praised the joys of rural life. It offered little in the way of practical advice; it included no planting charts or lists of expenditures, no advice about gardening or raising chickens. On the other hand, Baker's first readers knew a back-to-the-land book when they saw one. In its review of the volume, the *Chicago News* commented that *Adventures in Contentment* was "another of the books intended to prove to city folk that life in the country is so much better worth living."[33] The *Springfield (MA) Republican* editorialized: "The dream of getting back to the farm holds a cherished place in the fancy of many Americans who are condemned to the noise and bustle of the marketplace," adding that the "latest of these exponents of the simple life is David Grayson."[34]

For their part, readers could point out that *Adventures in Contentment* displayed the most important features of the back-to-the-land book. David Grayson's first words in print struck just the right note of intimate first-person revelation: "I came here eight years ago as the renter of this farm, of which soon afterward I became the owner. The time before that I like to forget."[35] Those words, with their dark hint at not-quite-forgotten bad times, signaled to readers that this would be the story of an escape from the city. Indeed, the first Grayson sketch begins with what its readers would have recognized as the standard opening trope of back-to-the-land stories: the narrator undergoing a nightmarish urban experience. *The Key to the Land* opens with a financial crisis, as the narrator loses his business to a rapacious trust. *Strawberry Acres* opens with three brothers and a sister suddenly left penniless by their father's death.[36] For David Grayson, the crisis was medical. He "lay prostrate with fever and close to death for weeks and watched the world go by." But his illness turned out to be more than physical: "The only sharp pang that I suffered was the feeling that I should be broken-hearted and that I was not; that I should care and that I did not."[37] Today a physician might call it depression; doctors at the time might have diagnosed brain fever or "nervous prostration"—the term the Springfield *Republican* used in its review of the book.[38] This combination of physical and spiritual disease, too, was endemic among characters in back-to-the-land stories; it often played a key role in prompting those characters to flee from the city.

The illness was caused by an intolerably fast-paced, high-pressure, and competitive working environment. The first Grayson sketch brought the issue into sharp focus: "From the moment, as a boy of seventeen, I first began to pay my own way, my days were ordered by an inscrutable power which drove me hourly to my task." Every fiber of his being felt the pressure: "My senses, my nerves, even my muscles were continually strained to the utmost of attainment." Competition and struggle had made him little more than a slave: "I was rarely allowed to look up or down, but always forward, toward that vague Success which we Americans love to glorify. . . . If I loitered or paused by the wayside, I soon heard the sharp crack of the lash."[39]

In contrast to many other back-to-the-land stories, the Grayson stories say nothing about financial desperation. Ray Stannard Baker was, after all, a highly successful and sought-after journalist who had presumably left such money worries behind him. Before his move to the *American Magazine*, Baker was earning $7,800 per year plus royalties on his books, insulating him from the financial worries typically described in back-to-the-land books.[40] Working for *McClure's* had paid off handsomely for Baker, providing him not only that very generous salary but a nationwide audience and the collegial support of the most respected journalists of his generation—hardly the sort of circumstances one would expect to generate such a bitter condemnation of the modern work world.

Nevertheless, Baker's work life really was full of tension. As he later told the story (under his own name this time), the atmosphere at *McClure's* was nerve-racking. He longed for more freedom to work on his own writing projects. He was depressed about the unfinished novel he had abandoned and increasingly frustrated with journalism. Returning from a research trip to Germany in 1900, Baker experienced something a little like the breakdown he attributed to David

Grayson: "I had attempted to do too much in Europe, driven too hard," and "the difficulty lay far deeper than any physical illness."[41] Moreover, even with his high salary, Baker still depended on selling his wares in a very competitive market, and of course that insecurity only intensified when he quit *McClure's* in 1906 to become part owner of the *American Magazine*. The added uncertainty may well have helped to bring David Grayson to life.

Unlike David Grayson, when Baker had his breakdown he did not go back to the farm, but he did take a long vacation in Arizona (arranged and paid for by *McClure's*). There in the desert, as he slowly recuperated, Baker reevaluated his life. He came up with plans for two new novels, and he determined to get out of New York City and the *McClure's* office so that he could write. After an unsuccessful experiment in the suburbs of Westchester County, Baker settled his family in the village of East Lansing, Michigan, where his wife's family lived and where he himself had attended college. He still commuted to the *McClure's* office in New York several times a month, but he hoped spending the rest of his time in a rural atmosphere would provide him with the peace he needed. Baker's experience was not quite like the story he came up with for David Grayson, but in its most basic form—the breakdown, the retreat from the city, the rural recovery—it shared a common outline. Perhaps the shadow of Baker's personal nightmare gave the Grayson story a ring of authenticity.

Readers and Fakers

Then again, although readers loved the sketches, they seemed uncertain about how authentic they really were. That was part of the reason they inundated the *American Magazine* with hundreds of letters.[42] Some letters were simple "thank you" notes or queries about the next installment. Some were more personal, recounting life stories or asking for advice. But it is striking how often people wrote to ask whether David Grayson was "real."[43] Like William Lighton's fans, they were not sure whether the stories were fact or fiction. One woman echoed many doubters when she wrote that she enjoyed Grayson's stories but did not believe he was really living on a farm. Coming close to guessing the truth, she asked, "Is it not a fact that you wrote this series in your comfortable, although unromantic study, in some comfortable and unromantic house in New York?"[44]

This skepticism was fostered in part by a debate that was raging in the magazines at the time. When one of David Grayson's correspondents wrote "I know that you are only a nature fakir after all," he was using a term that had just come into fashion. It was Theodore Roosevelt, again, who coined the phrase. In a 1907 *Everybody's Magazine* interview, Roosevelt attacked "nature fakers" (or "fakirs") who misrepresented or overromanticized their encounters with the natural world.[45] But the controversy over authorial fakery went beyond nature writing, intensified by the new pressures on literary production. As journalists faced demands to supply information more quickly and under the pressure of increased competition, "fake" information and stories proliferated. Historian Christopher Wilson points out, for example, that Baker's contemporary Upton Sinclair began his career by passing off a first-person narrative of a suicide, *The Journal of Arthur Stirling*, as the real thing, even faking an obituary for the character.[46]

Back-to-the-land stories were particularly vulnerable to rumors of fakery.[47] One reviewer speculated, for example, that "David Grayson" might be a pseudonym for J. P. Mowbray, the author of *Journey to Nature*.[48] (Actually, the name "Mowbray" was itself a pseudonym for journalist Andrew Carpenter Wheeler.) Rumor also had it that John Streeter had written his *Fat of the Land*, which went through four reprints, "from a city sick room," not from the farm he described in the book. In fact, it was one of David Grayson's readers who reported that rumor to him.[49] Grayson was of course a rather incongruous recipient of such a complaint, being himself entirely imaginary.

Nor was this a simple case of a pseudonym. One might write under a pseudonym and still record *someone's* real experiences. But Ray Stannard Baker was not the "real" David Grayson, either. At the time he wrote the sketches that became *Adventures in Contentment*, Baker was commuting from his editorial job in New York City to his new home in East Lansing. Baker did live in that rural area, at least part of the time, but he was not a farmer. He would not own a piece of property that could be described as a farm until he moved to Amherst, Massachusetts, in 1910. Even then, Ray Stannard Baker was many things—journalist, political adviser, biographer, even in time an amateur farmer—but he was never David Grayson.

Readers seemed to sense the truth, but they wanted to believe that the sketches were in *some* way "real." One correspondent—the one who let Grayson in on the secret of Streeter's fake back-to-the-land story—did not care to confront a second disappointment. He urged Grayson: "If your Adventures have been written in a city flat, please don't admit it!"[50] But many readers did want to know. Some had already staked a great deal on the authenticity of the stories, particularly those who were contemplating following in David Grayson's footsteps by leaving their city jobs and buying a farm in the country. Those readers needed to know whether Grayson's account was literally true and whether it could work for them. Such readers showered David Grayson with questions: "Do you still keep up that life? Are you *really now* living it? Were you rich to start with?"[51] A journalist for the Chicago *Tribune* wrote to ask "if you are a real person on a real farm." If the answer was yes, "I would beg you to tell me a little more about it—what state it is in (not condition) how much of it there is—what is the best way for a raw city man to go about such a thing." This journalist was wary: "You may be a young man who never saw a farm—sitting at a typewriter and smoking a corn-cob pipe, while he 'grinds' out these stories." Still, he very much wanted to believe, adding, "It is only my newspaper work which makes me skeptical."[52]

Some of Grayson's correspondents had in fact already left the city for the farm, claiming that *Adventures in Contentment* had convinced them to make the break. One such reader reported to the editor of the *American Magazine* that David Grayson's stories had persuaded him to buy a New England farm. Now he wanted to know—perhaps too late—whether Grayson was "real." "Perhaps I am foolish to make these inquiries about my Patron Saint, for should I learn that David Grayson—was simply a gifted magazine writer, or worse still a woman[,] the awakening would be a sad one."[53]

All told, about 15 percent of David Grayson's correspondents reported that they were considering going back to the land or had already done so.[54] (More about these people in chapter 3.) But they were not the only ones who wanted reassurance that David Grayson was "real." Most of David Grayson's readers probably lacked the resources—perhaps even the desire—to cash in their city assets and buy a farm. Still, the back-to-the-land story might encourage a more modest dream: a future retirement in the country, another job in a smaller town, perhaps simply a suburban home with a backyard. For those who saw no hope of ever getting out of their city jobs, the Grayson stories could at least offer an occasional hour's daydream to counter a working day of drudgery, stress, and insecurity.[55] But even for such a temporary retreat, readers needed assurance that Grayson's adventures were not pure fiction.

Such readers did not need to be told that David Grayson was literally a farmer. Theirs was a more modest hope: that Grayson was a real person who was sharing with them his own dream of escape, not someone who was cynically calculating to cash in on theirs. At the very least they wanted to know that the sketches reflected the honest daydreams of whoever wrote them. As one of these readers put it, "If you are somewhere on Wall Street manipulating stocks and . . . laughing in your sleeve at your admiring audience, I could never forgive you nor enjoy your writings again."[56] Another correspondent was more inclined to forgive; she imagined David Grayson as a fellow sufferer rather than a Wall Street tycoon. Lena Walters wrote to ask, "Do you sit all day in a stuffy city office and dream of . . . those beautiful quiet spots?" Walters was a salesclerk.

She described her own situation with heartbreaking clarity: "I stand all day behind a counter. . . . When I look out at all I see a narrow, dusty street, with old brick buildings on the other side. This has been my daily view for ten years." Walters feared she would never find a way out of that dead-end job, but she wanted Grayson to know she appreciated what he had created for her, whether he was "real" or not: "While I work I dream of the woods and fields . . . and that is why I love to read of your wanderings."[57]

A Chicago correspondent seemed willing to accept even less. "You may or may not have taken that trip in a corn field," he wrote, "and you may or may not have digged a ditch, but . . . I am glad to know that there is one other man who knows how to live, whether he lives up to that or not."[58] Even when absolute proof of David Grayson's inauthenticity confronted them, a few readers attempted to salvage their emotional rapport with the author, and with it their faith in his rural dream. Henry Nelson wrote from California that he wanted to correct one obvious error because "I love you, and don't like to have you laughed at"—but no one who had mistaken the parts of a wagon frame as Grayson had done could possibly be a farmer. Grayson had almost fooled him: "You show such an appreciation of the matters of nature, and teach so well the joy that *may* be got out of the rural life that I almost thought you was one of us." Now, he wrote, "I know that you are only a 'nature fakir' after all—but—I love you none the less."[59]

For many of David Grayson's readers, *Adventures in Contentment* would never be a blueprint for a literal escape from the city; at best it offered a daydreaming "way out." But some readers took that kind of escape very seriously. A woman wrote from Chicago, for example, to dictate precisely what she wanted to believe about Grayson and his characters. She hoped he was really named David Grayson "and not Samuel Simpson or Percy St. Claire," but she feared "that would be too good to be true." Even if that was not his real name, she hoped he would at least *look* like a David Grayson: "a wee bit gaunt and stooped, more than a little gray, and with a quiet light in calm eyes which haven't decided, after forty-five years, say, whether to be grey or blue." She feared that he might not fit that pattern, but she was even more concerned that David Grayson's sister "Harriet" would not be as she imagined. "Maybe dear, kindly Harriet, in real life wears a Marcel wave [a hairstyle created with an electric curling-iron] instead of a demure 'part,' and French heels and a Swastika bracelet [the latest arts-and-crafts fashion] instead of a housewifely white apron and a gingham sunbonnet!"[60]

Some of Grayson's readers tried literally to write themselves into his fictional world. One wrote, for example: "I'm not too busy to lag along by your side while you hoe a row of something. . . . am I not even now gingerly picking my way down the freshly turned earth and talking to your back as you bend over your hoe, or standing still when you rest on the hoe handle?"[61] Another went so far as to offer a plot synopsis for Grayson to consider for inclusion in a future sketch. She wrote out a plot that began with her meeting David Grayson in order to check him out "as a possible suitor for her sister," whom she described as a professional singer. In the end she offered two possible endings to the story and invited David Grayson to choose one. Ending number two began: "Grayson looks thoughtful and asks further particulars."[62] This correspondent may have been attempting to step out of the realm of the dream world into the reality of matchmaking, but she framed her request as a plot contrivance in a David Grayson story.

From here it was only one more step to a more bizarre case of identification with the author. In 1915, a man claiming to be "David Grayson" visited Denver, setting off a real-life drama that was in truth stranger than fiction.[63] This "David Grayson" allowed himself to be wined and dined by the town's leading citizens, giving lectures about the "poetry of existence" and passing himself off as the author of *Adventures in Contentment*. Local newspaper writers smelled a rat; they contacted the *American Magazine* and immediately received telegrams from the magazine and from Baker himself confirming that the man was a fraud. In the meantime, Baker had already been receiving desperate appeals from a family embroiled in another part of the story. (Those letters also went to John S. Phillips, the editor of the *American*, and even to Ida Tarbell: "Because you write for the American, because you are a woman, I appeal to you.")[64] It appears that the imposter had moved in with a family living on a Navajo reservation in Arizona and seduced the young wife, and then, when she left her husband, declared himself engaged to her widowed sister—all the while representing himself as the author of the David Grayson stories.

The newspapermen of Denver, who did not know (or at least did not write about) these more sordid aspects of the tale, seemed to be intrigued chiefly by the imposter's motive. One of them wondered "whether this contentment thing hasn't gummed up his machinery and spilled it all over his think factory."[65] They knew that this "Grayson" had not made much money from the deception, and he must have known that he would almost certainly be found out. The *Denver Post* reported the fraud on its front page, editorializing in the subheading that the "Man's Vanity and His Longing for Fame Prompted Impersonation." The interview between the reporter and the imposter was revealing:

> "But, David, you told me all about writing that story, even to the announcement that the hero really was yourself."

"And he is myself," announced David Grayson. "That is just the kind of a life I lead."

"But you did not write any of the Grayson stories."

"No. But I helped to write them."

"How?"

"By writing to the man who writes under the name of David Grayson and offering suggestions."[66]

The imposter claimed that his name really was David Grayson, and that the book described his real-life experiences; furthermore, he implied that he had somehow prompted, suggested, or ghost-written the writing done by the real author. Evidently some *Post* reporters still credited this version of the story even after the exposé, because later that year the newspaper ran a story reporting the imposter's marriage (to the woman mentioned in the desperate letters to Baker) and describing him without apparent sarcasm as "one of the collaborators in the writing of the famous David Grayson stories."[67]

"Collaborator" was apparently the word the imposter settled on, too. In a final effort to retain credibility, he wrote to a magazine editor proposing a professional partnership. The editor sensed something strange and directed a discreet inquiry to the *American Magazine*. As she described it, the imposter had told her that the David Grayson stories "were a sort of collaboration between his own life, travels, experience etc., and the actual work of a well-known writer who did not care to have his own name known."[68] In fact, the imposter had told her that the "well-known writer" was Ray Stannard Baker; he had implied that Baker, too, was a fake who wrote what he was now calling "the published versions" of the David Grayson stories.[69]

Of course, that insinuation was false. In one sense, however, the imposter was correct: there *was* an element of collaboration in the shared project between David Grayson's readers and the "well known writer who did not care to have his name known." The imposter claimed a relationship with David Grayson and imagined himself as somehow intimately involved with the stories. Other readers felt much the same. And in fact, the imposter did write to David Grayson, not once but several times, both before and after the fraud was exposed—and they were just the kinds of letters that many other readers sent. Addressing the author as "David the Civilized," he imagined himself as "David of the Wilds," his "Brother of the West."[70] Lena Walters, the salesclerk, did not venture to put herself on a level of spiritual equality with the author, but she did make a similar claim of kinship: "While I work I dream of the woods and fields," she wrote. "May be dreaming and writing of them is your way of earning money."[71]

A Writer's Dream

Which brings us back to Ray Stannard Baker. Writing was certainly Baker's way of earning money, but "dreaming" had not usually been part of that work. He had made his reputation reporting on subjects that might be considered the very opposite of appropriate dream material: labor bosses, company towns, corporate trusts, and railroad rates. When it came to the David Grayson sketches, however, Lena Walters was correct: Baker was indeed doing that "dreaming and writing" she imagined. Writing as David Grayson allowed Baker an escape of his own to a place where a hardheaded reporter could not go—at least not under his own name. Had he chosen to employ his formidable journalistic abilities in writing about rural life under his own name, the result would probably have been not the meditative essays he produced as David Grayson but a fact-filled account of the crisis of the countryside.

That option was in fact open to Baker. Two of his brothers made their careers as agricultural experts. During his own college days at Michigan State College he had known virtually all the future important players in the country life movement, including commission members Liberty Hyde Bailey, Herbert Collingwood, and Kenyon Butterfield. In fact, the country life movement was essentially born at Michigan State: the plan was hatched at the college's semi-centennial anniversary celebration in 1907.[72] Moreover, Baker's connection with his alma mater was unusually strong. He had married the daughter of his favorite botany professor, William Beal, and the first material for the David Grayson sketches came out of his reimmersion in East Lansing. And when he finally found a way to leave New York permanently, moving to Amherst, Massachusetts, he was drawn there partly by the presence of his old college friend Kenyon Butterfield, now president of the Massachusetts State Agricultural College—and a member of the Country Life Commission. Still, Baker never offered his services to any of the numerous country life reform efforts. In fact, he never mentioned the country life movement in his autobiography, although he devoted considerable effort to assessing the successes and failures of progressivism. As for David Grayson, *he* was no reformer at all. No rural crisis appeared on the pages of *Adventures in Contentment*. As in other back-to-the-land books, the farm was not a problem there; it was the "one way out."

Baker had a great deal of personal capital invested in David Grayson's rural vision. For one thing, the David Grayson books were the kind of "steady sellers" that would provide Baker a reliable income for the rest of his life—a welcome safety net that would allow him to take on or reject other projects as he liked. Writing as David Grayson also solved some of Baker's most long-standing and painful professional problems. David Grayson was born in a moment of epiphany. At the very moment Baker faced the fact that he would never finish his novels, no matter how much time he had to write—the novel form was "not my free and natural method of expression," he realized—he also recognized his "free and natural" voice in the notebook writing that would provide the basis for the David Grayson sketches.

As Baker saw it later, the destruction of his hope for the novels had allowed his real ability to emerge: "When the half-gods go, the gods arrive!" After that, and for the first time, he wrote with confidence and effortlessly: "I never wrote more easily or freely, or with greater delight. I used the first words that came to me and never attempted to alter a thought." Indeed, for Baker, writing as Grayson was "more or less left-hand work" and "more or less inexplicable," a daydreaming state not unlike the "dreaming and writing" Lena Walters imagined.[73] And perhaps there was a good reason why Baker did not name the Grayson sketches some variant of *Three Acres and Liberty*. The title Baker gave the first sketch—a title that "literally flew" into his mind, as he recorded later—seems to have been triggered by his own private dream.[74]

As a young journalist, Baker had confronted all the evils of untrammeled capitalism at their worst. He had walked alongside the desperate and ragged men who made up Coxey's army on their march to Washington. He had collected food for starving children during the great Pullman strike in Chicago in 1894. His famous *McClure's* "muckraking" articles of 1903 had taken him through scenes of great suffering, from the sweatshops of New York to the mining camps of Colorado. As he later reported in his autobiography, he and the other writers at *McClure's* were themselves "personally astonished, personally ashamed, personally indignant at what we found."[75] But Baker was also a man of an inherently moderate turn of mind, and he had a deep distrust of ideology and radicalism. As he admitted later in life—"a little sadly," as he phrased it—he "would have been glad to preach with the prophets and suffer with the martyrs," but he was "never quite converted to anything: I never joined."[76] Baker found it impossible to espouse the radical solutions he heard proposed by Jack London, Lincoln Steffens, and the many other associates whose certainty he respected but could not share.

To be sure, Baker's *McClure's* articles about the labor movement did defend workers' rights to organize, and that was a stand that put Baker decidedly to the left of mainstream middle-class American opinion in 1903. But they also reveal a deep ambivalence and a deeper reluctance to take sides. All of the articles expressed sympathy for workers. In "The Rise of the Tailors," for example, Baker reported on the heroic struggles of labor organizers to unionize the poorest of the poor in the sweatshops of New York, setting his article off with a translated Yiddish protest song. But he was drawn to stories without clear heroes and villains. In that January 1903 groundbreaking issue of *McClure's*, while Ida Tarbell detailed the power-grabbing tactics of Standard Oil and Lincoln Steffens revealed how city governments were controlled by graft and bribery, Ray Stannard Baker addressed the right to work. His article focused on the predicament of Pennsylvania coal miners who were *refusing* to come out on strike, and not on the desperate strikers themselves. More often than not, Baker's investigative articles focused on corruption *within* the labor movement. As he explained his choice later, "I have always liked, best of all, to study minorities."[77]

Again and again, Baker confronted and reported on great evils—the horror of lynching in the South, the shocking gap between rich and poor in the cities, the pitiable conditions of workers on strike in the Colorado mines—only to come up short on solutions. Socialist Upton Sinclair assessed Baker's temperament by noting that "you can beat even the rest of the folks on McClure's for getting together facts minus conclusions." Reporting this quip in his autobiography, Baker claimed to regard it as "high praise" and to be proud of his refusal to take sides: "*Ignorance* is the real enemy," he wrote.[78]

The Burden of the Valley of Vision

There are signs, however, that Baker longed for a firmer belief, for some tangible solution. The title of the first David Grayson sketch offers its own testimony to Baker's uneasiness with continually witnessing wrongs he could not bring himself to try to right. At first glance, most of the sketches that make up *Adventures in Contentment* may seem far too aimless, even frivolous, for such a weighty title as "The Burden of the Valley of Vision." For readers, the David Grayson sketches offered an imaginative escape from the burdens of city work (or perhaps even encouragement to make a real escape), but the work the sketches performed for the man who wrote them was of another sort altogether.

One by one, David Grayson shouldered the burdens Ray Stannard Baker carried. As David Grayson, the most intractable political and social dilemmas seemed easier to face.[79] Take politics. In David Grayson's world, the political problems that dismayed progressive reformers—corruption, graft, the indifference of educated and capable men—simply disappeared. David Grayson's small town preserved the purest democracy imaginable. At his first town meeting, "watching those bronzed farmers at work gave me such a conception of the true meaning of self-government as I never hoped to have." This rural democracy was so powerful and effective that it simply dissolved another progressive

I

"THE BURDEN OF THE VALLEY OF VISION"

This Thomas Fogarty illustration depicts David Grayson as an exhausted invalid lying under a tree. Barely able to lift his head, he seems absorbed by the view of the city in the distance, perhaps seeing there the troubling "vision" of Baker's title. From David Grayson, *Adventures in Contentment* (1907).

dilemma. There were three Polish immigrant families in David Grayson's town, and because their numbers were small, they were easily assimilated into the democratic process. "Here in the country we promptly digest our foreigners and they make as good Americans as anybody."[80] No "undigested" masses created foreign-born voting blocs, no party bosses ruled. Perhaps Baker despaired of creating a true democracy in America; David Grayson's faith never wavered.

Or take religion. Baker had grown up in a world of absolute moral certainty. As a young man he had worshipped his father and the faith of his father's Civil War generation in Yankee Protestantism and the Republican Party. Like many progressives, he later lost his faith in both politics and religion, and like many progressives, he found those certainties difficult to replace. David Grayson also rejected the orthodox faith of *his* fathers; but in David Grayson's world, this wrenching change broke no family ties, caused no guilt.

Of the fourteen sketches that make up *Adventures in Contentment*, four directly confront the question of religion. In "The Marsh Ditch," David Grayson addresses a charge from an orthodox neighbor that he is a "Materialist." He offers—half as a rebuttal, half as a confirmation—a highly selective list of "materialistic" experiences he cherishes. Intensely sensuous, they are neverthe-less morally unassailable: the physical sensation of hard work; a cool stream to drink from; the taste of bread.

Similarly, Baker turns orthodoxy inside out in "The Infidel." David Gray-son meets a man the neighbors condemn as a dangerous enemy of the faith but finds in him only a harmless, anxious man who, terrified by the horrors preached by orthodoxy, insistently and obsessively denies the existence of hell. Turning the tables once more in "The Joy of Possession," David Grayson meets a botanist who speaks for secular science but who also expresses a rap-turous pantheist faith: "Now—it seems to me—there is nothing but God."[81] Characteristically, David Grayson judges the local "Scotch preacher," like the Presbyterian faith he defends, to be as fundamentally harmless as the infidel and the Darwinist scientist: he is a "kind of human cocoanut, rough, brown, shaggy, but within he has the true milk of human kindness."[82] In David Gray-son's world, materialism, Darwinism, and orthodox Presbyterianism are simply shadows obscuring a deeper truth.

Most impressive of all, David Grayson works this same almost magical transformation on class conflict, the single greatest problem of Baker's time. In three sketches, David Grayson encounters men of three different classes. In "The Tramp," the problem of poverty appears on the doorstep in the form of a visiting vagrant. Grayson begins as if he were Baker, who has heard it all before. Without listening, he anticipates the tramp's hard luck story: "'You can't get any work, you're cold and you haven't had anything to eat for two days, so you are walking out here in the country. . . . At home you have a starving wife and three small children—' 'Six, mister—' 'Well, six—And now we will go in to supper.'"[83]

But the tramp eludes Grayson's generalities. His problem turns out to be not poverty or alcohol or unemployment or any of the other social problems for which Baker might have hoped to provide a solution. Instead, his problems are purely personal; he is haunted by an extremely peculiar psychological malady, the hypersensitive ability to imagine in advance what will happen next in his life. Neither a labor union nor a strike nor even a massive redistribution of wealth would help a homeless, jobless man like this one. When the tramp finally leaves, one can almost feel the weight of responsibility falling from someone's (Grayson's? Baker's?) shoulders.

In "An Argument with a Millionaire," David Grayson turns his attention to the top of the social ladder. Pretending not to recognize the local millionaire, David Grayson asks him to help repair his wagon. As they work in the dirt and grime, he draws the millionaire into conversation, recalling for him the plot of a Tolstoy story in which only those with calluses on their hands are allowed to eat. The millionaire is suitably impressed. "'What is a farmer doing quoting Tolstoi!' remarked his countenance—though he said not a word." Grayson has the upper hand, of course. Characteristically, though, the millionaire also reveals himself as more than a representative of his class. He is not a haughty lord of creation but a decent man who is able to laugh at himself. He takes the trick in good humor, washes his greasy hands, and—like the tramp—joins Grayson for dinner.

In "I Entertain an Agent Unaware," a young traveling book salesman comes to the door. His "brisk step" and "sharp blue eye" mark him as someone driven by money making, and his speech patterns tell the reader that he is not educated enough to understand the worth of what he is selling—"six volumes full of literchoor."[84] Neither rich nor poor, he is, in fact, exactly such a young man as would likely have been a fan of David Grayson books, working in one of the new retail jobs created by the rise of national markets (a subject explored in chapter 3). Again, David Grayson plays dumb; he begins by appearing to be attentive to the man's sales pitch but traps him instead into really listening to the poetry he is selling: "I took the book which he had been urging on me . . . I made up as innocent as a child." Grayson opens the book and reads a Wordsworth poem aloud: "The world is too much with us; late and soon, / Getting and spending we lay waste our powers." Then he turns to a Scottish dialect poem about "home," reading it so effectively that the salesman is reduced to tears. Grayson's skilful manipulation reveals beneath the young man's slick patter his homesickness, his concern for his wife and young daughter, the dreams he has for the future. Finally, David Grayson sends him on his way with a speech about the value of things that are priceless. He does not offer to help him out by buying a book.

Noticeably absent here—especially when one considers Baker's expertise on the "labor question"—is any comment about the economic structures that provided the millionaire with his wealth, obliged the young salesman to work so far from his home, or sent the out-of-work "tramp" to roam the countryside in search of handouts. (That may be what caused some critics to look at the David Grayson writing as pious claptrap, easy reading for the business classes. Vachel Lindsay commented in the Chicago *Evening Post*, for example, that he was tired of hearing "pie-faced, mutton headed businessmen . . . tell me they like David

Grayson . . . with a little-Eva-going-to-heaven look in their eyes.")[85] But that was precisely the point. Writing as David Grayson fostered the "left-handed," daydreaming state in which Baker could play out his deepest fantasies without having to test them against hard reality. In David Grayson's world, religious conflicts were trivial, democracy triumphed, and class struggles were simple misunderstandings among individuals of good will. Writing as David Grayson, Baker could assert—for himself, chiefly, but also for his readers—that rural life would dissolve modern tension, doubt, and conflict.

With this example in hand, it would be easy to dismiss the entire back-to-the-land literature of the early twentieth century as little more than a simple escape fantasy. Indeed, Baker, like Lighton, found that his country sojourn could not last, at least not in the way he had imagined it. After several years' search for a political leader he could respect, Baker discovered that leader in Woodrow Wilson, whom he came to revere. At first a pacifist, Baker reversed his opinion on war in Europe, committing himself to the cause of Wilson's vision of a democratic and peaceful future. In that cause, he would play the most important political role of his life. Baker was a close personal advisor to Wilson throughout the war and then the painful and ultimately futile struggle over the League of Nations. After Wilson's death, Baker withdrew from public affairs, immersing himself in the monumental project of editing Wilson's papers and writing his biography, spending fully twenty-one years of what he acknowledged to be "hard labor" on the arduous project of defending the Wilson legacy. In a telling gesture, Baker used the last words of his own autobiography, which were also his own last words to appear in print, as a plea for the acceptance of Wilson as "the pre-eminent man he was, as the true inheritor and prophet of the great American tradition."[86]

During the years when Baker labored over the Wilson project, he continued to write as David Grayson, but he revealed his identity in 1915, and the pseudonym seemed no longer to provide the same imaginative alternative it had once offered. The Grayson books evolved into increasingly straightforward accounts of Baker's own experiences with gardening, beekeeping, and taking care of his ten acres in Amherst, Massachusetts. In the final Grayson books, *The Countryman's Year* (1936) and especially *Under My Elm* (1942), Baker dropped David Grayson's pretentious "simple life" homilies altogether and returned to his own modest style. Reflecting on the back-to-the-land movement he had helped to encourage, Baker wrote of his contacts with readers who had followed in his footsteps (or what they *hoped* were his footsteps) and returned to the land. He reported cautious optimism about the railroad workers, architects, and machine tool workers who had taken up farms near him in western Massachusetts and those who had written to him from all over the country. Most, he thought, seemed to be "far more contented, hopeful, even happy, than average human beings."[87]

Here for the first time, too, Baker reflected at length on his own genuine efforts to return to the land. If his earlier works had betrayed a certain illusory quality that had fed readers' suspicions, Baker's last book breathed another spirit. "I knew well enough," he wrote with the carefully measured phrases that characterized his writing under his own name, that "any such experiment in living must represent all sorts of compromises—what life is not a compromise?" Finally, in 1942, he imparted to his readers what David Grayson's original readers had so much wanted to hear: an honest-to-goodness, real-life, first person affirmation of "what I had dreamed about, what I longed for, and what I had finally attained." Baker's dream, once separated from David Grayson's preoccupations, turned out to have been much like the modest dreams of his readers: "a few acres with hills not far off, a field or pasture, an orchard, a garden—a possible cow, a pig or so, chickens and turkeys."[88] David Grayson's readers had recognized that dream back in 1906, even when it was buried under the weightier concerns of *Adventures in Contentment*. The author's dream, as they had hoped, was not so different from their own.

3

Who Wants a Farm?

In November 1911, progressive editor and publisher Walter Hines Page posed a challenge to the readers of his magazine the *World's Work*. "Everybody has been crying 'Back to the land,'" he wrote, but was anyone serious about it? "Do people really wish to get on the land? . . . Or is 'back-to-the-land' all cry and no wool?"[1] In December, Page repeated the question even more directly. "Do *you* want a farm," or do you "merely want somebody else to go and live on one?"[2] Page asked his readers to write in if they wanted a farm. Should the results warrant it, he promised that the *World's Work* would endeavor to help. Throughout 1912, Page tabulated the responses and published extracts from the letters he received. At the end of six months, after receiving seven hundred letters, he answered his own question: "Are there competent persons who want farm-homes and do not know how to find them? The World's Work has proved that there are many such persons."[3]

There may indeed have been many people in those years who wanted to go back to the land, but they have left behind little hard data. (Whether they were the "competent" people Page was seeking is another matter, as we will see.) The aggregate census figures testify to movement in the opposite direction, of course: they reflect a long-term, persistent movement of people to cities. The turning point occurred in the very years when Page was surveying his readers: the 1910 census still reported a rural majority, but by the 1920 census, the majority was urban. In 1920, as if to mark that decisive change, the Department of Agriculture began a yearly count of both farm-to-city and city-to-farm migration. Those figures tell a somewhat more complicated story. During the 1920s, an average of two million people left farms for cities each year—but at the same time, an average of 1.3 million people each year were going the other way, leaving cities for farms.[4] The data are not sufficiently detailed to reveal much about these migrants, however, and the count began only after the first large-scale enthusiasm for back-to-the-land projects had subsided.

In 1914, the Department of Agriculture sent a questionnaire to its forty-five thousand "crop correspondents" across the country, asking them to report on back-to-the-land activities in their areas. The report based on this research concluded that a back-to-the-land movement did indeed exist: it was not a "strong movement," not a "concerted" one, but it was nevertheless significant in many parts of the country. This report did not provide much hard data, either, but it did express concern about both the quantity and the quality of the back-to-the-land recruits: "It is plain that the movement 'back to the land' very poorly offsets, to the extent of its meager proportions, the loss to agriculture of the farmers' sturdy sons who leave that occupation."[5]

Who were the first back-to-the-landers, then, if not those "farmers' sturdy sons"? It may not be possible to determine much about the overall size and demographic significance of the movement, but sources do exist that can shed light on an equally important question: who *wanted* to go back to the land, and why? In addition to the published sources, there are several surviving membership lists from back-to-the-land colonies. And then there are letters. While the seven hundred letters sent to the *World's Work* appear to be lost, Page published excerpts from them and reported the aggregate results of his survey. Nor was Page the only writer receiving letters from readers. In *How to Live in the Country* (1911), Edward Payson Powell published extracts from a few of the three hundred letters he said he had received in the previous year. (The letters were responding to Powell's 1904 book, *The Country Home*.) William Lighton reported receiving thousands of letters—a "perfect deluge"—after he published his "Story of an Arkansas Farm" in the *Saturday Evening Post* in 1910.[6]

Of course, there is always the possibility that those writers exaggerated the number of letters they received or at least selected carefully which ones they chose to publish. Fortunately, once again, there are the David Grayson letters. They came to him in the hundreds, and they have been carefully preserved. Between 1906 and 1912, about 15 percent of David Grayson's correspondents—forty-one people in all—reported specifically that they hoped someday to go back to the land, that they were making plans to, or even that they had already done it.[7] From Plainfield, New Jersey, for example, a man wrote: "After failing to find happiness in Wall Street I came across your book 'adventures in contentment.' To it I owe my present happiness. I bought an old fashioned farm and made it habitable and now live twenty four hours a day."[8] Another correspondent wrote that she and her family were building a "stone Bungalow on a 20 acre farm up on the very brow of a hill." She, too, testified that David Grayson had "helped mightily to clinch the decision to leave the fever and fret and make a real home somewhere out in the open spaces."[9]

These letters from David Grayson's readers, supplemented by other materials, offer a rare opportunity to examine the back-to-the-land impulse beyond the printed page. Correspondents shared personal details about their lives, responding perhaps to the intimate revelations they had read in published accounts. Some wanted farming information, others advice about money. Often they asked for approval of plans they had already formed and reassurance that they were doing the right thing. Jessie Boyd wrote to David Grayson in 1908, for example, that she and her husband, Ralph, planned to "build a log cabin, and shake the dust of the city from our feet." They had found their inspiration in Hall's "'Three acres and liberty' for the practical side," she told Grayson, and "some such view (as our commoner natures permit) as you have shown us" for the spiritual side. Two years later, she and her husband still held their city jobs in Seattle: the federal census recorded Ralph as a stenographer and Jessie as an index clerk at a library. By 1920, however, they had moved to the outskirts of town; Ralph now reported his occupation as "farmer."

Similarly, two women wrote to Edward Payson Powell asking him to bless their exodus from teaching and entrance into farming: "We have about two thousand dollars apiece. That will take care of us until we have had some experience, will it not?" Correspondents like these often offered to discuss intimate features of their lives. Perhaps these two women had not anticipated that Powell would publish their revealing self-assessment: "Honest, we are not over fifty-five, either of us, in good health, homely, and not a bit afraid of using our hands."[10] Some correspondents even asked for help directly. One sent Lighton a copy of his *Saturday Evening Post* article with a typewritten comment on it: "Reading this made me come to Fayetteville. Can't you give me a job on your farm raising poultry, gathering apples, etc etc? I've sat at a desk 20 years."[11]

Often, however, correspondents just wanted to tell their own stories. Their accounts were frequently similar to the ones recorded in published back-to-the-land accounts, but they were not carbon copies. Readers clearly embraced some parts of the stories they read; just as clearly, they ignored other parts and re-interpreted others still to suit their needs. Examining the private correspondence alongside the published accounts reveals something of how back-to-the-land readers connected with back-to-the-land writing.

This Straining Commercial Life

Both private and published stories commonly began with an illness. Some readers described experiences similar to those of David Grayson as they were recounted in *Adventures in Contentment*. Davis Parker Leach, for example, was deeply influenced by the David Grayson sketches. He sent four letters to their author in 1906 and 1907, writing in such personal terms that he apparently touched some chord in Ray Stannard Baker, who answered his letters and finally even revealed his identity to him. Leach's story, like David Grayson's own, began with an illness that was both physical and emotional. "This straining, nerve-racking commercial life . . . has aged and almost soured me." But simply reading David Grayson's story had begun the healing process. Leach's state of lethargic despair was being replaced by "hope and almost cheerfulness," he reported, and his "wholesome longing for life and nature" was reawakened.[12]

The census reveals that Leach was a salesman for a drug company, but readers with different occupations reported similar health problems. A missionary in Brazil wrote to David Grayson that he hoped to retire to a farm because his health demanded "an out-of-door life."[13] Another correspondent wrote that he had developed "a spinal trouble, which rendered it imperative I should give up my work in the City."[14] Yet another described his escape from journalism to farming: "Worked many years on a morning newspaper till the black devils of sleeplessness broke me."[15]

Professional writers sometimes made rather startling claims about the health benefits of a return to the land, alleging that country life could cure such serious illnesses as tuberculosis, rheumatoid arthritis, and typhoid fever. David Grayson's correspondents made much more modest claims, merely suggesting that going back to the land had improved (or would improve) their general health, sleep, and physical strength. One reader wrote from Massachusetts that he had been "doing a little farming during the past 1 ½ years, my oculist wanting me to live out of doors to strengthen my eyes and nerve."[16] Another wrote from Georgia that his farm had renewed his youth, bringing him "good digestion, sound sleep, and the discovery that I have a *second* and even a *third* wind."[17] (That was a reference to a 1907 article by William James published in the *American Magazine* exploring the phenomenon of "second wind"; James proposed that men had extraordinary powers in reserve that might be evoked only by a challenging situation. The phrase "second wind" seems to have been appropriated by back-to-the-landers as an expression of the ability of middle-aged men to find new health and vitality in the country.)[18]

For many correspondents, however, these chronic health problems were symptoms of a larger difficulty. Sometimes they were simply sick of their jobs. Published back-to-the-land accounts typically presented work in the city either as too fast paced and competitive or monotonous and unsatisfying—enough to make a person sick, indeed. And on this matter, letter writers fervently agreed.

Lena Walters was not the only person who wrote to Grayson to lament the utter dreariness of her work as a salesclerk, standing "all day behind a counter."[19] Caroline Storrs complained to Grayson that her work as a live-in nurse required her to keep to "one small room in the crowded city . . . in order to earn her daily bread."[20] A teacher from Philadelphia complained to Edward Payson Powell that she was "dead tired" of her "treadmill work."[21] In response to the editorial question "Who Wants a Farm?" in the *World's Work*, a traveling salesman wrote: "Ask the poor, tired, traveling man who sees his family once a month for a day or two before he hot-foots it again for another tiresome and lonely month."[22]

For other correspondents, a little boredom and drudgery at work would have been a welcome relief. Their work was so competitive and fast paced that they despaired of keeping up. Ray Stannard Baker's account of David Grayson's liberation from the city gave expression to the deep unrest some readers felt. "The chief impression [my life in the city] left upon my memory," David Grayson recalled, "is of being hurried faster than I could well travel."[23] As early as 1885, Edward Payson Roe had created a bookkeeper character in his novel *Driven Back to Eden* who was frightened by the speed, intensity, and competition of his job: "You know I . . . am not one of those smart men who can push their way. . . . I can't seem to acquire the lightning speed with which things are done nowadays." The man tried to keep up "by long hours and honesty," but he knew he was losing the battle: "I don't believe I could ever earn much more than I am getting now."[24]

Readers, too, expressed such fears. One wrote simply that he was thirty years old and "very tired of the continual fight."[25] Another took heart from David Grayson's story, in which mental and physical breakdown opened the door to escape. As Grayson sinks into illness, he reflects on his condition in Darwinian terms: "'This is Unfitness. I survive no longer.'"[26] The reader echoed Grayson: "Like you, I am a city failure in sence [*sic*]." But, as he told Grayson, being "unfit" had turned out to be the best thing that had ever happened to him: "Brother, being a failure is sometimes a great gain."[27]

City Workers

What kinds of jobs were these that were so dreary or so stressful? Professional back-to-the-land writers thought they knew the answer. While many advocates supported back-to-the-land projects for the masses of new immigrants in the cities, most believed it was preeminently a solution to the problems of "middling" workers. An article in *Collier's* suggested that it was the "in-between classes" who most needed and wanted a return to the land: "If a preacher of the gospel of this new exodus were to arise, he would do well to address them first."[28] In the *World's Work*, an article calculated that "nearly two thirds of a city's population" was part of an "intermediate aggregate," ranging from "intelligent skilled mechanics" at one end to "writers, teachers, and clergymen" at the other. Those were the people who were most likely to want to go back to the land: "both men and women"—it was important to specify both, as we will see— "looking with longing eyes beyond the steam and smoke of the city to that *ultima thule* where there is an abiding country home."[29]

Evidence from a number of sources suggests that back-to-the-land promoters assessed their target audiences shrewdly. Workers from those broad middle ranks dominated both the membership lists of back-to-the-land colonies and back-to-the-land accounts in the popular press. The Little Lands colonies of southern California, for example, attracted members from a broad spectrum of upper working-class and lower middle-class occupations. At the Los Terrenitos colony outside Los Angeles, a little under one-third of the members held white-collar positions as teachers, journalists, clerks, or salespeople. A slightly larger number were skilled blue-collar workers: house carpenters, dressmakers, electricians. (Another quarter had actually been farmers or gardeners *before* they joined the colony.)[30] San Ysidro, the Little Lands colony outside San Diego, had a similar profile: roughly 35 percent of its members were white-collar workers, roughly 30 percent skilled blue-collar workers.[31]

The David Grayson letter collection, however, suggests that a somewhat more select group of readers may have been the primary consumers of back-to-the-land literature. Of the 165 correspondents whose occupations could be identified, nearly all occupied the upper end of the "middling" spectrum.[32] Only a handful—around 4 percent—were the kind of "intelligent skilled mechanics" who made up the base of that larger "intermediate aggregate."[33] And as it turns out, the David Grayson correspondents were not simply middle-class; they occupied a distinctive sector of the white-collar workforce.[34] Over 40 percent of Grayson's correspondents held professional positions, at a time when only 4.5 percent of all American workers fell into that category. Some of those professionals were lawyers and doctors, but many more were journalists, teachers, and librarians: often as well educated as lawyers and doctors but seldom as well paid. Even more distinctive was the number of David Grayson's correspondents employed in clerical and sales work, jobs at the bottom of the white-collar sector. Just under 10 percent of all Americans held jobs in this category in 1910, but among David Grayson's correspondents, the number was nearly 30 percent.

Those correspondents were not simply interested in writing to David Grayson. They were also disproportionately interested in going back to the land. Among the thirty-four letter writers who mentioned going back to the land (and whose occupations could be determined), these two occupational categories are even more dominant: three-quarters of those who wrote to David Grayson about their own return to the land (twenty-six out of the thirty-four correspondents) were either clerical and sales workers or lower-level professionals. Teachers and journalists, clerks and traveling salesmen—these were the would-be back-to-the-landers most likely to write to David Grayson.

The predominance of such readers could be a statistical fluke or the result of some other characteristic of the Grayson sketches, but a 1912 issue of the *World's Work* offers a bit of corroboration.[35] In a brief article featuring extracts of letters from readers, six out of the seven correspondents held white-collar positions: there were two teachers, a traveling salesman, a worker in the "news business," a worker in "the U.S. federal service," and an office worker in "a large manufacturing concern."[36] Even among recent immigrants—perhaps the least likely of all to write to an author like David Grayson—there are hints that the pattern holds.[37] According to historian Robert Alan Goldberg, nearly a third even of the immigrant Jewish workers who settled the Clarion agricultural colony in 1911 occupied white-collar jobs before they went to Utah.[38]

Why would these relatively well-placed city workers be interested in returning to the land? To begin with, the white-collar sector was expanding rapidly—faster than any other occupational category.[39] There were a quarter of a million clerical positions in 1880; by 1910, there were nearly two million and by 1920 three and a quarter million. Similarly, there were under half a million salespeople in 1880, a million in 1910, and almost a million and three quarters in 1920.[40] The style of the work itself was changing just as quickly, becoming more mechanized, routine, and compartmentalized. Not coincidentally, many of these positions were also beginning to be filled by women. The juxtaposition of poorly paid jobs for men with even more poorly paid jobs for women encouraged the development of an increasingly stringent hierarchy in the workforce. For men, the old expectation that clerical occupations would be a route to middle-class ownership was becoming a distant dream, replaced by permanent employment in department stores and offices.

Other white-collar occupations were undergoing broadly similar changes. Traveling salesmen, for example, had once been known as the "lone rangers" of white-collar work, traveling long distances, relying on intuition, cherishing often eccentric personal styles. Now older men were being pushed to retire, and younger salesmen found that their work was increasingly regimented and controlled from the central office. In *Men Who Sell Things* (1907), a popular textbook for traveling salesmen, Walter Moody explained that the greatest problem the salesman of the day faced was "how to . . . prevent being crushed out and shoved to one side in the mad commercial whirl for conquest."[41] (No wonder David Grayson's traveling salesman got tears in his eyes when Grayson read to him the Wordsworth lines "getting and spending we lay waste our powers.")

Many lower-level professionals were in the same position. It was nothing new for teachers to be paid poorly, but they were now also experiencing some of the same pressures as clerks and salespeople. The number of teachers tripled between 1870 and 1900, and the growing presence of women on the job increased the stratification of the workplace there as elsewhere.[42] Journalism was undergoing an even more fundamental transformation. On every front, the occupations associated with producing printed matter were being reshaped. Innovative publishers like S. S. McClure and Edward Bok were transforming their magazines into mass-market creations with a national reach. Writers and editors, as much as proofreaders and pressmen, found themselves in a more market-driven, pressurized workplace.

Reporters on the newspaper beat experienced this change with special intensity, and of course, their experiences made it into print more frequently than most other people's did. Ray Stannard Baker's first year on the job at the *Chicago Record* was characteristic, combining low pay, eleven-hour work days, and tremendous time pressure—"everything done at top speed, almost nothing well or thoroughly done," as he later described it.[43] Speed, competition, and stress were becoming endemic to the profession. David Graham Phillips, who, like Baker, would soon become well known as a muckraker (his "Treason of the Senate" articles exposed the corruption of legislators), described a workplace where "worn, restless editors, writers and artists, toiling heedless of the hours for sleeping and eating," sacrificed the health of both "body and mind in the effort to feed and stimulate the public appetite." Edna Ferber's description of her effort to become a beat reporter repeated a tale much like David Grayson's: "I was pressing too hard," Ferber wrote: "I ate meals improperly balanced and at irregular hours." Finally, her journalistic plans were "temporarily sidetracked . . . through the fact that I quietly fainted one morning when I was dressing to go to the office."[44]

Blue Envelopes

David Grayson's correspondents reported experiences of exhaustion and "burn-out" similar to those chronicled by professional writers. In such situations, it was a toss-up whether to hate the job or fear the loss of it. In a world without Social Security, unemployment benefits, or medical insurance, back-to-the-land writers dwelled on the plight of the "frightened middle-aged man who goes timorously to work wondering whether the job is still there."[45] In theory, it should not have been new white-collar workers in particular who feared getting the "blue envelope" (we call them "pink slips" now), of course. Gabriel Davidson, for many years the director of the Jewish Agricultural Society, regarded that fear as the chief motive of Jewish back-to-the-landers in all occupations. The "white collar man," to be sure, was "obsessed by fear of the slowing down of mental faculties," and the "professional man" was "crowded out by younger competitors." But the factory worker was also "fearful of the tenure of his job." The shopkeeper was in the same boat, living in "daily dread of being driven out of business by big combinations." Even "the man of relative affluence—perhaps a manufacturer or merchant"—feared "a turn in the wheel of fortune."[46]

In reality, white-collar workers often enjoyed substantially greater job security than did their skilled blue-collar counterparts. As historian Jerome Bjelopera has pointed out, one of the most important advantages of white-collar work at the turn of the century was its steadiness in comparison with skilled blue-collar work, even though the latter often brought in similar or even better wages.[47] Nevertheless, the question of how to provide for unemployment, sickness, and old age perplexed and worried David Grayson's white-collar correspondents.

One teacher framed the question bluntly: "At best I can hardly expect to continue present work as a teacher more than ten years. What then?"[48] That sense of vulnerability was well founded. Teaching was an occupation for young people: in 1900, the median age in the profession was twenty-seven.[49] Correspondents in other occupations echoed the teacher's concerns. A salesman wrote to David Grayson that he had found himself too old—at fifty—to compete in his trade. He had two children in high school and was fast using up his savings. "I would like to get on the land—to make our living out of the soil and stop living on dwindling resources." His options were narrowing: if he could not take his family back to the land, "I either go on the bread line or commit suicide before all resources disappear."[50]

Writing in the *Craftsman*, a printer articulated a frequently expressed fear that he would soon lose his job to a younger competitor: "Time would inevitably fill my place at the print shop—for newspaper work requires young and active men."[51] He was all of thirty-nine years old. Another writer drove home the same fears. "Even now," he insinuated, "you may feel your hold upon the city and its mad endeavor slackening." Never forget, "strong hearts and ready hands" are always "eager to take up your task with greater courage and finer enthusiasm." Truman DeWeese was an advertising man, so perhaps his gift for persuasive phrasing ran away with him, but it is just as likely he felt it all himself. "Some day at quitting-time," he predicted, "the lights will be turned out for you forever, and . . . a new hat will hang from your peg in the office." The question was "Are you ready for it?"[52]

Of course, these middling workers ought to have been "ready for it"— saving money for their children's education and making provision for illness, job loss, and eventual retirement. But that raises the question of income. Many of the new white-collar workers earned salaries that struck them as barely enough to get by. A 1901 article in the *World's Work* estimated that such "intermediate" workers made around $20 per week, or $1,000 per year.[53] That seems to have been roughly accurate. According to Bureau of Labor sources, the average salary for clerical workers in the railroad industry in 1900 was a little over $1,000 per year. For postal workers the average was $925.[54]

Those were not starvation wages. The average wage of all nonfarm workers in 1900 came to less than half that amount: $483 per year at full employment, or about $9.50 a week.[55] But $20 a week appears to have been somewhere near the "bottom line" for urban respectability.[56] Even for recent immigrants, that figure of $900 seemed to demarcate a threshold of decency. In 1901, *Der Yiddisher Emigrant* estimated that a family needed at least $18 per week—around $900 per year at full employment—for a "more or less respectable living."[57] For people teetering on the edge of the middle class— who needed the right clothing for the office and respectable housing in good neighborhoods, and who cherished the hope that their children would attend high school and perhaps even college—it could mean a fairly desperate existence. And some white-collar jobs paid far less. Male office workers in Philadelphia in 1890 averaged over $900 per year, but female office workers made only a little over $400. Clergymen averaged only $731 in 1900 and teachers a miserable $328. (A dressmaker, in contrast, might make considerably more: at the $2.50 per day rate advertised in the *New York Times* in 1901, perhaps $600 or $700 a year.)[58]

Under the right circumstances, of course, a worker might feel good about $20 a week, or even $6. But the right circumstances did not prevail in these times. By 1907, when a stock market crash and bank panic sent shock waves through the system, many workers would not yet have forgotten the deep impact of the depression of 1893, which had lowered wages and employment levels for years. Such panics were enough to make anyone wonder about job security. Then there was the issue of rising food prices. The early twentieth century is regarded as a "golden age" for American farmers precisely because the price of food was relatively high and rising. And food was no small part of the budget in these years. According to the Bureau of Labor, in 1901, the average income for a family of two or more (often including more than one person's wages) was $651; that family would spend $266 on food—a whopping 40 percent of the entire income. Even those who made as much as $1,200 per year spent a third of their income on food.[59]

That average family, moreover, was spending a total of $618 out of its $651 in yearly earnings—leaving $33 in savings. Even families who earned $1,200 per year spent all but $148 of it.[60] These workers might have a month's wages put away for a rainy day, but what about substantial savings for retirement? And how much could a teacher making $350, or even a postal clerk making $900, save for unemployment or old age? No wonder the published literature was eloquent in its evocation of the fearful insecurity of urban life.

David Grayson's correspondents never mentioned salaries or prices directly, but they did write about their fear of old age and of losing their jobs. Bolton Hall had such people in mind when he described the problem in *A Little Land and a Living*: "I call 'poor' every one who cannot afford to be sick for a few weeks, or who has not over four weeks' wages in the savings bank." That definition, he thought, would include most of the "clerks, the stenographers, the bookkeepers, the tradesmen, and even some of the professionals of our great cities, who earn barely enough to give them a living, much less a decent home."[61]

No One to Lord It Over Me

Nor were wages and salaries the whole problem. Back-to-the-land advocates frequently argued that insecurity was intrinsic to the very nature of modern occupations. Everyone who worked for wages, they asserted, was fundamentally insecure. As William Ellsworth Smythe put it, all wage earners were "dependent on the enterprise, the life, the fortune—even the whim—of some one else." Another back-to-the-land author used stronger language to deplore the fate of his friends "who have labored all their lives for another." Because their "very existence depends upon a wage," they "have never been their own masters."[62] The Grayson sketches made the point even more explicitly: "If I loitered or paused by the wayside . . . I soon heard the sharp crack of the lash."[63] Correspondents, too, occasionally echoed this rhetoric of slavery. To the *World's Work*, one man wrote that he wanted to find the "independence mentioned in your paper." He had left the farm as a young man and entered the civil service: "'Now,'" he wrote, "after some twenty years of hard work I am confronted with the fact that I have been a slave."[64]

Of course, slavery was not a very apt analogy for the position of a civil servant, but this language was rooted in a venerable American rhetorical tradition. Back-to-the-land advocates linked the ownership of one's own means of production—the workshop or, best of all, the farm—not simply with security but with independence, autonomy, and the kind of personal integrity they often denominated "manhood." This "producerist" perspective was an old-fashioned way of looking at the world at the turn of the century, but an updated perspective might only make matters worse. Those who worked in "factories, department stories and offices," Smythe argued, now depended not on a single master's will, however capricious, but worse, on a soulless conglomerate.

To describe the plight of such workers, writers frequently used the phrase "cogs in a wheel." One character in a back-to-the-land tale explained, "For twenty years now I had been a cog in the clerical machinery of the United Woolen Company."[65] A David Grayson correspondent used that phrase to describe his own sense of loss of control. John C. Reese, a reporter in Atlanta, confessed wistfully that he could not afford to go back to the farm. Before he knew what he was doing, it was too late: "The big world had gripped me, and I was but a tiny cog in the machinery of things." Liberty Hyde Bailey used the phrase in an article in the *World's Work*. "A cog in the wheel of town life or an independent proprietor—it depends on yourself."[66]

But becoming an "independent proprietor" did not really "depend on yourself" any more, if it ever had. Independent proprietorship—for generations the goal not only of middle-class men but of skilled workers as well—was by the early twentieth century becoming increasingly a thing of the past. Yet the dream of independence remained alive in the population long after the reality had faded. In 1905, the Retail Clerks' International Protective Association reported that half of male sales clerks still dreamed of becoming small business owners.[67] Bailey asserted that farming could still bring that dream to life: going back to the land could provide people with "comfortable and personal homes" and free them from debt. Most important of all, they would be "beholden to no man."[68]

Back-to-the-land writers interpreted the time-honored dream of independent proprietorship in a variety of ways. Smythe explicitly connected the back-to-the-lander's self-respect with political independence: "If a man goes up in his own estimation when he puts on a new suit of clothes . . . how much higher will he rise when he steps from rented quarters into a home of his own?" A citizenry made up of men, each one of whom owned "his own ground, his own roof, his own fireside," would eradicate political corruption: "It will not be quite so easy to tell him how to vote on election day—not quite!"[69] (Smythe's book came out in 1921, so perhaps he did not have time to edit it to reflect the previous year's constitutional amendment providing for women's suffrage.)

Hall, too, connected the independence of the back-to-the-lander with political freedom, but of a somewhat different kind. In a letter of congratulations to a group of Little Lands colonists, Hall deplored the humiliating position of "those who must pray for their daily bread to an employer instead of the All-giver." But "if we can satisfy our desires out of a little land," he promised, "we need call no man master, and may speak our minds, however revolutionary our speech may be."[70] Hall had good reason to be concerned with the right to free speech. He would push his own right to speak his mind to the limit in the next few years, handing out proscribed birth control pamphlets and later defending the rights of those who opposed American entry into World War I.

No David Grayson correspondents wrote about conflicts between their work and their personal freedom, and the census materials do not reveal the fears and dreams of the members of the Little Lands colonies directly. Reading between the lines, however, it may be possible to guess at some motives. At least one real-life Little Lander must have found Hall's argument compelling. Henry Heath Bawden never told his whole story in writing, but he experienced first-hand the clash between his need to please his "masters" and his desire to speak his mind. He solved that problem in the end by going back to the land. Bawden was an important exponent of pragmatist philosophy, trained by John Dewey at the University of Chicago, where he received his doctorate in 1900. Within a few years, he had launched a distinguished career. He taught at Vassar College, where he published prolifically, before leaving to chair the philosophy department at the University of Cincinnati. There, however, Bawden ran into serious trouble. Vassar administrators, it turned out, had hustled him off to Cincinnati because they were unwilling to tolerate either his separation from his wife or his unorthodox views on marriage. When administrators at the University of Cincinnati discovered the situation, they immediately moved against Bawden, too. He fought back in the media, defending his beliefs in both the local Cincinnati *Times-Star* and the *New York Times*: marriages should be based on "comradeship," unmarried women with children should not be ostracized, divorce restrictions should be eased.[71] Cincinnati students apparently attempted to defend their professor, but he was forced out at the end of the term.[72]

The colony of San Ysidro gave Bawden a chance to start over. He gave his name to the census taker as Harry Bawden (replacing the former professorial "H. Heath Bawden") and his occupation as "truck farmer." He did continue to publish, but he also expended some of his intellectual energy on experiments with cloth greenhouses. Bawden became an enthusiastic spokesman for the Little Lands cause. He never regained an academic position, but as far as the census reveals, he seems to have made the most of his hard-won personal freedom. In 1920 he was reported living with a wife named Beth; in the 1930 census, he was still a truck farmer, but he had a wife named Josephine.

Edward Payson Powell hinted at a rather similar experience with a job that curtailed his intellectual liberty. The bosses he confronted were not university administrators but the committees who hired clergymen. "With ministers I have special sympathy," he wrote. Because of pressure from their congregations, they were "compelled to hold on largely to the conservative past, and . . . not allowed to adjust their work to the living present." Powell had himself been a Congregational minister before leaving that church for a position with the Unitarian magazine *Unity*. He made a name for himself as a defender of Darwinian theory and protected his intellectual independence by buying a farm. Farm self-sufficiency, he reasoned, would allow the minister to speak his mind without fear and thus "render him more independent in his preaching, and save his manhood as well as his intellectual vigor."[73]

Another clergyman used similar language in Lyman Abbott's liberal Christian weekly the *Outlook*. William Harsha reported that he had given up his work as a minister and taken up a homestead claim in the West. There were many difficulties, he reported, but "I am content and thankful that I . . . hit the trail to the brush. For my own inner manhood has come to its best."[74] Harsha seems also to have experienced a situation similar to the one Powell described. He did not tell this part of his story in the article, but in 1899 he had resigned from his post as pastor of the Second Collegiate Reformed Church in New York. The *New York Times* had reported that the resignation was precipitated by ill health, a heavy burden of debt, and "malicious rumors" circulated by an "old fogy element" in the congregation.[75]

It is no coincidence that Harsha and Powell both used the word "manhood" to describe the independence they found on the farm. The interlocking concepts of economic autonomy, political independence, and personal integrity had deep roots in the "producerist" worldview and had always been understood as masculine. Few correspondents addressed these issues directly, but one pair of letter writers hinted that they shared that understanding in a revealing double letter to Edward Payson Powell. On the front side of the page, the wife described her longing for a more natural environment: "I am willing to work hard if I can just hear a brook all day and I would like to do my sewing out under an apple tree." But her husband wrote on the back of the sheet his own most pressing concern: "What I want is to own a piece of land and nobody to lord it over me or tell me what to do with it."[76]

IT CAME OVER ME THAT I WAS ONLY A MACHINE THAT WAS
WEARING OUT

The middle-aged reporter in *A Living Without a Boss* (1911) faces a set of problems that appeared frequently in back-to-the-land books. He is in his forties, married, and dependent on a job he is about to lose to a younger man. He fears he is "only a machine that is wearing out." Worse yet, he reflects, "I felt that my very manliness was leaving me in my anxiety to hold my place."

Arthur Judy, another Unitarian clergyman, went beyond this shared gendered rhetoric to imagine the entire back-to-the-land experience as a venture in masculine renewal. Just as Theodore Roosevelt portrayed the outdoor experiences of hunting and camping as a means of reinvigorating natural manhood, Judy described a return to the land as something like the moral equivalent of war. A farmer's life was "one incessant fight," he wrote, requiring moral courage, daring, and tremendous endurance. "If you ask me, what the farm can do for a man, I will reply that it can give him hardness, or hardiness, or hardihood." The "all but impotent yearning of the city man for the country," as Judy wrote, was "a pleading of manhood for self-preservation."[77]

A few back-to-the-land authors took the theme of reinvigorated manhood one step farther. DeWeese promised his implicitly male readers that going back to the land would return to them the powers of youth: "Already you begin to feel the hot blood of youth coursing through your veins."[78] Frederick Rockwell's *Key to the Land* promised an even more heart-pounding rejuvenation. In this story of a Darwinian struggle of the small proprietor against the corporate behemoth, the owner of an iron manufacturing company is forced out of business by a trust. His family is forced to move back to the ancestral farm for its support. Almost immediately, they begin to revert to primal impulses: "The first scratches were beginning to fleck off the veneer of a superurban civilization."[79] The manufacturer rediscovers his "prehistoric instinct" to chop firewood. Those same primal urges lead to the rekindling of romance between husband and wife. As soon as they reach their new home he notices a difference: he sees her "face clear-cut in the moonlight[,] . . . her thin, delicately carved nostrils dilated with the sheer joy of life—life at the full tide, insurgent, resistless." It has a palpable effect: "The blood rushed and swirled about his heart in the ancient, primal way that he had not experienced in years."[80] At the end of the first year, as they count off the successes of the farm, his wife adds one more: she is expecting another child.

No private back-to-the-land letters reported any stories quite like this one. A few mentioned that rural life had given them better health, sounder sleep, or healthier children. One or two bragged about how many children they had, but no one mentioned anything about his or her primal urges or the hot blood of youth. Perhaps, after all, we have finally hit on a dream that was too personal to report to a stranger. Or perhaps readers simply understood this language—to a twenty-first century reader so overtly sexual—in a different way. Judy finished his *Atlantic Monthly* article not with more talk about "manhood" and "hardness" but with his real point. "This is our message for all who care to give heed to our experience," he wrote in italics. "The glory, the worth of life is not to the spender, it is to the producer."[81]

The Woman on the Farm

On the other hand, perhaps correspondents told no stories quite like Rockwell's because they were more interested in the problems of women. Back-to-the-land authors worried about the widespread notion that women were better off in cities than on farms. Country life reformers pointed to the isolation and backbreaking labor women endured on farms as major factors in the exodus from the land in the first place. One woman made that case in a letter to the *American Magazine*, turning the back-to-the-land rhetoric on its head. It was *farm* life and *farm* work, she was convinced, that made women sick and tired, not city jobs. "I have been a farmer's wife for twenty-five years," she wrote, "and . . . I know both from experience and observation that the average woman on a farm leads a life of nerve-racking, soul-killing drudgery and isolation."[82]

Back-to-the-land writers acknowledged the special difficulties that faced women on the land. They warned prospective farmers that without a wife who shared his vision, a man simply would not make it. "Your Laura has got to want it, too," as Lighton put it.[83] But they feared the influence of women. The *World's Work* acknowledged that "the aversion of women to farm-life" was a primary barrier to a widespread back-to-the-land movement.[84] As Harrison Whittingham explained it, "To the average city woman the social position of a farmer's wife is not an enviable one." City women imagined rural women "bare ankled in a hot timothy field, tortured by bumblebees and work."[85]

A long-running argument in the *World's Work* focused on *why* women saw the countryside in such a negative light. One correspondent opined that women were reluctant to leave the bright lights and shopping opportunities of cities. The editor took the position that most women were simply unaware of the wonderful new labor-saving devices and means of communication available in the country. A female correspondent agreed: "The woman who dreads going on a farm hasn't yet made the acquaintance of the new type of farmer's wife," who was now "a much more alert and useful woman than her city sister." The work on a farm was not overwhelming if approached intelligently, and "the telephone and the rural delivery are inexpensive and they bring the community to her door."[86]

A number of letters to David Grayson suggest that not all women were falling for that line. They make a striking exception to the uncritical acceptance correspondents usually afforded the Grayson sketches.[87] These correspondents wrote, first of all, to defend "Harriet," David Grayson's fictional sister, who kept house for him in these stories. A teacher wrote to suggest that he was insensitive to Harriet: "Can she only cook?" She acknowledged that Grayson wrote perceptively about men, but she complained: "I want to know Harriet's soul."[88] Another correspondent agreed that David Grayson did not appreciate his sister's contribution. His "blessed essays" would not have been written, she argued, if instead of the "good bread, roast lamb, and mayhap a shortcake" Harriet was constantly turning out, he "had been fed on 'Campbell's Canned Soups.'"[89] A stenographer from Shreveport, Louisiana, wrote that she had not been able to convince herself that the Grayson stories were true at all. "But if you are really living on a farm . . . I want to say here and now, that my

ADVENTURES IN CONTENTMENT

The half-title page of *Adventures in Contentment* (1907) features a Thomas Fogarty drawing, unlabeled but apparently a portrait of "Harriet," David Grayson's sister and housekeeper. Harriet was an object of considerable interest to David Grayson's readers. One reader wrote to Grayson pleading for reassurance that "dear, kindly Harriet" wore a "housewifely white apron" rather than the latest city fashions: here she seems to be doing just that.

sympathies are with Harriet." All that talk about nature and country life was very well, but "don't you think, as a sensible woman, Harriet had much rather be in town, where she could cook with gas?"[90]

The depiction of "Harriet" was clearly a weak spot in the David Grayson stories. (Christopher Morley found the character so intriguing that he wrote his own book about her. *Parnassus on Wheels* [1917] begins with a letter to David

Grayson, explaining that its "real" author was a woman whose situation was much like Harriet's. Reading the David Grayson books, Morley wrote, she would "mutter something about 'Adventures in Discontentment,' and ask why Harriet's side of the matter was never told?")[91] One woman from Syracuse offered a devastating ten-page commentary on Harriet's life. She did not question the truthfulness of the David Grayson sketches in general, but she had a lingering sense that something was not right about the character of Harriet: "Do you know, she doesn't seem real, some way, and so I am forced to conclude that either consciously or unconsciously you have given us a creature of your imagination."

The crux of her objection was that Harriet's experience of rural life would be profoundly different from her brother's. Her work would keep her indoors, while his drew him out: "She may wonder how your pastures would look and feel this morning, and the brook down there by the willows—but no she must bake more bread to take the place of that loaf which you enjoyed and praised as her handiwork." Harriet would not find in the country "any more of the out of door life than her sisters in the city—certainly not as much freedom as they have." She would have all the extra tasks that rural women performed—the butter to make, the chickens to feed, the hired man to care for—but she would miss out on "the companionship of congenial friends." She asked David Grayson, finally, to weigh it for himself: "Now, what compensating advantages does life in the country bring to Harriet—aside from her sympathy with your enjoyment of it?"[92]

To such a question, back-to-the-land advocates usually offered only confused and not very convincing rejoinders. A few articles did discuss women's experiences with going back to the land. One of the "Cutting Loose from City Life" series in *Country Life in America* told the tale of "How Two Women—A Mother and Daughter—Established a 'Department Farm' in Maryland and Made It Pay."[93] In 1912, Gustav Stickley argued that "Woman is taking a more important place in the 'back-to-the-farm' movement than is generally supposed." "Woman," Stickley argued, was more interested in a return to the land than men were and had been "pleading for a more natural life and home and a better playground for her children than the vicious, unwholesome streets of a city."[94] But articles that focused specifically on women were few.

Out in the country, in the meantime, a different kind of debate over women's work was in full swing. Should rural women continue to perform their traditional difficult and productive work on farms, or should they "modernize" their roles by becoming the chief consumers of their families, following the model of middle-class urban women? Many agricultural experts argued for a transformation of rural patterns, whereby women would take up middle-class urban gender roles that would relieve them of the more difficult physical labor associated with farm tasks, lighten their burdens with new household equipment, and honor their feminine desires for diversion, beauty, and social life. That was the perspective expressed by Persis Cone, the Grayson correspondent who deplored the "hard heavy work" and social isolation Harriet endured.

Other rural women, however, resisted this critique and struggled to hold on to their productive roles on the farm, preferring hard labor and a sense of accomplishment to an easier but less essential role (or, of course, hoping for meaningful work *and* labor saving devices).[95] Back-to-the-land advocates could have intervened on that side of the debate, arguing that autonomous work was as satisfying for women as it was for men. Ray Stannard Baker might have answered his correspondent by giving "Harriet" words to speak of her choice to bake her own bread rather than buying it. Plenty of real-life rural women made that choice every day.[96] Instead he gave the impression that David Grayson did not see the work at all.

Back-to-the-land writers floundered on this issue for the same reason that the rhetoric about workplace autonomy, independence, and "manhood" flowed so naturally from their pens. They simply failed to grasp that the debate over women's work in the countryside was rooted in "producerist" perspectives not very different from their own. Some women wanted the "manly" independence derived from autonomous and skilled work, too. More important, most back-to-the-land advocates seemed not fully to grasp the possibility that a return to the land might appeal especially to women, not as incarnations of an idealized "Woman," but as workers. This was an instance where real-life back-to-the-landers were far ahead of the imaginations of authors.

One Philadelphia schoolteacher wrote to Edward Payson Powell with all these things on her mind. If she could work on her own terms, she wrote— "have a school and carry out my own ideas"—she would enjoy teaching. Because she lacked that autonomy and was required to "carry out other people's feelings and views," she had decided to seek it elsewhere—to go "into the country to make a home for mine own self." What this correspondent wanted was precisely the autonomy and independence usually called "manhood" in the back-to-the-land literature. "Why cannot I keep bees, or raise chickens for broilers, or have a greenhouse, or grow small fruits?" she asked, listing the kinds of farming that seemed most suited to women. She pressed Powell directly: "Can a woman make a living in the country without a man to take care of her?"[97]

Powell said yes. Back-to-the-land writers did not discourage working women like this teacher from taking the plunge, but they often seemed unaware of the circumstances of the women in their audience. When they considered the matter at all, most attempted to make the highly problematic case that the life of the average farm woman was superior to that of an idealized middle-class married woman in the city. This strategy forced them to argue that farming and gardening were easy tasks, suitable for delicate ladies and young children. Gustav Stickley, for example, compared gardening to the new, more strenuous pastimes popular among the well-to-do: "Why should not a woman work in her garden as proudly and contentedly as she plays golf or tennis?"[98]

Most female correspondents, however, did not compare their dreams of rural life with the leisurely lives of well-to-do ladies—about which they knew little—but with their own situations as stenographers, teachers, salesclerks, and nurses. Ten female correspondents wrote to David Grayson about returning to the land. Six were unmarried (four were single, one widowed, and one divorced).[99] The widow appears to have been living on her income, but the other five had paying jobs—one was a teacher, two were librarians, one was a trained nurse, and one was a salesclerk—all at the very bottom of the white-collar pay scale. Surely here, if anywhere, were workers who had good reason to fear for their futures and to wish for more security. What is more, three out of the four married women who wrote to David Grayson about returning to the land were also listed with occupations in at least one census during their married lives: one was an index clerk at a library, another was a magazine writer, and the third was a physician. Theresa Jennings shared a medical practice with her husband, placing her in a category of her own, but the other two shared at least some of the experiences of the single women.

The Little Lands sources are particularly revealing on this point. One local historian collected a number of stories of the first generation of women who lived in Los Terrenitos, a colony outside Los Angeles. Many of these women were clearly operating outside the supposed sheltered environments of middle-class homes. Little Lander Zoe Gilbert, for example, came to California in 1913 and bought a plot of land in Los Terrenitos. She then apparently went back home to Indiana, got married—and promptly returned to California without her husband. She continued to live as a single woman in the Little Lands community for thirteen years, at which point she returned to Indiana and her husband for good. During her years in Los Terrenitos, she played a critical role in the community, working as assistant postmaster, gift shop operator, and librarian.[100]

Like Zoe Gilbert, who was listed (incorrectly, as it turned out) as single by the census taker in 1920, a number of other women at Little Lands colonies foiled the census categories. Several were listed in the census as married (although without husbands present) *and* as household heads—a condition that was technically impossible by census definitions. And some "single" women were in fact living as couples. Marie Frish and Anna Souto, immigrants from Austria and the Azores, were both working as housemaids when they met. Together they bought half an acre in Los Terrenitos and began to garden and raise chickens. Both their relationship and their occupation seem to have confused the census takers. In 1920 they were listed as having no occupations; in 1930 they were described as "poultrywomen," but the word "partner" beside Anna Souto's name was scratched out and replaced with "lodger."

Similarly, Cora Belle Linaberry and Myra Osgood joined forces after they moved to Los Terrenitos. Cora Belle Linaberry was a widow from Michigan. Myra Osgood, the daughter of a Maine clergyman, had been living with a female partner in Boston in 1910, where she owned a laundry. Neither the Linaberry-Osgood household nor the Souto-Frish household seems to have caused any scandal, but there was apparently more talk when Mabel Free Dean left her husband Charles Dean to move in with their next-door neighbor Emma Kraft. By 1920 the two were living together and were listed as "farmers" in the census.[101]

Several of David Grayson's correspondents told similar tales. Alice Dinsmoor, a former Brooklyn schoolteacher, reported to David Grayson that she and her friend, a woman "who is to me what your 'Harriet' is to you," were living very happily on a farm in rural New Jersey.[102] A second Grayson correspondent was divorced, and a third was about to be divorced, although she did not know it when she wrote to him. Florence Folsom had asked David Grayson for his help in 1908, reporting that her husband was thousands of dollars in debt and seemed tormented: "He alternately boasts of his 'success,' and tells me that spiritually he is lost; that he is 'less than human.'"[103] The census reveals a possible source for some of that guilt. By the 1920 census, husband Charles was living in prosperous Westchester County—with a new twenty-four-year-old wife and four-year-old daughter. Florence, in contrast, was living in Queens with her son, now twenty-one years old. Florence had held a job in the early years of her marriage (as a magazine writer), but after the divorce she was dependent on her son, not a lawyer like his father, but a machinist—a testimony to the downward mobility that often weighed on divorced women and their children.

The evidence from these various sources suggests that single, widowed, or divorced women, working mostly in lower white-collar jobs, were particularly drawn to the back-to-the-land movement. Local chronicler Mabel Hatch came to Los Terrenitos with her elderly father in 1913, just after the community was founded. Years afterward, Hatch published an account of the early days of the community and recalled the first meeting of the settlers. She described the gender dynamics of her back-to-the-land community with crystal clarity. Looking around her at that first meeting, she took stock of the people who would soon be her neighbors. She saw small businessmen with asthma and "widows striking out on their own after a long life of taking orders." Seated next to her was "a woman of fifty or so . . . with a tired, lined face but with the look of a fearful eagerness in her pale eyes." Her hands were "smooth and well kept." Hatch guessed she was probably "a stenographer or office worker or maybe a teacher." There were bachelors "who had just begun to realize they would be old someday and decided they better fasten onto something after the roving life." And then there were spinsters, "oh lots and lots of spinsters, who had been stenographers and book keepers and file clerks and teachers for more years than they wanted to remember."[104] Mabel Hatch was herself one of those "spinsters." Thirty-three when she came to Los Terrenitos, Hatch worked as an insurance agent.

Few professional back-to-the-land writers seem to have noticed how much their message appealed to women like these. The founder of the Little Lands colonies was one promoter who did seem to "get it."[105] In his last book, *City Homes on Country Lanes* (1921), Smythe addressed the gender issue openly, pointing out that the "appeal of the garden home is by no means . . . limited to either sex." He noted that "great numbers of unmarried women"—"bachelor-maids," he called them—as well as "bachelors of the male persuasion" were "conspicuously numerous in garden communities." He did attempt to put a conservative spin on the message. The "ideal proprietor" of the little lands home, he added hastily, was "the man with wife and children, all interested and helpful." The companionship of working with one's mate, Smythe felt sure, would save marriages and produce more children. But his message was clear: "The occupations of the garden home are all such as women can readily pursue." For examples, he offered "Miss Mabel Free" (who had left her husband for her next-door neighbor) and "Miss Emma Kraft" (the neighbor) by name, praising the house they built together "largely with their own hands."[106]

David Grayson's correspondents, in contrast, seem to have sensed how little he knew about the matter. One reader pleaded with him, "Tell me David Grayson, how can a woman find the road to contentment?" Although nature had given Caroline Storrs a "great love for little children, for animals for a home," she had no choice but to "work amongst uncongenial surrounds in order to earn her daily bread." She did not believe David Grayson could understand her problem. "You are very wise David Grayson," she wrote, "but you are a man." Storrs gave David Grayson some good advice: "Perhaps you had better ask Harriet."[107]

HER HOME-IN-A-GARDEN

This illustration from William Ellsworth Smythe's *City Homes on Country Lanes* (1921) is the work of Thomas Fogarty, who also illustrated David Grayson's *Adventures in Contentment*, but this young woman affects a modern, youthful style very different from that of Grayson's "dear, kindly Harriet." Smythe assured readers that an independent life on the land was well suited to single women; the illustration carries the same message, portraying gardening as a pleasant, easy pastime. Clearly the basket of vegetables the young woman carries is no burden, and her smiling self-confidence seems to be the result of the security she has found in her "Home-in-a-Garden."

Happy Endings?

Divorced women; clerks and bookkeepers; teachers of a certain age; journalists with migraines; professors drummed out of academia. These were probably not the "competent" people Walter Hines Page hoped would write to him when he asked his readers "Who Wants a Farm?" (In fact, he mentioned no letters from women at all.) Perhaps that is also why the USDA official feared that no matter how numerous the back-to-the-landers were, they would not make up for the loss of "the farmers' sturdy sons."[108] Whether promoters of the dream liked it or not, however, these appear to have been the people who were most serious about going back to the land.

Critics asserted that such unqualified, inexperienced people could not adapt to rural life, no matter how enthusiastic they were. But perhaps not surprisingly, no correspondents reported to David Grayson that they had met with failure on the farm. Often, they reported immense satisfaction. From New Jersey, one correspondent wrote: "Some years back when you published your 'a in c' I was working in a big city; but dreaming a beautiful Golden Dream." Now in the country, he exulted, "I live in the 'most sweet corner of the universe.'"[109] Another correspondent told a similar tale: "After nearly a half century of life in the city in exacting newspaper work, I am in 'God's country' on a little ancestral farm, taking the keenest possible interest in the simple, peaceful life which you picture so graphically."[110]

Retired schoolteacher Alice Dinsmoor reported to David Grayson that after twenty years in the system she and the friend she lived with were now perfectly happy on the farm. Her only fear was that Grayson had made rural life sound so "alluring" that he would cause "all New York" to "pour out upon us, and our Contentment may all be changed to miserable clatter and confusion."[111] (The census reveals that Dinsmoor stayed on that farm for the rest of her life, and at the age of eighty was still listed as "truck farmer.") Rodney Elward had been a journalist until the "black devils" of insomnia had made it impossible for him to keep at it. He was listed as a farmer in every census from 1910 to the end of his life. "I only wish," he wrote, that "the world weary people who are being ground up in the metropolitan machine could take your advice and get back to the soil."[112]

No letters reported failure, but the story of one correspondent does suggest some real-life complications. In 1900, Matthew Lytle was a music salesman in Terre Haute. He was thirty-six years old, living with his widowed mother, his wife, and their five children, all under ten years old. When he described himself to David Grayson as a "city failure" in 1907, one can only imagine the pressures under which he was laboring. In that first letter, Lytle explained why he thought his failure had been for the best: "Had you, or I either, have been a city success we might have been narrow minded *worldly* persons and might never had accomplished half the good that you have already done, and that I hope to do in the future."

Lytle and his wife were "believers in small farms," he explained, describing his "twelve and a quarter acres," his horse and cows, his ducks and chickens and turkeys, and his children: "Of the last named animals we have six, from the blue eyed baby of two years to a boy of 16 years." Glowing with enthusiasm, Lytle described how farm life provided them all with "good health and plenty of wholesome food and plenty of wholesome work to make them enjoy sweet slumber." The experiment was clearly a success. "We are nearer happiness," he wrote, "than we have ever been in our lives."[113] (This letter was one of the few Baker answered, noting on it, "lovely letter.")

Three years later, Lytle reported to David Grayson once more. "It has been a hard pull and the brow of the hill is quite a way up yet," but he felt confident of success: "when I get to the top . . . I can look back down with satisfaction and tell others how it was done." This letter, too, testifies to Lytle's satisfaction with their choice. But Lytle also included a long paragraph of a different sort:

> In your last story I can feel with you every sensation. The smell of the clover blossoms, the gradually increasing heat as the day progresses, the thirst and the satisfaction of the first draught from the water jug, the exquisite odor of that chicken and gravy, the relaxation as you lay in the shade of the tree, the stiffness you felt as you went to work after dinner and the feeling of satisfaction you experienced when the clover was all down and into cocks; all of this have I passed through and can therefore ~~appreciate~~ [correction in original] realize with force the trueness of your portrayal.

Lytle was certainly writing about country life in this passage, but he was also self-consciously *writing*—responding to David Grayson's prose style and shaping his own. Perhaps a perceptive reader might see there a sign that Matthew Lytle would not remain a farmer for the rest of his days. He now saw his back-to-the-land story as just that—a story—and one that ought to be in print. In fact, he was looking for "some one who can tell the story better than I can" to shape his prose into "smooth and easily flowing sentences." That person "might be David Grayson," he hinted. "Who knows."[114]

David Grayson did not take up this challenge. In the 1920 census, Matthew and Zula Lytle turned up in Gulfport, Mississippi, a resort community far from their farm in Iowa. It is impossible to know whether Lytle's family was forced off the farm (which did have a mortgage on it in 1910); perhaps it was not possible to support his large family there, after all. Or perhaps Lytle decided to try to tell his story himself. His occupation is illegible in the 1920 census, but in 1930 he was listed as a reporter for the local newspaper. Wherever Lytle was in 1920, however, his satisfaction in 1910 had been real. Not everyone who returned from going back to the land had necessarily been a "country failure." Some people simply moved on to other things.

4

From Little Lands
to Suburban Farms

By 1920, when Matthew and Zula Lytle ended their experiment in rural living, there were clear signs that the first wave of enthusiasm for a return to the land was coming to an end. Judging from the numbers of books and magazine articles appearing in print, the back-to-the-land movement might reasonably be declared to have been over by the end of World War I. Literary production dropped off sharply, and by 1920, back-to-the-land writing was barely visible in mainstream culture.[1] That sharp drop seems to fit the general turn of historical events. The popular trends of the 1920s—rapid urbanization, a "Jazz Age" worship of speed and technology, a reactionary and acquisitive cultural climate—would seem to have provided little support for a continued movement.

The shadow of the war, and the national turn away from radical and reform efforts in its wake, discouraged back-to-the-land enthusiasts as it did other progressive reformers. Those who had espoused radical positions—Bolton Hall's single-tax colleagues, for example—found themselves divided into irreconcilable pro- and antiwar factions. In a 1917 letter, Hall mocked the efforts of prowar single taxers to impose their version of patriotism on antiwar colleagues: "We Single Taxers are strong for free speech, except of course when somebody speaks freely what we do not approve of." Having purged the pacifists, he joked bitterly, the movement should also throw out members "who openly play ball on Sunday, say damn, are not legally married or are otherwise disreputable."[2] But Hall knew the defense of free speech was no joke. His letters document his continuing effort to find places for people on the land, but they also record his efforts to pressure the government into releasing Eugene Debs, then serving a ten-year sentence for speaking out against conscription, and to fight the Sedition Act Debs had violated.[3]

For Hall, the postwar world was a sadly altered one, but he did not despair. In 1926, he took up his pen to reply to a scornful article by H. L Mencken called "What Happened to the Liberals?" Times had indeed changed, Hall acknowledged. But the radicals and their ideas were not gone: "Yes, they have become less conspicuous, but they are not dead; they will grow again . . . though we will have to wait till winter comes to booming 'prosperity.'"[4] Hall was right, of course. The back-to-the-land message did re-emerge with the stock market crash that inaugurated the Great Depression. In the meantime, what could a radical do but "become less conspicuous?"

From Dreams of Farms to "Garden Goozle"

Books about rural life did not disappear entirely. Rural sociology and agricultural economics flourished at the land grant universities in the 1920s, and studies of the problems of the countryside appeared regularly in the press. Some of those books addressed the question of how to repopulate the countryside or at least stem the tide of population to the cities. New "country life" titles continued to appear, as they had done since the mid-nineteenth century. One such book had an apparently promising title: *Farming Fever* (1924). It purported to be a neutral assessment of the pros and cons of returning to the land. Its author, Wheeler McMillen, was a farm journalist who might appear to have been a likely back-to-the-land advocate.[5] McMillen believed, however, as most agricultural experts did by then, that the rapidly increasing efficiency of farm technology was leading inevitably to fewer but larger farms. Perhaps it was sad, but in McMillen's view, the last thing the countryside needed was more people. In any case, he explained, most people no longer wanted—or could no longer afford—to indulge in "the pleasures of dallying with things growing out of the earth." (That word "dallying," with its connotations of loitering, flirting, or playing, was characteristic of country life books.) Still, he remarked cheerily, "nothing need bar us" from fantasizing about such pleasures. After all, "I have long since given up hope of ever being a pirate but I have had lots of fun buccaneering in imagination."[6] Daydreaming had always been part of back-to-the-land reading experience, but McMillen's flippant comparison reduced it to nothing more than a childish fantasy.

Similarly, Richardson Wright's *Truly Rural* (1922) had the kind of subtitle that made it sound like it was a back-to-the-land book: "Adventures in Getting

Back to the Earth." But Wright's comic meditation about his impending purchase of an old house set a similarly facetious tone: "'Just why do people want to live in the country?' I asked myself." His answer launched him into a parody of country life writing: "'They want to escape the whirling vortex of a complicated city life. They want to sniff of its sweetness . . . and feel the pressure of its gentle winds on their cheeks. . . .'" Wright interrupted his own rhapsodies abruptly: "'Hold on!' I said to myself. 'That's utter drivel!'"[7]

Perhaps the most dramatic sign of change was the appearance of the fifth David Grayson book, *Adventures in Understanding* (1925). In this book, David Grayson leaves his rural retreat and returns to the city: "When the Great War broke into my quiet it changed all things for me," the character explains. "I had to live in a City—at first sadly enough—and there I wrote laborious articles and books."[8] The plot of *Adventures in Understanding* is a nearly exact reversal of the first Grayson sketch. In the original story, David Grayson had retreated to the country, where he experienced a sudden conversion to the beauty of rural life, awakening one morning "with a strange, new joy in [his] soul."[9] In 1925, Grayson experiences another such awakening, this time to the joys of *city* life: "Suddenly, something down deep within me seemed to come alive . . . I seemed to catch a harmony I had not heard before."[10] *Adventures in Understanding*, in other words, was a "back-to-the-city" book. With David Grayson's capitulation, one might well judge that the first back-to-the-land movement was officially over.

Yet books do not tell the whole story. Writers and perhaps many readers may have turned away from the cause, but there were still some people making their way back to the land—at times in spite of the advice of experts rather than because of it.[11] The back-to-the-land impulse did not disappear, but it took on new forms, becoming, like Hall's radicals, a "less conspicuous" part of a more conservative mainstream culture. To trace that process of "mainstreaming" requires a return to a story that began before the war.

California Dreams

There was one exception to the new silence about back-to-the-land projects. Before the war, both private developers and government agencies had made a number of attempts to establish agricultural colonies. Those efforts continued after the war, receiving an added boost when advocates of agricultural colonies turned their attention to providing farms to returning veterans. These projects received widespread media coverage, in magazines ranging from the *New Republic* to *Country Gentleman* and even *Ladies Home Journal*.[12] To a striking degree, those projects—and that media attention—were concentrated in the West, and especially in California.

For decades, real estate developers, hotel keepers, journalists, and railroad promoters had been working to present California as an agricultural Eden. By the end of the century, the state's agricultural trends increasingly favored small farms. California's vast ranches and wheat farms were being broken up into colonies of small intensive farms. The great landowners took the lead in forming the colonies, recruiting farmers and providing irrigation, roads, marketing cooperatives, and even instruction on how to grow the new crops in which they specialized. Fresno developers were in the forefront of this movement, establishing thirty-four raisin-producing colonies by 1890.[13] Many cities that are now part of the greater Los Angeles urban conglomerate—Riverside, Long Beach, Westminster, San Fernando, Alhambra, San Bernardino, Anaheim, Pomona, Ontario, Lompoc, and Pasadena—were founded as farm colonies.[14] By 1909, nearly half of the state's total agricultural output consisted of intensively grown fruit and vegetable crops cultivated on these small farms; by 1929, intensive crops made up almost four-fifths of the state's produce.[15]

The result was a distinctive landscape of smallholding agricultural communities—a landscape that seemed naturally designed for back-to-the-landers. As one enthusiast put it, "the men of the southern valleys" of California had "made the small farm unit supreme." "Ultimate California," he prophesied, would be a land of small, self-sufficient, democratically distributed farms.[16] Promoters of these colonies used back-to-the-land rhetoric to lure easterners to California farms, aiming their pitch at the "'mechanic, tradesman, clerk, [and] physician' who struggled in 'life-long drudgery.'"[17] Small, specialized farms, they argued, offered the city man an opportunity to escape to healthy outdoor work in the California sun. The up-to-date scientific knowledge required for growing irrigated fruit crops offered intellectual challenges to intelligent and educated city migrants. Almonds, apricots, olives, or raisins would provide for a family's cash needs, and in sunny California, they would find it an easy task to supply food for their own tables.[18] Back-to-the-land advocates themselves did not create California's landscape of intensively cultivated small farms. But at the turn of the century, California farms looked a lot like back-to-the-land dreams.

The Irrigation Connection

Back-to-the-land advocates did initiate at least one part of this process. California was the home of several much-discussed cooperative agricultural communities. Although these communities mostly ended in failure, their highly visible stories strengthened the connection between the back-to-the-land vision and the California dream. It all began with the campaign to "reclaim" the arid western lands. Without water, of course, California was no Eden; like other western states, its agricultural development depended on irrigation. In 1902, supporters of arid land reclamation succeeded in passing the Newlands Act, authorizing the sale of federal land in order to fund irrigation projects in the western states. Some leaders of the reclamation movement hoped to go farther, envisioning large-scale federally funded colonization projects to settle the "surplus men" of the eastern cities on self-supporting farms in the West. Not surprisingly, several of the irrigation movement's leading spokesmen were also back-to-the-land advocates.[19]

William Ellsworth Smythe, for one, played a central role in connecting the back-to-the-land movement with California's agricultural development.[20] Smythe was an enthusiastic booster of the state's attractions. Beginning in 1901, he wrote for the *San Diego Union* and for the promotional magazine *Out West*; he worked for progressive political causes, ran for office, and wrote the first comprehensive history of San Diego. During those busy years Smythe also revised his best-known work, *The Conquest of Arid America*, the book that set forth his vision of irrigation as the providential means of bringing people back to the land.

Smythe's peers seem to have found him something of an oddity; his fervent idealism and persuasive powers made for a disconcerting combination that suggested both prophet and real estate salesman. In a letter to Bolton Hall 1912, one of Hall's fellow single taxers described Smythe as a "splendid fellow, great planner and brilliant writer" but urged Hall to be cautious about getting involved with him, judging that Smythe "plans too large and is too sanguine to make his project pan out."[21] Elwood Mead, a reclamation movement colleague who occupied one of the first federal positions dealing with irrigation, feared Smythe as a "visionary enthusiast who, if left alone, would make the whole movement ridiculous."[22]

Visionary he certainly was. In a 1911 speech to the National Irrigation Congress, Smythe testified that "the Pilgrim Fathers were no more earnest in their desire to give religious liberty to the world than are the Little Landers to give back to the American people their lost inheritance of individual independence."[23] Smythe's rhetorical skill, legendary among his peers, rested on his passionate insistence that the back-to-the-land dream was a matter of social justice. "Haven't we encouraged capital by every means in our power? . . . To the rich men who wanted to build railroads we loaned millions of dollars. . . . Can't we help a poor man to get a home?"[24] It was not an accident that he titled one speech "The New Gospel: A Little Land and a Living." For Smythe, the "hope of the Little Lands" was indeed a kind of religious faith "that in response to the loving labor of their hands, the Earth shall answer their prayer, 'give us this day our daily bread.'"[25]

Little Lands

In 1908, Smythe brought all his talents to bear on the founding of the Little Lands colony of San Ysidro south of San Diego on the border with Mexico.[26] The colony itself would provide low priced land, a public irrigation system, and a cooperative market for the colony's products. The "Little Landers" would do the rest. The first lots were distributed in 1909. According to the colony's press releases, thirty-eight families were there by the fall of 1910, and that year's census confirmed around forty households living in the village of San Ysidro.[27] In 1913, Smythe reported that the community had grown to about three hundred people.[28]

Initially, San Ysidro received good press, much of it generated by Smythe himself, who published a community magazine, wrote articles, lectured, and networked with politicians and irrigation leaders. The *World's Work* ran a laudatory article in 1911, and the *Craftsman* followed with one of its own in 1912.[29] And there did appear to be some success stories, like Harry Bawden, the former philosophy professor who was dismissed from two academic jobs for his "free love" sentiments and who specialized in growing vegetables in cloth greenhouses.

There were obstacles in the early years, but the colony appeared to be overcoming them. A reorganization in 1910 formed a more effective governmental structure, and the colonists applied for state permission to become an official irrigation district, which would give them the right to float a bond for a better irrigation system. By the end of 1912, the state finally granted them approval to go ahead with their fund-raising, and things appeared to be taking a turn for the better. At a celebration in the summer of 1913, local politicians and business owners praised the achievements of the colony: there was a thriving market in downtown San Diego; an improved irrigation system; and established Little Landers who were profiting from their labors.

To be sure, there were still difficulties. (Their location along the border did not help. The local IWW complicated the situation by taking sides with the socialists during the Mexican Revolution.) Even the improved irrigation system was never fully adequate to colonists' needs. The cooperative marketing system exacerbated conflicts between those colonists who lived on the fertile flat land (and thus produced higher-quality vegetables) and those who lived on the poorer, and more inadequately watered, higher ground. Still, it appeared that none of these problems was insurmountable.

Buoyed by the early success of San Ysidro, Smythe went into business with real estate developer Marshall V. Hartranft to create a second Little Lands colony, Los Terrenitos, in the San Fernando Valley, outside Los Angeles. In 1913 they subdivided 273 acres, building roads and an irrigation system for the colony. They gave it a Spanish name (meaning "little lands") in hopes of invoking the romantic associations with the Mexican colonial past that were popular with southern California developers. Within a few years Smythe and Hartranft established two more Little Lands colonies farther north, in the Bay area: one in Hayward, named Hayward Heath, and one in Cupertino (in the heart of what is now Silicon Valley) called Monta Vista. By 1915, prospects for the Little Landers looked good.

That year, Smythe and Hartranft promoted the Little Lands concept at the Panama-Pacific International Exposition in San Francisco. In a pamphlet he prepared for the exposition, Smythe laid out the Little Lands scheme. The governmental structure of the colonies would unite the time-tested democratic practices of the New England town meeting with progressive reforms like women's suffrage and the new system of initiative, referendum, and recall. Little Landers would benefit from both buyers' and sellers' cooperatives; the developers would supply them with water and a town hall. Expert teachers would instruct newcomers in vegetable and poultry production. Proximity to major cities would provide access to culture, educational opportunities, and a market for farm products, while the colonists themselves would luxuriate in peace and quiet on their own land. Little Landers, it seemed, would have it all.[30]

But the colony of San Ysidro, at least, would prove to be a poor test of the plan. Two blows fell on the community almost simultaneously. In January 1916 the Tia Juana River rose, destroying the expensive and all-important irrigation system, along with the houses and property of many settlers. Worse, the flood waters deposited so much silt on the river valley that the best crop lands were made unusable for the foreseeable future. Several settlers did put their lives back together and remain after the first months of recuperation (Harry Bawden, for one, was still there in 1920, and still listed as a truck gardener), but the community never recovered. By the end of the year, in any case, the Little Lands colonies were experiencing a different kind of setback.

Not Even in Egypt

Ironically, the blow came from the hand of another advocate of back-to-the-land irrigated colonies. In 1915, Smythe's old colleague, Elwood Mead, returned from eight years in Australia, where he had organized an extensive government-sponsored program to build irrigated agricultural colonies. Mead and Smythe had known each other from the beginning of the campaign for federal reclamation. Now it would be Mead who helped to turn the tide against the Little Lands colonies. On his return, Mead accepted the position of professor of rural institutions at the University of California and from there launched his campaign. Mead had long advocated state-sponsored colonies, and hoped to prove to the governor and legislature that there was a need for state intervention in California. In 1916, shortly after the disastrous flood at San Ysidro, Mead received the legislature's permission to launch an investigation into privately sponsored agricultural colonies.

Mead's blue-ribbon State Commission on Colonization and Rural Credits was given a broad mandate. Perhaps not surprisingly, after investigating thirty-two colonies (including three Little Lands settlements), interviewing hundreds of settlers, surveying bankers and merchants, and sending University of California graduate students to investigate, the commission found the results they were looking for. Real estate developers like Hartranft came in for some harsh criticism in the commission's report. (One of the settlements investigated by the commission was the town of Wasco, in California's Central Valley. Hartranft had been the primary real estate developer there when the railroad came through.)[31] Although the heading for this section of the report was "Colonizers not Dishonest," it was a case of damning with faint praise. "Relatively few of the men engaged in this business were knowingly dishonest," the report conceded, but most of them were "unthinking and ignorant," and the consequences of their actions were devastating.[32]

Mead's report highlighted the overblown promises, high prices, and heavy debt burdens that characterized California's land market, and warned that the number of tenant farmers in the state would grow. Perhaps more surprising, the report also attacked the Little Lands belief that a single acre could support a family. "The widely-advertised statement that in California a comfortable living can be made for a family from an acre of land," the commission asserted, showed either "ignorance of agricultural possibilities" or "an inexcusable disregard of agricultural facts." Little Lands promoters misled vulnerable people— "oversanguine, inexperienced settlers" and "laborers and clerks in cities"—into believing that a Little Lands holding would provide a retirement policy for their old age. "Washerwomen, clerks, artisans, and school-teachers are struggling to pay for these little patches of land which often are so located that they could not be made to provide a living income."[33] Not even in the Nile valley in Egypt, with its heavily irrigated land and dense population, could an acre support a family, much less provide a retirement income for frail elderly people.

At least one part of this accusation was accurate: many Little Landers were retirees. From Smythe's point of view, indeed, one of the most admirable features

This photograph by Ralph P. Stineman was labeled "Mr. Scott"—probably Lafayette E. Scott, listed in the 1910 San Ysidro census as a 61-year-old widower from Massachusetts. A later account of the Little Lands colony praised Scott as a "journeyman shoemaker" who, in spite of his age, succeeded in establishing an independent life on the land. Critics of the Little Lands colonies were skeptical, contending that men like Scott were too old for the self-sufficient life. At any rate, the colony failed, and the 1920 census shows Scott back in Brockton, Massachusetts, in a neighborhood occupied mostly by workers in a shoe factory. (San Diego History Center)

of the Little Lands plan was that it provided for the needs of "those good men and women who have passed the dead line of 45, where no one will hire them."[34] In 1910, the average age of the settlers at San Ysidro was forty-nine, while at the founding of Los Terrenitos in 1913 the average age of colonists was forty-six.[35] Those who had been farmers before they came to Los Terrenitos—fully a quarter of the residents—were even older: their average age was fifty-nine. These averages do suggest that many colonists were thinking of the Little Lands as a retirement plan. And Smythe welcomed these older colonists, claiming that "there is no community on earth whose people are so secure against want, even in the day of old age, as the Little Landers Colony."[36]

Opponents charged that "dear old ladies with $500" were being strong-armed into buying useless plots of land.[37] Smythe countered with tales of "delicate women who have triumphed." The commission argued that colonists needed an income of $500 per year to live comfortably on their Little Lands plots. Smythe reported the story of a "grand old man" of sixty-five who came to the colony "with $250 capital" and was "to-day absolutely independent."[38] (Perhaps this "grand old man" was Lafayette E. Scott; see facing illustration.) In any case, he argued, the Little Lands offered a haven to people who did not have that $500 income. Such an "ageing person may well ask himself," he wrote pointedly, "if he knows of any better provision to make?"[39] But whether justified or not, the commission's criticism seems to have had its intended effect. No more Little Lands colonies were founded after 1916.

Helping Men Own Farms

As Mead hoped, another result of the commission's inquiry was that the legislature authorized the founding of the Land Settlement Board and made him its chair. In 1917, the legislature allocated $260,000 to support a state-funded agricultural colony. The Demonstration Colony in Durham, in California's Central Valley, opened in May 1918. Mead arranged everything to replicate his successes in Australia: carefully screened farmers were chosen from among a thousand applicants; an administrator was selected to provide expert advice and keep an eye on the farmers; architects designed the cottages. The financial arrangements were by the standards of the time extremely generous, reflecting Mead's conviction that farmers needed long-term loans and low interest rates to succeed.

At first glance, Mead's Demonstration Colony looks a lot like the Little Lands colonies he attacked. The colony offered inexpensive land on easy terms; a rich community life to replace the isolation of traditional farms; cooperative

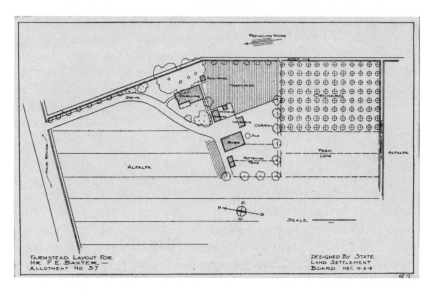

California's agricultural settlement in Durham was meticulously planned, as this "Farmstead Layout for Mr. F. E. Baxter" suggests. The architect has designed a curving driveway with shade trees around the house, and he has taken account of the prevailing winds. This farm was planned as a commercial cattle operation, but it was also designed for self-sufficiency, with space set aside for orchards, a chicken coop, and a very large vegetable garden. (Courtesy of the Bancroft Library, University of California, Berkeley)

marketing and buying arrangements. Like Smythe, Mead offered expert assistance to the colonists—in this case the resources of California's land grant college—and assumed a careful (some might say intrusive) oversight of the colonists' lives. Yet the distance between Smythe's Little Lands and Mead's Durham colony measured a philosophical difference among back-to-the-land advocates that was becoming increasingly clear. Like Walter Hines Page's 1912 *World's Work* survey, Mead was searching for "competent persons" to operate modern commercial farms. Durham required a significant cash investment from its carefully screened farmers. It was clearly not intended to offer farms to "grand old men" with $250 to their names, far less to "delicate women."[40]

Mead shared with Smythe the agrarian belief that the stability of the nation depended on widely distributed land ownership, but he was also deeply concerned about social disorder. The prospect of an increasing number of immigrant tenant farmers in California and the threat of Red revolution in Europe motivated him as much as—perhaps more than—the dream of independent proprietorship. Putting an end to the Little Lands would be one step in the process of undercutting the back-to-the-land movement's associations with radicalism and reform.

As it happened, Durham could not have been founded at a better moment. High food prices, created by World War I, helped colonists to get through their first years with flying colors. Press coverage (much of it authored by Mead himself) was glowing, presenting the colonies as models for a wider movement. Mead's 1920 book, *Helping Men Own Farms*, described the Durham experiment as if it had already multiplied and spread across the landscape. The state was "buying large tracts of unimproved land, cutting them up into small farms and farm laborers' allotments," and "selling these farms and allotments to worthy landless people." "Each settlement," he wrote (there was at that point only one, but another was in the wings), "has a competent director who is helping the colonists to grow better crops, to own better stock, to work together in buying and selling, and to build up a sound community life."[41]

Mead had reason to think that Durham would be the first of many colonies. He had little trouble convincing the California legislature to found a second colony at Delhi, farther south in the Central Valley, in 1919. By then, too, the colonies had acquired a new and more urgent purpose: the resettlement of veterans. Returning soldiers needed work, and the war had lowered food production and caused food prices to skyrocket. The California legislature saw Delhi as part of a large-scale effort to create federal and state-funded farm settlements for soldiers. Federal planners with an interest in projects for veterans looked to California for models. In fact, Woodrow Wilson's secretary of the interior, Franklin K. Lane, hired both Mead and Smythe to work on plans for a national veterans' resettlement project.

For a few years, such projects seemed just about to take off. According to one historian, between 1916 and 1922 there was always at least one bill before Congress that would have authorized back-to-the-land colonies for returning soldiers.[42] As it turned out, however, Delhi was one of very few such projects to be completed. The national plans failed to gain congressional approval, in large part because of concerted opposition by the organized voices of commercial agriculture. The Grange, the Farm Bureau, the agricultural press, the agricultural colleges, and the Department of Agriculture itself were all adamantly opposed to placing thousands of new tax-payer subsidized farmers on the land at a time when commercial agriculture was already perceived as overproductive and overstaffed.[43]

That opposition strengthened as another year went by. Food prices fell steeply in 1920 and did not recover. In the very year Mead published his success story in *Helping Men Own Farms*, his plans fell victim to the beginning of a long and severe agricultural depression. Within a few years, the Delhi colony fell to the same forces. Mead refused to concede defeat, launching a widespread propaganda campaign for the projects in the early 1920s. By 1923, however, he appears to have given up; he chose that moment to leave for a trip around the world. The California legislature subsequently launched an investigation and after much debate ended up writing off the debts of the Delhi colonists. By then the colonists at Durham were also feeling the effects of the steep drop in food prices and agitated for the same treatment. The whole mess ended up in court, and the state and the colonists finally parted bitterly in 1930. Mead became the commissioner of reclamation for the federal government, in which capacity he worked on much bigger projects.[44]

Chickens and Eggs

A flood destroyed much of San Ysidro; the bad press generated by Mead did the rest. Perhaps it was poetic justice that doomed Mead's Central Valley agricultural projects to a similar fate. But not all California colonies failed. In the shadows of the ambitious government-sponsored plans, a handful of private agricultural colonies managed to thrive. The Charles Weeks poultry colonies, for example, were doing just fine. Weeks had perfected his system of raising poultry in the 1910s, in a community he called Runnymede, in what is now East Palo Alto. In the early 1920s Weeks moved on to an area near the newly developing community of Owensmouth in the San Fernando Valley, where he founded a second colony.

Weeks modeled his colonies on Smythe's Little Lands. He dedicated his first publication, *Egg Farming in California*, to "all who are interested in intensive production on small acreage . . . and especially to those who contemplate a state of higher independence on the land." In the booklet, Weeks told the story of his life: his rural childhood, his college education, and his fruitless search for rewarding work in the city. He concluded the story with an appeal that would have sounded familiar to any back-to-the-lander: "There ought to be some way, some plan by which we could obtain the heart's desire early in life without drudging away the best part of life in distasteful work."[45] Weeks' had his moment of truth at a poultry show in Madison Square Garden: entranced by that "glorious collection of perfect birds," he determined to return to his ancestral farm in Indiana and raise chickens.[46]

Weeks credited Smythe for inspiring his vision. Smythe publicly endorsed the first chicken colony at Runnymede and later hired Weeks to teach the Little Landers at Hayward Heath. In the poultry colonies, as in the Little Lands, colonists worked a one-acre home plot and expected to feed themselves from their own gardens and fruit trees. They had access to a cooperative marketing system, and Weeks himself demonstrated the techniques necessary for success. But Weeks portrayed his system as a significant practical improvement over the Little Lands model, describing Smythe as a visionary but impractical man. (The "Weeks method" probably *was* more sustainable. Because he confined chickens in large open buildings, they provided manure that fertilized the gardens, creating a closed cycle that would make farmers nearly independent of external inputs. Water was the only necessity outside the loop, so Weeks located his colonies in water-rich areas and encouraged colonists to build water storage tanks.)[47]

The chicken colony in Palo Alto gradually lost steam after Weeks left, but the Owensmouth colony thrived through the 1920s. Its success may not have been entirely due to the presence of Weeks, however. In cities all over the country, there was a rapidly growing market for fresh poultry and eggs. A competing poultry system was proposed by Milo Hastings, food editor for Bernarr Macfadden's magazine *Physical Culture*. In *Dollar Hen* (1909), Hastings recommended raising free-range chickens rather than investing in expensive housing. Some chicken and egg producers, indeed, flourished without the benefit of any such expert guidance. Back east, for example, a young poet named Robert Frost raised eggs on a small farm in Derry, New Hampshire.[48] On a grander scale, and even before Weeks had appeared on the scene, the northern California town of Petaluma already had a reputation as the "egg capital of the world."

By the 1920s, large numbers of Jewish farmers were moving into Petaluma's egg business, building a tight-knit community and network of producers. Many of these settlers had left Russia as young and ideologically committed Zionists, communists, or socialists, and a number of them had traveled to Jewish land settlements in Kenya, Argentina, or Palestine before ending up in Petaluma. Their politics gave their farms a special significance. For a generation or more, Jewish back-to-the-landers had extolled the redeeming power of work on the land. The imperative to demonstrate to the world that Jews could support themselves on farms was part of an effort to reinvent Jewish culture and shake off the historic burdens of the ghetto. Petaluma chicken farmers still saw it the same way in the 1920s: "They always charged Jews were parasites," one settler explained. "I wanted to show them that Jews can produce on the land."[49]

While the Jewish farmers of Petaluma felt a unique obligation to prove they were fit for farming, in other ways they were much like Charles Weeks colonists. As Milo Hastings argued, all chicken and egg farmers operated in a market well

adapted to smallholders. The marketing end of the business could be organized on a large scale by cooperative or corporate oversight, but large businesses could not compete in the actual production of high quality chickens and
eggs. "There are no Rockefellers or Armours in the hen business," Hastings explained. "It is the people's business." The "captains of industry" had not yet
been able to monopolize land, and "labor imbued with the spirit of ownership
they cannot monopolize."[50]

The dream of self-sufficiency and independent proprietorship was alive
and well in these chicken colonies. The title of Charles Weeks's second book,
One Acre and Independence, echoed Bolton Hall's *Three Acres and Liberty*. There he
made the same point: "panics, strikes, wars or famines do not molest me on my
ONE-ACRE FARM. . . . I have no fear of 'losing my job'; for I am my own
boss and am king of my own little world."[51] William Smythe had engraved the
same sentiments on a plaque in the clubhouse at San Ysidro. The "Hope of the
Little Landers" was

> That individual independence shall be achieved by millions of men and
> women, walking in the Sunshine without Fear of Want.
> That in response to the loving labor of their hands, the Earth shall answer
> their prayer, "Give us this day our daily bread."
> That they and their children shall be Proprietors rather than Tenants,
> working not for others but for themselves.[52]

One Jewish farmer arrived in Petaluma in 1925. He had traveled a long and cir-
cuitous route from Bialystock to California: after three years in Siberia and a
year in the American army, Ben Hochman walked across the country from
New York to California. His rhetoric was less exalted than Smythe's, but his
sentiments were the same: "I figured, 'On a chicken ranch in Petaluma, you
can be a free man.'"[53]

Back-to-the-Land Real Estate

San Ysidro succumbed to the flood and Mead's commission. Durham and
Delhi were unable to withstand the falling food prices of the postwar years.
Weeks himself would go bankrupt during the Great Depression of the 1930s:
one former colonist recalled that he had overextended himself cosigning loans
for colonists who could not pay their mortgages. But many of his colonists continued to live on their land and raise chickens.[54] The Petaluma chicken producers survived much longer, until the 1950s, when Purdue and other giant national producers (alas for Milo Hastings' faith that the "captains of industry"

could not raise chickens!) began to dump their poultry on California markets at prices calculated to drive small producers out of business.[55]

There was one Little Lands colony in Los Angeles that neither succeeded nor failed in quite the ways the other colonies did. Within a few years of its founding, Smythe's Los Terrenitos colony had changed its name to "Tujunga" and was undergoing an intriguing transformation. The colony's much-praised town meeting had quickly passed into disuse, and already there was talk of allowing Los Angeles to annex the community. But far from being deserted, Tujunga was overrun with people. One historian who visited the Little Lands colonies in 1931 described what was going on: investors had discovered "that the tract possessed great possibilities as a suburban district of Los Angeles."[56]

This was not really a very dramatic change. As the report of Mead's commission had made clear, real estate developers and the founders of agricultural colonies were no strangers to each other. Back-to-the-land colonies were typically organized much like profit-making real estate ventures. William Smythe and his partner George P. Hall had organized the San Ysidro colony as the Consolidated Realty Company of San Diego, which bought the land and divided it into lots. Smythe acknowledged later that he was uncomfortable combining the real estate business with community building and that "just as far and as fast as possible I intend to separate my work entirely from the sale of land," but "there is no other way in which people can have homes that I know of."[57] Charles Weeks, too, had begun his chicken colony in Palo Alto by buying tracts of land and subdividing them, but he was completely unapologetic about it, arguing that his work was "far greater . . . than the mere subdivision of land." It was nothing less than "the greatest economical work of the age."[58]

Marshall Hartranft, the developer of the Tujunga Little Lands colony, seamlessly wove together his varied careers in real estate development, regional promotion, farming, and community building. Hartranft had migrated to California from New Jersey in 1890, settling in the southern California town of Sunland in 1907.[59] In 1910, when Hartranft first appeared in the federal census in California, he called himself a farmer. In 1920 he was listed as a manager of a fruit store. In 1930, Hartranft reported to the census taker that he was a magazine publisher. All these reports were doubtless accurate: Hartranft did raise fruit in Sunland, he did have a fruit store, and he did publish something called the Los Angeles *Daily Fruit World*, as well as the promotional magazine *Western Empire*. (Years later, Hartranft would make a foray into literature. Shortly after John Steinbeck's *The Grapes of Wrath* came out in 1939, Hartranft published a response: *Grapes of Gladness*, a novel that described the happy experiences of a migrant family in California.)[60]

EGG FARMING
IN CALIFORNIA
•
A POULTRY BOOK
WRITTEN BY

WEEKS POULTRY FARM PALO ALTO CAL.

Charles Weeks was the founder of two California poultry colonies: he subdivided suburban land into one-acre plots, trained the buyers to raise chickens according to his methods, and provided a cooperative marketing system for the eggs. Inspired by the Little Lands model promoted by William Ellsworth Smythe, Weeks promised that his own improved system would guarantee to "people of small means . . . a luxurious living on a little land with health and independence."

Curiously, at no time did Hartranft report himself to the census as the pioneering real estate developer he was. One local historian counted no fewer than five different company names under which Hartranft did business at the time he enlisted Smythe to help with the Tujunga Little Lands colony.[61] The Little Lands colony made up only a small part of his Western Empire Suburban Farms Association landholdings in the area. Hartranft raised working capital for his real estate ventures by his "Western Empire Home Extension Plan." A shareholder could swap shares for land—simply getting in early on the purchase of a farm—or choose to be repaid in cash, thus turning the transaction into a speculative real estate investment.[62]

That was the sort of muddying of the waters that bothered Elwood Mead most about the Little Lands. Not only did Little Landers blur the distinction between land for speculation and land for subsistence, but they failed, the commission's report complained, to differentiate land with "productive values," that is, farms, from land valued only as a consumer item, namely, house lots.[63] The commissioners feared, in other words, that Little Landers got back-to-the-land colonies confused with suburbs.

Little Landers were not the only Californians who were obscuring those distinctions. For their part, southern California's conventional developers were trying hard to apply the Little Lands "brand" to their own real estate. Land speculators and community boosters at San Diego's 1915 Panama-California Exposition saw no reason why suburban tracts could not also be intensive farms. The model farm they constructed at the San Diego exhibition featured a stylish bungalow with every modern convenience, located on seventeen acres of intensively cultivated land. The promotional materials made it clear that developers envisioned this sample farm (perhaps without the larger orchards) as a model for self-sufficient suburban properties throughout the region. They even used the phrase "little lander."[64]

As for back-to-the-landers themselves, if there was confusion there, it went all the way back to the beginning of the movement. Mindful of the disadvantages that drove people from farms to cities in the first place—rural isolation, drudgery, lack of opportunity—back-to-the-landers had consistently advocated a "third way" that would avoid the disadvantages of both country living and city living. Bolton Hall, for one, had been openly skeptical about the joys of life out in the countryside. Hall frequently pointed out that poor people stayed in cities for very good reasons—"not because a man is no good but because he is no fool." Indeed, in *Three Acres and Liberty* Hall had asserted that traditional farms furnished a "horde of recruits for insane asylums, owing to the isolation and monotony of everyday life, with its lack of social intercourse and educational advantages."[65] His idea was to get people "back to the soil" but also "close to the cities," where they could gain their independence without losing access to urban social life and educational opportunities.

Mead called it "closer settlement" and viewed it as a critical part of the success of agricultural colonies. Weeks echoed that conviction: "Instead of big holdings in lonely places," people needed "small holdings near to the heart of civilization."[66] Smythe saw it the same way: "It is idle to talk 'Back to the Soil' if by that is meant going back to the old conditions of drudgery, isolation, and heart-hunger." All these leaders hoped to provide colonists the best of both rural and urban worlds.[67]

Back-to-the-Land Suburbs?

If back-to-the-landers were looking for suburban lots, it appears that suburbanites may have thought of their own small lots as farms, too. Several historians have argued that early twentieth-century suburbanites were drawn to suburbs for reasons strikingly similar to those that lured other people back to the land: food self-sufficiency, low-cost housing, and the relative security provided by the ownership of land.[68] In many suburbs, low-priced lots without building restrictions made it possible to build inexpensive houses using one's own "sweat equity." (William Smythe's Little Lands colonies had no building restrictions, either: "When God forbids the roses to climb on anything but a $10,000 mansion it will be time enough for Little Landers to adopt the same policy.")[69] The cost of food was such that growing one's own could make a significant improvement in the family's standard of living. In the absence of job security or a government safety net, a house and garden could provide a modest degree of security to working people.

The parallels are more than incidental. Historian Andrew Weise's description of African American suburbanites, for example, suggests that they operated more like back-to-the-landers than like middle-class white suburbanites. They were more likely to "underconsume," in the worried phrase of the social workers—meaning that, like back-to-the-landers, they tended to be careful savers, skeptical of consumerism, and confident of their ability to produce for themselves. They were less likely to view their property as a commodity or investment, and more likely to see it as part of a plan for self-sufficiency.[70] Similarly, historian Becky M. Nicolaides's work on blue-collar Los Angeles suburbs suggests just how closely such suburban developments resembled the back-to-the-land colonies in their midst. Nicolaides argues that the independent suburbs around Los Angeles were far different from the middle-class enclaves of our collective imagination. Those suburbs, as Nicolaides writes, "stood midway between farm and city, as transitional communities where rural practices were adapted to metropolitan conditions."[71]

South Gate, the Los Angeles suburb Nicolaides studied most closely, included three developments, originally named—not accidentally—Southgate *Gardens*, Home *Gardens*, and Bell *Gardens*. Promoters bragged about the "marvelous crops" that were "produced by home owners in Southgate."[72] They carved out deep and narrow lots to make room for gardens and livestock in the back, enforced few or no building restrictions, and kept costs low enough for people who hoped to get a living from their land. Nicolaides identifies one type of blue-collar suburb as "farm-fringe," a place where there was a "palpable blurring between urban and rural life."[73] Most of the San Fernando Valley fit that description—including not only the Little Lands colony of Tujunga and the Charles Weeks chicken colony near Owensmouth but also the suburbs of Owensmouth, Van Nuys, and Reseda.[74]

The people of these suburbs had a great deal in common with Little Landers. In South Gate, Nicolaides identified a mixed-class community whose social profile appears similar to that of the Tujunga Little Lands colony. By her count from 1926 documents, about 22 percent of South Gate's workers held upper white-collar jobs (professional, managerial, proprietary) and nearly 19 percent held lower white-collar jobs (clerical, sales); almost 55 percent were blue-collar workers.[75] In the Little Lands colony of Tujunga, 17 percent held upper white-collar jobs, 12 percent lower white-collar jobs, 11 percent were small-scale proprietors, and 30 percent were skilled blue-collar workers. Moreover, 24 percent of the Tujunga Little Landers had been listed as farmers or farm workers in the 1910 and 1920 censuses, that is, *before* they moved to the colony. If they are added to the blue-collar pool, as they probably ought to be, the occupational makeup of the suburb of South Gate and that of the Little Lands colony of Los Terrenitos would be nearly identical.

To a significant degree, Little Landers also shared the ethnic backgrounds of the Los Angeles suburbs. To be sure, they were somewhat more diverse than the surrounding communities. Only 10 percent of the suburb of South Gate was foreign born, while 23 percent of Los Terrenitos colonists were first-generation immigrants.[76] With only a few exceptions, however, both the immigrants of Tujunga and those of South Gate were from the "old" migration centers of northern and western Europe and English-speaking Canada. This was at a time, of course, when new immigrants to the United States were coming overwhelmingly from eastern and southern Europe. The English, German, and Anglo-Canadian immigrants of Tujunga and South Gate were unlikely to be regarded with much hostility by native-born Americans.[77]

The Secret of Nippon's Power

William Smythe often expressed the hope that the Little Lands colonies would make it possible for people from different backgrounds to live on amicable terms: "Though diversified in race, religion and commercial pursuits," as he put it, they would be "united by a common interest and enthusiasm."[78] He recalled after his wife's death that she had graciously set the tone at San Ysidro by establishing the colony's social life on "a note of absolute democratic fellowship," including everyone in her social circle regardless of class or income. But "absolute democratic fellowship" is rarely to be met with, now or then. Little Lands colonies, like the blue-collar suburbs they resembled, were defined not only by their relative ethnic homogeneity but also by their rigid racial restrictions.

Hartranft's promotional pamphlet for Tujunga, "My Hand Made Home in the Hills," specified that "purchase of property is restricted to native Americans, white, and of good reputation."[79] (Since by my count nearly a quarter of the community's residents were foreign born, however, there is reason to doubt that this criterion was applied in practice.) In his first pamphlet, Weeks had written only that "sincere, earnest, sober people" were welcome in his chicken colony, but by the time he published *One Acre and Independence*, he felt it was necessary to specify not just "high class people" but "those living as nearly as possible on the same plane, all belonging to the Caucasian race."[80] Smythe appears never explicitly to have articulated any racial restrictions himself, but in 1914, after he had left San Ysidro, the community charter was amended to exclude "Orientals" and "Negroes."[81] (In 1908, moreover, Smythe had published this reassuring remark in bold-faced type: "The Chinaman can no more compete with the 'little lander' than he can compete with the white laundry, which has reduced his business in that line to the most insignificant proportions.")[82]

Perhaps in nothing else did the colonies resemble their suburban neighbors so closely. While South Gate and suburbs like it were generous in welcoming neighbors of varied class backgrounds, they were resolutely segregated racially.[83]

As for Japanese immigrants, the passage of the Alien Land Law in 1913 would have rendered their admission to a back-to-the-land colony pointless: the law banned all Asians from owning land in California, even if they had already bought it. And the powerful anti-Japanese sentiments that swept California in these years created another kind of dilemma for back-to-the-landers.

On the face of it, Japanese farmers were doing precisely what back-to-the-land enthusiasts advocated: they worked hard, spent little, and above all, cultivated intensively, producing lavish crops from little lands. But that was precisely the problem. Japanese farmers had become famous for their success with intensive vegetable farming. By 1920, in spite of the restrictive legislation and the intense hostility they faced, Japanese farmers controlled 450,000 acres of land in California, and 10 percent of the state's crop revenues.[84]

Theoretically, back-to-the-landers should have admired what Japanese immigrants had achieved in California. After all, from the beginning, back-to-the-land enthusiasts had recounted stories of how Asian and European peasants had coaxed enormous yields from small acreage. "Where Americans have sat with folded hands in dejection, lamenting that there was no profitable employment," wrote Gustav Stickley in 1911, "these Asiatics have taken modest acreages of soil and by careful cultivation extracted comfortable livelihoods from them in return for their labor."[85] Stickley seems to have been suggesting that Americans of European descent should take "Asiatic" farmers as role models. Or was he attempting to spur Euro-Americans to greater achievements by humiliating them with the observation that inferior racial groups had surpassed them?

Critics of the back-to-the-land movement argued that the kind of manual labor that was required on intensive small farms was not suitable for white people—that it was, in fact, suitable *only* for Asians (or Mexicans or African-Americans or Italians). Back-to-the-landers responded in a variety of ways to that argument. Some said nothing at all; others continued to make admiring remarks of the ambiguous sort that had characterized the literature from the beginning. Weeks, for example, presented Japanese "Little Farms" (in Japan, not in California) as positive examples for his all-white chicken colonists in *One Acre and Independence*.[86]

Others still took the hostility toward Japanese farmers as an opportunity to make their case, using the threat of Japanese dominance as an argument for encouraging white workers to return to the land themselves. For example, Mead presented the presence of Japanese farm workers in California as an important incentive for developing farm colonies for Euro-American workers. The "alien renter," as Mead termed Japanese workers, put "rural life on the downhill grade" and endangered the future of agriculture.[87] Mead's commission deplored the fact that California's tenant farmers were almost entirely "Asiatics" or—almost as bad—"peasants from those portions of Europe where life is sordid and the standards of living are low." Such workers had "no interest in community needs." Unlike their Euro-American neighbors, they were possessed by "racial indifference and aloofness." Even their good farming and frugal living were condemned, since these practices enabled Japanese and southern European workers to pay high land rents and still make a living.[88]

George H. Maxwell was at least consistent. Already in his *First Book of Homecrofters*, Maxwell had written about what he termed the "secret of Nippon's power." He had argued that Japan won its 1905 war against Russia because Japanese citizens all had access to gardens, and that those productive gardens fostered independent workers, stalwart soldiers, and loyal citizens.[89] Later, after war broke out in Europe, Maxwell returned to his case for large-scale federally sponsored settlement of western lands. This time he argued that national defense required the settlement of millions of Americans on small farms on the reclaimed lands of the West, where they would constitute a reserve defense for the continent. Maxwell's position—that the United States was in imminent danger of being drawn into war against Japan and that only a huge reserve army of Little Landers could avert catastrophe—was extreme, but he had defended it for many years.[90] It was not southern California soil alone that generated this racialized version of the back-to-the-land creed.

Back-to-the-Land Goes Mainstream

Some things, however, did apparently grow differently in California soil. By the 1920s, the back-to-the-land message was clearly shaking off some of its associations with radicalism, even with reform. In fact, it was coming to wear at least some of the politically conservative fashions of the day. In 1910, Smythe, who was not much of a militant, had nevertheless felt comfortable with the language of revolution. In an address at the National Irrigation Congress, he had asked: "Don't you know that back of the insurgency in both parties, back of the struggle between labor and capital, back of the mountain of votes for the program of social revolution, is the suffering of the masses?"[91] Times and styles had changed. In 1920, Mead hoped that returning people to the land would *discourage* revolution—not help bring it about, as Hall had once anticipated. "The chaos of Russia has grown out of land hunger," Mead reasoned. "No one fears for the safety of France where nearly half the people are landowners."[92]

Hobnobbing with all those real estate promoters might have influenced even old-fashioned radical and progressive back-to-the-landers to move a little to the right. In fact, there was one spot in Los Angeles where the projects of city promoters, real estate developers, and back-to-the-landers all converged: at 126 South Broadway, the office of the Los Angeles Chamber of Commerce. The chamber published the promotional magazine *Out West*, to which Smythe contributed in the early years of the century. Hartranft's real estate office was in the chamber's building. And it was the chamber that invited Weeks to establish a chicken colony in southern California. The chamber's Agriculture Department, in particular, consistently promoted small suburban farms; it maintained a permanent exhibit of the agricultural products of southern California and sent pamphlets, brochures, and exhibits of local produce back east.[93]

The chamber of commerce, of course, had its own reasons for embracing the back-to-the-land idea. One of those was spelled out in a brochure for industrialists thinking of relocating: "The real secret of the efficiency of the workers of Southern California may be found in their home life." California workers, the brochure explained, "live in their own little bungalows, surrounded by plenty of room for fruits, vegetables, and flowers." In the chamber's delicate phrasing, workers' living expenses were "sharply reduced" by the "luxuries" available to them from their own backyards, and thus they required less from their employers. The slogan at the end of the brochure said it all: "WHERE NATURE HELPS INDUSTRY MOST."[94] Judging from the chamber's use of the back-to-the-land idea, one might assume that the whole effort had simply been swallowed alive by the pervasive conservative drift of the 1920s.

But it was not quite that simple. The man in charge of the "small farm homes" projects in the Agriculture Department of the Los Angeles Chamber of Commerce was Ross H. Gast.[95] Gast was also a farm and garden writer for the *Los Angeles Times*—and the *Times* was a conspicuously right-wing newspaper. Under the guidance of Harrison Gray Otis, who was one of the city's most ardent boosters and one of its most rapacious real estate developers, the paper had played an important role in destroying the labor union movement and enforcing an open-shop policy in the city. Otis was gone now, and his son-in-law Harry Chandler ran the paper, but when the *Los Angeles Times* supported back-to-the-landers, it would certainly be reasonable to look for a probusiness motive.

Gast's articles, however, championed back-to-the-land ideas that seemed little different from those of the early days. Beginning in the early 1920s, the *Times* and the chamber of commerce cosponsored a yearly Small Farm Home contest. Gast managed that program and wrote a column, "The Southland Garden and Small Farm Home," which became a permanent fixture in the paper. The column doled out advice about tomatoes and chickens and reported on the achievements of successful owners of "little suburban farms." In 1921, Gast wrote an article titled "The Lure of the 'Little Farm' in the Suburbs," which explained that the "little farm" was attractive because it gave people a means of escaping by now traditional sources of unhappiness: the profiteering landlord; the "old shop-worn H. C. of L. [high cost of living]"; and the urban

This postcard from around 1919 advertised *Little Farms* magazine, the journal of a national organization called the "Forward-to-the-Land League." The snug cottage is nestled among gardens, orchard, and poultry yard. Palm trees draw attention to the year-round climate that made the southern California back-to-the-land "lifestyle" so attractive. On the reverse side is a ready-made message: "Me for the land independence and a living." (San Fernando Valley Digital Library, Special Collections, Oviatt Library, California State University, Northridge—from original in West Valley Museum, Woodland Hills, California)

experience itself—the "night-blooming tom-cat on the alley fence." Gast praised a man who had built a "small but comfortable home" and found the now-traditional "health[,] . . . happiness and . . . content derived from the work in the open air."[96]

Gast's model suburban farmers were not intended to liberate themselves completely from wage labor with the proceeds of their acre. Indeed, the Small Farm Home competition specified that the judges did not expect a family to get its entire living from the land; they expected the breadwinner to keep his paying job when that was possible. (During the Depression years, Gast would promote this model nationally, calling it "going half way back to the land.") One might say they were simply suburban homeowners with gardens. Still, throughout the 1920s, Gast continued to use the phrase "little landers" to describe his model families. And although Gast assumed that the breadwinner in these suburban families would keep his day job, his columns described a "normal suburban" regimen that was as ambitious as any Little Lands household's. In one column, Gast suggested that a reasonable household goal would be two hundred laying hens, a garden to provide all the family's vegetables year-round, a berry patch, and a fruit orchard intercropped with alfalfa for the chickens. Rabbits and goats were optional.[97] As late as 1943, Gast would take for granted that most suburban gardeners were dividing their very large (three thousand square feet) gardens in half and planting one half with alfalfa for their livestock.[98]

The *Los Angeles Times* had not become an advocate of progressive or radical reform, of course, nor had back-to-the-land ideas been completely taken over by conservative forces. Instead, Gast's columns reflect an increasingly intimate interplay between back-to-the-land rhetoric and the emerging southern California suburban "lifestyle." After all, these suburbanites experienced the same insecurities, the same fears of illness and old age, the same desire for autonomy and independence, as their peers who went "all the way back to the land." Perhaps the best way to understand the new reality is to return once again to Bolton Hall. In 1926, when he responded to H. L. Mencken's attack on liberals like him, Hall wrote that those liberals had not gone away: "We have not lost faith either in the plain people or in the Zeitgeist." What had happened, he said, was something a little more complex: "The radical ideas of 1910 are conservative planks now." In southern California, at least, the ideal of the self-sufficient "little lander" had gone mainstream.

Coda: Frank Lloyd Wright's Broadacre City

The "Little Lands" dream of planting back-to-the-land ideas in suburban soil would find its most illustrious advocate in Frank Lloyd Wright, who began to articulate his own version of that dream during a time of great personal struggle. In 1932, after years of scandal and personal troubles had kept him from working in the United States, Wright launched a full-scale reentry into the American limelight: he published an autobiography; announced the opening of a school for architects at Taliesin; and brought out a small, self-designed book called *The Disappearing City*, his first account of the project he would call Broadacre City.

By then, the Great Depression guaranteed an enthusiastic reception for back-to-the-land ideas, and Wright's vision attracted a great deal of attention. Over the winter of 1934–35, the students at Taliesin made Wright's abstract ideas three dimensional, creating a twelve- by twelve-foot model of Broadacre City. In the spring of 1935, it was displayed at New York City's Rockefeller Center, where the *New York Times* reported that over forty thousand people viewed it. After its debut in New York, the model went on tour; it was widely reviewed both in New York and in the other cities where it appeared.[99]

Wright's plan for Broadacre City appeared strikingly avant-garde to its first viewers. The design featured the ubiquitous presence of new technologies—telephones, electrical appliances, and particularly automobiles. It even included some spaceshiplike flying machines, along with many of the futuristic design elements that characterized Wright's later style. But in spite of the ultramodern look of Broadacre City, its concept was deeply rooted in the turn-of-the-century ideas and values Wright shared with early back-to-the-landers.

The first page of *The Disappearing City* displayed a Dante-esque image of the industrial city, almost completely obscured by smoke and cloud, with only the tops of the highest buildings visible above the reeking atmosphere. In the text that accompanied his images, Wright evoked the misery of urban life in language that echoed the most dramatic back-to-the-land rhetoric of the previous generation. Wright's city dwellers lived in nightmarish subjection to machinery, progressively weakened by their environment until they were able to do no more than "to stay in lockstep. To pay up." Even their most basic social instincts were blighted: "Humanity preying upon humanity seems to be the only 'economic system' [the city dweller] knows anything about."[100]

Wright's conception of the evils of the industrial city was inspired in large part by the arguments of Henry George in favor of a single tax on land. In *The Disappearing City*, Wright reasoned from that position, asking "Why not make more free to 'the poor' the land they were born to inherit as they inherit air to breathe and daylight to see by and water to drink?"[101] (Years earlier, single-tax advocate Joseph Dana Miller had made much the same argument: land was a "free gift of nature," like air and sunshine.) Like the first generation of back-to-the-land advocates, Wright believed that land ownership made democracy possible and that land distribution would ultimately abolish class differences and end poverty: "Any man once square with his own acre or so of ground is sure of a living for himself and his own."[102]

In fact, Wright's faith in a future in which there would a broad distribution of land was more utopian than that of earlier back-to-the-landers, who had typically envisioned a return to the land as an individual and partial solution rather than as a broad program of social reform. For Wright, Broadacre City was not just "one way out" for a few lucky or thoughtful people; it entailed a complete reorganization of society. Virtually every human being living in Broadacre City would own at least an acre of land (sometimes Wright suggested that the acre would belong to a family and at other times that each man, woman, and child would own one); almost everyone would combine part-time farming with other occupations. Indeed, Wright rejected the term "back to the land" as a description of his plan because he perceived his project as being universal in scope.

As Wright saw it, speculation in land was not only unjust, but had also caused the blight of the cities by concentrating people and resources in crowded urban centers. Cities had emerged in the first place, he argued, because of the need to coordinate the collection of profits in land, which in turn required centralized government authority to support the system and a white-collar army to staff its infrastructure. As Wright explained it, "The profits of [speculating in land] create a series of white-collar satellites all subsisting by the sale, distribution, operation and collection of the various unearned increments." ("Unearned increments" was the standard phrase used by single taxers to refer to the profits from speculation in land.) The built environment of the industrial city reflected the profound injustice at the heart of the system that created it: "The skyscraper is [its] modern monument. The city is its natural home."[103]

Perhaps at one time the centralized city had been necessary for production and distribution—necessary, even if ugly and unjust. But Wright argued that new technologies had made that function obsolete. Now cities were ugly, un-just, *and* unnecessary. New technologies—especially the automobile—would liberate people from the need to live in them. Once liberated, they would grav-itate to suburban spaces that combined the best of both urban and rural envi-ronments. Not only would every citizen in Broadacre City be entitled to an acre of land, but every adult would own at least one automobile.

Wright's faith in the transformative power of new technologies also had deep roots in the previous generation. Back-to-the-landers from Bolton Hall to William Smythe to Elwood Mead had anticipated that new technologies would make it possible for ordinary working people to combine education, culture, a rich social life—experiences once available only in cities—with the small farm's independence and self-sufficiency. As far back as 1904, Edward Payson Powell had argued that electricity was the providential solution to the overcrowding of the cities; it would decentralize the cities' concentrated populations and en-courage a return to household production and small farms.[104] By the time Frank Lloyd Wright unveiled his plan for Broadacre City, then, back-to-the-landers had long anticipated that the new opportunities created by those tech-nologies would be located in the suburbs.

Back in 1910, for example, inventor Edgar Chambless had published a de-scription of his city of the future. In his book *Roadtown*, Chambless envisioned an entire city taking the shape of one long line of continuous buildings—"a line of city through the country"—several stories high, built over and con-nected by an underground electric monorail. Transportation, electricity, and gas lines would be located beneath this "city," and every household would share them. But this was not just a dream of futuristic ease and luxury: "Roadtown" was a back-to-the-land community, offering to "the suburbanite all that he seeks in the country and all that he regrets to leave in town." Each household would have access to a small plot of land directly outside its doors, with which it could opt either to "play at farming" or to "do real farming," as Chambless put it. The new technologies (although not yet the automobile) would make it possible for people to "go to the land and take the best things of the city with them."[105]

A strangely similar vision was delineated in the early years of the Russian Revolution by an agricultural economist named Alexander V. Chayanov. In *Journey of My Brother Alexei to the Land of Peasant Utopia* (1920), Chayanov imagined the city of Moscow in the year 1984, transformed by a peasant revolution that has overthrown urban factory-based communism. The new Moscow, shaped by the hands of the peasants, is no longer an old-style city. It is now a "continuous agricultural settlement:" a patchwork of farms, garden plots, "rectangles of common forest," and "stripes of co-operative pastures." Flowing through this "peasant Utopia" is its lifeblood: a "river" of automobiles."[106]

Henry Ford had probably never heard of Alexander Chayanov or Edgar Chambless, but he, too, had a vision of a new kind of suburban space. Ford hoped to capitalize on the new technologies he had played a critical role in developing—not only to benefit his automobile company's bottom line but also to alleviate some of the social problems that factories like his had helped to produce. In the 1920s and 1930s, Ford designed and established a series of nineteen decentralized village factories outside Dearborn, Michigan.[107] These small-scale factories employed anywhere from a thousand workers down to a mere twenty, at a time when over one hundred thousand workers labored at the huge complexes at River Rouge and Highland Park. The plan was to allow Ford's workers to keep their factory jobs while they also tended small subsistence farms—and to create new kinds of communities that combined the best of city and countryside. (Critics charged that the plan was also intended to force workers in such villages and suburbs to accept lower wages and to keep them from forming unions.) Although they shared little else, both Chayanov and Ford anticipated Wright's vision of a world where everyone would own both an acre of land and an automobile.

For Wright, as for these other visionaries, automobiles symbolized something much more than modernity. Like Ford, Wright anticipated that automobiles would make possible the widespread distribution of people across the landscape, integrating home and work, factory and farm, into one seamless experience. But Wright also believed that the widespread dispersal of population across the landscape would help to liberate individuals from their former dependence on their employers—an outcome Henry Ford probably did not anticipate. Wright shared the producerist belief of earlier back-to-the-landers that labor for wages or for salary made workers helpless against the ups and downs of the economy and dependent on the whims of employers. Once the poor man gains access to the land, Wright argued, his soul "again grows to be his own."[108] Workers on their own home acres could feed their families, get a good job (factories and offices would now be spread across the countryside), and build a house one piece at a time. "Where is your poor man now?" Wright asked. "No longer poor."[109] Like the first back-to-the-landers, too, Wright associated independence with manhood, imagining a world in which poor men with access to their own land would live in "manlike freedom," as he put it, "like the bravest and the best."[110]

Broadacre City promised to deliver on nearly all the old dreams of the back-to-the-land movement. The home acre would guarantee not just survival but also an "invigorating association with beauty." The city would be spread so thinly across the landscape that human habitations would blend seamlessly into the natural world. Children on the home acres would grow up with "all the freshness and sweetness of their birthright." Even more important, it would be theirs *as* a right, "not by grace of some municipal-minded landlord" who might allow them access to a city park, "as a goldfish inhabits a glass globe, with a pebble and a reed."[111] And Wright added one new promise all his own: as people experienced their newfound security, a burst of creativity would follow. New buildings would be "in harmony not only with the ground but harmonious with the pattern of the personal life of the individual."[112] The architecture of homes would become truly individualized, regenerated along with everything else.

The rhetoric is compelling, yet one look at Wright's images of Broadacre City is enough to remind a reader abruptly of the deep divide between those days and our own. In the 1930s, Wright's critics were mostly on the left, and their chief criticism of Wright's vision was that it lacked the means of implementation. Without class struggle or a transfer of power, where would all this free land come from? Meyer Schapiro attacked Wright in the *Partisan Review* for recycling the bourgeois reform ideas of the 1880s (chiefly the single tax). Writing in *New Masses*, Stephen Alexander praised Wright for having been driven "by the inner logic of his craft to an anti-capitalist position" but argued that he was naïve to think all this could be achieved without political action. (In 1935, Wright responded that Broadacre City was anticapitalist, but that it was also "anti-Communistic" and "anti-socialistic."[113] With those phrases, Wright identified himself as a "decentralist," in common with a growing number of back-to-the-landers in the 1930s—about which more in chapter 6.)

Looking back today, however, most critics are far more disturbed about an altogether different problem with Broadacre City. Wright's utopia resembles nothing so much as the "edge-city" nightmare of sprawl that has come to dominate so much of the contemporary American landscape. Broadacre City would conform entirely to the patterns imposed by the use of automobiles (along with those spaceshiplike flying machines). The small plots that would allow for household self-sufficiency would also make it difficult for people to congregate in any central location, even with all those cars. The democratic distribution of land to every household would generate endless uninterrupted settlement across the continent. The thinly spread city—"everywhere and nowhere"—would leave no part of the natural world uninhabited.

The connection between the back-to-the-land idea, the suburbs, and the automobiles that shaped the suburbs remained strong throughout the 1930s and into the 1940s. Wright himself remained committed to the Broadacre City dream for the rest of his life, publishing one more version of his manifesto as *The Living City* in 1958, the year before he died. But by the last third of the century, most people had come to doubt the wisdom of the massive allocation of resources to the suburbs; many saw the whole enterprise as a collective mistake of the first magnitude. In the 1970s, a new crop of back-to-the-landers would break the link between the suburbs and their back-to-the-land promise. Those later back-to-the-landers would associate the suburbs not with self-sufficiency and independence but with precisely the stifling conventionality and consumerism they hoped to escape by returning to the land.

Yet in the early years of the twenty-first century, ironically, a handful of writers with back-to-the-land inclinations are once again promoting the latent potential of suburban spaces. These new authors acknowledge that suburban spaces have been blighted by automobiles and their attendant highways and strip malls, but they argue that they are also the only places where ordinary people can acquire usable space for gardens and small farms. This new perspective on the suburbs is suggested by the title of a recent book by Heather C. Flores: *Food Not Lawns: How to Turn Your Yard into a Garden and Your Neighborhood into a Community* (2006).[114] Another author spells out the darker side of the argument. In her 2008 book *Depletion and Abundance*, Sharon Astyk acknowledges that suburban spaces over the past century have been wasteful and polluting, encouraging consumerism and destroying community. Nevertheless, she argues, they cannot be abandoned now: when the last of the fossil fuel is gone, it will not be possible to bring everyone "all the way back to the land." No doubt it would be a complicated feat for suburbanites to transform their energy guzzling houses into energy efficient shelters and their front yards into small farms. But no matter how difficult such a transformation might be, Astyk argues that it is the only realistic post–peak oil option. She calls her new model the "little house in the suburbs."[115]

Neither Frank Lloyd Wright nor any of the back-to-the-landers of the early twentieth century envisioned a world after peak oil, of course. Their vision of the self-sufficient suburb was rooted in a nearly unconscious belief in an endless supply of fuel for all those new technologies. But they would probably have found the instinct to turn toward the land in hard times familiar, and they would surely have grasped the meaning of the title of another of Astyk's books: *Nation of Farmers*.[116]

Part 2

Returning to
Back to the Land

5

Subsistence Homesteads

The New Deal Goes Back to the Land

As Bolton Hall had predicted, "winter" did come once again to the American economy. Those who had scoffed at reformers during the boom years of the 1920s now turned to them once more. And Hall himself lived to see his words vindicated. In 1935, at the age of eighty, he was in the news again. One journalist described his career with a tone of bemused admiration: "When he was a wealthy young lawyer and writer Mr. Hall used to get locked up or driven from a hall for preaching single tax or birth control." Now, the story continued, "he alone survives the rousseausque excitements of four or five decades ago." (Perhaps it *seemed* like "four or five decades ago," but it hadn't been quite that long.) To this writer, Hall now seemed like a "prophet." For all these years, he and his comrades—a "little band of equalitarians"—had been pressing for a more "equitable distribution of wealth." Without it, they had warned all along, "something would blow up."[1]

Now that something *had* "blown up," everyone seemed to agree that people should get back to the land. Businesses, charities, city and state governments rushed to cobble together back-to-the-land projects for people who were unemployed or on relief. The *Survey* (the journal of record for social workers) kept track of some of those efforts, which at first amounted to no more than simple community garden projects. In 1931, the magazine reported, the mayor of Minneapolis was planning a garden project for two hundred families. In 1932, it noted, "gardens for the unemployed have graduated from

141

the hit-or-miss methods of last year into a nation-wide relief project." The state of New York expected to award small plots of land to fifty thousand workers that year, and the International Harvester Company was offering gardens to its laid-off workers in a dozen cities. The American Friends Service Committee had established subsistence gardens in the devastated coal mining communities of Kentucky and West Virginia. In half a dozen cities from Akron to Seattle, real estate boards had turned over vacant lands to relief agencies for cultivation.[2]

Celebrities weighed in, too. Henry Ford had long been interested in creating a class of workers who would have one foot on the land, one in the factory. The decentralized factory villages Ford designed in the 1920s had provided workers with small plots of land they could cultivate in slack times. Now these models took on new relevance.[3] After the crash, Ford funded a series of newspaper advertisements urging governments and business owners to find land for the unemployed. In 1932, he set an example by providing gardens for fifty thousand of his Detroit automobile workers.[4] (Unfriendly critics called these "shotgun gardens," because Ford made them mandatory for all his workers.) Another prominent supporter was the well-known health and body-building enthusiast Bernarr Macfadden, who had become a media mogul by the 1930s. In both his tabloid, the *New York Graphic*, and his more respectable weekly journal, *Liberty*, Macfadden plugged the back-to-the-land idea as the single most effective solution to the problem of unemployment. By one count, Macfadden ran no fewer than fourteen back-to-the-land articles and editorials in *Liberty* between August 1931 and August 1933. In 1932 and 1933, Macfadden even sent his firm's public relations expert to lobby Congress for government-sponsored back-to-the-land colonies.[5]

Farm journalist Russell Lord commented rather skeptically on the high profile of these new back-to-the-land advocates: "Hardly a week goes by but some new leader of public opinion discovers the space between cities"—the countryside—"as a God-given dump for the unemployed." Lord depicted those "leaders of public opinion" as a little hysterical: "The land! That is where our roots are!' Henry Ford has cried"; "'Get Back to Earth,' Mr. Hearst's *New York American* urges in bold-faced type." And as Lord reported, it was not just media figures who jumped on the bandwagon. Government agencies were hiring more clerks to deal with the increase in applications for homesteads, and Manhattan businessmen were discussing soil types. Little wonder that publishers got on board, too, sending word around that they wanted more "idyllic" farm literature from their writers.[6]

After the Crash

Once again, writers responded to the buzz, and a new crop of books appeared. Their titles echoed those of earlier years: *Flight from the City* (1933); *A Living from the Land* (1934); *Five Acres and Independence* (1935). Magazines also reflected the renewed interest. The *Atlantic Monthly* chronicled the progress of a "folk movement back to the land" that appeared to be a spontaneous expression of the "common man's humble yet eloquent opinion that recovery will, at best, be slow."[7] The *Literary Digest* (a general interest magazine that merged into *Time Magazine* in 1938) reported the results of a survey that counted eighty thousand Jewish settlers who had successfully moved "from ghetto to farm."[8] Other magazines ran articles more like those semifictional, semiautobiographical stories that had been so popular in the 1910s. An artsy New York couple's "Retreat to the Land" appeared in *Scribner's* in 1933. After a teatime conversation with their friends—"a stock broker, a publisher, a writer and a dancer"—the couple left their studio, packed up their Ford roadster, and staked a claim to a homestead in the Ozarks, "thirty miles from the nearest railroad, telephone, or radio."[9]

These Depression-era writers had a great deal in common with their predecessors. They portrayed the farm as a refuge from the evils of city life—"a narrowing, uneducative, imitative, more or less selfish and purposeless existence," as one writer characterized it.[10] Once again they deplored the urban workplace and its lockstep regimentation. One writer told the tale of a "sorrow-dazed, impoverished . . . widow" who was forced to try to fashion herself into a "cog" to fit the "industrial machine."[11] Another described the plight of "Don," who was "the fourth-ranking member of the second-ranking department of the third-ranking bank in his city." To achieve that undistinguished position, Don had labored "fourteen modest-salaried and hardworking years" in a "solitary compartment ornamented by one window with steel bars." One day Don realized with "meteoric force" that he had managed all too well to become a cog in a wheel, or something worse: "a life-term convict."[12]

Depression-era writers also echoed their predecessors' critique of urban consumerism. One writer deplored the city's "endless display of things in store windows," which kept desire "at fever pitch" and made restraint impossible: "Such neat gadgets, such desirable things; there is always one at least that we must have and cannot do without." Out in the country, in contrast, there was no such need to resist—to "hurry by and say, 'Get thee behind me, Satan'" to the temptations of advertising. There were no "satanic windows," as he put it, "calculated, like the body of Thäis, to crack the austerity of a saint."[13] (This was a reference to Jules Massenet's eponymous opera about a courtesan and a monk.)

The new back-to-the-land prescription, too, was in its essentials identical to the old one: security could come only from self-sufficiency. "Buy as little as possible," wrote Charles Allen Smart—not only of "fertilizer, tools, labor, food, clothing" but also of "health, pleasure, and everything else."[14] In *RFD*, a Book-of-the-Month Club selection in 1938, Smart explained why: "On a farm, using is much easier and more natural than selling; also, much safer."[15] That year, Henry Tetlow gave the same counsel in *We Farm for a Hobby and Make It Pay*: "The farmer who diversifies as much as possible, aiming always first at home use, will find the unexpected acts of God more often than not beneficent."[16] Smart, a socialist, called it "production for use" rather than production for profit; Tetlow, a Republican, described it as sound business practice. By either name, it was the old project of household self-sufficiency.

Security still occupied the minds of writers in the 1930s, much as it had gripped the attention of earlier back-to-the-landers. But something had changed: the fear of "black Friday and red ruin" now cast a wider and deeper shadow, evoking a greater sense of helplessness and desperation. The characters in these Depression-era stories no longer seemed to control their fates. The heroine of *Abandoned Orchard* (1932) actually *wanted* to become a "cog in an urban wheel," but she was not able to keep up: "Though I gritted my teeth, worked faithfully, and never complained, jobs seemed to slip from under my tired feet."[17] Charles Morrow Wilson's character Don did not leave his position at the "third-ranking bank" on his own initiative. Perhaps because he knew that far too many of his readers would have been happy to have even such a dead-end job, Wilson had Don stay on "until the job died a natural death."[18] These characters did not choose to go back to the land; they were forced there. They did not simply lose their jobs; they searched endlessly for work in "office after office after office" and in "city after city after city."[19] In these books, well-to-do suburbanites faced more than tightened budgets: they descended into poverty and finally into destitution, with "virtually nothing left to set upon the table."[20]

Perhaps also because of the desperation of the times, Depression-era writers characteristically attacked the city's consumerism with even more intensity than had their predecessors. Often they portrayed the pre-Depression era as what Charles Morrow Wilson called "a record-breaking era of avarice" that had brought inevitable and disastrous consequences in its wake.[21] Advertising, over-consuming, debt, fast living—these had in some sense caused the downward spiral in the economy; perhaps they were also signs of a deeper breakdown. Because the depth of the crisis was unprecedented, some writers came to envision returning to the land as something more than a personal solution—more than "one way out." Now it appeared to be the first stage of a sweeping social and cultural transformation. "It is quite likely," counseled the New Jersey secretary of agriculture in *A Living from the Land* (1934), that in the future "we shall have a shorter working week and probably periods of unemployment for hundreds of thousands of ambitious people." From now on, workers would need to count on "a partial living from the land."[22]

Depression-era back-to-the-land stories reflected a perception, common to many Americans, that the system was truly broken—that the country had gone too far down the path of industrialism, urbanism, and specialization and that a sharp and perhaps permanent change was inevitable. The Depression had unmasked something fundamentally wrong with the American economy, perhaps even with the nation's polity and culture. It might be that some kind of final collapse was at hand: that capitalism would be replaced by socialism or democracy replaced by dictatorship or anarchy. Or perhaps a collapse could be averted by a return to a more modest and stable way of life at a lower level of consumption. In either case, "life is not what it was," as one writer acknowledged, "and perhaps it will not again be what it was for those of my generation." He could only hope that it was not the end of civilization but instead merely a readjustment that might in time seem like a wholesome change: the birth of a "better social order."[23]

In these dark times, back-to-the-land writers did not depict even the rural homestead as a bed of roses. Publishers may have wanted "idyllic" stories of the farm, as Russell Lord asserted, but that is not what they got. Some narratives seemed to waver between hope and despair even after their characters have returned to the security of the land. One writer expressed gratitude for his "cellar stocked with winter supplies," his "woodpile[,] . . . the cow, the chickens," but even they did not make him feel safe. All he could claim was that his self-sufficiency calmed his "desperation and frenzy."[24] Another writer mused that "the economic and political situation seems more full of danger, promise, and deep change than at any time since the destruction of feudalism."[25]

Through the darkest days of the Depression, a perennial crop of "country life" books continued to appear. In these relatively light-hearted accounts, one could still read about the author's adventures with remodeling a colonial house or about his or her comical encounters with rustic neighbors. But even these books were darkened by the shadow of confusion and fear. Frederic F. Van De Water's *A Home in the Country* (1937), for example, offered the usual humorous account of city people buying land in the country. But this narrator was afraid, too: "There may have been louder voices in the mounting chorus of fear that rose from Manhattan in the early 1930s," he reported, "but there were none more candidly terrified than our own." The couple's decision to buy a house in the country was prompted by their need to invest their savings in something safer than a bank or the stock market—a far less pressing concern than the unemployment, homelessness, or downright starvation that threatened characters in other narratives. But even from his relatively sheltered position, the narrator confronted questions that would have been unthinkable a few years earlier: "When the dwelling built upon the sure rock of savings accounts and bonds begins to reel and crack, . . . what else is left?"[26]

Other writers expressed a similar sense of disequilibrium. Smart explained in *RFD* that he had not made any large-scale improvements to his Ohio farm "because everything in the world seems too uncertain for heavy building and extensive planning." Smart really did mean "everything." He found nothing he could count on in the world around him: "We farmers may be collectivized, we may be completely isolated and plundered, and we may simply go further into disorganization, inefficiency, tenancy, and dependence." Smart even reported his fear (a little eerie to read in the twenty-first century) that the Depression was somehow causing climate change: "If these extremes of heat and cold, and of droughts and flood, continue, agriculture in this region will have to be profoundly changed, and how, no one knows."[27]

Gove Hambidge's *Enchanted Acre: Adventures in Backyard Farming* (1935) offers a poignant example of how the shadow of the Depression darkened back-to-the-land books. Hambidge was a freelance writer who had left his editorial job for a country life before the crash of 1929: "We began this free and good life—relatively free and very good—when everything was booming and editors bought with a liberal hand." In better times, a title like *Enchanted Acre* might have led a reader to expect a book filled with cheerful descriptions of experiments with chickens or strawberries. Indeed, the book opens with a light-hearted scene: the family is eating breakfast on the porch, listening to birds sing, and basking in the sunshine. But the passage takes a sudden apocalyptic turn: "Trouble broods over the earth. There is violence and suffering and rumor of wars. Men's bowels are gnawed by pangs of poverty." Even the author's "free and good life" on the land was fraught with danger: "Over us, too, trouble has long hovered, a dark-winged hawk."

No individual solution—no "one way out"—could offer shelter from such a crisis: "The wings of the hawk," Hambidge wrote, "shadow the world." He struggled to pull himself back into the proper spirit: "There is peace here and now," after all, and "the man and the woman feel that they are rooted on this hillside." But Hambidge could not take comfort even in that sense of temporary safety. He was forced to revise this sentiment, too, in an awkward and telling phrase: they were "almost not uprootable." A one-acre farm in Westchester County was hardly an adequate defense against the fears Hambidge faced: "Nothing human roots deep enough to hold against all winds."[28]

Federal Back to the Land

Because of a widespread sense that the foundations of life had been fatally undermined, the Great Depression helped to accomplish what no earlier upheaval had been able to: it drove the national government to invest its resources in a large-scale effort to move people back to the land. For a generation, rural sociologists and agricultural experts had been attempting with scant success to shape the future of the American countryside with state and federal programs. Now, progressive programs that had failed to get through Congress in the years after World War I reemerged for new consideration. Back-to-the-land projects appeared alongside all kinds of plans for land reclamation, city gardens, and consumer cooperatives. This time, they had new and powerful allies. Hearst papers trumpeted the virtues of a return to the land. Macfadden and Ford lobbied for the cause. More important, the new president himself appeared to be one of those allies. As one back-to-the-lander described it, the Depression had created a vital opportunity. "The . . . collapse of the dream of golden plenty from mass production" was a tragedy, to be sure, but it was also a long-awaited opportunity: it had brought about the election of Franklin Roosevelt, "with his belief in the possibilities of subsistence homesteading."[29]

Roosevelt had indeed long been committed to policies that would place more Americans on small plots of land. Like the views of the first President Roosevelt, those of the second had been shaped by progressive agricultural experts' arguments in favor of more efficient use of natural resources, improvements in the quality of life in rural areas, and more efficient farming practices. Beneath it all, this president, too, cherished the old agrarian conviction that rural life sustained both character and community. The Depression gave those ideas greater urgency and simultaneously made concrete action possible. In 1931, while he was still governor of New York, Roosevelt addressed the American Country Life Conference, setting forth his analysis of the causes of the current crisis: "Our urban industrial economy is fraught with tremendous perils, as we now see. The faster the wheels of the economic machine turn the greater the disaster when it meets impediments."[30] Like many back-to-the-land advocates, Roosevelt saw the Depression as a long-awaited correction. It both interrupted the unsustainable growth of previous years and revealed the fatal flaws inherent in that pattern of development. During the years of rapid growth, as Roosevelt phrased it, "the economic liberty of the individual" had been "swallowed up in the specialization of industry, of agriculture and of distribution." The whole system had become increasingly fragile, endangering not only the individual "cog" but also the entire structure of the economy: "The cog can move only if the whole machine is in perfect gear."[31]

Roosevelt repeated the arguments of a generation of back-to-the-land advocates. Urban specialization made people dependent on jobs created and sustained by someone else. The wholesale movement of population from farms to cities made the American economy more fragile and individual workers less secure. To an audience of young people, Roosevelt spoke plainly: "It is in the city, and especially in the large city, that unemployment most quickly results in acute need and acute suffering." He began with the old argument, now brought vividly to life again: those who go back to the farm "will never starve to death, while they may if they remain in the city." To be sure, "in the city they have a chance of becoming millionaires." But as Roosevelt put it, "There are lots of things better than growing exceedingly rich." Best of all was "having the assurance of a competence, of a sufficient living, of a good life and good neighbors."[32]

A "sufficient living," a "good life," a "competence"—these time-honored words echoed the agrarian and producerist sentiments of days gone by. They also repeated the arguments of a generation of back-to-the-landers. In William Ellsworth Smythe's phrase, "A little land and a living, surely, is better than desperate struggle and wealth possibly."[33]

But Roosevelt did not propose to bring the city's unemployed workers literally "back to the farm." His agricultural advisers were certain that technological innovations had made commercial farms too productive and efficient even to employ the number of workers already there. At the same time, upheaval in the farm regions, fueled by plummeting prices for farm products, made it politically impossible to consider shipping large numbers of people back to the open countryside. Russell Lord voiced the objection of commercial farmers: "What would Mr. Ford say if he were a shoe manufacturer, and hard times came . . . and then it were seriously argued . . . that everybody ought to be given access to a small cobbler's last, at least, and encouraged to make his own shoes?"[34]

Recognizing the logic of this complaint, New Dealers proposed a compromise: bring the unemployed out of the cities to small towns or suburban areas where rent and food would be cheaper and where they could cultivate small plots of land for their own use. Presumably those workers would still be purchasing some goods from commercial farmers, particularly if they could find jobs in those less crowded places. At least they would not be selling their own produce. While he was still governor of New York, Roosevelt had engineered just such a program, settling "stranded" industrial workers on subsistence plots. Not coincidentally, such plans would bring unemployed workers precisely into the middle landscape long favored by back-to-the-land advocates. Sharing the perspective that had inspired Henry Ford's decentralized factories and Frank Lloyd Wright's Broadacre City, many New Dealers were convinced that automobiles, electricity, telephones, and radios would inevitably pull people—and jobs—away from urban centers, in time alleviating much of the suffering, overcrowding, and poverty of the industrial cities. They hoped to organize and hasten that process.

At the same time, New Dealers designed similar programs to deal with the plight of the countryside. Agricultural experts argued that it was the poverty and backwardness of farm regions that had helped to destabilize the national economy in the first place. From now on, farmers who lived on productive, well-managed land would be encouraged to proceed with the mechanization and commercialization of their farms. Farmers who lived on poor land—"marginal" or "submarginal" land that could never produce a decent "standard of living," in the new sociological phrases—would be encouraged to move to better farmland or to different jobs. In a mirror image of the programs for the urban poor, those farmers would be given assistance to move *closer* to towns and cities, where they too could enjoy the advantages of new roads, new technologies, and new markets. The state would buy up their mountainous, inaccessible, or exhausted land and allow it to revert to forest for timber production or recreational uses.

This complex and often contradictory New Deal agenda attempted to unite old agrarian ideas with progressive faith in the solutions of experts and a new acceptance of government action. It was in many ways the culmination of the work of a generation of agricultural experts and progressive reformers. It was also a sign of the times. European governments were experimenting with similar efforts to disperse industrial populations into the countryside, create garden space for unemployed workers, provide homesteads for veterans of World War I, and reinvigorate rural life. (Many observers noted that the New Deal programs bore more than a passing resemblance to large-scale back-to-the-land projects underway in both Nazi Germany and fascist Italy.[35] Others compared them to the Soviet Union's massive reorganization of the countryside.) Out of this long list of transnational concerns, and from a broad and multifaceted vision, the New Deal's "subsistence homesteads" were born.

Subsistence Homesteads

The subsistence homestead projects may have been Roosevelt's "pet children," as *Time* labeled them in 1934, but as the magazine also reported, they quickly turned out to be "problem children."[36] Programs designed to tackle such a broad agenda were necessarily diverse. Unsurprisingly, their management was sometimes chaotic and even schizophrenic.[37] The legislative foundation of the programs was never very secure, leaving them open to numerous challenges throughout their existence. Encountering too much opposition to a bill specifically authorizing the establishment of back-to-the-land communities, Alabama Senator John Bankhead managed to insert $25 million for that purpose into the National Industrial Recovery Act. The phrasing was vague, authorizing the president to use the money to redistribute the "overabundance of population in the industrial centers."

On that unstable foundation, Roosevelt created the Subsistence Homesteads Division and placed it under Harold Ickes's Department of the Interior. (That choice reflects Roosevelt's perception that the subsistence homesteads were more social reform than charity. If the program had been designed primarily as relief for the poor, it would probably have been placed in the Federal Emergency Relief Administration under Harry Hopkins.) It had only a short stay there. Already under fire from its enemies and weakened by an internal struggle between Ickes and the division's director, Milburn L. Wilson, the division was in peril within a year of its birth. When the Supreme Court ruled the entire recovery act unconstitutional in 1935, Roosevelt preserved the Subsistence Homesteads Division by moving it to the newly created Resettlement Administration, under the control of Rexford Tugwell.

A second move became necessary in 1936. Under increasing scrutiny from resurgent conservative forces in Congress (and made even more vulnerable by its association with the unpopular "red" Tugwell), the program was saved once again by a move to the Department of Agriculture, where it became part of the new Farm Security Administration (FSA). In the meantime, several other agencies had also been organizing subsistence farming and gardening communities. The Federal Emergency Relief Administration had established a rural rehabilitation division that created rural colonies for people on relief. The Resettlement Administration sponsored its own programs, mostly for landless tenant farmers and sharecroppers. Most of these programs, too, came under the control of the FSA in 1936.

The programs that jostled with one another under all these different mandates targeted very different populations. Some assisted so-called stranded communities that had depended on a single industry, now dead or dying. The community of Arthurdale, in West Virginia, for example, was built on the American Friends' Service Committee's work with stranded coal miners there. It became alternately famous and infamous for its ambitious social engineering, its cost overruns, and the active sponsorship of its most famous advocate, Eleanor Roosevelt. Other programs provided subsistence gardens for industrial workers who still had jobs. Like the earlier Ford village factories, these projects were intended to increase workers' security in hard times. Granger Homesteads in Granger, Iowa, for example, was designed to supplement the unreliable and meager incomes of workers at the nearby coal mines. It was the product of a collaboration with Luigi Ligutti, a Catholic priest who was a leader in the agrarian Catholic rural life movement.

Some projects were intended for farmers. There were programs to resettle the people whose "submarginal lands" the government bought. Shenandoah Homesteads, for example, was established to house farmers whose land was taken for the Blue Ridge National Park. There were projects to settle farmers on the "cutover" lands that had been deforested by lumber companies in northern Wisconsin and the Pacific Northwest in the early twentieth century. (There were even programs to *remove* some settlers already living on such cutover lands.)[38] And some projects were intended to settle landless tenant farmers on farms of their own. Dyess Colony in the Arkansas Delta, for example, was originally set up under Hopkins's Federal Emergency Relief Administration, coming under FSA supervision only in 1939. William Reynolds Dyess, the state's first Works Project Administration administrator, originated the plan to provide sixteen thousand acres of uncleared bottomland for settlement in twenty-acre parcels. The project directors selected applicants from among the poorest white tenant farmers in the area (among whom were the parents of the renowned singer/song writer Johnny Cash, who moved to Dyess in 1936 when their son was four years old).

In yet another twist on the subsistence homestead idea, Tugwell developed his own favorite "greenbelt towns," perhaps the most ambitious of all the resettlement projects. The greenbelt towns—in Greenbelt, Maryland, Greendale, Wisconsin, and Greenhills, Ohio—were designed from the ground up to combine all the advantages of rural and urban life and provide the lucky inhabitants with garden plots as well as houses and jobs. (Tugwell connected the new towns to the larger impulse behind the homesteads by reasoning that in time, more and more rural workers would be pushed off "submarginal" land. Those people would end up in city slums unless low-cost housing was provided for them, and low-cost housing was possible only outside the high-priced real estate markets of cities—in the suburbs.)[39] They were inspired in part by the turn-of-the-century garden city plans of Ebenezer Howard and also bore a close resemblance to Frank Lloyd Wright's Broadacre City vision. (In fact, Wright offered to help Tugwell design and build those projects in the image of Broadacre City, but he reportedly asked for such an astronomical figure—a total of $1 billion—that he must not have been expecting a serious response.)[40]

Not surprising in retrospect, there would never be enough money to fund all these projects adequately, and often they turned out to be far more expensive than anyone had estimated. As time went by, they were increasingly constrained by congressional restrictions and political hostility from several ideological directions. Depending on how they are counted, somewhere between sixty and two hundred homestead communities had reached some level of development by the time the programs were cut off by Congress during World War II.[41] Two hundred may sound like an impressive number of such programs, but they could not make even a small dent in the massive unemployment and poverty of those years. At best, New Deal officials could only hope that the success of the subsistence homesteads would encourage private sponsors to create similar communities.

New Dealers usually rejected the term "back to the land" for these projects. That was partly to avoid the nostalgic connotations of the phrase. Tugwell, in particular, disliked the notion of a retreat from industrialization and believed the president himself was too inclined toward what Tugwell saw as romanticism. Tugwell, in fact, viewed the homestead projects as stepping-stones *away* from widespread subsistence farming, toward the ultimate goal of a planned, collectivized, high-tech system for both agriculture and industry.[42] (Tugwell had studied with Scott Nearing at the Wharton School back before Nearing was fired from his teaching job there. While Nearing's radicalism had left him unemployed and without a public voice by the 1930s, his student had better luck.) Others in the administration, including Milburn L. Wilson, were more inclined toward the "romantic" belief that people were better off growing their own food. But they too saw the wisdom of making it clear that they envisioned neither a return to Arcadian simplicity nor a mass conversion of factory workers into commercial farmers. Wilson explained to the American Farm Economics Association, for example, that the phrase "back to the land" had utopian connotations associated with earlier "altruistic" attempts to stem the inevitable flow of people into cities, connotations he wished to avoid for his new projects.[43]

Instead of "back to the land," then, New Dealers used the phrase "subsistence homesteads." The word "homestead" was clearly intended to echo the great American experience of settling the public lands of the West—a word that evoked both the many hardships of the settlers and the rewards won by those who persevered.[44] "Subsistence," on the other hand, was intended to reassure the farm lobbies. Subsistence communities would produce for themselves, not for the market. Commercial farmers argued that with food prices at rock bottom, the last thing they needed was more people adding to the overproduction that drove down prices. (The Grange, the agricultural press, the agricultural colleges, and the U.S. Department of Agriculture itself had long acted as the most vehement and outspoken opponents of federal back-to-the-land programs and had scuttled the programs that emerged after World War I.)[45]

It may have been necessary to avoid provoking the commercial farming lobbies, but "subsistence" was a word that seemed to invite bad publicity. One back-to-the-land writer based his skepticism about the entire subsistence homestead program on the name. He acknowledged that there were good reasons for the program: "work for men to do where otherwise they would have no work, and hope where there was only hopelessness, and perhaps food for empty bellies." Still, he feared that subsistence homesteading "would be merely turning back to the peasant way of life." He acknowledged that he himself would "would rather be a peasant in the country than a pariah of the industrial system in the city," but he thought it was "a sorry business to be forced to be either."[46]

Other critics also imagined subsistence homesteading as a return to medieval peasantry and as an implicit admission that the Depression had halted the entire upward trajectory of civilization. One writer who was otherwise sympathetic to the projects acknowledged that the word "subsistence" implied "a lower standard of living in relation to what an American might be expected to demand."[47] The director of the Division of Subsistence Homesteads Division himself agreed with this assessment. "Personally," Wilson admitted, "I dislike the word 'subsistence.'" The word suggested to him, too, that the country was giving up on "the standard of living which should be within the grasp of men . . . in this age of science."[48] Supporters of the programs might almost have been better off with the nostalgic connotations of "back to the land."

Whatever their names, the New Deal's subsistence homestead projects were clearly modeled on the plans and dreams of the back-to-the-land activists of the previous thirty years. They also reflected the work of a group of progressive agricultural experts who had persisted in attempting to make room for more farmers, in spite of the near-consensus in their field that farming was destined to become large scale and mechanized. Director Wilson, for one, was well versed in the trials and tribulations of earlier large-scale back-to-the-land colonization efforts. His ideas had been shaped by Elwood Mead's farm colonies in California and by the efforts of Mead and Franklin K. Lane, Woodrow

Wilson's secretary of the interior, to establish farm colonies for veterans after World War I.[49] Wilson believed that those earlier back-to-the-land efforts had failed because of the remoteness of the colonies, the poor choice of settlers, and antagonism with local communities. Based on that assessment, he organized his subsistence homesteads in a way that placed as much power as possible in the hands of local organizers.

At the local level, the organizers who applied for funds from the division were often back-to-the-land enthusiasts from way back, inheritors of the vision of Bolton Hall, men who had worked in their own cities and regions to bring city workers back to rural living. Now circumstances conspired to offer them one more chance—this time with government funds—to try out their own back-to-the-land projects. In the process, they illustrated just how ideologically diverse that earlier vision had become. Subsistence homestead planners looked back to predecessors ranging from the anarchist Kropotkin to the single taxer Joseph Fels; from the progressive Walter Hines Page to the Arts and Crafts designer Gustav Stickley. They had in mind models as diverse as Bolton Hall's Free Acres and the Jewish Agricultural Society's nearby New Jersey towns; Booker T. Washington's vision of independent African American farmers and the "little lands" communities of William Ellsworth Smythe. Some subsistence homesteads even looked like Los Angeles suburbs.

Halfway Back to the Land

By 1934, Ross Gast had already spent much of his career encouraging people to raise their own food. After helping to create the southern California model of suburban "little farm homes" in the 1920s, Gast went on to become the director of the federally sponsored El Monte subsistence homesteads project. The El Monte project was situated in the rural but rapidly developing San Gabriel valley outside Los Angeles. (The project also included a second, smaller community in nearby Reseda.) That area was part of what historian Becky M. Nicolaides has termed the "farm fringe" of Los Angeles—"blue-collar suburbs" where residents built their own houses and raised food on their small plots of land. There were commercial farms in El Monte as late as the 1940s; surrounding those commercial farms were many subdivisions whose long narrow lots testified to their use as small-scale farms.[50] One *Los Angeles Times* columnist reported that in the year *before* the government announced its plans for a project in El Monte, nearly three thousand people had already taken matters into their own hands and moved onto small farm plots there.[51]

The El Monte project faithfully replicated the southern California model. As one *Times* columnist explained, "Washington calls these farmlets 'subsistence homesteads,'" but "we call 'em 'small farm homes.'"[52] In the 1920s Ross Gast had still called them "little lands," but by 1933 Gast had abandoned Smythe's term and was using an expression devised by George P. Clements, the secretary of the Los Angeles Chamber of Commerce's agricultural department: "going half-way back to the land."[53] And in 1934, Gast coined his own phrase — "rurban homes" — to name the new federal project.

The conservative *Los Angeles Times* was bound to express skepticism about the New Deal's subsistence homesteads program. The editors dubbed the El Monte project "socialism pure and simple," mockingly explaining that "theoretically," everyone there would "dwell together in beautiful harmony." They linked the idea of family food self-sufficiency ("production for use") to the recent campaign of socialist Upton Sinclair for governor of California — a campaign they had helped to derail. Nevertheless, the paper supported Gast and the project. They could hardly do otherwise. The *Times* had been promoting precisely the same sort of "little farm homes" since 1921.

Writers for the *Times* found ways of distinguishing their praise for the project from their criticism of its federal sponsors. One laudatory article reflected in its title the paper's double message. The heading was "Uncle Sam Points the Way Back to the Land," but the subheading defiantly took the compliment back and asserted local ownership: "Model Community Based on Idea of Southern California's Garden Homes." The writer praised Ross Gast and Joseph Weston, the local architect who designed the program's houses, for their hard-headed resistance to liberal flights of fancy. Neither of these two local men would talk about "the all-time programs and social millenniums the New Deal heads discuss so fluidly back in Washington," the columnist wrote, "but they light right up when you ask them where the hen houses are going on their little farms." The *Times* conceded that the New Dealers were doing at least one thing right: "When the folks in Washington stopped rubber stamping long enough to give [Gast] a free hand in planning the plantings and production facilities . . . they showed good judgment."[54]

In 1935, however, they stopped doing that one thing right. In an effort to streamline the unwieldy operations he had inherited when Roosevelt was forced to move the Subsistence Homesteads Division to the Resettlement Administration, Tugwell announced that his agency would eliminate plans for new communities in the San Fernando valley and turn the El Monte project over to local control, ending the government's five-year commitment four years

Another woman works in her garden. This 1936 Farm Security Administration photograph by
Dorothea Lange documents the productive gardens and family-friendly surroundings of the El
Monte Subsistence Homestead in Los Angeles. The project gave skilled and white-collar workers
the opportunity to own homes and gardens much like those in the surrounding suburbs—southern
California's popular "half-way back to the land" model. (Farm Security Administration—Office of
War Information Photograph Collection, Library of Congress)

early. Gast resigned his post soon after, just at the point when all one hundred of
the planned houses had been built and were occupied.[55]

In spite of the sudden change of plans, El Monte appears to have been one
of the most successful of the New Deal subsistence homestead communities.
Gast must have been as discouraged as the homesteaders were when the federal
government withdrew its support, but in public at least, he continued to call the
project a success.[56] The homesteaders rebounded and successfully reorganized
themselves into a self-governing unit.[57] As one commentator put it in 1940, the
community paid "back its own costs in a manner totally unorthodox on government projects."[58] The support of the well-known and well-connected Gast
averted what might have become entrenched political opposition from the
powerful *Los Angeles Times*. Enthusiastic local support made the work relatively

easy. (One study reported, as a sign of that enthusiasm, that the project had registered twenty-seven thousand visitors in a four-month period.)[59]

At the same time, the project's designers had hedged their bets. Because they believed the subsistence plots would require an average of three hours per day to work effectively, the planners for El Monte had given preference to skilled workers and clerks, who they thought would have more leisure time than factory workers.[60] As a result, they collected a relatively young, relatively highly educated group of participants; all of them had jobs when they took up residence. In a 1942 government-sponsored review of the subsistence homesteads, Paul Johnstone and Russell Lord judged that the success of El Monte was not surprising.[61] Choosing to accept these clerks, department store salespeople, and carpenters (rather than, say, out-of-work factory workers or migrant farm workers) had made it likely that the project would do well, and it had. The choice also revealed how deeply El Monte was rooted in the soil of the first back-to-the-land movement, which had found its greatest support among just such workers.

In the end, El Monte melted into the surrounding communities. In fact, it had never been very different from its neighbors. El Monte embodied back-to-the-land ideas at their least socially disruptive and most politically conservative. As Gast pointed out in his last words as head of the project, "None of the exotic social and economic theory which has ruled in the establishment of subsistence homesteads in some parts of the country was considered in carrying out Rurban Homes."[62]

Who Says Jews Can't Farm?

When Gast wrote about "exotic social and economic theory," he may have had projects like Jersey Homesteads in mind. That project was already underway in south Jersey, near Trenton, when El Monte was begun. Like Gast, the director of Jersey Homesteads had a long history in the back-to-the-land movement, but Benjamin Brown's story could not have been more different from Gast's. Brown had been the leader of the Jewish back-to-the-land community in Clarion, Utah, back in the 1910s. That project had failed, but he had stayed on in Utah. He and his brother became successful farmers there, and Brown went on to organize the Utah Poultry Association to market regionally produced eggs across the country. In 1925 he opened a New York City office, and from there he reentered the larger Jewish back-to-the-land effort. In 1927, Brown traveled to the Soviet Union to help to establish a Jewish back-to-the-land colony in

This 1936 Farm Security Administration photograph by Russell Lee shows Benjamin Brown as the "father" of Jersey Homesteads: a well-dressed, prosperous businessman and philanthropist. But long before he launched his successful business career, Brown had been committed to the back-to-the-land movement. As a young man, he had first tried farming for himself, and then helped to found the Jewish agricultural settlement in Clarion, Utah. (Farm Security Administration—Office of War Information Photograph Collection, Library of Congress)

Siberia. (This was the so-called Jewish Autonomous Region in Birobidzhan.) On that trip he met Milburn L. Wilson, also a consultant on the project, who would soon become the director of the Subsistence Homesteads Division.[63]

After the division was up and running in 1933, Brown came to Wilson with a ready-made plan for a colony of Jewish garment workers that had already been approved by a committee of New York labor and charity leaders. The time must certainly have seemed right for such a plan. By then, the privately funded Jewish Agricultural Society could boast of having settled some sixteen thousand Jewish families on farms—a record of success that was not lost on New Dealers.[64] In addition, the Jersey Homesteads project seemed a perfect fit for the goal of providing industrial workers with small farm plots to cushion them against hard times. Garment workers—whose jobs were highly seasonal and unstable—were a natural constituency for a part-time farming project.

In addition to providing a subsistence cushion for impoverished workers, the Jersey Homesteads planners had broader social goals in mind. In formulating his vision, Brown relied on the strengths of the community he wished to serve, hoping that the solidarity of Jewish garment workers—mostly socialists and all union members—would lead them to support a fully cooperative village economy. Jersey Homesteads would have at its center a cooperatively owned garment factory, offering both employment and ownership to its colonists. There would also be cooperatively owned farms and shops, offering some members more opportunities for paid work and assuring all members low prices for consumer goods. All this cooperation would certainly have appeared "exotic" to Ross Gast and his co-workers at the *Los Angeles Times*. It would not have seemed at all alien to Benjamin Brown. Most of the earlier Jewish back-to-the-land efforts had featured many cooperative elements, and a great many had been avowedly socialist or communist. (According to the community's most important historian, about half of the Clarion colonists had belonged to radical political groups.)[65] The new colony would appeal to the same kinds of reformers and radicals: as one resident recalled of Jersey Homesteads' first settlers, "Their heads were stuffed with . . . ideologies, ideologies, ideologies: socialism, communism, anarchism, Zionism, trade-unionism."[66]

In fact, everything at Jersey Homesteads reflected the values and experiences of the past generation of Jewish back-to-the-landers. Several successful Jewish colonies had been established by philanthropists in New Jersey back before the turn of the century. The towns of Alliance (founded by the Hebrew Emigrant Aid Society in 1882) and Woodbine (founded by the Baron de Hirsch fund in 1891) in particular had achieved relative success with a formula of combining small farms with factory jobs. Although the populations of those south Jersey communities had shrunk in the prosperous 1920s, they provided a model for Brown and his committee.[67] At the same time, Brown must also have brought with him from Utah his own bitter memories. He and his comrades had encountered hunger, cold, and loneliness in Clarion—a project that had moved largely inexperienced workers two thousand miles from their city homes and committed them to a type of dry-land farming not even their best-trained farmers knew anything about. This new project would be different. It would be located close to New York, enabling workers to learn to farm while holding on to their factory jobs, their family connections, and their social ties.

Underlying every aspect of the plan was the same motivation that had inspired the founders of the Jewish Agricultural Society and the National Farm

The man in this 1936 Farm Security Administration photograph by Dorothea Lange seems to be issuing a challenge from his grain field. The caption states it boldly: "Member of the Hightstown Farm Group Says: 'Who Says Jews Can't Farm?'" Like earlier Jewish back-to-the-landers, this Jersey Homesteads colonist hoped to demonstrate to the world that Jews could succeed at "productive" work on the land. (Farm Security Administration—Office of War Information Photograph Collection, Library of Congress)

School, as well as Brown and his Clarion comrades of twenty years earlier: the perennial drive to prove that Jews could cast off their ghetto heritage and make a living from the land. Nearly thirty years earlier, Benjamin Brown had addressed an open letter to the New York Yiddish journal *Dos Naye Lebn* (*New Life*) inviting its readers to join him in his efforts to found a Jewish colony. The letter carried a challenge in its title: "Far Vus Nit Mir?" ("Why Not We?")[68] A 1936 photograph taken at Jersey Homesteads by FSA photographer Dorothea Lange repeated that same challenge. A confident, muscular man stands in a field of grain, arms akimbo, and turns to look into the camera. The caption reads: "Who says Jews can't farm?"[69]

In contrast with the El Monte project, Jersey Homesteads endured a barrage of criticism from nearby observers. One resident recalled that the place had been known to its neighbors as "that Jew Communist town."[70] Many observers found the community's Bauhaus-style concrete houses, designed by German refugee architect Alfred Kastner, absurd and ugly. The cost of the project especially drew fire. "Hightstown Homesteaders Live Millionaire's Life," the *Newark Sunday Call* reported in 1936. "Costly Homesteads Blunders Left to Rot Tax Money Away," added the local *Asbury Park Press* in 1938. The *Saturday Evening Post* called it the "four million dollar village." (To be sure, the *Asbury Park Press* also reported in 1936 that Albert Einstein liked the project and was impressed by its success).[71]

Certainly the enterprise faced its share of difficulties from the beginning. There were struggles among the members of the original oversight committee, some of which reportedly arose from Brown's autocratic style. David Dubinsky, the powerful head of the International Ladies' Garment Workers' Union, walked off the committee, refusing to grant his support to a project that might take union jobs from the city. The people of the community, who had each staked $500 of their own hard-earned money to get there, were apparently not disposed to think of themselves as humble objects of charity and made use of their experience in the labor movement to organize themselves to resist government policies they disliked.[72]

Then, just as happened at El Monte, at the very moment the Jersey Homesteads project seemed to be hitting its stride, the Subsistence Homesteads Division was moved to the Resettlement Administration. But instead of cutting this project loose without further assistance as he had done with El Monte, Tugwell asserted tighter control over Jersey Homesteads, ejecting Brown from his leadership position and intensifying government oversight. But even under Tugwell's firm control, things did not run smoothly. The cooperative clothing factory did not open until 1936. When it finally did open its doors, only a few workers were available, because most of the houses had not yet been completed. Although there were several attempts to keep the factory afloat, it was never profitable. This was, after all, the middle of the Depression.

Still, Jersey Homesteads was a vibrant community. In a 1938 Federal Writers' Project collection called *Stories of New Jersey*, the authors described it as a vigorous and lively place (although they compared it, in an apparently unconscious ill omen, with earlier short-lived communes—Brook Farm and the North American Phalanx). The authors did not mention that the colonists were Jewish but admitted that at first, the surrounding residents had "looked askance at this community of pioneers." Now, however, things were improving. The community boasted an air-conditioned clothing factory, staffed entirely by union members who were paid union wages; a farm that employed six members of the community and showed a profit in 1937; a tearoom run by the community's young people; and a new school building.[73] FSA photographer and social realist painter Ben Shahn painted one of his most famous murals in that school, a triptych depicting the progress of Jewish immigrants beginning with their persecution in Russia, through their labor struggles, and to the founding of Jersey Homesteads.[74]

In 1942, when Paul Johnstone and Russell Lord undertook their assessment of the subsistence homestead programs, the garment factory was still operating. (Benjamin Brown had given it an infusion of $50,000 of his own in 1937, allowing it to reorganize and keep itself going for a few more years).[75] Most families still kept gardens—at least partial testimony to their continued commitment to the ideals that had brought them to Jersey Homesteads. And in 1945, in a gesture that said a great deal about the feelings of those who lived in Jersey Homesteads, the town voted to rename itself "Roosevelt."

Subsistence Memories

It is impossible to deny that projects like Jersey Homesteads were expensive and often exasperatingly poorly planned and managed. Since the 1940s, historians, in spite of their generally sympathetic perspectives, have been counting the cost overruns and registering the poor decisions of nearly all of the New Deal subsistence homestead communities. Personality conflicts, meddling bureaucrats, autocratic planners—the projects had all of these problems and more, sometimes to an almost ludicrous degree. Already in 1942, Lord and Johnstone felt compelled to make a bid for sympathy in judging the projects, asking their readers not to forget that the subsistence homesteads programs had been the product of hard times, "conceived in terms of a kind of pessimism born of bitter and hopeless experience."[76] Yet the record is not solely one of failure; by 1942 there had been only an 18 percent turnover rate at the homestead communities, and most of the homesteaders who left did so because they had found jobs elsewhere.[77] And as time has gone by, those high price tags and administrative blunders have come to occupy a less salient place in the historical record.

Professional historians have not overhauled their assessment of the New Deal subsistence homesteads as a whole since the 1950s.[78] Lately, however, ordinary citizens have been offering their own evaluations. As the seventy-fifth anniversary of the New Deal approached at the end of the twentieth century, citizens of communities like Arthurdale, West Virginia, Penderlea, North Carolina, Aberdeen Gardens, Virginia, and Roosevelt, New Jersey, began to take stock of their New Deal heritage, and to preserve and protect it. Applications poured in to the National Register; new museums and oral history projects flourished. A flood of personal memories, often recorded by those who were children in the 1930s, offered new perspectives on the legacy of the subsistence homesteads.[79] Some of those accounts challenge the judgments of professional historians. The website of Arthurdale Heritage, Inc., for one, concedes that all of the cooperative experiments at Arthurdale lost money, even quoting one historian's judgment that the cooperatives "were poorly conceived, poorly managed, and . . . poorly operated." But the author of this website also insists on acknowledging another view: "Although financially unsuccessful, the cooperatives did provide employment to the homesteaders at a time when it was most needed as well as skills they used even after the craft industry stopped operations."[80]

The case of Penderlea offers a similar example of memory challenging history. From one standpoint, the story of this North Carolina subsistence homestead is all about Hugh MacRae, a real estate and railroad magnate. MacRae's commitment to back-to-the-land efforts went back to 1903, when he had founded the first of six farm colonies. At that time, MacRae had hoped to provide a model for a new kind of intensive farming in the South. He recruited workers from all over Europe to grow crops on ten- to twenty-acre plots close to his railroad line outside Wilmington, North Carolina, hoping to encourage white native-born farmers to modernize their farming crops and techniques.

By the time he proposed Penderlea to the Subsistence Homesteads Division, MacRae had accumulated a great deal of experience operating on a massive scale: he had devoted two hundred thousand acres to his experiments and employed eight hundred workers. He owned almost everything necessary to establish the new colony: another vast tract of land, railroads, and even Tidewater Power and Light, which would supply electricity to the colony. MacRae also had connections. He had corresponded with Bolton Hall and Walter Hines Page in the early years and worked with Elwood Mead and Franklin K. Lane in the 1920s to push for southern reclamation projects for returning veterans. Indeed, MacRae had himself been considered for the position of director of the Subsistence Homesteads Division and was involved in the planning that led to its creation. So it was not a surprise when Penderlea became the first of the subsistence homesteads designed to move landless workers onto farms of their own.

But from the recent perspective of one woman who grew up in Penderlea, the real story is not about Hugh MacRae. In *The Roots of Penderlea: A Memory of a New Deal Homestead Community*, Anne Cottle relates the long and complicated tale of the conflicts between MacRae and Harold Ickes under the remarkably appropriate heading "Two Curmudgeons." The more important part of Cottle's story begins in chapter 3, "The Homesteaders Arrive." Her interviews with former residents recount the growth of a community over time: the early struggles with the half-cleared land, the founding of the school and churches, the development of social ties.

Her portrait is not always rosy. The relationship between settlers and government was complex and sometimes difficult. (Government regulations, for example, required that colonists own only purebred stock. In theory, colonists would get loans to buy those animals, but the loans were slow in coming, so settlers found themselves forced to hide their unqualified milk cows in the woods, out of the view of the project managers.)[81] One of Cottle's informants, however, testified that life in the community was better than historians have suggested. In fact, he directly contradicted historian Paul Conkin's assessment of Penderlea. Reece Lefler, one of the original farmers at Penderlea, argued that Conkin's report of poor morale and resentment among homesteaders was overblown: "Lord God! . . . I don't know where he got that." Lefler also countered another one of Conkin's observations, pointing out astutely that "if the government lost money" on the project, "it was their own fault." They had paid inflated prices for both materials and labor, as everyone in the community knew.[82]

A resident of Jersey Homesteads launched a similarly spirited defense of her community. "Roosevelt is not a utopian success story," Pearl Seligman acknowledged in an online historical essay. Indeed, she pointed out, "isolated utopias based solely on secular ideologies do not have a good track record in this country." (She, too, may have been thinking of Brook Farm.) But in recalling her own memories of life in Jersey Homesteads, Seligman concluded with an assertion that something important *had* worked there. Seligman argued that the most important gift Jersey Homesteads had given its residents was "the responsibility for governing themselves in their own community." That was "by far the most dignifying, life-defining occupation," engaging them as "full people, ennobling them with the activities of citizenship."[83] Seligman's assertion recalls Dorothea Lange's arresting image of that unidentified Jersey Homesteads man in the field. In retrospect, its caption might have been not only "Who says Jews can't farm?" but perhaps just as important "Who says out-of-work immigrant factory workers can't govern themselves"?

A similar account is given by the residents of Aberdeen Gardens, built in Newport News, Virginia, to assist workers in the shipyards. Theoretically, one-tenth of the subsistence homestead projects were to be allocated to African Americans, but no administrators managed to come anywhere near that goal: Aberdeen Gardens was the single such "Garden City for Negroes" to be constructed. Because of that fact, and because Aberdeen Gardens was created entirely by African American architects, engineers, contractors, and builders, it received a tremendous amount of attention. The elaborate "greenbelt" landscape and handsome brick houses created both a powerful public relations statement and, according to the testimony of residents, a successful and enduring community.[84] Like Seligman, to be sure, the residents who told the story of Aberdeen Gardens based their judgments on childhood recollections, which bear all the characteristic shadings of personal memory. And, of course, heritage organizations have their own incentives to invent a rosy past. A few professional studies, however, have also begun to offer evidence that might support some of these positive reassessments.

Sociologists Jess Gilbert and Spencer D. Wood, for example, trace the impact of a single small project for African American tenant farmers in the heart of the Mississippi River Delta.[85] Finding evidence of success in such a project would be no small irony; historians have justly pointed out that overall, the New Deal came up exceedingly short in its efforts for African Americans. Yet the few projects that were completed may have cast a longer shadow than was immediately apparent. Gilbert and Wood argue that a single Resettlement Administration project in Mileston, Mississippi, may have provided a critical opening for African Americans in that "most southern place on earth."

Colonists at resettlement communities like the one in Mileston experienced the Resettlement Administration at its most committed. Landless workers were given farms of their own, settled in houses of almost unheard-of luxury for the southern poor, white or black. Resettlement Administration advisors helped them to organize a wide array of cooperative enterprises, providing participants with the opportunity to gain experience both in self-government and in business management. By the time the FSA liquidated its holdings there in 1944, the Mileston community was operating a thriving cooperative store (supplanting the ubiquitous company store that held many sharecroppers in perpetual debt bondage), a cooperative cotton marketing system, and a vocational school. Perhaps most important of all, the farmers had taken title to their farms.

As Gilbert and Wood argue, the landowning African American families of Holmes County would become vitally important leaders in the struggle for voting rights in the next generation. Free of the control of white landlords, they managed in the 1940s and 1950s to provide an excellent education for their children. Their land provided a physical buffer that helped to protect their churches and other public meeting places—so exposed in other parts of the South—from terrorist attacks. And it would be Mileston landholders who would be the first to register to vote in their county. Their county's chapter of the Mississippi Freedom Democratic Party was the strongest in the state, and Robert Clark, a Holmes County landowner, became the first African American to be elected to the Mississippi Assembly.[86]

That story would have pleased Bolton Hall. He had believed that land ownership and food self-sufficiency would make it possible for the oppressed to resist the coercion of the powerful. Even very small numbers of such independent landowners—a few Jewish immigrants in New Jersey, a handful of African American farmers in Mississippi—would be able, he thought, to hold their own against overwhelming pressures. New Deal administrators, in contrast, were often reluctant to make such claims for the projects. They were eager to distance themselves from what they saw as the romantic dreams of the previous generation's back-to-the-land movement, preferring to speak about measurable "standards of living" and the "rehabilitation" of "marginal" populations. Even judged by the standards of the New Deal social scientists, however, the Mileston story offers food for thought; land ownership there appears to have ended the cycle of debt, provided access to education, and fostered a distinctly higher "standard of living." There are only a few tantalizing hints of evidence, but if the subsistence homesteads did engender results like these—even if only for a handful of people in a few places—one might reasonably judge that those results outweighed a great many bureaucratic blunders and cost overruns.

Still, as Russell Lord and Paul Johnstone concluded in their 1942 study, the experience of the subsistence homesteads was not such as to encourage further experiments in producerism. "Good housing with earth to dig in, a chance to garden, elbow room, a wholesome and beautiful place in which to rear children—such things are good and widely desired," they acknowledged.[87] But when times returned to normal, they believed, Americans would quickly go back to their pursuit of better jobs, higher wages, and an ever-widening array of consumer goods. It was time to get out of the business of encouraging self-sufficiency. In the years after World War II, liberals would create government programs to foster economic growth, full employment, and broad access to home ownership, but they would never again encourage citizens to produce for themselves on subsistence homesteads.

Coda: Ralph Borsodi Rejects the New Deal

At the beginning, the subsistence homesteads project in Dayton, Ohio, looked promising. If all had gone well, it would have represented a seamless transmission of the ideas of one generation of back-to-the-landers to the next. The Dayton project was the brainchild of Ralph Borsodi, the son of Bolton Hall's old comrade William Borsodi, a fellow single taxer who had written the preface to Hall's *A Little Land and a Living*. Following in his father's footsteps, Ralph Borsodi had begun his political life as an advocate of the single tax. As a young man, he held a series of jobs in the burgeoning advertising industry, but in 1920, troubled by ill health and a housing shortage in New York City, Borsodi and his family went back to the land. At his new home in the suburbs, he and his wife Myrtle Mae created a prototype for the kind of productive household they would advocate in the coming years.

In the meantime, Borsodi began to publish the books that would articulate his increasingly radical critique of industrial society. He began with the segment of the economy he knew best. In *National Advertising vs. Prosperity* (1923), he argued that while advertising had once played a vital role as a source of information, it was now beginning to distort the economy by creating false needs and by inflating the price of goods. In *The Distribution Age* (1927) and *This Ugly Civilization* (1929), Borsodi presented his case against the centralized production of the modern factory system. Machinery itself was not responsible for the "ugliness" of civilization, in Borsodi's view; used correctly, machine technologies were a blessing. The problem was centralized production, which might appear at first to be efficient and inexpensive but would always end up costing more in distribution and advertising costs over time. In *This Ugly Civilization*, Borsodi proposed a return to small-scale household production; he began to use the word "homestead" to describe such a household on a small plot of land organized for self-sufficiency.

In *Flight from the City* (1933), Borsodi described how his own family had returned to the land and devised a successful alternative to the factory system. Not content with growing their own food, the Borsodis had become nearly completely self-sufficient: they made their own clothing, invented their own entertainments, generated their own electrical power, and homeschooled their sons. To perform all these tasks, they embraced the latest high-tech machinery:

Borsodi made it clear that they did not "contemplate any return to primitive ways of life."[88] But even using the most elaborate and expensive equipment, he argued, household production was more efficient and less expensive than factory production, because it eliminated the distribution and advertising costs necessary to centralized production.

In all his writing, Borsodi maintained the old producerist connection between land and independence. He concluded *Flight From the City* with a parable reminiscent of Hall's metaphorical tales. This one was the story of Esau and Jacob. Esau was the oldest son, destined to be his father's heir. But Esau was a "reckless hunter," while his "more conservative brother Jacob . . . was a farmer." One day when Esau was faint with hunger, and Jacob had food, Esau found he had no choice but to sell his brother his birthright in return for the well-known "mess of pottage." "Surely it is unnecessary to draw a moral," Borsodi wrote, though of course he did: "No man can afford to be dependent upon some other man for the bare necessities of life without running the risk of losing all that is most precious to him." Every man who worked for a wage was risking his birthright.[89] Only household self-sufficiency would transform dependent wage earners into independent, self-reliant, and secure proprietors.

Ralph's wife, Myrtle Mae, by all accounts the source of most of the practical information with which the Borsodis began their experiment, also expanded on the producerist rhetoric of the 1910s. Like men, she argued, women risked their birthright by working for wages. The educated "new women" of her generation had been deceived into thinking they could do better for themselves and their families by working in professional occupations, but all that hard-won organizational and intellectual training could be put to better use at home, in the tasks of self-sufficient production. Myrtle Mae had formerly worked in advertising herself; she published her articles chiefly in magazines for advertising professionals like *Electrical Merchandising* and *Advertising and Selling*. But beginning with "A Full-Time Job at Home," published in the *New York Herald Tribune* in 1929, she occasionally gained a wider audience. When she published her provocative essay "The New Woman Goes Home" in *Scribner's*, writer and editor Dorothy Van Doren felt compelled to respond with her own piece, "Breadwinner or Breadmaker?"[90]

As it happened, Borsodi was brought to Dayton by a woman who had not given up her professional position and "gone home." Elizabeth Nutting, who had earned a doctorate in religious education at Boston University, was educational director of the Dayton Council of Social Agencies (a fundraising arm for charities).[91] She read Borsodi's work and invited him to speak in Dayton in 1933. The Dayton project emerged as a solution to the desperate difficulties city charities faced in satisfying the enormous increase in demand for their services. Fearing that it would run out of money altogether, the council was searching for a way to supplement and ultimately replace its traditional food distribution program. It began by organizing cooperatives where unemployed workers could produce food, clothing, and other goods for their own use and for barter. It had organized somewhere between three and five hundred families into twelve production units when Borsodi appeared on the scene. Not long after, he became the group's official advisor.[92]

Under Borsodi's guidance, the group bought a farm outside the city and began to build houses on small plots of land. There, the settlers modeled themselves on the Borsodi household, producing as much as they could for themselves and their neighbors. True to Borsodi's principles, the project was set up as a single-tax colony: a corporation was created to take permanent possession of the land; the colonists would own only the improvements to their land. When Subsistence Homesteads Division money became available for the first time, Wilson, who was familiar with Borsodi's work, expedited the Dayton project. It became the first of the new federal subsistence homestead projects.

From Wilson's standpoint, the Dayton project seemed ideal. Much like the later El Monte venture, it was directed by local leaders who knew their city well, and it enjoyed the support of the community. It was guided, moreover, by a leading light of the back-to-the-land movement, whose writing had already attracted a great deal of publicity. The division, it seemed, would have to do little other than hand over the money. But by the time the federal funds got to Dayton, Borsodi and his supporters were enmeshed in an internal power struggle. Some colonists criticized Borsodi and Nutting's leadership; there were charges that they favored their personal friends. The local controversy was exacerbated by Borsodi's attempt to set up an African American homestead community near Dayton, which generated heated resistance among many white residents.[93]

Word of these controversies made it to Washington, and became part of a larger struggle that had already developed between Wilson and his boss Harold Ickes. Ickes had never liked Wilson's commitment to local autonomy; he was exasperated by the anarchic messiness of local control and fearful of the overspending and corruption that might stem from local disregard for Washington regulations. The situation in Dayton brought that larger conflict to a head and precipitated Ickes's move to force Wilson to reassert central control over the projects. Wilson resigned. Ickes then presented a stark choice to the Dayton group: give up the money and escape governmental control or take it and live with closer supervision from Washington. Faced with what he saw as a federal power grab, Borsodi fought back, attempting first to get the money from another branch of the government and then to sue the Subsistence Homesteads Division for breach of contract. Finally, the Dayton homesteaders and the Bureau of Community Service chose to get rid of Borsodi rather than forego the federal funds they had been promised.[94]

Borsodi's problems were no different from those of many others. Local opposition, personality conflicts, power struggles, and multiple changes in central administration and policy would be familiar stories at other subsistence homesteads, too. But Borsodi was as much a propagandist as a community organizer, and he was able to channel his disappointment in a new direction. In *Flight from the City*, Borsodi had identified his primary target as the industrial system, which moved society inexorably toward greater consolidation and centralization. Now he envisioned another threat: the New Deal government itself, which seemed to be imitating the worst aspects of big business, centralizing power and resources of its own in Washington. In the 1947 reprint of *Flight from the City*, Borsodi spelled out his new critique, by then fully formulated. "The masses of people are frantically calling upon Washington for old age pensions, unemployment compensation, and other forms of security from the cradle to the grave," he wrote. Meanwhile his own family was able to provide all these things for themselves, "as most self-respecting Americans used to do" until "the gospel of depending upon the government began to be substituted for the gospel of independence."[95]

There had been no talk of rejecting "the gospel of depending upon the government" while the Dayton project was still in his hands. In a 1934 article in the *Survey and Graphic*, Borsodi had condemned the $25 million allotted for subsistence homesteads as pitifully inadequate and suggested that the government devote at least $1 billion to the project.[96] And in the 1933 edition of *Flight from the City*, he had argued that all the money state, local, and federal government agencies were spending on direct relief could easily fund small homesteads for everyone who was out of work. "Why shouldn't we use the public's 'will-to-give,'" he argued, "to enable the unemployed to support themselves?"[97]

That passage was still there in the 1947 edition, but by then Borsodi's experience with federal power had given his argument a different slant.[98] In 1933, to be sure, he had opposed greater government control over the economy, whether in the form of socialism or even of liberal constraints on business—but only because those changes would not go far enough to fix the essential problem. No matter who owned or controlled the system, he had argued then, it would still generate the same dependence, the same "inherent insecurity." If the state took control of the marketplace, wage earners would be no closer to independence; they would simply be dependent on government instead of on corporations. After the Dayton debacle, Borsodi came to believe that dependence on government was itself the central problem. Now his writing took on a new note of nostalgia for the rugged self-reliance of the pre-Depression days. One wing of the back-to-the-land movement was officially parting company with the other.

Borsodi had once seen the subsistence homestead programs of the New Deal as a critical opportunity for back-to-the-landers. He had greeted the "collapse of the dream of golden plenty from mass production" as the once-in-a-lifetime opportunity that brought a sympathetic president to the White House. Now the New Dealers no longer seemed like allies to Borsodi. From now on, he would have to form other alliances to bring his plans to fruition. Many back-to-the-landers would go with him.

6

"I'll Take My Stand" (in Vermont)

Decentralizing the Back-to-the-Land Movement

The New Deal subsistence homestead programs met with criticism from all sides. From the right, Ohio senator Robert Taft led Republican congressional resistance, attacking the entire New Deal for its socialistic innovations, reckless spending, and dangerous expansion of government power. Virginia senator Harry F. Byrd, a leader of the conservative Democratic coalition, targeted the subsistence homesteads in particular for their wasteful spending and collectivism. On the left, many commentators viewed the projects with an equally critical eye. Malcolm Cowley of the *New Republic* set out his magazine's position in a 1933 article "How Far Back to the Land?" He ridiculed the "small farm racket" as a "wistful" search for "primitive, arcadian simplicity." Cowley argued that any such effort to transform people back into "peasants of the thirteenth century" would be dissolved by the irresistible forces of modernity: "money, automobiles, radios, Greta Garbo."[1]

Louis Hacker, a Marxist economist on the faculty at Columbia, launched a similar attack in *Harper's Monthly*. First of all, Hacker wrote, this "romantic dream" of "little modern Arcadias" would be very expensive. Perhaps they might actually be able to revive "the ancient handicrafts of spinning, weaving, wood working, pottery making" and "similar pursuits of a contented peasantry," but he estimated it would require $10 billion to create the "thousand-odd Brook Farms" that would be necessary to make a dent in the nation's problems that way. Worse than the cost, Hacker entertained a dark suspicion that the Roosevelt administration, "hard driven by the contradictions of its own position," might find the homesteads' dependent populations politically useful and even "seek to build up exactly such a sheltered peasant group" to bolster its power to "withstand the revolutionary demands of the organized industrial workers."[2] Such things were being done in Germany and Italy, Hacker pointed out. While critics on the right feared that Roosevelt had Stalinist ambitions, leftists feared that he would take Mussolini and Hitler as models.

The Decentralists

Ralph Borsodi shared these fears of the Roosevelt administration's will to power. But he did not share the critics' animosity toward subsistence homesteads or the back-to-the-land agenda. Borsodi believed deeply in the "small farm racket" that Malcolm Cowley despised, and he spent much of his career encouraging people to revive the "ancient handicrafts" Hacker dismissed. By the time Borsodi broke with the Dayton subsistence homestead project in 1935, he had forged a new connection with a loosely organized group of thinkers who were neither laissez-faire Republicans nor New Deal liberals, neither fascists nor communists. In 1937, Borsodi helped to found a journal called *Free America*, which would speak for this "third way." By the second year of publication, the editors had settled on the term "decentralist" to describe their views.[3]

Borsodi's fellow editor Herbert Agar, a journalist and public historian, played a key role in bringing together the coalition that created *Free America*. In the first issue, Agar defined the ideological parameters of the magazine. He began by invoking the Vanderbilt University writers known as the Southern Agrarians. Their defense of the traditional rural life of the South in the 1930 manifesto *I'll Take My Stand* had offered the first clear alternative to the "triumphant plutocracy," materialism, and "uncritical worship of bigness" that had dominated the nation in what Agar called the "high unpleasant noon of Coolidge prosperity." Next, Agar credited a group of "third-way" British reformers known as distributists with teaching him personally to "recognize the enemy I wanted to fight." (Distributists advocated the widespread "distribution" of property and the reestablishment of an economy of self-sufficient farms and autonomous, small-scale workshops.)[4] Finally, Agar enumerated the other allies of *Free America*: the agrarian Catholic Rural Life Conference; the cooperative movement; the single-tax movement; and Ralph Borsodi himself, who, like the Agrarians "back in the days of Coolidge," had attacked "plutocracy and the worship of bigness."[5]

Agar summarized the common goal of this alliance with a deceptively simple phrase: "economic democracy."[6] Like the distributists, American decentralists envisioned a world in which everyone had access to productive property—to the tools and materials that would allow them to feed, clothe, and shelter themselves. Like the old producerist radicals of the turn of the century, they viewed themselves as the defenders of small-scale independent proprietors against their chief enemy, monopoly capitalism, which gave vast economic power to a small oligarchy, dispossessed ordinary people, and corrupted democracy at its core. "Our common ground is a belief that monopoly capitalism is evil and self-destructive," Agar wrote.[7]

Many observers must have perceived this perspective as oddly anachronistic in these years of titanic struggle between communism, fascism, and capitalism. As Agar saw it, the most powerful enemy of the American dream was not a foreign ideology—not Reds infiltrating the president's cabinet or Brownshirts marching in the streets—but the homegrown "friends of Big Business, who dishonor the dream [of democracy] by saying that it has been realized . . . today."[8] From the standpoint of decentralists, neither fascism nor communism was truly opposed to capitalism; both were logical results of the constant evolution of industrial capitalism toward a greater concentration of power and resources at the top. Socialism, in their view, simply shifted the monopoly power of private oligarchies to the state without weakening that power or distributing it more democratically.[9] A clever phrase used by an anarchist website in 2009 sums up the decentralist position in the 1930s: they were "free market anti-capitalists."[10]

The decentralists of the 1930s have sometimes been referred to as conservatives. A number of them even used the word to describe themselves. Over time, however, the word "conservative" has taken on certain associations that do not fit. Decentralists were indeed critical of the growth of government bureaucracy and regulation, and they did fear the New Deal's centripetal force. They deplored the forces that were compelling people to "decide fewer and fewer things for themselves and instead obey orders from distant and absentee authorities," in Borsodi's words.[11] Yet they were not simply "Jeffersonian" opponents of big government. Far less were they Reaganesque advocates of its dismantling.[12] Indeed, *Free America* more often positioned itself as an ally of the Roosevelt administration than as its opponent.

Journalist Dorothy Thompson, an occasional contributor to *Free America*, explained the alternating hope and fear with which decentralists viewed the New Deal: "Two souls dwell in the bosom of this Administration, as indeed, they do in the bosom of the American people." One of those souls "loves the Abundant Life, as expressed in the cheap and plentiful products of large-scale mass production and distribution." Decentralists hoped the other soul would prevail—the one that yearned "for former simplicities, for decentralization, for the interests of the 'little man,'" the one that "revolts against high-pressure salesmanship, denounces 'monopoly' and 'economic empires' and seeks the means of breaking them up."[13]

On some basic issues, moreover, New Deal policy makers were themselves "decentralists." They were committed, for example, to "decentralizing" jobs and people, to moving workers and factories out of crowded cities into under-populated rural areas. And the *Free America* editors were not opposed to massive government intervention in pursuit of that kind of decentralism. Conservative critics denounced the dangerous concentration of power in New Deal programs like the Tennessee Valley Authority, but *Free America* writers praised its "decentralization" of electricity, industry, and jobs into the countryside. Those New Deal projects did not embrace the whole vision of decentralism, to be sure. They would not distribute control or ownership more broadly among workers, but they would at least increase their independence by bringing them into the countryside where they could provide food for themselves. That was a goal close to the hearts of many decentralists: they were committed back-to-the-landers.

Decentralists argued that economic democracy depended above all else on a widespread return to self-sufficient homesteads. Every issue of *Free America* expressed strong support for the back-to-the-land project in all its aspects. Borsodi himself provided one model: he founded the School of Living in suburban New York in 1934 to foster the creation of back-to-the-land communities for white-collar workers. The Bayard Lane community just outside Suffern, New York, was the first to be completed; another in West Nyack soon joined it, and there were plans for more. Borsodi viewed his School of Living as an alternative to the New Deal's subsistence homestead projects, which he rejected after his bad experience in Dayton. School of Living homesteaders, Borsodi asserted, were not "looking to Washington, looking to socialism, communism, technocracy—to some form of collectivism or purely political action." They were "believers in self-help."[14]

Most decentralists, however, were far from hostile to the New Deal subsistence homesteads. Seconding Borsodi's earlier call for a billion dollars to be committed to subsistence homesteads, Southern Agrarian Frank Owsley went even farther, proposing that every landless or tenant farmer in the country be given land (to be purchased by the federal government) and the necessary housing and tools to become self-sufficient.[15] And the collective editorial voice of *Free America* was clear: the subsistence homesteads projects should be "attacked in terms of billions of dollars."[16]

Most decentralists supported not only a return to the land for urban workers but also a parallel movement of farmers away from commercial crops, back to farming for self-sufficiency. One *Free America* writer explained why decentralists embraced "production for use," describing the long train of tragedies that followed a farmer's decision to place his faith in a cash crop: "In some prosperous moment," the farmer "abandons the traditional subsistence basis of farming that made him and his family secure at least against want." His "soil begins to degenerate." After a while, "less prosperous times appear." He must sell his cash crop in a market "controlled by the exporters or domestic middlemen." In the end, he loses his land and becomes a tenant.[17] (This argument was a plainer version of Southern Agrarian Andrew Nelson Lytle's eloquent depiction of the undoing of the subsistence household, which began with the prediction "as soon as a farmer begins to keep books, he'll go broke shore as hell.")[18] To reverse that process of destruction, Americans must reject the new notion of "farming as a business" and revitalize the idea of "farming as a way of life." With those contrasting phrases, which echoed through the pages of *Free America*, decentralists pledged their support to a wide-ranging back-to-the-land agenda: rural repopulation, a rejection of consumerism, and an embrace of "production for use" and the diversified family farm.

Returning to Region

There was yet another plank in the decentralist platform. In a *Free America* article entitled "E Pluribus Unum," Princeton professor of modern languages Christian Gauss argued that the tentacles of big business were reaching out and strangling American regional cultures. A bland mass culture now threatened to stifle the diversity and vitality of small-town and rural America. As Gauss put it, "Lynn has lost all her New England character, as Gastonia has lost her Southern, and Massillon her Middle Western character." Something more than the quaintness of regional character was at stake. Using language that echoed the broader decentralist critique of big business, Gauss argued that the people of these provincial cities and towns felt that they had been "looted." Working for national chain stores or factories that had no local loyalties, they were "serving masters that they [did] not know."[19] A vital regional culture depended on local ownership of small workshops and businesses as well as widely distributed subsistence farms.

This regionalist element was something new for back-to-the-landers. There had been a few favored destinations in the early years, to be sure: the Pacific Northwest had received a lot of press attention, and the Ozarks had been popular for a few years. But when the first back-to-the-landers had envisioned a rural home, they had most often imagined it just outside their own cities. Now the back-to-the-land movement was beginning to reflect an emerging regional-ist sensibility. *I'll Take My Stand* forged a pioneering link. The Agrarians made no specific calls for a return to the land, but they viewed the defense of the subsistence farm and the cause of the South as one (perhaps lost) cause. The South's self-sufficient farms, they argued, sustained a culture more authentic and morally rooted than anything that could grow from the sterile soil of northern cities. At least to begin with, all the Agrarian writers supported the New Deal's subsistence homesteads.[20]

The Agrarians took a distinctly southern "stand," of course, with the North (or New York City or New England) usually playing the role of the adversary. But the writers made it clear that their real enemy was the growing power of urban industrial society, and they hoped to find allies outside the South. As it happened, they found those allies in the stronghold of their old enemy: it was New England, not the Old South, that would attract the greatest share of at-tention in this generation's back-to-the-land enthusiasm.

New England: There She Stands

At one time, New England had been the area *least* likely to attract back-to-the-landers. Of the 101 correspondents who wrote to the *World's Work* looking for farms in 1912, only 8 hoped to settle in New England.[21] Perhaps the lack of interest in those days reflected a perception that New England was "tired" or "worn out"; books and articles bemoaning the "decline" of rural New England were everywhere at the turn of the century. By the 1930s, of course, the situation ought to have seemed even worse: now the news was all about New England's *industrial* decline. For New England manufacturers, the depression had begun years before the crash of 1929. The region's textile and shoe industries were devastated, and the cities that depended on them had the dubious distinction of being stricken with unemployment and hunger years before other American cities. In 1933, in a moment of great symbolic significance, the Appleton Com-pany, founders of the textile industry that had begun New England's historic rise to industrial power, closed its doors and moved to Alabama, where no unions or child labor laws stood in its way. Even the Southern Agrarians could see that New England was no longer the industrial giant that had been the South's ancient foe.

It may have been precisely this tale of economic hardship that renewed interest in the region. New England's long-standing economic troubles now seemed to reveal its underlying strength. Its people and their institutions seemed to be weathering the storms of the Depression more gracefully than other parts of the country. For years, modernist critics had portrayed the region as the haven of dour Puritans and antiquated blue laws; now New England began to find new literary defenders. In "New England: There She Stands," a much-quoted 1932 editorial in *Harper's Monthly*, writer Bernard DeVoto praised the region's traditional austerity. Others might still associate the region with the "slag of Puritanism," but DeVoto saw something different. When "panic possessed America," he wrote, "New England wasn't quite so scared. The depression wasn't quite so bad in New England, despair wasn't quite so black, the nightmare wasn't quite so ghastly." Long years of tribulation had given its people strength: "By the granite they have lived on for three centuries, tightening their belts and hanging on." Now that Americans were "staring apprehensively through fog that may not lift in this generation," DeVoto suggested, they "may find [New England's] knowledge of hard things more than a little useful."[22]

Perhaps that was why over half the back-to-the-land and country life books printed between 1930 and 1946 took New England as their subject.[23] To be sure, not all of these new books imparted the region's knowledge of "hard things." Some were part of the first wave of what would become a flood of Connecticut country life books written by New York–based authors. (Elswyth Thane called these I-bought-a-barn books when she wrote her own in 1950.)[24] Hal Borland, who lived in northwestern Connecticut, would write a weekly outdoor column for the *New York Times* from 1942 to 1978. Gladys Taber began her popular "Stillmeadow" series in 1940; her first book, *Harvest at Stillmeadow*, would be followed by more than a dozen from the 1940s through the 1970s.

These I-bought-a-barn books did reflect a kind of regionalist sensibility. A number of their authors were westerners, drawn to New York for professional reasons. Hal Borland was born in Nebraska, Gladys Taber in Colorado. Lucile Grebenc, the author of *Under Green Apple Boughs* (1933), and Ruth Cross, the author of *Eden on a Country Hill* (1938), were both Texans by birth.[25] Perhaps because they were transplants, these authors expressed an acute awareness of New England's distinctive built and natural landscape, praising its vivid seasonal changes and the colonial farmhouses and stone walls that spoke of its long history. Several of these Connecticut books told back-to-the-land stories; the Depression, after all, affected writers and literary agents as well as farmers and workers.[26] For the most part, though, Connecticut's I-bought-a-barn books employed the region as a backdrop for the restoration of old houses, flower gardening, and other genteel pastimes. Connecticut had its stone walls, but DeVoto's "granite" New England was located farther north.

Speaking from Vermont

For over a generation, New England's imaginative center had been migrating farther and farther north, away from the industrial cities of southern New England with their enormous factories and foreign-born workers, toward the depopulated seaports and inland villages. A major marker of that change, as historian Joseph Conforti has argued, was the 1914 publication of Robert Frost's *North of Boston*, in which Frost articulated a vision of New England rooted in the beauty and hardship of life in the rural north country.[27] The change was cemented by the 1930 decision of retired businessman Robb Sagendorph to buy a farm near his family's summer home in Dublin, New Hampshire, where, in 1935, he founded *Yankee Magazine*.

The new regionalist books also reflected that northward shift. Northern New England would provide the setting for several classics of country life literature in the 1940s. Naturalist author Henry Beston's *Northern Farm* (1948), which chronicled a year in rural Maine, became an almost instant classic. Both Bertha Damon's *A Sense of Humus* (1943), set in New Hampshire, and Louise Dickinson Rich's Maine story *We Took to the Woods* (1942) carried enough literary weight to warrant reviews in *New England Quarterly* by prominent Harvard literary scholar Kenneth Murdock. It was in Vermont, however, that a revitalized New England regional consciousness merged most closely with the back-to-the-land movement.

While not a single back-to-the-land narrative written before 1930 was set in Vermont, during the 1930s the state suddenly took center stage.[28] DeVoto, for one, located the heart of his "granite" New England not in Connecticut or even New Hampshire but next door to his summer home in northern Vermont. Visiting the farm of his neighbor Jason one night, DeVoto reported, he "came away with a dazed realization" that he had discovered a household that was "wholly secure." True, Jason was "so little of an economic entity"—spending so little, producing so much—that he barely qualified even as "what the liberal journals call a 'peasant.'" Yet Jason's family lived "what those same periodicals call 'the good life.'" For DeVoto, Jason's rocky upland acres did not conjure up visions of the unending and hopeless toil of a "peasant," but of the back-to-the-lander's dream of security, independence, and self-sufficiency. Farmer Jason was more than a Yankee stereotype. He had become a model for the nation: "a free man, self-reliant, sure of his world, unfrightened by the future."[29]

Vermont was particularly—almost uniquely—well placed to attract this kind of notice in these years. Politics was part of the story. In 1936, when the rest of New England finally pulled up its Republican roots and voted for

This Farm Security Administration photograph by Jack Delano is dated 1941, two years before Norman Rockwell's famous painting of Thanksgiving ("Freedom from Want")—yet it depicts a similar scene and evokes the same sentiments. The family is far from wealthy: the children on this dairy farm are apparently drinking water with their supper. Still, there is enough to go around: the tablecloth is clean, the mother is smiling. The title of the photograph, "The Gaynor Family at Dinner on Their Farm," emphasizes the security and independence the family members derive from living on their own land. (Farm Security Administration—Office of War Information Photograph Collection, Library of Congress)

Roosevelt, Maine and Vermont held out in a legendary minority vote, the only states among the forty-eight to do so. Along with Maine, Vermont became the target of many a joke for that quaint loyalty to the faith of its fathers. One *New York Times* editorial entitled "Old Faithful," for example, employed a time-honored metaphor to express its gratitude that "in this shifting and phantasmagoric world the Vermont Republicans are as stable as their mountains."[30]

Such jokes were based partly on a misconception: Vermont's political identity may have been stable, but it was not uncomplicated. Despite that legendary 1936 vote, Vermonters happily accepted their share and more of many New Deal projects. For their part, New Dealers held no grudge: they poured out their munificence on the state. The first Civilian Conservation Corps camp was sited in Vermont, and work began on it one week after the passage of the bill creating the program. By 1934, there were eighteen camps in the state. And more help was on the way. The Federal Emergency Relief Administration drew up plans to help thousands of Vermont's poorest farmers relocate from mountain farms classified as "submarginal" onto better land or into better jobs. The National Industrial Recovery Act made funds available to build an ambitious and costly scenic highway along the ridge of the Green Mountains.

Vermonters were generally enthusiastic about federal jobs projects, but they greeted the larger plans with misgivings.[31] They were guided on this cautious path by the rising star of George D. Aiken, who became governor of the state in 1937 and U.S. senator in 1941. A Republican in a one-party state, Aiken nevertheless came from a long line of progressives, and he harbored pronounced pro-labor sympathies. "Today the Republican Party attracts neither the farmer nor the industrial worker," Aiken lamented in a national radio address in 1938, arguing that his party's leaders had become rubber stamps for business interests.[32] (Many years later, in the midst of the Vietnam War, Aiken reportedly made the wry proposal that became his best-known legacy: the U.S. government should simply declare victory in Vietnam and withdraw its troops.)[33] *New York Times* jokes aside, even outsiders could easily perceive that a vote for Aiken was by no means a pledge of allegiance to hidebound Republicanism.

Aiken, in fact, was a spokesman neither for the right nor for the left—nor was he simply a moderate. His politics were deeply rooted in decentralist soil and in the new regionalist sensibility associated with that position. (Aiken's apparent comfort with what Harvard historian Crane Brinton called the "strange company" of the decentralists and their Southern Agrarian allies led Brinton to joke that "the Civil War has apparently ended, even in Vermont.")[34] Like the writers of *Free America*, Aiken supported many New Deal programs, especially the subsistence homestead projects.[35] Even when he opposed federal projects—as he did the massive flood-control dams proposed for the Connecticut River—he worked to devise regional cooperative alternatives that would achieve the same goals more democratically, as he saw it, without ceding local power to the central government.

Most characteristic of all, however, was Aiken's opposition to the Resettlement Administration's plan to turn Vermont's mountainous "submarginal" farmlands into national forest. (In the system of categorization devised by agricultural economists, "submarginal" was the lowest type, denoting land that could neither support its owners adequately nor be farmed sustainably. The recommended policy for such land was to retire it from agriculture altogether and manage it as recreational or conservation land.) In *Speaking from Vermont* (1938), a collection of essays he published in conjunction with his Senate campaign, Aiken defended the right of Vermont farmers to their "submarginal" farms. First, he argued, New Deal experts were simply wrong to believe that mountain farms could not be productive. Displaying his intimate familiarity with northern farming practices, Aiken explained that many crops—potatoes, hay, apples—grew best in the highlands. More important was Aiken's central point. These farms provided not just a good living but a good way of life: "Some folks just naturally love the mountains and like to live up among them." It was true that hill farmers did not have access to the consumer goods available in the city, but what they possessed was more valuable: the security and self-reliance of the diversified farm, where "freedom of thought and action is logical and inherent."[36]

Aiken's submarginal farmers were a lot like DeVoto's prototypical Vermonter Jason. Although they, too, lived "far below 'the American standard'" and beyond the reach of manufactured consumer goods, Aiken's hill farmers also lived in "comfort and security." As Aiken put it, they had the "inherited faculty of being able to do without things which people accustomed to more cash feel they must have." That faculty, he wrote, "stands us in good stead." (The "us" here was a true campaign flourish. Aiken did own a farm, but he was certainly no subsistence farmer.)

Little wonder *Free America* ran a laudatory portrait of Aiken a few months before the Senate election in 1940, describing him as "the strongest advocate of decentralism in public life today."[37] Outsiders, the writer explained, erroneously perceived Vermont as "the rock-ribbed home of the rugged individualist." Based on that misunderstanding, other politicians had warned Aiken that he could not get a Vermonter to join his voluntary cooperative ventures, "any more than you could grow potatoes on a granite ledge." But Aiken understood his state's traditions better, recalling that "Vermont was the first state to prohibit slavery in the United States, and the first state to grant universal suffrage," and that "any state founded on such principles might be a pretty fertile place to start the cooperative movement."[38]

The decentralists of *Free America* cherished a special affection for Vermont. Because of Aiken's leadership and the state's traditions, in fact, one author explained that Vermont had "come to have an almost symbolic significance in the pages of FREE AMERICA." That partiality may seem a little odd. Maine, after all, joined Vermont in its stand against the New Deal in 1936, and like Vermont, it often adopted a "third-way" political posture. New Hampshire's *Yankee Magazine* took an editorial position similar to the decentralists, opposing "mass production, mass distribution, mass advertising, and mass almost-everything-you-can-think-of."[39] Some journalists, in fact, wrote for both *Free*

Perhaps this 1943 Farm Security Administration photograph by John Collier, labeled simply "Bethel, Vermont: A Farm," depicts the kind of landscape journalist Dorothy Thompson had in mind when she described Vermont's rural landscapes as especially "sightly:" "The neat, well painted farm house, the adequate barn, the well-kept pasture, and even the small lawn and flower garden" all testify to the independence and security of the inhabitants. (Farm Security Administration— Office of War Information Photograph Collection, Library of Congress)

America and *Yankee*.[40] It may have been their vacation experiences that tied *Free America*'s writers so closely to one state. As it happens, a number of them spent their summers in Vermont. Editor Katherine Gauss Jackson vacationed in Greensboro, a summer colony in the northeastern corner of the state populated primarily by academics. (Her father was the Princeton dean who wrote that article about the loss of regional distinctiveness.) Bernard DeVoto's summer home—the spot where he encountered his prototypical "granite" farm family—was not far from there.

Journalist Dorothy Thompson, along with her husband Sinclair Lewis, spent summers in central Vermont. Thompson's 1937 *Free America* article "Concerning Vermont" expressed the magazine's abiding love for the state. It was not simply the beauty of the landscape, she explained: the state's distinctive "sightliness" reflected its decentralist values. In Vermont, Thompson asserted, there was "almost no such thing as single-crop agriculture." Every farm was self-sufficient, with its own wood lot, sugar bush, apple orchard, vegetable garden, chickens, and cows. As a consequence, even in remote places where Thompson expected to find the blight of rural poverty—"hillbillies inhabiting unsightly shacks," as she wrote—she found "the neat well painted farm house, the adequate barn, the well-kept pasture, and even the small lawn and flower garden." The beauty of the landscape was an outward expression of the inner grace of self-sufficiency. Those carefully maintained farms expressed the values of the families that worked them, people "as independent, and self-respecting . . . as I have yet met."[41]

In 1940, the *Free America* editors decided, after much debate, to accept advertising for a few select products. Three of the eight advertisements came from Vermont. One advertiser (with no sign of a qualm, although readers now will certainly wince) offered to sell a circular staircase taken from an Asher Benjamin house. Another advertised maple syrup from a place called Forest Farm, up in Jamaica, Vermont: "Vermont Maple Syrup, we boil our own." The notice did not use their names, but Forest Farm belonged to Helen and Scott Nearing, who had moved to the Green Mountains some eight years earlier. The third ad offered old-fashioned stone-ground cornmeal for sale, processed at a recently restored gristmill in Weston, Vermont. The restoration of the mill was the work of Vrest Orton, who, like George Aiken, provided a tangible link between the decentralists and their favorite state.

Free Vermont

The decentralist vision of Vermont was not simply a vacationer's fantasy. Vermont itself was abuzz with efforts to revive its regional culture and economy. One source of the excitement was the Stephen Daye Press, founded in Brattleboro in 1931. Named after the first printing press in North America (originally located at Harvard), the new press generated an impressive list of regionalist publications, including collections of Vermont biography, poetry, and prose as well as the first volume of what would become Helen Hartness Flanders's definitive collection of Vermont and New England folk music. It published George Aiken's popular *Pioneering with Fruits and Berries* (the product, along with his earlier *Pioneering with Wildflowers*, of his first vocation as a horticulturist). It also published several back-to-the-land books. Elliott Merrick's *From This Hill Look Down* (1934) and Charles Morrow Wilson's *Country Living Plus and Minus* (1938) appeared in the company of a slight but beautifully printed "country life" book by Charles F. Speare called *We Found a Farm* (1936) and Muriel

Helen Knothe Nearing poses beneath a sign advertising the Nearings' maple business at Forest Farms in Vermont. Photograph by Llewellyn Ransom. (Courtesy of Special Collections, University of Vermont Libraries)

Follett's quietly poignant description of a year in the life of her family's farm, *New England Year* (1939).

One of the founders of the Stephen Daye Press was Vrest Orton, a native son of Vermont who had grown up in Massachusetts and worked for years as a journalist and freelance writer in New York City before returning to Vermont to start a series of small businesses. Orton was also a frequent contributor to *Free America*. His career offered living proof that the decentralist's view of Vermont was not a projection of outsiders or summer visitors. Years before he began his association with *Free America*, Orton had launched a tongue-in-cheek campaign to defend Vermont's distinctive character and values by way of a truly decentralist method: secession.[42] Like those other defenders of regionalism, the Agrarians, Orton chose a literary venue in which to issue his challenge to the status quo, John Walter Coates's elegant little poetry magazine *Drift-wind*. Orton's challenge predated the Agrarian manifesto by two full years. In "Vermont—for Vermonters," he castigated the unholy alliance between chamber of commerce "Babbitts" and Vermonters who left the state and became infected by "the fever of modern life, in its rankest materialism and commercialism."[43] Returning home, the apostates brought with them their tastes for a crass and selfish modernism that threatened to undermine all that was unique about Vermont.

In 1929, Orton constituted himself a member of a "Vigilance Committee" and proposed a way to "squash" all "un-Vermonterish" imports: everything from "tourists who patronize natives" to "jerry-built roadside shacks, summer camps [and] hot dog stands" to "factories belching smoke, crushing the workers and breaking their souls."[44] After secession, he hoped, foreigners would be forbidden to acquire land in Vermont unless they agreed to raise food on it. (Back-to-the-landers, that seemed to mean, would be allowed entry.) Orton wrote with bravado: everyone knew, he asserted, that Vermonters were "taciturn, brave, self-reliant, reserved, sturdy, reticent, determined and strong" and that their love of their native ground was more like that of a Balkan peasant than that of a normal American.[45] But his tone did not obscure his serious point: Vermont must not become "a Summer Playground for the Nation" (the title of a state-published handbook for tourists), a "great booze highway to Canada," or the site of the "best display of advertising billboards and attendant hot dog stands." Nor should it host the "cheap factory sites" or "squalid industrial communities" that blighted southern New England.[46] Vermont's true future lay in the decentralist landscape out-of-staters found so appealing: the farms of its hillsides and the self-sufficient small-scale village industries of its river valleys.

In his *Free America* articles, Orton praised Vermonters who possessed "the initiative and willingness to decentralize themselves" by resurrecting the infrastructure of small-scale rural economies. One such article told the story of Edward J. Taylor, who left his job with an oil company to take up the challenge of revitalizing a village woodworking industry. Another article described the Crowley cheese factory, where production techniques had remained low tech, small scale, and local—a business that had "purposely been kept small." It was, Orton wrote, "a remarkable example, in good working order, of the best agrarian-decentralist doctrines and technique." These businesses reinvigorated regional economies, making them stronger and more resistant to the inroads of national advertising and distribution networks. They also taught the most important lesson Vermont had to offer: "By letting the rest of the world dash by, breathless for progress . . . in a maddening speed toward super-efficiency and short cuts for profit," the Crowley cheese factory had "arrived so far ahead" that it had made "a new kind of progress."[47]

Orton himself was one of the "ingenious, hard-working fellows" he liked to write about. His work with the Stephen Daye Press, and later with the Countryman Press he set up in the town of Weston, was only a part of the story. Orton also helped to found the Vermont Guild of Old Time Crafts and Industries to revitalize traditional industries. The guild rebuilt the gristmill in Weston, and within a couple of years the company was producing the cornmeal it would later advertise in *Free America*. Orton made a more lasting name for himself with a pioneering mail-order business designed to market the products of local craftsmen. He called it the Vermont Country Store, and it thrived. (Until recently, its catalog bore the slogan "The Voice of the Mountains" on its cover.) The revitalized Vermont of the future, Orton argued in *Free America*, would continue to embody those values the magazine's readers held dear. It would not be simply "the old agrarian way of life, nor the new highly centralized, technical mode of living," he explained, "but a rather pleasant, sound combination of both."[48] It would be, in other words, a true realization of a "third way."

Unfree Vermont

Skeptics like Harvard historian Crane Brinton scoffed at the idealized image of Vermont's farmers circulating in the decentralist press. Brinton conceded that DeVoto's self-reliant "Jason" was "wholly real," but he argued that DeVoto ignored the "poor-white squalor" of rural Vermont: "Jason's cousin Harry, who has been on relief for fifteen years . . . and Dolly, who has achieved two bastards before her twentieth year."[49] Orton would not have written so contemptuously about his neighbors, but he knew that Vermont was not quite the refuge from large-scale market forces its admirers wanted it to be. Orton was well aware that local mills that processed farm goods—businesses that ground grain, wove wool, or made butter and cheese—had all but disappeared from most villages by the 1930s. Vermont farmers, despite their much-praised self-sufficiency and independence, had been hit hard by the Depression, too. Most of them produced milk for the greater Boston "milkshed," and they were anything but independent of the market. Milk checks declined by an average of 50 percent between 1929 and 1932.[50] As Orton acknowledged in *Free America*, "The big milk entrepreneurs hold the Vermont farmers in thrall as completely as if they owned them as body slaves."[51]

Another *Free America* writer from Vermont confirmed Orton's assessment of the desperate situation in Vermont's dairy farming communities, arguing that the problem lay with the very centralization the state was allegedly resisting so successfully. In a 1937 article, Elliott Merrick explained that the dairy farmers in his village had once sent their milk to a local cooperative that was an integral part of the village economy. It had used ice cut by local workers, and helped to support the village sawmill, gristmill, blacksmith shop, and stores as well. But "forces it could not fight" drove the creamery out of business. Now, Merrick wrote, farmers sent their milk to a big company in Boston, which set prices and controlled distribution from a distance far beyond their reach. The problem was "immense, far away, vague, impenetrable." The Vermont dairy farmer was as much a victim of centralization as any factory hand working for a faceless corporate giant. "They do not know who is working for them, who against them. All they know is that they are powerless," Merrick wrote. "They cannot help themselves as they used to, and you can see it in the stoop of their shoulders." The bitter moral he drew was one that bore repetition, even in Vermont: "There is no substitute for independence."[52]

Yet both Merrick and Orton found hope in an improbable place. In *Free America*, Orton described the 1935 debate over the proposed Green Mountain Parkway. It had looked as though the proparkway forces (which Orton detested) would prevail, but as he described it, "there arose at the last hour the true countrymen," the farmers, who beat back the New Deal project, with its threatened hot dog stands and roadside shacks. But it was not just the farmers. In spite of Orton's earlier denunciations of "Babbitts" who despoiled Vermont, he now acknowledged that the farmers could not have prevailed without help from another group: Vermont's "newly arrived urban people." It was a "strange combination," he commented—but it worked.[53] A "curious alliance" seemed to be emerging between native traditionalists and urban expatriates. A decentralist Vermont, it seemed, might be sustained not simply by Vermont's traditional rural values but also by the energy and skills of newcomers. If they promised to grow their own food, as Orton had once stipulated, he now thought they might even make good neighbors. Another decentralist writer called them "neo-Yankees."[54]

By the mid-1930s, a decision to move to a farm in Vermont was becoming something like a political statement in itself. It indicated a preference for subsistence farming—"farming as a way of life" rather than "farming as a business"—and for small-scale communities and businesses. It suggested, at the very least, discomfort with centralized government and downright hatred of urban industrial conglomerates, a wary distrust of consumer culture and a fondness for simplicity and frugality (at least the idea of it). Moreover, it testified to a perspective that linked these values to a specific landscape. In the eyes of back-to-the-landers, the small scale of the farms, the wood lots and orchards, even the austerity of the windswept upland "submarginal" farms, expressed the tenacity of Vermont's farmers in holding on to the self-sufficient "safety first" strategies of an earlier time—their rejection of consumerism and commitment to self-reliance.

Of course, if moving to Vermont was a political gesture, it was not a simple one. The authors who embraced this new vision of Vermont interpreted it in a range of ways. One might look to Vermont's farms for a bare subsistence for city refugees—or for a summer retreat for artists. Vermont villages could serve as incubators for small businesses or for a national "third-way" political movement. Some people, indeed, were not looking for much more than a weekend in the country.

Neo-Yankee Summer People

At that end of the spectrum was Frederic Van De Water, who wrote a series of books about his Vermont farm, beginning with *A Home in the Country* and continuing to *We're Still in the Country* (1938) and *The Circling Year* (1940). Van De Water's narratives are not too different from the standard I-bought-a-barn book. One *Free America* reviewer, comparing *The Circling Year* to other Vermont books, remarked that it "would give no more lasting satisfaction than a cream puff."[55] Even the most lightweight writer, however, could not seem to buy a Vermont farm without also taking on some of its political and cultural baggage.

The Van De Waters purchased their Vermont farm in the depths of the Depression, at a time when, as Van De Water described it, "the merriest parties" in Manhattan "degenerated into muttering huddles that broke apart to peer down into the street where the barricade-raisers might be at their dire employment."[56] Others may have been facing joblessness, bankruptcy, and despair; for the Van De Waters the farm was merely a safer investment than the stock market. Still, although it lacked the sense of urgency that infused many back-to-the-land books in the 1930s, Van De Water's writing did reflect the decentralist view of the state: "The chief intangible product of Vermont," he wrote, "is independence."[57]

That earnest-sounding observation of Vermont character was occasioned by the narrator's experiences with a real estate agent. Many I-bought-a-barn books began with mock-tragic tales of real estate agents who led the characters astray; Van De Water's joke was that this real estate agent was unaccountably honest. The point he made was at least partly serious, however: "The spirit of the arch-rebel, Ethan Allen, still walks the hills and his individuality has tinctured even the real estate business."[58] That he raised the specter of Ethan Allen was no accident: Van de Water later wrote two histories of Vermont that enshrined this vision of the liberty-loving Ethan Allen as the embodiment of the state's identity. "In some strange way," he wrote in *Reluctant Republic*, "the climate, the soil, the contours of that land itself, had nurtured—still preserves—that disconcerting passion" for freedom.[59]

For generations, New England's summer vacationers had been amused by depictions of quaint "Yankee" neighbors and servants, portrayed sometimes as taciturn and sometimes as garrulous, alternately shrewd and naive. In *A Home in the Country*, Van De Water described his rural neighbors in terms that recycled all those old stereotypes of Yankees, with just a hint of a new kind of respect. He advised urbanites who had acquired farms in the area not to bring their "patrician airs and graces" along with them. To be sure, Vermonters would be happy to work for these relocated gentry. "Thrift, industry, craftsmanship and a desperate hunger for real work" ensured that "he who buys property in Vermont need never lack for mechanic, craftsman or day laborer." At the same time, though, they would find that Vermonters possessed an "odd, abiding dignity" rooted in their respect for work. Van De Water described his own amazement when his hired man reacted to being addressed as "Harry" by calling Van De Water "Frederic." In the end, he decided that he liked it; it had the "sound and ancient flavor of a democracy that was based on equality rather than a scrambling for class-privilege." (Perhaps, too, he hoped that workers who called him by his first name would be less likely to man those barricades he had feared in Manhattan.)[60]

Van De Water cherished the idea that Vermonters had somehow escaped the worst aspects of modern civilization. Like Orton in his secessionist manifesto, Van De Water praised God for having "so far . . . withheld from this clean land the blessings of Hotte Doggeries and Dew Drop Inns and Min's and Bill's Place." The "tent-caterpillar ravages of vacationists," as he phrased it, had not yet marred the state's beauty. (This at a time when Vermont's promoters, both privately and publicly employed, had been working hard for a generation or more to spread those "tent-caterpillars" throughout the state.) Vermont had so far escaped all that, he argued, because the "values in this part of the world are not those of America at large." (Here, Van De Water echoed his hero Ethan Allen's most trenchant remark: "The gods of the hills are not the gods of the valleys.") In this "neglected portion of the nation," Van De Water wrote, "the democracy the founding fathers dreamed . . . still actually works."[61]

Neo-Yankee Entrepreneurs

Samuel Ogden might have written those same words, but he would have meant them in a different way. Ogden and his family moved to Vermont in 1929, just before the crash. In fact, the family more or less repopulated the mountain village of Landgrove, which had been almost deserted when they bought most of the buildings in town. *This Country Life* (1946) was nothing less than a decentralist manifesto. Ogden reported in the 1973 edition of his book (published by Rodale Press at the height of a later back-to-the-land movement) that his family had made the move back to the land "inspired by the writings of Ralph Borsodi."[62] He quoted from George Aiken's essay "Not So Submarginal" in support of his preference for "farming as a way of life" as opposed to "farming as a business," arguing that if farming were not aimed at self-sufficiency, it was nothing but a business, "and a poor one at that."[63]

Ogden condemned the widespread belief that a higher "standard of living," greater consumption, or more leisure would lead inevitably to a happier or more fulfilling life.[64] He addressed readers dissatisfied with "the modern trends toward specialization and mechanization, toward centralization and socialization," warning such would-be back-to-the-landers that a move to the country would require a "drastically revised" set of values. They would have to turn their backs on the "glamour of the city, with its high-speed life and its specialized occupations." They would have to accept a lower standard of living and harder physical work, with only the satisfaction of that work to reward them. Ogden reminded his readers sternly that "the material rewards of living in the country cannot be expected to be great," but they would gain the back-to-the-lander's dream of security, independence, and self-respect: "a life more rewarding socially and culturally" than they had ever imagined.[65]

The first half of *This Country Life* was devoted to practical back-to-the-land advice: how to find a place to live, how to fit into a rural community, how to provide food for the household.[66] In the second half of the book, Ogden explored a wide variety of nonfarm rural occupations, from practicing medicine to making false teeth. Like Orton (and like Borsodi, who was fascinated with small-scale machinery), Ogden saved his greatest enthusiasm for the revitalization of small-scale manufacturing. He wrote with pride about his own blacksmith forge and praised Orton's mail-order catalog and the popular Crowley cheese. He even suggested marketing maple syrup in smaller and more stylish glass containers—precisely the project that Helen and Scott Nearing were taking up in another part of the state.

But Ogden did not write much about the unique characteristics of Vermont or the old-fashioned virtues of its people. Nor was he concerned with keeping the "tent-caterpillar ravages of vacationists" away from the state, or protecting its pristine Arcadian simplicity. In fact, Ogden served on the Vermont Development Commission, a group that played an important role in promoting tourism and skiing.[67] He proposed a number of occupations for homesteaders that—in hindsight it seems clear—would almost certainly lead to the erosion of the household and regional self-sufficiency he prized. He suggested that would-be back-to-the-landers might make a living by running children's summer camps or providing lodging for skiers. Ogden and his family did both. After all, if small, independent artisans were to thrive in rural Vermont, what better way than to bring discerning consumers to their doors?

Neo-Yankee Artists

Charles Morrow Wilson was a regionalist writer, but his books were mostly about Arkansas, his birthplace. His first book, *Acres of Sky* (1930), was a description of Ozark customs.[68] During the 1930s, however, Wilson divided his time between Manhattan and his farm in Vermont. The book he wrote about Vermont, *Country Living Plus and Minus*, was packed with the standard material of a traditional back-to-the-land book, discussing start-up costs, providing lists of vegetables, and offering advice on egg production and forage crops. He repeated the decentralist mantras as well, quoting from George Aiken's "The Farm's a Place to Live" and echoing the much-repeated declaration that in Vermont "farming . . . remains primarily a pattern of life, rather than a means of earning money."[69]

The opening words of *Country Living Plus and Minus* call up elemental pleasures: "I have finished with barnyard chores and wood-chopping," Wilson wrote. "The wood is in. The milking is done. Supper is ready." The sketch by landscape painter Carola Spaeth Hauschka that accompanies the passage is equally simple but also artfully chosen. (*Country Living Plus and Minus* was a product of the Stephen Daye Press, which took illustrations and bindings seriously.) A sketch of a pile of chopped wood testifies to the satisfaction of productive work, now done. This family will be warm. It will also be well fed: "Apples, mellow and red, fried in butter with just a sprinkling of brown sugar. Bacon fresh sliced from a side of home-cured pork. Cornbread thin and crisp. A corner of yellow butter, a spoonful of comb honey, a cup of alien tea seasoned with honest, home-skimmed cream." With a sigh of contentment, Wilson concludes, "I am having a good time in the country."[70]

This was unpretentious writing, but it echoed perhaps the most powerful defense of the subsistence farm ever written: Andrew Nelson Lytle's essay "The Hind Tit," published in *I'll Take My Stand*. Lytle imagined a farm whose patriarch had not yet made the fateful decision to buy a ledger and keep accounts. He described the hard but fulfilling work of the family members, their web of mutual obligations, and their soul-satisfying meals. In that prelapsarian time and place, the pleasures of a "one-year ham" or a "heaping plate of fried chicken," of "deep-yellow butter and creamy milk, fat beans and juicy corn," arose from the farm family's relationship to the food's production. Precisely because the farmer "has not yet come to look upon his produce at so many cents a pound, or his corn at so much a dozen," his enjoyment of his food was unspoiled.[71] (Conversely, John Steinbeck envisions the transfer of Dust Bowl farms from small-scale proprietors to corporate owners as a dystopian nightmare: "Men ate what they had not raised, had no connection with the bread. The land bore under iron, and under iron gradually died; for it was not loved or hated, it had no prayers or curses.")[72]

Wilson placed food—produced on the farm and regionally distinctive (in spite of his odd choice of honey in place of the iconic maple syrup)—at the center of the back-to-the-land vision. But Wilson also took pains to let the reader know that he himself was only a part-time farmer. He even let his readers in on an open secret: "The most articulate exponents of a return to the land are authors, not farmers."[73] His neighborhood in southern Vermont, Wilson reported, was home to seven households of back-to-the-landers, and almost all of the breadwinners of those families were artists or professionals. One neighbor was a sculptor and another a professional harp player. Like Orton, Wilson believed that such city refugees would help to build a new kind of rural community. The last lines in Wilson's book suggest that he imagined professional and artistic "neo-Yankees" like himself as ties that would bind the new rural community together: "My neighbor on the left has just finished milking. I don't know how many hundreds of times he has done this chore. My neighbor on . . . the right is up for the weekend, hammering away at new boards on old beams. I live in the middle, between the oldtimer and the newcomer, trying to catch the points of view of both."[74]

Neo-Yankee Back-to-the-Landers

Elliott Merrick's *From This Hill Look Down* struck a different note. It tells a classic back-to-the-land tale of a hero who loses his job and searches in vain for another one. After weeks of rejection, John Dacey comes to the end of his rope: "One day . . . while interviewing a fur merchant who wanted an elevator boy who would also run errands and do janitor work for eight dollars a week, John inadvertently said *Sir*." That slip triggers a terrifying response in him: "Something ageless and primitive in his brain was saying, *You must kill this man now*." Frightened by the intensity of his own rage, John "turned and ran from the shop."[75] Still running from his humiliation and despair, he climbed into his old truck and headed north in search of a farm. By then, there was no need to explain why he chose to look for that farm in Vermont.

John Dacey's return to the land was not the product of a desire for a safe investment or a pleasant retreat but of sheer desperation. Merrick's own return to the land was apparently driven by a similar distress. As he reported in a *Free America* article, he and his wife moved to a backcountry Vermont farm in the depths of the Depression with $200 to their name. "Our income was uncertain," he wrote in 1937, "and for months at a time it has been non-existent." At the end of five years, however, he reported that he and his wife had their farm half paid for and that although they were "never very far from pennilessness, we have plenty to eat, we are still alive, in fact very much more alive than when we came."[76] Merrick advised his readers to follow in his footsteps, to "live on what they can raise, make their homes out of logs or boards or sod or canvas" if necessary—whatever it took. They, too, could bear the primitive housing, the hard work, and the plain living and in the end "win out and be proud of themselves, not starve to death on charity rolls.'"[77]

From This Hill Look Down, like *Country Living Plus and Minus*, was a product of the Stephen Daye Press. It, too, was carefully illustrated but in a different style. Instead of dwelling on the comfort and security of rural life, Allen Congdon's woodcuts emphasized the independence of that life—what an earlier generation would routinely have referred to as its "manhood." On the cover was a stark woodcut of a man with a pitchfork looking out his barn door. There is no telling whether this figure was a seventh-generation Yankee farmer or a recently arrived author.

Merrick, of course, was not exactly the figure portrayed on the cover of the book. He was in fact a New Jersey–born, Yale-educated professional writer. (He had recently published an account of a back-to-nature journey even more daunting than this Vermont adventure would be: *True North* (1933) chronicled Merrick's adventures with the Grenfell Mission in the wilds of Labrador.) Moving to Vermont converted Merrick's desperate character John Dacey into someone like DeVoto's Vermont farmer, a "free man, self-reliant, sure of his world, unfrightened by the future." Judging from the book's cover, it had also transformed Merrick himself. The dust jacket described the author as a man "who labors with his hands for sustenance." He did not have much time to spend with the "world of paper," the back of the book explained. *From This Hill Look Down* featured an introduction by the well-known regionalist poet Walter Hard, who also emphasized Merrick's farming credentials, writing that the

In Allen Congdon's striking cover design for Elliott Merrick's *From This Hill Look Down* (1934), a man surveys his domain from the barn door. The man appears tired, but also proprietary: his hard work has earned him the right to the homestead he surveys. The dust jacket text implies that this is a picture of Merrick himself, an author "who labors with his hands for sustenance."

book was "wrested from the soil by hands which know labor." Hard commended Merrick's decentralist politics, praising him for choosing "a dinner of green herbs, gathered by the sweat of his own brow," over a "stalled ox furnished by a charitable government."[78] His choice to become self-sufficient, Hard concluded, was proof that Merrick deserved to be regarded as a native Vermonter.

Yet Merrick, too, hoped that "neo-Yankees" would strengthen and transform Vermont's rural economy and culture. Merrick believed that a large-scale return of city people to the land would encourage an exchange of knowledge and skills that might help both farmers and city refugees. Not only did city people needed to learn the skills farm families possessed; country people needed to know that what they did was valuable and significant. "It would be important news to the average New England farmer that Ralph Borsodi, as an expert and technician, encourages the grinding of one's own grain," Merrick suggested. Farmers had "no idea that any modern city-bred man is interested in such humble, age-old shifts to make ends meet." Traditional farmers might regain faith in their "self-sustaining, close-knit way of life" if they knew that their self-sufficient practices—"stove-ashes for the garden, a wood lot to supply the stoves, cattle to supply manure for the fields and the produce of the fields to feed the cattle"—were not just old-fashioned ways of getting along but an "efficient, unbeatable combination." The blending of farmers' traditional knowledge with the new ideas of decentralist back-to-the-landers, Merrick hoped, might ultimately "transform rural America from a land of despair . . . to a land of hope and new faith."[79]

All these authors shared the conviction that Vermont's farms were the embodiment of decentralist back-to-the-land values. The state was not perfect, they knew, but it was one of the few places left where self-sufficient farms and communities still hung on, through the boom years of the 1920s and the depression years of the 1930s. Yet perhaps paradoxically, all these authors envisioned a future for Vermont that depended on new people moving to the state—people who would be a lot like the authors. Ogden wanted self-reliant craftsmen and farmers to thrive but that would require buyers of cheese, maple syrup, and iron fireplace tools—at least, they would need to visit the state as skiers and summer vacationers. Wilson hoped that more writers, artists, and other professionals with an appreciation for part-time rural life would reinvigorate rural communities like his own. Merrick called for hardy back-to-the-landers like himself (perhaps they would also be part-time authors) to help build a new rural economy for Vermont.

For the rest of the twentieth century, Vermont's economic and cultural destiny would waver among these visions. Was the state to be a rural retreat for artists and professionals? A haven for craftspeople who catered to specialized markets? Or would it repopulate itself with urban refugees seeking self-sufficiency on the land? When Vermont's population began to rise again after nearly a century of decline, all those visions would be brought to life. Skiing boomed in the years after World War II; second homes spread throughout Vermont as the interstate highways inched their way up the state in the 1960s. Artists colonized small towns; professionals bought farms. And when a new generation of back-to-the-landers looked for their own routes back to the land in the 1970s, they, too, would follow that same road north.

Coda: The Nearings Invent Their Own Vermont

Helen and Scott Nearing would one day become the best-known Vermont back-to-the-landers. They moved there in the 1930s, but in those days they wrote no books about it. The Nearings published their story only in 1950 (*The Maple Sugar Book*) and in 1954 (*Living the Good Life*). Even then, their books would receive little attention until the rerelease of *Living the Good Life* years later, in 1970. Finally, in the midst of yet another wave of back-to-the-land enthusiasm, *Living the Good Life* would acquire iconic status. By then, the Nearings themselves would seem almost ageless—he was eighty-seven and she sixty-six when the book was rereleased—and their story would seem at once contemporary and timeless.

That story spanned almost the entire twentieth century. Nearing's promising career at the Wharton School had come to an abrupt end back in 1915, when he was dismissed for his outspoken support of protective child labor laws (and for publishing a provocative open letter to evangelist Billy Sunday enjoining him to apply the principles of the gospel to the current economic scene). He lost his next position at Toledo University when his opposition to World War I made him too hot to handle. His career options narrowed. He joined the Socialist Party, took a teaching post at the Socialist Party's Rand School of Social Science, and launched an active career as a public speaker. In 1918, his antiwar pamphlet *The Great Madness* resulted in a highly publicized trial under the Espionage Act; in court, Nearing presented a powerful defense of the right to free speech and was acquitted. In the 1920s, Nearing left the Socialists, joined the Communist Party, and started writing for the *Daily Worker*, but within a few years he broke with that party, too. By 1930, the middle-aged Nearing was in a nearly impossible position. His earlier struggles against war and on behalf of social justice and free speech had been nothing short of heroic, but now, fewer and fewer mainstream magazines—and finally even leftist journals— would publish his writing. His opportunities to make a living by public lecturing dwindled and then almost disappeared.[80]

Meanwhile, in 1928, Scott Nearing met Helen Knothe, the daughter of a well-to-do family with close ties to the theosophical movement. Trained as a classical violinist, she had studied with the concertmaster of Amsterdam's Royal Concertgebouw Orchestra while traveling widely in theosophical circles. She had risen to the highest levels of the Theosophical Society as the chosen companion of the dazzling young leader Krishnamurti—only to find herself suddenly and unceremoniously rejected. She was recovering from that emotional roller coaster ride when she fell in with Nearing, twenty years her senior, who was now separated from his wife and children. In 1932 the couple determined to move to Vermont.[81]

Scott Nearing had already acquired the skills of a back-to-the-lander by then. First there had been the summers spent in Arden, Delaware, where he learned to garden and to build with stone. Then, in the early 1920s, after his academic career ended, he and his first wife, Nellie Seeds Nearing, had tried going back to the land, moving to the home of Scott's parents in Pennsylvania, where they grew a large garden and converted the barn to living quarters. Now he taught those gardening and building skills to Helen. Using capital they obtained from family and friends, the Nearings (they eventually married after Scott's first wife died in 1946) gradually acquired over a thousand acres in the Green Mountains. They developed a sizeable maple syrup business, working the sugar bush on shares with their neighbors. Under Helen's guidance, the couple developed a successful marketing strategy, packaging the syrup and the maple sugar in distinctive boxes and bottles and advertising them to a variety of discerning clients, including the readers of the 1940 *Free America* ads.[82]

By the 1970s, when most of their readers finally "discovered" them, the Nearings had left their maple syrup business and their Vermont farm and moved to Maine. In that new time and place, Scott's advancing age, his decades of radicalism, Helen's eastern spiritualism, and their shared commitment to personal austerity would combine to create a sense that the two were living incarnations of the back-to-the-land spirit. And indeed, there is something prototypical about their story. In its general outlines at least, the story of the Nearings does read like a typical back-to-the-land narrative. It begins with a hero who has lost his job—or in Scott Nearing's case, many jobs. In the characteristically detached tone of *Living the Good Life,* "changing social conditions during the twenty years that began in 1910 cost us our professional status and deprived us of our means of livelihood."[83] (The "us" here was, of course, Scott.) The breadwinner is out of work; with all other options blocked, they have no choice but to retreat to the land (although they would not have liked the word "retreat").

The Nearings' critique of urban life is wholly typical of early twentieth-century back-to-the-land writing. "The average urbanite," they wrote in *The Maple Sugar Book,* "is like any ant in any anthill—a helpless creature of circumstances set up by landlord, merchant, factory owner, and banker." City life would inevitably "snare the unwary, reduce them to dependence, and force them into a life of servitude in the impersonal mechanism of an acquisitive society."[84] Wage-earning "dependence," servitude to a machine—these phrases reflect the producerist sensibility that fueled the first back-to-the-land movement. Like almost all back-to-the-land writers, too, the Nearings praised the satisfaction to be derived from self-sufficiency: "Both bread and butter may be homemade, and much of their savor lies in joy that always links effort and reward." Like any bourgeois I-bought-a-barn writer, they even tell a joking tale about the realtor who sold them their land: "The tricks he played must have made him number one man on Beelzebub's roster of real-estaters."[85]

In many ways, indeed, these books express more of the sensibility of 1915 than of 1935, and no wonder: Scott, at least, was closer to Bolton Hall's generation than to Elliott Merrick's. Unlike many 1930s back-to-the-landers, Scott Nearing was no decentralist, although he shared many of their assumptions about independence, self-sufficiency, and subsistence farming: he maintained his commitment to a future global socialist state until his death in 1983 at the age of one hundred. Nor did the Nearings write much about the character of Vermonters or the special features of the state so admired by the decentralists. In comparison to fellow "neo-Yankees" of the 1930s, their enthusiasm for New England feels a little flat. They point out that land had been cheap there in the midst of the Depression and remark that they did like the changing of the seasons. In *The Maple Sugar Book,* they propose (perhaps with a little tongue-in-cheek humor) that "soft climates probably produce soft people, and certainly produce parasitic people."[86] In *Living the Good Life,* the Nearings fall back on more conventional phrasing, simply praising the "perpetual surprises and delights to which New England weather treats its devotees."[87]

They did like the Vermont landscape, both physical and social: "The valleys were cosy, the people unpretentious. Most of the state was open and wild, with little of the suburban or summer vacation atmosphere." Like Frederic Van

De Water, they admired what he called the "long, blue ranges unlacerated by scenic highways, immune to the pox of 'summer camps.'"[88] And while they never mentioned it in their books, the Nearings also found in Vermont a network of friends, family, and associates much like those enjoyed by other "neo-Yankees." The place they chose to live already harbored a number of urban expatriates by the time they got there. Perhaps the most important of these were the author Pearl Buck and her husband Richard Walsh, who was president of the publishing house of John Day. That press would later publish *The Maple Sugar Book*, the Nearings' first attempt at mainstream writing. And it was Walsh and Buck who convinced them to write *Living the Good Life* a few years later.[89]

Yet at the same time the Nearings offered a startlingly frank critique of their rural neighbors. In fact, they expressed disappointment about precisely the characteristics the decentralists found so attractive. That dissatisfaction arose mostly from their near complete failure to establish cooperative or collective enterprises in their Vermont community. In one chapter of *The Maple Sugar Book*, "A Balance Sheet of the Vermont Project," the Nearings contended that the valley they were living in was a terrible place to experiment with collectivist endeavors. "Vermonters were strong individualists," they wrote, and circumstances encouraged that trait: "The percentage of home ownership and farm ownership was unusually high; the population was thin and widely scattered, and all the major Vermont traditions emphasized the individualism of the Green Mountain folk." Precisely because the families of the valley operated as the autonomous, self-sufficient households that the decentralists admired so much, the Nearings found it impossible to organize cooperative endeavors. "'Autonomous' is hardly the word" for such rural households, they groused: "'Sovereign' would be a more exact descriptive term."[90]

Furthermore, to the Nearings, the native Vermonters around them bore little resemblance to those Yankee icons of hard work and frugality admired by so many regionalist writers in the 1930s. That self-reliant Yankee farmer who provided a model for Bernard DeVoto's Jason, who was praised by George Aiken and emulated by Elliott Merrick, simply does not appear in *Living the Good Life*. Even when the Nearings did use the rhetoric of region, it had an oddly negative ring: "Hill dwellers are rugged individualists, mistrustful, cautious, and shrewd," they wrote, suggesting more the stereotype of an Appalachian hillbilly than of a "granite" Yankee. Moreover, the extraordinarily self-disciplined Scott and Helen, perhaps alone in all the world, viewed their Yankee neighbors as messy, haphazard, and self-indulgent: they complained that the neighbors left their machinery in the rain, altered their work plans when weather or guests intervened, and indulged their physical appetites with meat and sugar. In contrast to Helen and Scott with their well-regulated lives, those neighbors looked almost like the "peasants" that the critics had long anticipated would show up with a return to subsistence farming.

What they did not find in their neighbors, however, the Nearings characteristically provided for themselves. If they discovered few hill-country Vermonters who personified the virtues of self-reliance, hard work, and the resolute rejection of consumerism, all the more reason to embody those values themselves. Near the end of *The Maple Sugar Book*, the Nearings explained that in their years in Vermont they had learned from their sugaring business "the secrets that some of our forebears in the Green Mountains knew so well." The telling phrase was *"our* forebears." As the couple explained, they had learned "the secrets of simplicity, adequacy, decency, neighborliness, self-respect" from their sojourn in Vermont. (They did *not* say they had learned those secrets from their neighbors.)[91] New Jersey–born Helen and Pennsylvania-born Scott had essentially become their own quintessential Vermont Yankees. Their personal reinvention took on great symbolic significance, adding a new twist to the image of their adopted state.

In time, the Nearings would become an attraction in their own right. Although the couple moved to Maine in 1952, readers in the 1970s encountered them through their Vermont story as it was told in *Living the Good Life*; pilgrims sought them out at their new home in Maine and even hiked up into the mountains to find their former homestead in Vermont. In that way, the Nearings ultimately played an essential role in the Depression-era project of Vermont's back-to-the-land regionalist decentralists. Their hard work, their simple habits, their commitment to "plain living and high thinking," and their back-to-the-land experiment would become part of the profile of Vermont. When another generation of back-to-the-landers emerged in the 1970s, the Nearings would be the brightest star in their sky, and that star would be in the north.

7

Back to the Garden

The 1970s

The New Deal's homestead experiments were short lived: the federal government pulled out of most of the communities as the nation committed itself to World War II. But the war did not dampen popular interest in back-to-the-land projects. Shortly before the Japanese attack on Pearl Harbor, Marguerite Lyon published a humorous account of her flight from Chicago to the Ozarks, *Take to the Hills*. Deftly shifting the focus of her argument from what must originally have been the Depression to the imminent war, Lyon evoked a new reason for the old fears: "The Man on the Street now seems to feel that a farm is the only security if . . . well, if Things Get Worse."[1] Almost immediately, things did get worse, of course, and back-to-the-land books continued to appear in a steady stream. In 1943, Ed and Carolyn Robinson printed a small pamphlet that would later become their influential *Have-More Plan*. In the same year, Bertha Damon published *A Sense of Humus*. And in 1942, Ray Stannard Baker brought out his last David Grayson book.

In the opening words of *Under My Elm*, Baker (now writing openly about his own life, although still using the Grayson pseudonym) affirmed the back-to-the-land vision he had helped to awaken nearly forty years earlier. "I knew well enough," he acknowledged, that "any such experiment in living must represent all sorts of compromises—what life is not a compromise?" Nevertheless, "it was truly what I had dreamed about, what I longed for, and what I had finally attained."[2] He still hedged his endorsement with cautions: going back to the land could succeed "*if* undertaken with determination and sincerity *by a man who has in the beginning some love of the country—and* a fair degree of health, *and* a little money." But he recalled the hundreds of readers who had sought out his advice over the years, from railroad workers to "graduates of famous classical colleges"—all "living on farms and doing well."[3]

Nor did things change immediately after the war. In fact, the first few years after the war's end saw a sharp rise in the production of back-to-the-land books.[4] Ed and Carolyn Robinson reissued their *Have-More Plan* as a full-sized book with a major press in 1947: now it was *The Have-More Plan for a Little Land, a Lot of Living*. In 1948, Elliott Merrick brought out the book that became his best known work, *Green Mountain Farm*. Popular memories may dwell on GIs returning to a consumer bonanza of refrigerators, new cars, and suburban homes, but these years also witnessed an abrupt, if temporary, reversal of farm-to-city migration, as soldiers and industrial workers returned to their rural homes.[5]

Many of the new books were humorous accounts of misadventures with rural life, like Betty McDonald's bestselling *The Egg and I* (1945), which chronicled the narrator's futile efforts to adjust to her new husband's poultry farm in the wilds of the Pacific Northwest. Several back-to-the-farm movies employed the same comic approach. *The Egg and I* became a popular movie in 1947, but it seems to have owed much of that popularity to Ma and Pa Kettle, parodies of rural shiftlessness who lived next door to the protagonists. (The actors who played Ma and Pa made eight more movies in those roles.) Another 1945 movie spoofed the trend toward home-loving retreats. In *Christmas in Connecticut*, Barbara Stanwyck played the role of a food writer who dispensed recipes along with heart-warming tales of her New England farm and family—while actually living in Manhattan, without a farm, a baby, or even a husband of her own.

In 1950, a radio show called *Granby's Green Acres* depicted the similarly humorous adventures of a bank cashier turned farmer. (Its characters and plot would later be resurrected for the 1960s television series *Green Acres*.) "Granby" repeats all the standard back-to-the-land formulas to his skeptical wife and daughter: he feels trapped in his job as a bank cashier, and the price of food is skyrocketing. Most important, Granby longs for self-reliance: "I want to prove that I can make something of myself with my own hands, that I can succeed starting with nothing, just my brain." But Granby, too, is fundamentally a comic figure. His arguments begin eloquently ("The farm would give me independence. If I need an apple, I can pick it"), but they end badly ("If I want an egg . . . I can lay it").[6]

Perhaps all these jokes reflected a tension between the new consumer opportunities available in the postwar years and the persistent longing for a return to home and security. It was not all jokes, to be sure. In the same year that debuted *Granby's Green Acres*, Helen and Scott Nearing brought out *The Maple Sugar Book*. But within a few years, the postwar publishing flurry was over. The Nearings brought out *Living the Good Life* in 1954, but that year would be remembered for the dramatic end of Joseph McCarthy's anticommunist witch hunt, not for social experimentation.[7] The publication of *Living the Good Life* was possible only because the Nearings had founded their own small press to bring out Scott's political and economic treatises, untouchable by any mainstream publisher in the 1950s.

Outside the pages of books, only a few small communities of brave individuals continued to honor the political commitments of earlier back-to-the-landers. Around the Nearing homestead in the mountains of Vermont, a cluster of radicals and pacifists took refuge from World War II and the Cold War. The Labor Zionists, Quakers, and students of Gandhi who settled around Pikes Falls, Vermont, were more often decentralists like Ralph Borsodi than socialists like Scott Nearing, but they did share Nearing's fierce devotion to conscience. They braved job loss, isolation, and jail sentences; grew their own food; and lived on virtually nothing in order to be true to their convictions.[8] Had he lived to see them, Bolton Hall would have been proud.

A small number of committed back-to-the-landers also found refuge in Borsodi's experimental communities. In 1950, Borsodi himself left the Suffern, New York, School of Living settlement he had established in 1935, after being outmaneuvered by residents who were agitating for private ownership of the land. (True to Borsodi's single-tax heritage, the Suffern community had originally been organized as a land trust: the School of Living held the land titles, and homesteaders owned the buildings and other improvements.) After a few years of travel, Borsodi reestablished himself in a new community in Melbourne, Florida, recently founded by colleagues who had worked with him in Dayton in the 1930s.[9] Borsodi's protégé Mildred Jensen Loomis and her husband, John Loomis, also organized a satellite community in Brookville, Ohio, from which she edited the School of Living's journal the *Interpreter*. Like the refuge in the Green Mountains, these were tiny enclaves, barely visible in politically inhospitable times.

In some ways, it is surprising that the vision survived at all, in the midst of such fundamental economic and cultural change. It was not simply that the political environment of the 1950s was uncongenial to social experimentation or political deviance. So many of the old reasons for seeking a haven on the land now seemed to be vanishing. There were fearful prospects on the horizon, to be sure. In 1947, Borsodi advised "sensible people" to begin to go back to the land *before* "inflation and the loss of their savings, the collapse of the post-war boom, followed by unemployment, or World War III with atomic bombing, makes it too late for them to do so."[10] But never before had Americans been so protected from "black Friday and red ruin." The generation that came of age in the years after World War II would be the beneficiary of the New Deal and all its successor programs, from Social Security to Medicare, from unemployment benefits to workers' compensation. The booming postwar economy itself seemed to promise a future of endless prosperity, distributed ever more broadly across the social spectrum. No "dark winged hawk" of Depression circled over that generation; indeed, within a few years, many pundits were announcing that the very "problem of scarcity" itself no longer existed. Not until the mid-1970s would oil shortages and inflation herald the end of that era of abundance. By that time, another back-to-the-land publishing boom was already underway.

Total Loss Farms?

As with other social movements for which the decade of the sixties has been given the credit (or the blame), the defining year was really 1970.[11] That year *Mother Earth News* was born. The magazine quickly established itself as the journal of record for the new back-to-the-land movement, and within a few years, it boasted half a million subscribers.[12] New books abounded—and so did older ones. The Nearings reissued *Living the Good Life* in 1970, selling fifty thousand copies in its first year.[13] Borsodi's *Flight from the City* was reprinted in 1972, *This Ugly Civilization* in 1975. Rodale Press, the publisher of *Organic Gardening* magazine, reprinted Ogden's *This Country Life* in 1973. *Mother Earth News* interviewed Borsodi and the Nearings, reprinted Ed and Carolyn Robinson's 1947 *Have-More Plan*, and printed excerpts from the 1930s decentralist magazine *Free America* and even from the 1864 classic *Ten Acres Enough*. In an introduction to one new book—John and Sally Seymour's *Farming for Self-Sufficiency* (1973)—Mildred Loomis linked the book's arguments directly back to the "decentralist, organic on-the-land" ideas she attributed to Borsodi.[14] Perhaps the clearest indication of the degree to which the new writers were repeating the past amounted to a purely rhetorical flourish. Back in 1864, the grandfather of back-to-the-land books had been called *Ten Acres Enough*; in 1907 the phrase had been *Three Acres and Liberty*; in 1935, *Five Acres and Independence*. In 1972, Bradford Angier called his book *One Acre and Security*.

In spite of these direct connections with the past, however, casual observers have not usually associated this wave of the back-to-the-land movement with earlier times. In the popular imagination, it is associated, not with the single-tax colonies of the 1910s or the subsistence homesteads of the 1930s, but with yurts, teepees, domes, and communes, the 1967 Summer of Love and the 1969 concert at Woodstock. (After all, there was Joni Mitchell's "Woodstock" anthem: "got to get back to the land, and set my soul free.") Framing the movement as part of "the sixties" is certainly not wholly inaccurate, but it does obscure some of its important features. For one thing, it is probably more precise to associate the rebirth of the back-to-the-land movement with the *end* of that era or with the beginning of the next: the 1970 massacre at Kent State, the Watergate crisis, the 1973 oil embargo. That minor adjustment to the chronology would prompt a substantially different interpretation, rooting the movement not in a moment of apparent triumph for the counterculture but in political disillusionment and yet another economic crisis. (In fact, in her September 1969 performance of "Woodstock" at Big Sur, Joni Mitchell did not sing "got to get back to the land" but rather "got to camp out on the land." It was only when the song appeared on her *Ladies of the Canyon* album in 1970 that the line was changed to "got to get back to the land," perhaps signaling a new awareness.)[15]

Professional historians have so far subjected these most recent back-to-the-landers to relatively little close scrutiny.[16] Several accounts assert, for example, that one million people went back to the land in the 1970s. Tracing that suspiciously round number back through the footnotes brings one to a single estimate extrapolated from the study of a small area in British Columbia in 1979 — an excellent scholarly study but hardly adequate to the task of calculating an entire continent's efforts.[17] And if little is known about the scope of the movement, even less is known about who participated in it. One contemporary study of rural communes, titled *Children of Prosperity* (1973), asserted that communes and back-to-the-land experiments were the product of the unprecedented material abundance of the 1960s. (Earlier critics had asserted that back-to-the-land movements were the product of *hard* times, appearing "whenever the flood-tide of prosperity subsides."[18] Now, critics grumbled that the back-to-the-land movement arose from too *much* prosperity.) According to the author, moreover, these "children of prosperity" were "overwhelmingly white, under thirty, and from economically, educationally, and socially privileged families." The evidence for this judgment? "All observers agree."[19] Even a generation later, not much more hard data is available.

And memory can be deceptive. Helen and Scott Nearing also reported that the hundreds of young visitors who flocked to their home in Maine had been "raised in comfort if not pampered in luxury." They recalled no visitors from less privileged backgrounds: no African Americans, and no "young people whose parents worked in textile factories or steel mills."[20] Yet there is at least one significant case they appear to have forgotten. When Jean and Keith Heavrin came to visit in 1971, the Nearings welcomed the couple enthusiastically, offered them a parcel of their property, and invited them into the very select small community that surrounded their homestead. The Heavrins lived next door to the Nearings for six years, working closely with them on many projects. As it happened, Jean's own father worked all his life in a steel mill in Youngstown, Ohio, and her mother worked part-time sewing cloth toys in a factory.[21]

Popular legend attributes to the back-to-the-landers of the 1970s many of the cultural stereotypes associated with the 1960s: not only are they remembered as privileged and pampered but also as drifters and dilettantes. As the story goes, far from being concerned with security or self-sufficiency, they sought total freedom from work and discipline. When their trust funds dried up or their allowances were cut off (and "everyone knows" they had them), they found themselves completely unprepared for rural life, utterly ignorant of the basic skills they needed to survive. ("For the most part," a current unfootnoted Wikipedia entry pronounces authoritatively, "the back-to-the-landers of the 1970s were unprepared for the realities of a rural lifestyle.") The Nearings described young back-to-the-landers in just these terms. "Never before in our lives," they reported, had they met so many "unattached, uncommitted, insecure, uncertain human beings." Their visitors were "apolitical, impatient of restraints," and they understood little of the duty, self-sacrifice, and discipline that had shaped the lives of earlier back-to-the-landers. Worse still, they were woefully deficient in simple skills like hoeing and chopping wood.[22]

The Nearings, of course, contrasted their visitors with their own legendary self-discipline, ideological certainty, and multiple decades of experience. Perhaps they were not the best informants. But some of those "wandering" young people told similar stories about themselves, too, acknowledging—sometimes even celebrating—their own naïveté. Back-to-the-land writers in earlier generations had told their own tales of ignorance and lack of preparation: "Like most people who do foolish things," one author began in the 1920s, "we did it first and sought our justification afterward."[23] But the outpouring of regrets, doubts, and second thoughts that flowed from the pens of 1970s back-to-the-landers was unmatched. By the end of the twentieth century, they had generated a wide-ranging literature of reassessment: a new category of "back *from* the land" books.[24]

In spite of the rueful tone, these accounts render a mixed verdict on just how ill equipped, naïve, or ignorant back-to-the-landers of the 1970s really were. Ray Mungo's *Total Loss Farm: A Year in the Life* (1970) provides a characteristic example. In his Kerouac-inspired, rambling narrative, Mungo did his best to create the impression that he and his friends were precisely the sort of Peter

Pan–like lost children who would have frozen in the dark on their Vermont farm if left to their own devices. Referring to the other residents of the farm as "the children," Mungo named himself Pan—"who does in Captain Hook with a sweep of his wooden sword, saying: I am youth! I am joy! I am freedom!"[25] Yet Mungo also makes it clear that even these poetry-writing urban refugees had somehow learned to feed themselves from their gardens and orchards, care for farm animals, warm themselves with wood cut on their own property, and get the chores done: the "chimney cleaned, wood gathered[,] . . . new tires for the old car, radiator work on the tractor, insulate the shed."[26]

Mungo celebrated the naïveté of the "children" of his commune; others were not so pleased with themselves. One man recalled, for example, that he and his friends had built their house in such deep mountain shade that they got no sun for three months of the year. "'It was a classic city-kid thing,'" he recalled. "'We grew up in the flatlands in southern California. We had no idea.'"[27] Still, by his own account, these helpless "city kids" did manage to build a house, create a functional irrigation dam, feed themselves, and transform themselves into skilled practitioners of a variety of crafts.

Perhaps some contemporary observers judged themselves and others harshly because they were not in a position to grasp just how much had changed in the years since World War II or how difficult it had become to acquire the knowledge once taken for granted. In 1910, and indeed in 1930, a great many men had grown up with horses' harnesses, axes, and hoes; many women had learned as children to bake bread, raise chickens, and preserve food. By 1970, few young adults could call on childhood training in such rural skills. As one author commented with a touch of artistic hyperbole, "Not since the fall of Babylon have so many city dwellers wanted to 'return' to the country without ever having been there in the first place."[28]

At the same time, a critically important structural change had reconfigured the economic calculus of the back-to-the-land venture. Americans in the last half of the twentieth century, no matter what their income, now spent far less on food than ever before. By 1970, back-to-the-landers could count on saving at most 15 or even 10 percent of their total expenditures by growing their own food, as opposed to the nearly 40 percent back-to-the-landers in 1910 could have saved. So the savings generated by growing their own food did not make much of a dent in the overall budget. Other expenses—land prices, mortgages, taxes, insurance—loomed much larger. It was all very well to plan to acquire cash by growing strawberries or "camomile blossoms," as one back-to-the-lander later reflected. What to do, though, when "your taxes are going up 20 percent a year, but your income from selling camomile blossoms isn't?"[29] Hardy souls might build modest houses from scratch and pay for their land with cash, but even they could not avoid rapidly rising property taxes. Health care costs in particular placed back-to-the-landers in increasingly difficult circumstances. As one author recalled, she had once scoffed that health insurance was for "anemic organization men who smoked cigarettes and ate white bread"—but that had been before her two young sons had turned up with a crushed finger and a broken leg.[30]

Yet in spite of these fundamental economic changes, the back-to-the-landers of the 1970s still shared a great deal with those who came before. What is different about them is instructive, too.

A Cog in Something Turning

In 1977, *Mother Earth News* reported the results of a reader survey. Their half a million readers, they found, were not much like the "unwashed, unschooled, emotional, starry-eyed idealists" the editors thought people were probably expecting. They were "overwhelmingly well schooled, well cultured, and level-headed 'backbones'" of their communities. At a median age of thirty-two, *Mother's* readers were not remarkably young. Nearly 60 percent were college graduates (only 2 percent were currently students), and three-quarters were homeowners, with a median yearly income of $18,000 in 1977 dollars (substantially higher than the national median income). Over a third of the magazine's subscribers were "professional, semi-professional or technical people."[31] Sociologist Jeffrey Jacob came up with a similar profile derived from the subscription lists of the smaller, less glossy *Countryside Magazine* from the mid-1980s to the early 1990s. This group also included many relatively well-educated, property-holding married couples with children. One-quarter of them held professional positions.[32]

These studies suggest that the readers of *Mother Earth* and *Countryside*, at least (we do not know much about those who did more than read) did share some characteristics with back-to-the-landers of earlier generations.[33] They came from mostly white-collar urban (and now suburban) backgrounds, and they lived and worked in settings not entirely unlike those that had distressed back-to-the-landers in 1910. It is not surprising, then, that they registered complaints about urban life that resemble those of previous generations. They deplored the "noise, pollution, and crime" of city life, its "sirens in the night, hot asphalt, and smog."[34] "Smog" and "pollution" were popular terms in the 1960s and 1970s, of course, but this was an old grievance. They expressed a similar dislike for their jobs, too, although in a new idiom. Not only was the air "full of crud," as one *Mother Earth News* correspondent put it, but "the nine-to-five" was "a drag."[35] Another correspondent described the entire "rat race" with distaste: "Work hard in high school[,] . . . get good grades . . . go to a good college," all in order to "make lotsa bucks, and strangle in red tape for 30 years." And a third writer connected the term "rat race" favored by children of the sixties with the phrase favored by an earlier generation of back-to-the-landers: now that she and her husband had left their city jobs, they could be "individuals rather than 'cogs-in-a-wheel.'"[36]

All this is familiar, but there were also significant differences in the sensibility expressed in these new texts. Many of the hopes of early back-to-the-landers, for example, had revolved around the "halfway back to the land" option of the suburbs. Now, the suburbs seemed to offer nothing that was good: they were associated not only with traffic jams and strip malls but with mindless consumerism and a soul-destroying culture of conformity—everything new back-to-the-landers longed to escape. Now, they hoped to reconnect with the natural world far beyond the boundaries of suburbia. Correspondents to *Mother Earth News* wrote from the wilds of Alaska and northern Wisconsin, from the high deserts of California, the rain forests of British Columbia, and the abandoned farmlands of northern New England. They built houses miles from paved roads, up canyons and mountainsides, in swamps and on islands—as far away as they could get. The new writers dwelt lovingly on the prospect of "getting to know mother nature again."[37]

There was another difference, too. New back-to-the-land writers rarely expressed much concern about losing their paychecks. Nor did they typically address the topics of old age, illness, or retirement. Perhaps this was a reflection of their relative youth or of the good economic times in which they had grown up, or perhaps it reflected confidence in the Great Society's "safety nets"—Social Security, food stamps, Medicaid. By the mid-1970s, some of that was changing, to be sure. These "children of prosperity" encountered energy shortages, rising food prices, and crippling inflation—fitting parallels with the economic fears of earlier generations—and back-to-the-land writing began to reflect those concerns.[38] One 1975 book noted, for example, the "chronic shortages of everything from food to fuel to jobs that have suddenly come to plague us."[39] But the movement was born before those crises emerged, and the writing of the 1970s typically emphasized other matters.

Like many of their predecessors, indeed, this generation of back-to-the-landers shared one motive that ran deeper than the fear of losing a job. They cherished the old producerist vision of household self-sufficiency and personal independence. They celebrated the satisfactions derived from genuinely productive work. They attacked consumer culture with even greater conviction than did earlier back-to-the-landers, deploring the "gadget-filled suburban house, flashy cars, and the other nonessentials that symbolize success to most people."[40] And added to the distaste of previous generations for the constraints of the white-collar workplace was this generation's well-known impatience with the routine and conformity they associated with urban middle-class life in general. The drive "to become master of one's own schedule and deprogram oneself from imposed city routines" was pervasive in back-to-the-land literature in these years.[41]

What is more, some back-to-the-landers still perceived a return to the land as a means of safeguarding their personal and political independence. One 1971 account described a university professor who had been denied tenure because he had taken part in an antiwar demonstration: "I had the choice of becoming a radical or getting out," the man reported. (By "becoming a radical," he meant taking up arms: "Because of my beliefs on violence," he explained, "I chose to leave.")[42] An architect who went back to the land in Maine reported that he had chosen not to earn money at his profession "because I don't want to pay taxes to a government that's been lying about Vietnam and its intentions of solving social problems."[43]

Just as it had been back at the turn of the century, some back-to-the-landers in these days still connected the concept of personal autonomy with masculinity. In the first issue of *Mother Earth News*, one author's word choice demonstrated how closely his dream of personal freedom was connected with his notion of "manly" independence. Was it possible, he asked rhetorically, "to tell the boss to shove it," to "square your shoulders," and to "step out a free man?"[44] (It was probably no accident that this article was reprinted from a men's magazine called *Cavalier*.) But the connection between producerist values and masculinity, precarious to begin with, was becoming more difficult to sustain.

In some cases, female authors simply appropriated the rhetoric for themselves without comment. Patricia Crawford, for example, wrote merely that "some of us" have an "instinctive urge to return to the land and gain independence from the five-day week, the subway and the supermarket," without acknowledging that such an "instinctive urge" for independence had once been understood as a masculine instinct.[45] Others confronted the matter directly, linking producerist rhetoric directly to a resurgent feminism. "In a rural setting," one writer explained, "it is possible for a woman to live almost free of . . . male corporate dominance, *if* she has taken the trouble to develop competence in the daily details of survival."[46] (This author suggested that it was no accident that the acronym for *Mother Earth News*, "with its ploughboy interviews and emphasis on a land movement dominated by men," was MEN.)[47]

Indeed, this feminist producerism, with its association of skilled autonomous work with personal and political independence, fostered a new variant of the back-to-the-land movement. In 1976, Jeanne Tetrault and Sherry Thomas promised on the cover of their book *Country Women* to teach women "how to negotiate a land purchase, dig a well, grow vegetables organically, build a fence and shed, deliver a goat, skin a lamb, spin yarn and raise a flock of good egg-laying hens"—all "with minimum reliance on outside and professional help."[48] In addition to all that practical advice, in the sidebars *Country Women* chronicled one woman's journey away from dependence, self-doubt, and degrading work to the independence and self-reliance she achieved by learning those skills. In the late 1970s, dozens of separatist "women's land" colonies sprang up to foster women's autonomy and independence from men.[49]

For women who chose to remain in mixed-gender households, back-to-the-land values coexisted rather uneasily with second-wave feminism. Yet it is possible that the common trajectory of the two movements was not entirely coincidental. "Back from the land" narratives suggest that while both men and women worked hard on homesteads, a great deal of the sheer drudgery—carrying water, washing diapers by hand—fell to women. Still, in contrast with their mothers' work in city and suburban households, the "handmade life" often appeared liberating (at least at first) to back-to-the-land women of this generation. Outhouses and woodstoves seemed far from the sanitized suburban emptiness of Betty Friedan's "problem with no name." And self-image might matter almost as much as work, as one author reflected: "That was part of the fantasy too, the rosy wife at the kitchen door, watching her mate trudge wearily back from the fields, the setting sun at his back, to a redolent and reviving farm meal."[50]

But it was not simply romantic Earth Mother fantasies that attracted some women to this life. Jeffrey Jacob found that homestead women reported doing substantially more than their share of the hard work. Yet this unequal division of labor was less disturbing to them than it might have been had they been working in conventional urban or suburban households—not because they were living in a fantasy but precisely because they shared the fundamental producerist convictions. They perceived their work as intrinsically valuable and productive, and they saw it as a sign of their ability to make independent lives for themselves. Autonomy, skill, independence, self-sufficiency: the gender was different, but the values were the same.[51]

Back to the Garden

Some new back-to-the-landers, both men and women, saw the act of homesteading not simply as a means of protecting their independence but as a political act in itself—perhaps the last viable political act left to them. Ray Mungo stated the case eloquently in *Total Loss Farm*: "When we lived in Boston, Chicago, San Francisco, Washington," he wrote, "we dreamed of a New Age born of violent insurrection . . . we set up a countergovernment[,] . . . had marches, rallies and meetings." But as the peace movement gained momentum, something changed: "Then Johnson resigned, yes, and the universities began to fall . . . and by God every 13-year-old in the suburbs was smoking dope and our numbers multiplying into the millions." In that moment of triumph, in the spring of 1968, Mungo "woke up . . . and said, 'This is not what I had in mind.'" It was "not flowers and doves and spontaneity"—not the joyful anarchic liberation he had dreamed of—but just "another vicious system, the seed of a heartless bureaucracy." To create the kind of deep change he envisioned, only one option remained: "It was then that we put away the schedule for the revolution, gathered together our dear ones and all our resources, and set off to Vermont in search of the New Age."[52]

Another author imagined the political situation at the turn of the decade—the "political assassinations, burning cities, tear gas and bullets on university campuses, and the dragging on of war"—as "dark woods" where she and her "compatriots" had "dropped the torch." But while "so many of our egalitarian hopes were being dashed," she wrote, the "gentle revolutionaries were going right ahead"—back to the land.[53]

In what sense could these back-to-the-landers call themselves "revolutionaries"—"gentle" or otherwise? "Of course you alone cannot save the world," wrote Richard Langer in *Grow It!* "But," he added, "you can do your part."[54] They were able to envision their return to the land as an effort to "save the world" because they had adopted one idea that was almost entirely new to 1970s back-to-the-landers: the "green politics" of environmentalism. (Many early back-to-the-landers had also believed that they were engaged in an effort to "save the world," but they had been working for different goals: social justice, a broader democracy, or simply food and shelter for the poor.) Ray Mungo portrayed the back-to-the-land experiment as an almost monastic commitment to the new cause: "Pushing long hair out of their way and thus marking their foreheads with beautiful penitent dust," Mungo wrote, they "till the soil to atone for our fathers' destruction of it."[55]

The new environmentalist perspective added moral weight to the cause, as Mungo's quasi-religious language implies. "There is no adventure greater than ours," Mungo wrote. "We are the last life on the planet, it is for us to launch the New Age, to grow up to be *men* and *women* of earth, and free of the walking dead who precede us."[56] At the same time, environmentalism linked the new urgency of protecting the earth to the old goal of self-sufficiency. John Shuttleworth, the founder, editor, and publisher of *Mother Earth News*, explained in 1975 how inextricably the two were intertwined. Take a man "out of the big car and off the freeways," he proposed, and "show him how to quit the corporate job he hates." What would be the result? First, "You've given that guy's life back to him," and second, "you've lessened the impact on the planet as much as if you had cut the population of India by 50." That, he wrote, was "what MOTHER was created to do."[57]

John and Sally Seymour's *Farming for Self-Sufficiency* also made the case that environmentalism was a natural companion to the search for self-sufficiency. "Just as we cannot, for ever, go on . . . suppressing every species of life on the land except one money-making crop, so we cannot go on for ever ourselves living in human battery cages," they wrote. Humans in industrial society were no better off than the suffering animals trapped in the industrial food system— "hens in wire cages, or pigs in total darkness." Their analysis was apocalyptic: "It's all going to collapse." Perhaps there would be an environmental disaster— "the oil will run out, or the grub, or the uranium-235." They hoped, instead, that it would be human patience with industrial society that would reach its limit: "the power of Man to withstand the unutterable *boredom* of it all."[58]

The apocalyptic note in this passage would probably not have sounded strange to readers at the time. These years witnessed more than their share of wrenching change: the traumatic final stages of the Vietnam War; wildly unpredictable economic fluctuations; a government in profound political and moral crisis; and the first clear signs that the world was reaching what has now become known as "peak oil" production. But early back-to-the-landers, too, had shared a sense of urgency. Recall the rhetoric of the mild-mannered William Ellsworth Smythe at the 1911 National Irrigation Congress, predicting bloody revolution if land were not distributed more equitably, or the "dark-winged hawk" that "shadowed the world" and hovered over the nightmares of Gove Hambidge in 1935.[59]

This time around, however, the apocalypse seemed to threaten even more than revolution or the collapse of American capitalism; now it threatened global environmental catastrophe. Jackson Browne's haunting 1974 song "Before the Deluge" linked the back-to-the-land impulse with the coming environmental cataclysm: "With the energy of the innocent," went Browne's lyrics, "they were gathering the tools / they would need to make their journey back to nature"— but time was running out, sand slipping inexorably through the hourglass. "When the sand was gone and the time arrived / In the naked dawn only a few survived." But even this 1970s-style millennialism was not without historical roots. Richard Langer opened the first chapter of his 1972 back-to-the-land book *Grow It!* with a return to a very old apocalyptic vision, William Jennings Bryan's populist agrarian warning: "destroy our farms and the grass will grow in the streets of every city."[60]

A Hundred (Decentralist) Flowers Bloom

The back-to-the-landers of the 1970s were the rightful heirs of a long history of plans, ideas, experiments, and projects. They could lay claim to a wide array of legacies from the past, from single-tax colonies to garden suburbs to New Deal federal programs. First, however, they would need to be informed of those earlier efforts. That task was up to the writers, editors, and publishers who interpreted the movement to itself.

A few writers in the 1970s were keenly aware of the link between their own efforts and those of their forerunners, at least as far back as the 1930s. "If you're too young and tender to remember," John Shuttleworth editorialized in 1973, "almost every subject (except alternative sources of power) featured so far in MOTHER was covered just as earnestly during the Great Depression of the 30's . . . and again throughout World War II."[61] David Robinson, author of *The Complete Homesteading Book* (1974), reminded his readers that "The movement from the cities to the country is not something that started in 1970. . . . In a way it started in the 1930s when many realized that being short of cash is less painful in the country."[62] (Robinson's insight probably grew from his connection with the Garden Way Publishing Company, one of several companies with roots in the business Ed and Carolyn Robinson had founded when they brought out their "Have-More Plan" in the 1940s.) Anarchist intellectual Paul Goodman made the same point in his introduction to the 1970 edition of *Living the Good Life*: young people probably believed they had invented the back-to-the-land movement, "just as they imagine they invented pacifism, sit-ins, self-reliance, participatory democracy, progressive education, and sexual freedom"—but in fact they had not. Goodman advised them to look back in time for inspiration, "to take seriously the Thirties' ideas of the Nearings, Borsodi, Frank Lloyd Wright, and the Southern Regionalists."[63]

That would not take them all the way back to the beginning of the story, of course. Nor were all of the strands of back-to-the-land thought equally well represented among the cultural mediators of the 1970s. By far the most prominent were those texts that reflected the decentralist philosophy of Ralph Borsodi. During the 1940s and 1950s, as political dissent became increasingly constrained, decentralists in Borsodi's circle had made connections with a variety of radicals at the margins of contemporary political debate: radical pacifists, diet and sex reformers, and advocates of biodynamic and organic farming. A young man named Robert Swann, for example, was introduced to Borsodi's work over the course of the two years he spent in prison as a conscientious objector during World War II. (Swann had been arrested while staying with friends on a farm near the radical back-to-the-land community in the Nearings' neighborhood of Pikes Falls, Vermont.)[64] He later collaborated with Borsodi in developing two of the most innovative tools to come out of the decentralist/ environmentalist matrix of the 1970s: the community land trust and local currency (a system that uses vouchers of its own to replace legal currency and facilitate a more equitable local exchange of goods and services).

Swann played another important role in disseminating decentralist ideas. In 1969, having read an essay by E. F. Schumacher in the British journal *Resurgence*, Swann traveled to London to meet with Schumacher and later arranged for Schumacher to undertake a speaking tour in the United States to publicize his new book *Small Is Beautiful: Economics as if People Mattered* (1973). Schumacher's book was perhaps the most influential reintroduction of decentralist ideas during the 1970s. In it, he contended that large-scale systems and a model of endless growth are neither environmentally sustainable nor good for human society. Schumacher labeled his vision of small-scale communities and small-scale technologies "Buddhist economics." (Some critics have suggested that it might have been more accurate, if less popular, to call it "Catholic economics," perceiving in Schumacher's ideas a similarity to those of the distributists and Catholic agrarians of the 1930s.) *Small Is Beautiful* quickly became a classic; the concepts of "enough-ness" and "appropriate technology" spread rapidly into mainstream discourse.

By then, a resurgent decentralism was circulating among reformers and dissenters of many stripes, from Students for a Democratic Society in the 1960s to the antinuclear Clamshell Alliance in the 1970s.[65] It was Borsodi's protégé Mildred Jensen Loomis who played the most critical role in linking 1930s-style decentralism with the new causes.[66] Loomis edited the magazine originally called the *Interpreter* (renamed *Balanced Living* in 1958, then *A Way Out* in 1962), which almost single-handedly kept the homesteading dream alive in the late 1950s and early 1960s. Then in 1963 Loomis introduced *Green Revolution*, a magazine aimed specifically at creating a new reading audience among students.[67]

By 1977, the year Borsodi died, *Green Revolution* had embraced a wide variety of pacifist, anarchist, and communitarian movements, linking them to organic gardening, self-sufficiency, and back-to-the-land projects of many stripes. They had forged especially close ties with the Clamshell Alliance, which that year staged its greatest demonstration against a proposed nuclear power plant in

Seabrook, New Hampshire. (Clamshell Alliance would introduce many organizers to the tactic of forming autonomous small "affinity groups"—an anarchist
model that was very much at home on the pages of *Green Revolution*.) Mildred
Loomis wrote a tribute to Borsodi in that 1977 issue, classing him with Confucius,
John Ruskin, and Thomas Edison—men who had improved human life through
quiet work unrecognized in their lifetimes.[68] But it was Loomis herself who
fostered this rich cultural matrix.

In the pages of *Mother Earth News*, John Shuttleworth made a similar effort
to bring decentralist ideas into a new milieu. Shuttleworth steered his magazine
away from ideological statements, preferring brisk and practical "how-to" articles. As he explained, "hating theory the way I do, I thought we should plunge
right in with firsthand reports from people who had already carved out some
part of the decentralist life for themselves."[69] Especially in the early years,
Mother's editorial voice was broadly tolerant, reporting with approval all kinds of
back-to-the-land experiments, whether conducted by rugged individualists, followers of a charismatic leader, or tight-knit anarchist collectives. In a major 1975
assessment, Shuttleworth indicted such a wide array of evil forces that almost
anyone might have agreed with him. "The military-industrial complex and agri-
biz and the corporate structure" were to blame, he wrote, but also "sprawling
suburbs and blind human greed and planet-damaging shortsightedness."[70]

By 1979, however, Shuttleworth's tone was changing. While Loomis's *Green
Revolution* moved toward alliances with the left, Shuttleworth's populism grew
angrier. He himself grew increasingly nostalgic for his childhood, "that magical
time and place in history when a man's word was his bond." Shuttleworth recalled those days as a cross between a Jeffersonian paradise and an episode of
the 1950s television sit-com *Leave It to Beaver*: "The strong helped the weak[,] . . .
people stayed married once they got that way[,] . . . and people could . . . leave
their homes unlocked for weeks at a time and find nothing out of place when
they returned." For the destruction of that utopia, he now blamed "the unholy
trio of modern society—Big Government, Big Business, and Big Labor"—
which "trample[d] a free and proud way of life underfoot."[71] Shuttleworth was
still in the fold, but by his last year or two with the magazine, he had moved to
the far right wing of the decentralist spectrum.

The Nearings—Again

Whether younger readers were aware of it or not, decentralists—both left and
right wing—provided most of the ideological framework of the back-to-the-
land project in the 1970s. So it is all the more interesting that the most celebrated

and influential of all 1970s back-to-the-landers came from a different ideological direction altogether. Helen and Scott Nearing were the darlings of the back-to-the-land press; the lucidity of their prose, their embrace of health food and vegetarianism, and perhaps most of all, the sheer novelty of such elderly people with such radical beliefs made them especially attractive. The Nearings collaborated with Ralph Borsodi on several occasions, and they occasionally mentioned the work of decentralists approvingly, but Scott Nearing was no decentralist. He was not an orthodox Marxist, either, to be sure; he had been thrown out of the Communist Party in 1930 for what one critic called his "mystic individualism."[72] Nevertheless, to the end of his days, Nearing maintained his faith in centralized global socialism.

Back-to-the-landers did not usually perceive Helen and Scott Nearing in these ideological terms, however; often they seemed to be viewed simply as older and more experienced versions of their fans. In 1977, Shuttleworth described the Nearings as if they were the embodiment of the values of middle America: "hardworking, proud people who pay their dues, think for themselves, and stand on their own two feet." He acknowledged that they had not always been "honored in every corner of this nation," recounting the story of how Scott's pacifism had gotten him blacklisted in the First World War.[73] But he did not mention the couple's opposition to the "good war," World War II (which had alienated Scott even from his Communist associates); their visit to the Soviet Union and the People's Republic of China in 1957, at the height of the Cold War; or their decades-long resistance to American imperialism. Few people in the 1970s knew much about any of that. One report has it that after Helen's death, when the Good Life Center was established to carry on the Nearings' legacy, even many members of the governing board were unaware of the couple's political radicalism, still seeing them only as exponents of that "good life."[74]

Indeed, in one interview in *Mother Earth News*, Scott Nearing himself seemed to downplay his own radicalism.[75] Shuttleworth asked Nearing what he thought about communes and the "shared ownership of machinery," giving him a clear opportunity to talk about socialism. Nearing replied: "Admirable, admirable[,] . . . provided you can find a group of congenial people who . . . will stay together long enough so that they can make their experiment a success." Some communes, he explained patiently, "have gone along until September and October before they began to cut their winter wood," when it "should have been cut in April or the previous October." Nearing evidently wanted to talk about something other than collectivism: "You can't wait until the last minute to make provision for food, shelter and fuel. These things have to be

The photograph is labeled "Professor Scott Nearing," but those who admired Nearing later in his life might have found it difficult to recognize him in this elegantly dressed young academic. The studied pose and unwavering gaze say more about Nearing's Victorian roots than his radicalism. (George Grantham Bain Collection, Library of Congress)

very carefully worked out in advance. It can't be done off the cuff."[76] (Helen added a similar nod to the mainstream, advising the would-be homesteader to "work hard" and to "find the right mate.")

Perhaps Nearing changed the subject not to gloss over his political beliefs but because efficient work habits were nearly as important to him as socialism. Nearing had come of age in the progressive era, but like many reformers of his generation, he had been trained in Victorian habits of order, discipline, and self-control. Like many progressive reformers, too, he never lost his faith in those earlier standards. Nearing was admired in the 1970s for his austere personal habits, his work ethic, and simply his longevity (not many people had ever seen a ninety-year-old man wield a garden spade with such proficiency). But his habits were rooted in a long-ago culture that few observers in the 1970s recognized or understood.

Many fans, for example, admired the Nearings' rejection of meat, refined flour, and processed sugar. These dietary habits made the Nearings seem up-to-date, as if they had jumped aboard the latest countercultural bandwagon. In 1971, Frances Moore Lappé's *Diet for a Small Planet* had offered Americans a new politics of food, and in 1973, the influential vegetarian Moosewood Restaurant had opened. But the Nearings' dietary habits had been formed long before all that. Their practices were not based on recent ideas but on much earlier, mostly nineteenth-century, scientific and ethical arguments. (Few vegetarian cooks of the 1970s would have argued as they did, that the "craving for concentrated protein foods is an acquired and a dangerous habit.")[77] Helen had been brought up from childhood as a vegetarian, as was consistent with her parents' theosophical beliefs, while Scott had become a vegetarian in the 1910s, during his summers at Arden.

In *Loving and Leaving the Good Life*, Helen acknowledged that she and Scott were inclined by temperament to the austerities they practiced: "Something in me likes to be cold when other people are toasting around a fire; to fast when others are feasting; to work when others are lounging. As with Scott, there is something of an ascetic and puritan in me."[78] Their diet was not just simple, it was monastic: "To eat little and of few things is a good guide for health and for simplicity," they wrote in *Living the Good Life*.[79] They never touched alcohol, or coffee, or tobacco, or any of the recreational drugs so popular in those years. They made it a habit to fast on days when others feasted: Thanksgiving, Christmas, New Year's Day.[80] It was characteristic that Scott, having reached the age of one hundred, chose to end his life by fasting—simply intensifying a lifelong habit of self-denial.

Struggling with the Good Life

In the 1970s, most people who encountered the Nearings in print or in person would have understood little about their Victorian mind-set and almost as little about their radical politics. That lack of comprehension might not have mattered much, but, as it turned out, the Nearings were to be virtually the sole representatives of the early back-to-the-land perspectives that were not rooted in decentralist ideology. There were no reprints in *Mother Earth News* of the anarchist Kropotkin's argument that food self-sufficiency would strengthen the position of the people when the barricades went up. No one recounted the stories of the Jewish socialists, Zionists, and anarchists who founded back-to-the-land communities across the nation from the 1880s through the 1930s. No one remembered the Little Lands colonies; few even recalled the single-tax enclaves. *Mother Earth News* was able to locate and reprint selections from *Ten Acres Enough*, a book that had first seen the light of day in 1864. Yet somehow, they overlooked single-tax advocate Bolton Hall's *Three Acres and Liberty* and socialist Charles Smart's *R.F.D.*[81]

That was not the only blind spot in the literature of the 1970s. Neither the socially mainstream suburban farm projects of the 1920s nor the ambitious liberal subsistence homestead programs of the New Deal formed part of any acknowledged legacy. The common term for back-to-the-landers in the 1970s, for example, was "homesteader." Helen and Scott Nearing even used the phrase "subsistence homestead" to describe their experiment in *Living the Good Life*. But it appears that no one associated the phrase with the New Deal's subsistence homesteads program, which came into being in the same year that the Nearings went back to the land.[82] "Homestead" was also the word Ralph Borsodi had used to describe his family's establishment in *This Ugly Civilization*, back in 1929. Borsodi knew, of course, that the New Deal programs were also called "subsistence homesteads," but since he had been bitterly disappointed with his experiences working on one of those projects, he wanted no confusion between his "homesteads" and theirs.

Ultimately, these silences were about something even more fundamental than political ideology. Out of a past crowded with ordinary people of many different backgrounds and views, the culture brokers of the 1970s drew attention to a handful of radical individualists who—whatever their ideological commitments—essentially operated alone. In *The Complete Homesteading Book*, for example, David Robinson explained that many people had embraced back-to-the-land projects during the Depression, when "the economic system itself seemed to have gone askew." To illustrate that point, however, he pointed to the Nearings, the Robinsons, and Borsodi. He wrote not a word about the thousands of participants in the New Deal's homestead programs.

That choice was probably largely unconscious, but it had far-reaching consequences. Perhaps most important, it meant that stories about back-to-the-land *communities*—with all their rich potential both as models and as cautionary tales—did not appear in the literature of the back-to-the-land movement in the 1970s. No Little Landers, with their high hopes and homemade houses. No Arden, where Scott Nearing learned to garden and build with stone. No Jersey Homesteads, where a man could turn to the camera and ask, "Who says Jews can't farm?" Back-to-the-landers who attempted to create communities on the land in the 1970s were in great need of models. They might have had many, but they knew of very few.

At the same time, the focus on a few extraordinary individuals seemed to encourage a relentless scrutiny of the personal purity and ideological consistency of back-to-the-landers, leaving them open to criticism from every side and vulnerable to the disillusionment that follows unrealistic expectations. The furor over the Nearings' legacy is typical. Over time, the Nearings' own rigid principles were turned against them, as critics came to point out the many ways they failed to live up to the standards they erected for others.[83] In spite of their vociferous vegetarianism, for example, it appears that the Nearings did not reject all animal products. Helen ate ice cream. She even had a cat, and no one who read *Living the Good Life* could forget their assertion that domestic animals were "slaves."

Worse yet, the Nearings did not move to Vermont penniless, and over time, they managed to buy nearly a thousand acres of land with money the source of which they were quite vague about in their published accounts. Nor did the Nearings subsist entirely on the products of their farm. Scott lectured, they wrote, and both had access to other sources of income. None of this would have mattered, of course, had the Nearings not been designated—had they not set themselves up—as models of personal and ideological purity. In part, it was simply the old problem: back-to-the-land narratives had always been held to very high standards of veracity. Like Ray Stannard Baker's David Grayson stories and William Lighton's stories of his home in the Ozarks, the Nearings' books were scrutinized with great care—and for exactly the same reason. Thousands of readers wanted to know whether it would be possible for them to do what the Nearings had done. Like readers before them, they looked for literal fidelity to truth, and like their predecessors, they found contradictions, silences, and misstatements, as they would doubtless have found in almost any personal narrative. It simply mattered more with back-to-the-land books, particularly to those readers who—unlike the Nearings—would have to make do without donations from old friends, family inheritances, or the help of hundreds of young visitors.

But there was another difficulty here, too. To take the Nearings as models was a problematic choice, and not simply because they turned out to have human failings. There is the curious fact that many 1970s back-to-the-landers seem to have had the benefit of *fewer* comforts and conveniences than their predecessors, even fewer than those who lived through the dark days of the Great Depression. Eleanor Agnew reports from her interviews with back-to-the-landers that most of them heated with wood, used outdoor latrines and chamber pots, and got their water from wells and streams.[84] Even in the earliest years of the twentieth century, a great many farm families had managed better than to fetch their water in open buckets from streams. (Many simple intermediate technologies were more efficient than a hand-carried bucket, if not so convenient as a city water system.) The outhouses of long ago were at least often located in connected outbuildings rather than somewhere out in the snow, as were those of many later back-to-the-landers.

Some of the primitive conditions of the 1970s were doubtless simply a consequence of a lack of cash. Others were probably the product of that much-discussed ignorance and lack of preparation: one poor soul, for example, recalled risking life and limb, standing up to his armpits in snow wielding a chainsaw in his numb hands in order to cut down green wood to keep his wife and himself from freezing.[85] But more often, these back-to-the-landers seem to have been motivated by a desire to shake off all contact with modern life, to return to a kind of prelapsarian state of simplicity. One reminiscence described the homesteading life as a series of rejections: "Nothing metal or plastic or china will ever touch our lips again. No alarm clocks, radios. No newspapers except to start the cookstove." In an amused tone, author Linda Tatelbaum summed up her earlier exalted state of mind: "The seasons rule us. We are one with the woods."[86]

Perhaps there *was* something uniquely "penitential" in the back-to-the-land project of the 1970s, as Ray Mungo imagined. Many homesteaders seem to have shared the Nearings' moral absolutism. Jackson Browne's 1974 "Before the Deluge" passes a weighty, almost biblical judgment on those who tried to make the journey "back to nature" and found themselves too weak for that arduous trip. In the words of the song: "In the end they traded their tired wings / For the resignation that living brings." Like Esau with his pottage, they "exchanged love's bright and fragile glow" for the false "glitter and rouge" of modern civilization.

Browne left little doubt as to the fate of those who could not keep the faith: "In a moment they were swept before the deluge." The perception that a return to the land was an all-or-nothing proposition encouraged some back-to-the-landers to try to avoid all contact with modern life. One reported, with a dash of humor, that in the early days of her journey back to the land, she had frequently burst out with threats of rejecting not just modernity but civilization itself: "I'm going to go live in a cave!" she would shout. "I'll dress in animal skins, I'll eat wild greens, I'll cut myself off from complicity with this world!"[87] She was laughing at herself, of course, but the word "complicity" carries a heavy moral significance that cannot be laughed away entirely.

Jean Hay Bright recalled that she and her husband had gone to a great deal of trouble to avoid even the aesthetic marks of modernity: they had squared the exposed beams of their ceiling by hand, with a hatchet rather than a chainsaw. "We didn't want to have to stare up at the marks of mechanical civilization as we lay exhausted in our bed at night," she explained, ruefully adding, "such principles."[88] In this case, it appears the Nearings were directly inciting such romantic gestures. Bright reports that the couple had asked her husband to reshape some *machine*-made beams (imported from "Oregon to the Pine Tree State of Maine," no less) so that they would *look* handmade.[89]

In fact, the struggle over the Nearing legacy was not simply about *their* trust funds or *their* handmade homes; it reflected an anxiety common in this generation of back-to-the-landers. Complete personal and ideological consistency proved elusive. Linda Tatelbaum concluded in later years that achieving freedom from "complicity" with the modern world was not possible: "Even woodsmoke from my two stoves is an air pollutant, and my solar electric panels are made from silicone, copper, plastic, rubber." Referring once again to her original threat to go "live in a cave," she concluded, "I'll never be pure unless I go live in a cave and wear animal skins. But then I'd have to kill animals, wouldn't I?"[90]

The struggle for consistency, moreover, can lead to a kind of competition that spirals downward: *you* pump your water by hand, *she* brings it in from an outdoor well, but *I* carry it in buckets from a stream. Perhaps it may also help to explain the legend of the trust funds—belonging, apparently, to whoever was *not* telling the tale. Agnew reports that it was not just the Nearings who found it necessary to be vague about their resources. Others "who also happened to have a nest egg were careful to keep it quiet and spend it unobtrusively."[91] "Keeping up with the Nearings," Tatelbaum concluded perceptively, was "just another form of rat-race."[92]

This kind of "rat race" was something new. Earlier back-to-the-landers had not typically valued hardship for its own sake or flaunted it as a badge of honor.

Returning to the land had entailed a rejection of the role of consumer, to be sure, but most early back-to-the-landers had intended to *better* their material conditions, not sacrifice all comfort to a higher good. Borsodi had explained in 1929, for example, that he did not advocate "poverty and barrenness for the sake of its 'beauty'" or "hard manual labor for its 'moral' value." He advocated homesteading precisely because it provided "economic independence, and . . . a richer and fuller life."[93] Back-to-the-landers in the 1970s might have heard of Borsodi, but most knew little or nothing about the many earlier projects that had not followed the Nearings' model. They did not know that thousands of people—not just a handful of brave iconoclasts—had attempted to work out lives on the land. Among those thousands were many who had gone only "halfway" back to the land, who had kept their day jobs, or saved up to retire on small farms—people who had not cut themselves off from the mainstream, or from mainstream comforts, any more than was necessary in order to pursue their goals.

Perhaps it was the lofty standards—and the inevitable falling short of those standards—that generated the flood of memoirs revisiting, second-guessing, and judging the choices made in the 1970s. One writer, for example, later judged her earlier ideals to have been "indulgent, naïve and self-righteous." The problem, she thought, lay in thinking of the back-to-the-land project in moral terms at all. Rural life, she wrote, "should be viewed as an aesthetic choice, not an ethical one."[94] Another rejected not only the back-to-the-land project but the entire idea of trying to change anything: "The error was, I think, imagining that there was somewhere new to go, someone new to be." That mistake was understandable "in light of youthful exuberance and hope," he acknowledged, but it had been childish to hope to change human nature and society.[95]

Perhaps the fault did not lie with moral seriousness and high ideals, as these writers suggest. If there was any real fault here, it may have been the notion— common enough in the last quarter of the century—that individual consumer choices, no matter how self-denying, could substitute for political action. Many—perhaps most—back-to-the-landers of this period understood clearly the necessity for public action, in spite of a widely shared sense of disillusionment with politics. Jeffrey Jacob found that the back-to-the-landers he studied in the 1980s, at least, were extraordinarily committed to environmental causes, belonging to advocacy groups at a rate of three to five times the national average, with nearly half giving money to reform groups.[96] Even if some began their back-to-the-land journey believing they were leaving politics forever, those who stuck it out often learned otherwise, as they confronted the need to protect the land and neighborhoods they came to cherish.[97]

Yet in the 1970s, a return to the land was sometimes perceived as an effort to send a message by *not* consuming—like a general consumer boycott of everything at once. Early back-to-the-landers had not typically viewed their cause in quite this way. Of course, they had believed that being able to provide one's own food and shelter was a worthy goal, but they did not generally equate that "one way out" with politics. Whatever their other political commitments—single-tax, anarchist, socialist, decentralist, progressive, or New Deal liberal—they had imagined a return to the land as a necessary but not sufficient component of those efforts. The back-to-the-land project could certainly contribute to the realization of political goals, but change would not come simply by purifying oneself of "complicity" with corrupt politics, or industrial capitalism, or modernity.

In the end, the remarkable thing about the back-to-the-landers of the 1970s is not that they often failed, as it seems, to live up to their own expectations. The remarkable thing is that they made the effort at all. So many forces were operating against that decision. So much that had motivated earlier back-to-the-landers did not worry the new generation—and so many new worries had appeared. In striking contrast to the past, the hard times of the 1970s increasingly turned the economic calculus *against* back-to-the-landers rather than in their favor, as prices rose for things that had now become necessities.[98] Rising land prices, taxes, and medical costs—along with cheaper food—made the whole project less financially viable with each passing year. On top of that, larger-than-life images of a few extraordinary individuals effectively shut out a range of more gradual—or collective—alternatives to going "all the way back to the land." A generation's widespread disillusionment with politics-as-usual seems also to have combined with a still-powerful sense of personal responsibility to create, for some, a burdensome guilt that insinuated itself into the details of everyday life. That people continued to go back to the land in the face of all those challenges says a great deal about the persistence of the dream.

Epilogue

Home, Land, Security

Another boom, another bust. In the Reagan era, in spite of increasing in-equality, high unemployment, and an eroding middle class, the gospel of wealth attracted more followers than the gospel of simplicity. During the 1980s, *Countryside Magazine's* subscriptions fell from forty thousand to four thousand. (They were able to survive, as editor J. D. Belanger recalled, only by grace of a new word processing machine quaintly named "Macintosh," which cut their costs enough to save them to fight another day.)[1] *Mother Earth News* struggled to find new readers, replacing its gritty stories of living in the backwoods on next to nothing with instructions for backyard do-it-yourself projects. (Even today, letters appear in other magazines deploring the "selling out" of *Mother*.)

Still, as in the 1920s, a careful observer would find a lot beneath the surface. In 1981, a new "simple life" book appeared that would eventually be followed by many of its kind: Duane Elgin's *Voluntary Simplicity: Toward a Way of Life That Is Outwardly Simple, Inwardly Rich*. Topics that in the 1970s were closely associated with back-to-the-land projects—alternative energy, owner-built housing, or-ganic food—were still attracting plenty of attention. *Organic Gardening* magazine floundered a bit in the 1980s, but its parent company Rodale Press continued to publish books on subjects from solar energy to herbal medicine. Gene Logsdon, who had published *Two-Acre Eden* (1971) and *Homesteading: How to Find New Independence on the Land* (1973) with Rodale, took the change in stride. Logsdon went on writing books that taught homesteading skills—*Wildlife in Your Garden* (1983), *Practical Skills: A Revival of Forgotten Crafts* (1985), *The Low-Maintenance*

227

House (1987)—but the titles avoided back-to-the-land rhetoric. Like Bolton Hall's radical colleagues in the 1920s, for a few years the whole project became "less conspicuous."

In 1984, however, Don Mitchell published the first of his books about going back to the land in Vermont: *Moving Upcountry: A Yankee Way of Knowledge.* (This subtitle was a pun on Carlos Castañeda's tale of peyote-inspired enlightenment, *The Teachings of Don Juan: A Yacqui Way of Knowledge.*) And in the same year, Ian and Margo Baldwin left New York City—also for Vermont, where they founded Chelsea Green Press. That press would eventually become very "conspicuous" indeed, evolving into a latter-day (although much smaller-scale) equivalent of the back-to-the-land publishing powerhouse of Doubleday, Page nearly a century earlier. In an account reminiscent of William Ellsworth Smythe's 1921 description of his own readers, who used to "send for seed catalogues—and dream," Ian Baldwin explained to a *New York Times* reporter in 1999 that Chelsea Green's readers were not all back-to-the-landers; many of them, too, simply "like[d] to dream."[2] By the 1990s, books were pouring from the press to inspire those dreams: of wind power and solar heat, straw bale houses and composting toilets, permaculture and community gardens. Eliot Coleman, who for many years had worked closely with Helen and Scott Nearing, published his pioneering gardening guides *New Organic Grower* (1989) and *Four-Season Harvest* (1992). Shepherd Ogden, grandson of the Vermont back-to-the-land author Samuel Ogden, published *Straight-Ahead Organic* (1999). And Gene Logsdon returned to his old outspoken ways: in *The Contrary Farmer* (1993), he proposed a widespread return to small-scale self-sufficient homesteads, now calling them "cottage farms."

Judging from history, only one thing more was needed to trigger another full-scale back-to-the-land movement: a depression, perhaps, or some other kind of social crisis. As it happened, there would be no shortage of such disasters in the next few years. At the turn of the millennium, a false crisis—the anticipated "Y2K" collapse in the year 2000—was followed by a real one, in the wake of the 2001 attacks on New York and Washington. Two drawn-out and costly American wars ensued, and even these were often overshadowed by other calamities. Energy prices rose and fell with alarming volatility, and a series of hurricanes, floods, and droughts seemed to portend catastrophic climate change. When in 2007 a housing bubble burst, triggering a bank panic and a stock market crash, Americans were suddenly confronting nearly every kind of crisis that had threatened and inspired back-to-the-landers over the previous hundred years.

It should come as no surprise that by decade's end there was a spike in demand for garden seeds.[3] In 2009, veteran *New York Times* columnist Verlyn Klinkenborg gave the reason: "Growing a vegetable garden isn't going to balance the budget or replace lost benefits or even begin to make up for the shock of a lost job," he explained, "but part of the crisis we face is a sense of alienation and powerlessness."[4] In a move reminiscent of Franklin Roosevelt's reassuring Depression-era gestures, in 2009 the new Democratic president and his wife dug up part of the White House lawn and planted a vegetable garden. The First Lady and her elementary school assistants harvested a thousand pounds of food in the first year. The next season, they increased the size of the garden.[5]

All kinds of projects for self-sufficiency were becoming popular: not just vegetable gardens but also chicken coops appeared in suburbs, cities, and even apartment buildings. At last count, 245 "chicken enthusiasts" were signed up to be part of an online "Los Angeles Urban Chicken Group" founded in 2009.[6] In 2010, a *New York Times* reporter interviewed people who were responding to the financial crisis by spending less and doing more for themselves. A retired nurse from Texas pointed out what by then seemed all too clear: "We cannot rely on money and the banking system and government to come up with all the answers." This woman was no back-to-the-lander—yet—but she had started to bake her own bread, and she looked wistfully back to a time "years ago" when people were "more self-reliant and were more able to take hold of the reins and do things themselves."[7]

Although there was nostalgia in that remark, it was partly based on fact. Perhaps the back-to-the-landers of the 1970s had once seemed ill-equipped for a self-sufficient life, but how much more unprepared was this new generation, at a time when even the simplest home cooking was becoming an esoteric skill? But if the back-to-the-landers of the new century would need more help than ever before, they would also be more likely to find it. Emblazoned on the cover of the January 2009 issue of *Mother Earth News* was the old slogan "Back to the Land." In 2008, *Countryside* began a new "Greenhorn Series" specifically to advise first-time back-to-the-landers. Old books reappeared. *One Acre and Security* (1972) was reissued in 2000, *Five Acres and Independence* (1935) in 2009. Even the 1864 back-to-the-land book *Ten Acres Enough* was published in a "revived" edition in 2008. And this time around, it was not just books: blogs, online magazines, and videos abounded, rich with possibilities that would have pleased Bolton Hall, who had once had to resort to lending copies of his books to people who could not afford to buy them. So far, no press has picked up Hall's *Three Acres and Liberty*—but anyone can read it on Google Books.

New Growth

It is not quite the same movement this time around. Just as previous generations changed the message to suit their conditions, the writers and activists of the new century have forged a distinctive approach to the old concerns. For one thing, the words "food" and "politics" no longer sound strange in the same sentence. In fact, food has provided the focus of a new critique of industrial urban and suburban society. With the publication of *The Omnivore's Dilemma* (2006), Michael Pollan became the best-known spokesperson for this politics of food. Pollan's approach was restrained, but there was no avoiding the implications of his reporting: *The Omnivore's Dilemma* was a full-blown denunciation of the environmentally destructive, inhumane, unhealthy industrial system by which most food is produced and distributed in the United States. Even the systems that produce organic foods, Pollan maintained, are implicated in the global network of unsustainable oil-guzzling and soil-destroying agricultural practices.

Pollan has been far from alone. In the first decade of the new millennium half a dozen articulate, passionate, and influential authors embarked on extensive inquiries into industrial food production and distribution systems and into the American way of eating. Eric Schlosser's *Fast Food Nation* (2001) launched a comprehensive attack on fast food corporations, denouncing their injustice to workers, the cruelty of the meat processing system they underwrite, and their manipulation of cash-strapped schools to get their products into the hands of children. Schlosser even echoed the analysis of the decentralists of the 1930s, who had blamed modern industrialism for destroying regional cultures: he accused the fast food industry of "obliterating regional differences, and spreading identical stores throughout the country like a self-replicating code."[8] *Fast Food Nation* became a movie, and was joined by other documentary films—*Supersize Me* (2004), *King Corn* (2007), and *Food, Inc.* (2008)—each of which brought the American food system under intense scrutiny.

These exposés shared a new consciousness of the vulnerability of systems based on cheap energy. Suddenly (though not for the first time), the prospect of running out of oil seemed imminent—and now it was clearly linked with running out of food. Canadian journalist Paul Roberts followed up his monitory *The End of Oil* (2005) with the even more ominously titled *The End of Food* (2006). This clear and apparently unbreakable link between oil and the industrial food system contributed to the emergence of another new idea. Now it was eating from local food sources that appeared to be what back-to-the-landers a century before had called "one way out." Nutritionist Joan Dye Gussow in *This Organic Life* (2001) and ethnobotanist Gary Paul Nabhan in *Coming Home to Eat* (2002) offered the first of many arguments in favor of shifting toward regionally produced seasonal foods: better tasting and more nutritious, they are also less dependent on fragile transportation networks. In 2007, two narratives about local eating—Barbara Kingsolver's *Animal, Vegetable, Miracle* and Alisa Smith and J. B. Mackinnon's *The Hundred-Mile Diet: A Year of Eating Locally*—made the best-sellers' lists.

The "locavore" movement is not quite a back-to-the-land movement in itself. But it may prove to be a major promoter of the old back-to-the-land goals. Its most immediate effect is to create markets for products that in most areas can be supplied only by rapidly increasing the number of farmers. In its early stages locavore demand focuses on well-known summer vegetables and fruits. The farms that can best meet that demand for tomatoes, corn, and berries will typically be small and intensively cultivated, requiring relatively little start-up money or high-tech equipment but a great deal of personal attention and skill— an excellent opportunity for back-to-the-landers, as Peter Kropotkin and Bolton Hall had argued back at the turn of the previous century. As the locavore idea grows in sophistication, moreover, consumers look beyond tomatoes in August. Local sauerkraut and applesauce appear on shelves: someone nearby must grow those apples and cabbages, too. Demand for local cheese, meat, and eggs requires a different crop of farmers. Cheesemakers are needed, and small-scale processing plants; raising those animals on grass (not feeding them corn as the factory farms do) demands skills of a different kind.

Local eating brings both consumers and producers onto new terrain. Not many people, for example, live where olive oil can be said to be a "local" product: what will consumers choose to replace that popular item? Sunflower oil? Butter? Lard? (Indeed, the hitherto unthinkably plebian lard has actually begun to appear in co-ops and upscale markets.) And such dilemmas for consumers create widely expanded opportunities for back-to-the-landers. Because consumers wanted bread, pasta, and even beer made from local wheat, by the beginning of 2010 the *New York Times* was reporting on a rebirth of *grain* production in upstate New York—this a crop that had not been grown for market there for two hundred years.

In a broader sense, too, the demand for a deglobalized food system reflects a renewed interest in the most important feature of the back-to-the-land agenda. Consumers who find local eating appealing are often attracted first by its promises of healthier food and a smaller environmental "footprint." They want food that is "good, safe, and fair," to use the slogan of the Slow Food movement. But in the end the most enduring motive for local eating may be the old desire for independence: "the kind of independence," as Gene Logsdon

This New York Farm Bureau poster depicts what appears to be a fully mechanized commercial dairy farm in the early years of the twenty-first century: rows of Holsteins diligently eating around the clock in a state-of-the-art barn, a wall of hybrid corn in the field beyond. Still, it resurrects an old claim. At the center of the image is a lone farmer leaning on his broom, silhouetted in the light of early morning or late evening. From the beginning to the end of a long working day, the poster declares, the farmer guards our true "homeland security": not with the intelligence-gathering infrastructure of the so-called Department of Homeland Security created after 2001, but with the old safeguard of food self-sufficiency. (New York Farm Bureau, Inc., photo copyright Larry LeFever, Grant Heilman Photography, Inc.)

writes, "that defines success in terms of how much food, clothing, shelter, and contentment I could produce for myself rather than how much I could buy." Logsdon makes the old producerist connection between self-sufficiency and personal integrity, praising "the kind of freedom that allows me to say what I think in public without fear that my words will be 'bad for business.'"[9] Author Sharon Astyk elaborates on the point, arguing that self-sufficient "food preservation and food production" are nothing less than the "keys to democracy." Astyk contends that the days of peak oil have arrived: to get through the shortages and hard times ahead will require a great political struggle. Without food self-sufficiency, people will find themselves helplessly dependent on the same global corporations whose power it is so vital to resist. "The only possible escape from this bind," Astyk argues, "is to declare food independence."[10]

There is a new twist here. The focus on local eating has made self-sufficiency as much a community goal as an individual one. One advertisement for J. D. Belanger's *The Complete Idiot's Guide to Self-Sufficient Living* (2009) sums up the new perspective. From the time he started *Countryside Magazine* in 1969, Belanger has been advising people how to become personally self-sufficient. Now, he states flatly, "self-sufficiency for individuals is impossible." In order to bring about the critically important social transformation required by the daunting magnitude of the environmental challenges he sees on the horizon, Belanger argues that what is "absolutely essential" now is "self-sufficiency for Planet Earth."[11]

Meanwhile, supporters of the new self-sufficiency have become increasingly likely once again to target communities that are located not out in the woods or open countryside but in the suburbs. The new advocates of the suburbs of course recognize that those communities are highly dependent on automobiles and blighted by highways and strip malls. But they argue that they also happen to be the places where ordinary people—those who cannot leave their jobs and family obligations behind—can most easily acquire land for food production. This point of view is captured in the title of a short film made in 2006: *Eat the Suburbs: Gardening for the End of the Oil Age*.[12] The new push to "reinhabit the suburbs" brings us full circle, back to the early days of the movement. Back in the 1920s, the new suburbs had been popular because they offered space for people to cultivate gardens and raise chickens while still working at city occupations. For activists organizing "transition towns" to plan for the end of oil, the suburbs once again seem to provide that intermediate kind of space. In the old days they had called it "going half way back to the land." Sharon Astyk uses the phrase "little house in the suburbs," conjuring up associations with Laura Ingalls Wilder's classic children's book *Little House on the Prairie*.[13]

Nor is the food debate the only sign that back-to-the-land ideas are blossoming at the turn of the new century. The times are certainly right for

Matthew B. Crawford's best-selling *Shop Class as Soulcraft* (2009), which argues that the preference for white-collar jobs over skilled trades degrades the independence and dignity of work itself. Crawford is not himself a back-to-the-lander, but his plea against "the rising sea of clerkdom" and "on behalf of work that is meaningful because it is genuinely useful" echoes a century of producerist defenses of skilled, autonomous work as the basis of personal independence.[14] Even the old conundrums related to these producerist ideas are still around: some of Crawford's critics are put off not by his celebration of skilled work and the autonomous worker but by his association of that work with hypermasculinity. (Crawford works with motorcycles, not with wood, which is, he writes, "for hippies." The *New York Times* review of his book bore the sardonic title "Real Men Don't Eat Quiche—They Ride Hogs Over It.")[15]

Just as in previous generations, the relationship between domesticity and producerism is problematic. And once again, women facing the challenge of reconciling domestic obligations with paying jobs might find the new enthusiasm for preserving food, gardening, and raising chickens either a help or a hindrance—or perhaps both. One blogger calls herself "Peak Oil Hausfrau" in joking reference to those very complexities. A *New York Times* article raised the issue (and threw down the gauntlet) by labeling Berkeley, California, the "Vatican of Locavorism," an upscale university town where "chicks with chicks" now set the standard for "foodie" political correctness. The article suggested that the "omnivore's dilemma" provided what looked at first glance to be an "unexpected out from the feminist's predicament" but warned that chicken wire could "coop up" the unwary woman "as surely as any gilded cage."[16]

Shannon Hayes is the author of a book quoted extensively in that *New York Times* article. But the agenda Hayes proposes in *The Radical Homemaker* (2010) goes far deeper than the patronizing *Times* article acknowledged. Society is based on the principle that whoever has the gold makes the rules, Hayes writes, but "he or she who doesn't *need* the gold can *change* the rules." That conviction lies at the very heart of the back-to-the-land sensibility. From the beginning, self-sufficiency has been envisioned as the sine qua non of radical resistance. On that premise, Hayes argues for a full-scale rejection of consumerism; she envisions homes where both men and women place other values ahead of profit. Radical homemakers, she writes, are "men and women who have chosen to make family, community, social justice and the health of the environment the governing principles of their lives. They reject any form of labor or the expenditure of any resource that does not honor these tenets."[17]

In *Deep Economy* (2007), environmentalist Bill McKibben similarly endorses the old anticonsumerist message implicit in the new critique. McKibben argues that both the planet's health and the current human predicament demand a new way of living: a rejection of consumer values and an equally fundamental rejection of the entire model of economic growth in favor of decentralized economies, community self-sufficiency, and a reoriented culture. Perhaps it is not a coincidence, then, that McKibben located himself in Vermont—back in the 1930s the favorite state of back-to-the-landers—where a new movement has arisen from the old decentralist matrix. In 2005, Ian Baldwin helped to establish a new magazine, *Vermont Commons*, committed to promoting greater local autonomy and ultimately the "untying" of the United States via secession. Baldwin's Chelsea Green Press had already demonstrated its commitment to that revitalized decentralist perspective—at first, simply by the gesture of setting up shop in a village in Vermont and then by publishing books with a regionalist agenda. Frank Bryan and John McClaughry's *The Vermont Papers: Recreating Democracy on a Human Scale* (1989) was one of the first of these: a classic third-way manifesto that champions regional autonomy and a return to small-scale politics and culture.[18] In *The Vermont Papers*, one may detect an echo of that earlier southern regionalist manifesto *I'll Take My Stand*: at the head of the first chapter the authors placed a passage from a poem by Robert Louis Stevenson: "You must some time fight it out or perish / And if that be so, why not now?/And where you stand?"[19]

Old Roots

For all its innovations, nearly every element of the current back-to-the-land movement has its roots in the past. Even the most distinctive characteristics of the movement have been shaped by the efforts of those who came before. Many back-to-the-landers of the 1960s and 1970s—perhaps looking for the cash they needed when their Volkswagen rusted out, their property taxes went up, and their "camomile blossoms" did not bring in enough money, as one former back-to-the-lander described their dilemma—long ago turned their efforts away from individual self-sufficiency and toward grassroots institutional change.[20] In the process, they built a new infrastructure that would prove eminently serviceable when times changed once again.

Today's back-to-the-landers need not rely on international conglomerates for their seeds; they can purchase open-pollinated seeds for "heirloom" breeds of vegetables adapted to regional conditions. (Johnny's Selected Seeds started business in Maine in 1973; Territorial Seed Company in Oregon in 1979; Southern Exposure in Virginia in 1982.) Replacing the hand-me-down rusted-out woodstoves of their parents' generation, there are state-of-the-art, efficiently designed new ones. (Vermont Castings led the way in the 1970s.) On his Maine homestead next door to the Nearings' old home, Eliot Coleman worked for years to refine techniques for using unheated greenhouses year-round in the far north. Joel Salatin, whose Polyface Farm was featured in Pollan's *The Omnivore's Dilemma*, perfected a wide variety of innovative techniques for raising animals on pasture, so that farmers can avoid feeding their cattle the corn-based diet that is so closely linked to the failures of the industrial food system. If new homesteaders wish to build their own houses, there are schools to teach self-sufficient building skills. (Rob Roy's Earthwood Building School was founded in upstate New York in 1981.) Certified solar and wind installers help people to go off-grid. Publishers both online and off provide information on everything from chicken pasturing to potato blight.

In fact, while the looming energy questions of the twenty-first century seem to demand a collective solution, the old question of food self-sufficiency simply no longer requires quite the same go-it-alone approach that characterized the 1970s. Cooperative stores and farmers' markets are everywhere (mostly founded in the 1970s), and community-supported farms (introduced in the United States in the 1980s) are almost as widespread.[21] In the 1970s, a back-to-the-lander who craved such dietary specialties as whole grain bread, organic vegetables, bean sprouts, or even yogurt had to be prepared to make them at home. Now, novice back-to-the-landers may still prefer to make their own, but their options have expanded dramatically; not only will their local co-ops carry all those foods (locally sourced, to boot!), but they are increasingly likely to encounter a cheese maker next door or a baker down the road. The networks that provide support for back-to-the-land projects grow denser with each year, as young farmers and food producers find new markets and fill them.

Styles change, to be sure. For an observer of an older generation, nothing is more startling than to overhear bandanna- and earring-clad young people in the local co-op swapping recipes—not for tofu and vegetarian chili anymore but for pork belly and organ meats from heritage-breed pigs and cattle. Yet the new back-to-the-landers seem to recognize a connection with the past. In 2009, the *New York Times* featured an article about college students working as interns on small farms. Some students, the article reported, saw the creation of a trans-formed food system as "the political movement of their time." (Indeed they were so enthusiastic that they earned the classic term of opprobrium—"strident"—from the reporter.) One of the interns interviewed for this story, twenty-year-old Jamie Katz, agreed, telling the reporter that his involvement with the politics of food production had allowed him to find his inner radical. As he said, with evident relish, "I no longer wish I was born in the sixties."[22]

Finally, however, today's back-to-the-land enthusiasm is about more than political fashion. Like those that emerged in earlier days, some of the new projects are born from the desire of relatively prosperous people for food that is "good, clean, and fair." Others arise from the fact that even prosperous people once again have very good reasons to fear "black Friday and red ruin." Carla Emery, who printed the first copies of her *Encyclopedia of Country Living* in 1970 on a mimeograph machine, still warned in her 2008 edition: "many people spend their lives a paycheck away from hunger or homelessness—because they must pay other people to supply their most basic needs."[23] Bolton Hall had that same dilemma in mind when he wrote in 1907: "I call 'poor' every one who cannot afford to be sick for a few weeks, or who has not over four weeks' wages in the savings bank." Back then Hall had thought that his definition would include most of the "clerks, the stenographers, the bookkeepers, the tradesmen, and even some of the professionals of our great cities, who earn barely enough to give them a living, much less a decent home."[24] Today things are not altogether different.

And as they did in the past, back-to-the-land projects are also turning up among people with no paychecks at all. In Detroit, where the mayor's office estimates that over 40 percent of the population is out of work, gardens are once again all that stand between many residents and what is now euphemistically referred to as "food insecurity," but was once known as hunger. That is indeed a sad commentary on how little has changed in a century. Back in the long-ago depression of 1893, Detroit was the site of Mayor Hazen Pingree's pioneering efforts to provide vacant lots for urban homesteaders. Its residents now find themselves forced to reinvent an almost exact replica of that program, in a city so depopulated that "sprawling lots with waist-high weeds have rendered parts of [it] almost pastoral," as one writer described it in a report in the *Nation*.

That reporter, Ben Ehrenreich, saw the tragic irony in Detroit's situation: "in a city where workers once demanded control over the means of production of one of the largest industries in the world, residents are now fighting for the right to grow their own food." And it is both ironic and tragic that the same desperate struggle that overshadowed the lives of the poor in 1893 is once again shadowing those same streets. Yet a leader of the Detroit Black Community Food Security Network chose to place her emphasis elsewhere, making the old connection between self-sufficiency, independence, and power: "Don't look at us and say, Poor Detroit, no grocery stores. . . . People here are coming up with their own solutions to social problems." Unlike the anonymous writer who reviewed Bolton Hall's book for the *Nation* over a century ago, this *Nation* writer got the message: the organization's efforts, Ehrenreich wrote, "are about more than keeping Detroiters in tomatoes and kale—they're about self-determination."[25] That's what it has always been about.

Notes

Introduction

1. Bolton Hall, *The New Thrift* (New York: Huebsch, 1923), 108.

2. Ibid., 108–9.

3. Lyman Beecher Stowe, "Training City Boys for Country Life," *Outlook*, Nov. 9, 1912, 537.

4. Michael Kazin identifies a "producerist" tradition in *The Populist Persuasion* (New York: Basic Books, 1995). John L. Thomas uses the term to frame the ideas of Henry George, Edward Bellamy, and Henry Demarest Lloyd in *Alternative America* (Cambridge, MA: Harvard University Press, 1983). Most comprehensively, Christopher Lasch writes of an ongoing radical, non-Marxist producerist tradition in *The True and Only Heaven: Progress and Its Critics* (New York: Norton, 1991).

5. Clipping, *New York World*, Mar. 14, 1926, Bolton Hall letters, box 2, Bolton Hall papers, New York Public Library.

6. William Ellsworth Smythe, *City Homes on Country Lanes: Philosophy and Practice of the Home-in-a-Garden* (New York: Macmillan, 1921), 56.

7. Fred Myrtle, "The Little Lander's Hired Man: Electricity Will Do the Drudgery in Densely-Peopled Garden Cities," *Little Landers in America*, Mar. 1916, 94.

8. Louis Hacker, "Plowing the Farmer Under," *Harper's*, June 1934, 69. Actually, the article reads "little *Acadias*," but this appears to be a misprint.

9. Russell Lord and Paul H. Johnstone, *A Place on Earth: A Critical Appraisal of Subsistence Homesteads* (Washington, DC: U.S. Department of Agriculture, Bureau of Agricultural Economics, 1942), 184.

10. *Free America*, Jan. 1939, 9.

11. John Shuttleworth, "Why the Magazine Was Founded, What It Has Accomplished during the First Ten Years, and What It Expects to Do during the Next Decade," *Mother Earth News*, Nov./Dec. 1979, 44.

12. John Shuttleworth, "The Plowboy Interview," *Mother Earth News*, Mar./Apr. 1970, 6.

13. Gove Hambidge, *Enchanted Acre: Adventures in Backyard Farming* (New York: McGraw-Hill, 1935), 5–6.

14. Smythe, *City Homes on Country Lanes*, 59.

15. Paul Conkin, *Tomorrow a New World: The New Deal Community Programs* (Ithaca, NY: Cornell University Press, 1959), 36.

16. Sociologist Jeffrey Jacob provides the textbook definition: "large-scale collective behavior directed toward promoting or resisting social change, requiring some organizational structure, well developed ideologies, and an intellectual vanguard with recognizable public identities" (*New Pioneers: The Back to the Land Movement and the Search for a Sustainable Future* [University Park: Pennsylvania State University Press, 1997], 5).

17. Stanford J. Layton, *To No Privileged Class: The Rationalization of Homesteading and Rural Life in the Early Twentieth-Century American West* (Salt Lake City, UT: Brigham Young University, 1988), 37; Terry Allan Simmons, "But We Must Cultivate Our Garden: Twentieth Century Pioneering in Rural British Columbia" (PhD diss., University of Minnesota, 1979), 7.

18. John Steinbeck, *The Grapes of Wrath* (New York: Penguin Books, 2002), 419.

19. Shuttleworth, "Why the Magazine Was Founded," 42.

20. Lena Walters to David Grayson, 1906, box 1, file 1, David Grayson papers, Special Collections, Jones Library, Amherst, MA.

21. Smythe, *City Homes on Country Lanes*, 184–86. Laura Lovett discusses the pronatalist implications of the arguments of Smythe and some of his colleagues (*Conceiving the Future: Pronatalism, Reproduction, and the Family in the United States, 1890–1938* [Chapel Hill: University of North Carolina, 2007]).

22. Qtd. in Mary Lou Pozzo, *Founding Sisters: Life Stories of Tujunga's Early Women Pioneers* (Tujunga, CA: Zinnia Press, 2005), 261.

23. David Danbom, "Romantic Agrarianism in Twentieth-Century America," *Agricultural History* 65, no. 4 (1991): 1–12.

24. David Shi, *The Simple Life: Plain Living and High Thinking in American Culture* (New York: Oxford University Press, 1983), esp. chaps. 8 and 9.

25. Gould suggests that back-to-the-landers have consistently embraced three goals: the sacralization of nature, the making of the self, and the expression of resistance to the dominant culture (*At Home in Nature: Modern Homesteading and Spiritual Practice in America* [Berkeley: University of California Press, 2005], 113).

26. Jacob, *New Pioneers*, 180.

27. This assessment depends in part, of course, on which books and articles are judged to be part of the "back-to-the-land" discourse. My own study includes a number of popular and ephemeral texts that have not been examined carefully in the past, and on my own list of "canonical" back-to-the-land books and articles there are very few in the first half of the century that feature romantic reveries about nature.

28. Truman A. DeWeese, *The Bend in the Road, and How a Man of the City Found It* (New York: Harper and Brothers, 1913), 9.

29. B. Touchstone Hardaway advocated following Thoreau's advice about borrowing tools in "I Live with a Cookstove and Love It," *Mother Earth News*, Jan./Feb. 1971, 65. Poet and environmentalist Gary Snyder used Thoreau's authority to argue against the

use of DDT in "Four Changes," *Mother Earth News*, Jan./Feb. 1970, 2–4. The editor relayed Thoreau's advice to "build your castles in the air . . . and then put foundations under them" in "Becoming a Free-Lance Cartoonist," *Mother Earth News*, Jan./Feb. 1970, 12.

30. Gould, *At Home in Nature*, 39. Here Gould offers a nuanced reading of precisely *how* the Nearings used Thoreau's example.

31. Walter Harding, "Five Ways of Looking at Thoreau," *Massachusetts Review* 4, no. 1 (1962): 149–62.

32. In *Quest for Walden: The "Country Book" in American Popular Literature* (Jefferson City, NC: McFarland Press, 1997), Loren Owings assembled an impressively comprehensive list of back-to-the-land titles. As his title suggests, Owings asserts that nearly all twentieth-century back-to-the-land writing follows in the footsteps of Thoreau.

33. Gould, *At Home in Nature*, 39.

34. Ibid., 25.

35. DeWeese, *Bend in the Road*, 74–75.

36. Philip G. Hubert, *Liberty and a Living* (New York: G. P. Putnam's Sons, 1889), 18.

37. Owings, *Quest for Walden*, 62.

38. Edmund Morris, *Ten Acres Enough: Small Farm Self-Sufficiency through High-Quality Produce*, ed. Robert Plamondon (Blodgett Creek, OR: Norton Creek Press, 2008).

39. *American Agriculturist*, May 1864, 134; *American Agriculturist*, June 1864, 168. For a more extensive account, see Owings, *Quest for Walden*, 62–65.

40. Owings, *Quest for Walden*, 62–64.

41. Donald Grant Mitchell, *Rural Studies with Hints for Country Places* (New York: Scribner, 1867), 29.

42. Clipping, *Syracuse (NY) Standard*, Apr. 13, 1907, Bolton Hall scrapbook 1, Bolton Hall papers.

43. For the new market garden literature, see Beverly Seaton, "Idylls of Agriculture; or, Nineteenth-Century Success Stories of Farming and Gardening," *Agricultural History* 55, no. 1 (1981), 21–22.

44. Actually, it most closely resembled a British book published a few years earlier. *Our Farm of Four Acres* (London: Chapman and Hall, 1859) told the tale of a pair of sisters who moved to the suburbs of London and raised cows, chickens, pigs, and vegetables, thus learning to support themselves and their children. Its author, "Miss Coulton," wrote primarily for "gentlewomen" who needed money.

45. Edmund Morris, *Ten Acres Enough: A Practical Experience* (New York: James Miller, 1864), 23.

46. Ibid., 13, 4.

47. Hubert, *Liberty and a Living*, 1–2, 5, frontispiece.

48. Ibid., 77, 3.

49. Morris, *Ten Acres Enough*, 9.

50. Ed Zahniser, "Good Things from the Garden in the Closet," *Mother Earth News*, Nov./Dec. 1971, 50.

51. Robert Gross, "The Great Bean Field Hoax: Thoreau and the Agricultural Reformers," in *Critical Essays on Henry David Thoreau's Walden*, ed. Joel Myerson (Boston: G. K. Hall, 1988), 193–202.

52. Verlyn Klinkenborg, "Sow Those Seeds!" *New York Times*, Feb. 14, 2009.

Chapter 1. The Back-to-the-Land Project

1. "Hobbling Back to Nature," *Nation*, Mar. 21, 1907, 259.

2. Ibid.

3. Walter A. Dyer, "Eighty Acres and Bondage: A Spiritual Investment," *Craftsman*, Feb. 1913, 536.

4. Bolton Hall, *Three Acres and Liberty* (New York: Grosset and Dunlap, 1907), v.

5. Ibid., 406.

6. *Country Life in America*, Nov. 1910, 43; *Country Life in America*, June 1911, 223.

7. W. Bert Foster, *The Heron Nest* (New York: Rural Publishing, 1909), 5.

8. Grace Richmond, *Strawberry Acres* (Garden City, NY: Doubleday, Page, 1911).

9. William L. Bowers, *The Country Life Movement in America, 1900–1920* (Port Washington, NY: Kennikat Press, 1974), 3, 13. The rural population made up 63.9 percent of the population in 1890, 59.7 percent in 1900, and 53.7 percent in 1910.

10. Theodore Roosevelt, state of the union address, 1906, http://teachingamerican history.org/library/index.asp?document=1315.

11. *The Public Papers and Addresses of Franklin D. Roosevelt*, 13 vols. (New York: Random House, 1938–50), 5:431.

12. The word "agrarian" may describe a movement designed to redistribute land to landless workers or, as here, may describe a cluster of beliefs about the intrinsic value of rural over urban life.

13. Truman A. DeWeese, *The Bend in the Road, and How a Man of the City Found It* (New York: Harper and Brothers, 1913), 6.

14. David Grayson, *Adventures in Contentment* (Garden City, NY: Doubleday, Page, 1906), 220.

15. Two comprehensive studies of the country life movement are David Danbom, *The Resisted Revolution: Urban America and the Industrialization of Agriculture, 1900–1930* (Ames: Iowa State University Press, 1979), and Bowers, *Country Life Movement in America*. Both discuss the relationship of the first back-to-the-land movement to the country life movement. In *Born in the Country: A History of Rural America* (Baltimore, MD: Johns Hopkins University Press, 1995), his synthetic history of rural life, Danbom also explores back-to-the-land projects in the context of the prosperity of farmers in the "golden age" from 1900 to 1920 (162).

16. William Lighton, *Happy Hollow Farm* (New York: Doran, 1914), 55.

17. Liberty Hyde Bailey, *The Country-Life Movement in America* (New York: Macmillan, 1911), 203.

18. David Danbom explores this uncomfortable fit from a somewhat different perspective in "Romantic Agrarianism in Twentieth-Century America," *Agricultural History* 65, no. 4 (1991): 1–12.

19. As Bowers frames it, only the "romantic" country life reformers were committed to the traditional agrarian view of the farm. "Scientific" country life reformers saw farming primarily as a business that was being conducted inefficiently. They believed that the population of the countryside was dwindling precisely because of the greater efficiency they were encouraging. That efficiency might cause social dislocation, they conceded, but it was fundamentally healthy—a position that would of course bring them into conflict with back-to-the-landers (*Country Life Movement in America*, 28–29).

20. Liberty Hyde Bailey, "Can I Make a Farm Pay?" *World's Work*, Mar. 1901, 548.

21. Bailey, *Country-Life Movement*, 1.

22. Ibid., 23.

23. Douglas W. Steeples and David O. Whitten, *Democracy in Desperation: The Depression of 1893* (Westport, CT: Greenwood Press, 1998).

24. Freeman Tilden, *Second Wind: The Plain Truth about Going Back to the Land* (New York: Huebsch, 1917).

25. Clipping, *Syracuse (NY) Standard*, Apr. 13, 1907, Bolton Hall scrapbook 1, Bolton Hall papers, New York Public Library. Loren Owings makes a similar distinction between country life essays and practical guides (*Quest for Walden*, 5).

26. Hall, *Three Acres*, 277, 125.

27. Hubert, *Liberty and a Living* (New York: G. P. Putnam's Sons, 1889), 149.

28. *Historical Statistics of the United States, Colonial Times to 1970* (Washington, DC: Bureau of the Census, 1975), 321.

29. Foster, *Heron Nest*, 14.

30. Harrison Whittingham, *That Farm: Recounting the Adventures of a Dry-Goods Merchant Who Went Back to the Land* (Garden City, NY: Doubleday, Page, 1914), 228.

31. Lighton, *Happy Hollow Farm*, 102.

32. Bolton Hall, *The New Thrift* (New York: Huebsch, 1923), 109.

33. David Shi, *The Simple Life: Plain Living and High Thinking in American Culture* (New York: Oxford University Press, 1985), 4.

34. Shi characterizes Gustav Stickley and David Grayson, whom I discuss here, as part of a "progressive simplicity" impulse. See *Simple Life*, especially chap. 8, "Progressive Simplicity."

35. Hubert, *Liberty and a Living*, 2.

36. Grayson, *Adventures in Contentment*, 244–45. For more on David Grayson (who was really Ray Stannard Baker), see chaps. 2 and 3.

37. "Craftsman House #108," *Craftsman*, Feb. 1911, 506–7.

38. "The Simple Life," *Craftsman*, Aug. 1902, 252–57; "The Essence of Simplicity," *Craftsman*, Oct. 1902, v. The November 1904 issue included the photograph, a review of

a lecture, and an article by George Wharton James, "Two Days with M. Wagner" (*Craftsman*, Nov. 1904, 184).

39. Gustav Stickley, "Why 'Back to the Farm'?" *Craftsman*, Feb. 1911, 506–7, 522–23. This was a response to a *New York Times* article by Josiah Strong asserting that urbanization and industrialization were inevitable and should be embraced.

40. Edward Bok's use of "simple life" rhetoric in his *Ladies Home Journal* is particularly instructive. See Shi, *Simple Life*, 182–85, 204–5.

41. W. H. Jenkins, "A Living from a Three-Acre Farm: Possibilities of Health and Happiness for the Man with Small Means," *Craftsman*, Feb. 1911, 512–15.

42. For the story of Craftsman Farms, see Mark Alan Hewitt, *Gustav Stickley's Craftsman Farms: The Quest for an Arts and Crafts Utopia* (Syracuse, NY: Syracuse University Press, 2001).

43. For a biography of Carpenter, see Sheila Rowbotham, *Edward Carpenter: A Life of Liberty and Love* (London: Verso, 2008).

44. Gustav Stickley, "The Simplification of Life," *Craftsman*, Dec. 1905, 405.

45. Two studies of the early back-to-the-land movement in England are Jan Marsh, *Back to the Land: The Pastoral Impulse in England, from 1880 to 1914* (London: Quartet, 1982), and Peter C. Gould, *Early Green Politics: Back to Nature, Back to the Land, and Socialism in Britain, 1880–1900* (New York: St. Martin's Press, 1988).

46. Gustav Stickley, "The Conquest of Bread," *Craftsman*, Sep. 1907, 670.

47. Peter Kropotkin, *Mutual Aid: A Factor of Evolution* (1902; repr., Whitefish, MT: Kessinger Publications, 2004), 3.

48. Irene Sargent, book review of *Mutual Aid*, *Craftsman*, May 1903, 143–45; "A Chapter from Prince Kropotkin," *Craftsman*, June 1903, 209–20.

49. Edward Payson Powell, *How to Live in the Country* (New York: Outing Publishing, 1911), 1. N. O. Nelson, an industrialist and single-tax advocate, wrote the preface.

50. Hall, *Three Acres*, 43–44.

51. Herbert Quick to Bolton Hall, 1913, Bolton Hall letters, box 1, Bolton Hall papers.

52. Gustav Stickley, "Small Farms a Solution for the Evils of Overcrowded Cities and Unnatural Living," *Craftsman*, June 1911, 310.

53. George H. Maxwell, *Our National Defense: The Patriotism of Peace* (Washington, DC: Rural Settlements Association, 1915).

54. Foster, *Heron Nest*, 90.

55. Arthur P. Dudden, *Joseph Fels and the Single-Tax Movement* (Philadelphia: Temple University Press, 1971), 35. These efforts to provide small plots of land to the poor were also popular in Britain. The slogan "Three Acres and a Cow" originated with a campaign to persuade the British government to provide garden allotments. The Allotments Extension Act of 1882 was the first product of that campaign. In 1891, Salvation Army founder William Booth proposed his own elaborate plan—set out in *In Darkest England and the Way Out* (1890)—to relocate people living in slums to small farm colonies in rural England where they would prepare for emigration to Australia or Canada.

56. Undated clipping, *New York World*, Bolton Hall scrapbook 1, Bolton Hall papers.

57. Clipping, "Disinherited for His Charities: Bolton Hall, Son of the Greatest Presbyterian Divine, a Bankrupt This Week: His Creed," *New York World*, Dec. 4, 1898, Bolton Hall scrapbook 1, Bolton Hall papers.

58. Clipping, "Millionaire Lawyer," *Montreal Tribune*, 1897, Bolton Hall scrapbook 1, Bolton Hall papers; Elbert Hubbard to Bolton Hall, May 16, 1910, Bolton Hall letters, box 1, Bolton Hall papers.

59. *New York Times*, Mar. 23, 1895.

60. Clipping, *National Single Taxer*, Sep. 17, 1898, Bolton Hall scrapbook 1, Bolton Hall papers.

61. Unidentified magazine pages, 1908 penciled in, Bolton Hall scrapbook 1, Bolton Hall papers.

62. Joseph Dana Miller, ed., *Single Tax Year Book: The History, Principles and Application of the Single Tax Philosophy* (New York: Single Tax Review Publishing, 1917), 197.

63. "Disinherited for His Charities."

64. The story is told at the website of the Kansas State Historical Society, http://www.kshs.org/cool/monopoly.htm

65. *Who's Who Among North American Authors* (Los Angeles: Golden Syndicate Publishing, 1921), 93.

66. John L. Thomas, *Alternative America: Henry George, Edward Bellamy, Henry Demarest Lloyd and the Adversary Tradition* (Cambridge, MA: Harvard University Press, 1983), 193–94.

67. For an account of Fels's career, see Dudden, *Joseph Fels*. See also Evelyn Bodek Rosen, *The Philadelphia Fels, 1880–1920* (Cranbury, NJ: Fairleigh Dickinson University Press, 2000).

68. The villages now known as "the Ardens" were placed on the National Register of Historic Places in recognition of their status as the only nonreligious utopian community to survive for more than a century with original values intact. For the story of another single-tax enclave bankrolled by Joseph Fels, see Paul E. and Blanche R. Alyea, *Fairhope, 1894–1954: The Story of a Single Tax Colony* (Montgomery: University of Alabama Press, 1956), and Paul M. Gaston, *Man and Mission: E. B. Gaston and the Origins of the Fairhope Single Tax Colony* (Montgomery, AL: Black Belt Press, 1993).

69. Charles White Huntington, *Enclaves of Single Tax or Economic Rent* (Harvard, MA: Fiske Warren, 1922).

70. Upton Sinclair, *American Outpost* (New York: Ferris Printing, 1932), 232.

71. Scott Nearing, *Man's Search for the Good Life* (1954; repr., Harborside, ME: Social Science Institute, 1974), 1.

72. William Ellsworth Smythe, *The Conquest of Arid America*, rev. ed. (New York: Macmillan, 1905), 267.

73. William Ellsworth Smythe, *Constructive Democracy: The Economics of a Square Deal* (New York: Macmillan, 1905), 41–42.

74. *World's Fair Colony, 1915: Little Landers, Hayward Heath* (San Francisco: Society of the Little Lands, 1915), 12.

75. "New Plymouth," Idaho State Historical Society Reference Series, no. 984, Jan. 1993, http://www.idahohistory.net.

76. William Ellsworth Smythe, *City Homes on Country Lanes: Philosophy and Practice of the Home-in-a-Garden* (New York: Macmillan, 1921), 221.

77. Ibid., vii.

78. David Gray, "The Promised Land: Making a Country Home," *Collier's*, Mar. 13, 1909, 16.

79. Bolton Hall to Charles F. Weller, July 9, 1924, Bolton Hall letters, box 2, Bolton Hall papers.

80. Charles Weeks, *One Acre and Independence; or, My One-Acre Farm* (n.p.: n.p., n.d.), 133.

81. Dudden, *Joseph Fels*, 100–101; Joseph Fels to Booker T. Washington, in *Booker T. Washington Papers*, vol. 9, ed. Louis R. Harlan and Raymond W. Smock (Urbana: University of Illinois Press, 1980), 340.

82. Lyman Beecher Stowe, "Training City Boys for Country Life" *Outlook*, Nov. 9, 1912, 539.

83. The Tontitown project did not originate with a benevolent back-to-the-land patron but with a planter who needed to sell land in the Arkansas delta. He arranged to sell it to Italian workers who would sharecrop it until they paid their debts. Things went badly; the planter died, and his heirs were not inclined to be patient. Thirty-five families split off from this original colony and founded Tontitown (Ernesto R. Milani, "Peonage at Sunnyside and the Reaction of the Italian Government," in *Shadows Over Sunnyside: An Arkansas Plantation in Transition, 1830–1945*, ed. Jeannie M. Whayne [Fayetteville: University of Arkansas Press, 1999], 44).

84. Anita Moore, "A Safe Way to Get on the Soil: The Work of Father Bandini at Tontitown," *World's Work*, June 1912, 215.

85. Ibid.

86. C. L., "Two Views of the 'Back to the Land' Movement—I. 'Go Slow,'" *World's Work*, Apr. 1912, 717.

87. Hall, *Three Acres*, 62.

88. Ibid., 72–73.

89. There is an extensive literature on Jewish back-to-the-land efforts. For an overview, see Jacob Ornstein-Galicia, *The Jewish Farmer in America: The Unknown Chronicle* (Lewiston, NY: Edwin Mellen Press, 1992) and Uri Herscher, *Jewish Agricultural Utopias in America, 1880–1910* (Detroit, MI: Wayne State University Press, 1984), as well as Gertrude Dubrovsky, *The Land Was Theirs: Jewish Farmers in the Garden State* (Tuscaloosa: University of Alabama Press, 1992), a fine work which goes beyond the New Jersey colonies. See also Ellen Eisenberg, *Jewish Agricultural Colonies in New Jersey, 1882–1920* (Syracuse, NY: Syracuse University Press, 1995), a close study of the roots of the Jewish settlement movement in the Pale; Gabriel Davidson, *Our Jewish Farmers and the Story of the Jewish Agricultural Society* (New York: L. B. Fischer, 1943); Joseph Brandes, *Immigrants to Freedom: Jewish Communities in Rural New Jersey since 1882* (Philadelphia: University of Pennsylvania

Press, 1971); Abraham D. Lavender and Clarence B. Steinberg, *Jewish Farmers of the Catskills: A Century of Survival* (Gainesville: University Press of Florida, 1995).

90. Eisenberg, *Jewish Agricultural Colonies*, chap. 2, provides a helpful discussion of the impact of Am Olam.

91. For a broad account of the sponsors of Jewish colonies, see Eisenberg, *Jewish Agricultural Colonies*, chap. 3.

92. Davidson, *Our Jewish Farmers*, 35.

93. This story is told in an excellent monograph: Robert Alan Goldberg, *Back to the Soil: The Jewish Farmers of Clarion, Utah, and Their World* (Salt Lake City: University of Utah Press, 1986). My discussion here is based on his work.

94. Goldberg, *Back to the Soil*, xxiv.

95. "First Successful Jewish Colony in the United States," qtd. in Goldberg, *Back to the Soil*, 77.

96. Goldberg, *Back to the Soil*, 40.

97. Felix James, "The Tuskegee Institute Movable School, 1906–1923," *Agricultural History* 45, no. 3 (1971): 201.

98. Booker T. Washington, "A Sunday Evening Talk," Oct. 28, 1906, in *Booker T. Washington Papers*, 9:109.

99. Here I am following the lead of Michael Kazin (*The Populist Persuasion* [New York: Basic Books, 1995]) and Christopher Lasch (*The True and Only Heaven: Progress and Its Critics* [New York: Norton, 1991]), who have used the term "producerist" to describe such non-Marxist American radicals as the Knights of Labor and the populists. Similarly, in *Alternative America* John L. Thomas describes Henry George's single-tax position as a "producerist" vision of widely distributed ownership in a society of craftsmen and independent farmers. Others have used the word "producerism" to describe a variety of modern right-wing populist movements, but I am not making that connection here.

100. Edward Payson Powell, *The Country Home* (New York: McClure, Phillips, 1904), 12.

Chapter 2. Adventures in Contentment

1. Rebecca Kneale Gould, *At Home in Nature: Modern Homesteading and Spiritual Practice in America* (Berkeley: University of California Press, 2005), 292 n.18. Gould discusses Hall's beliefs in the context of her exploration of the spiritual practices of back-to-the-landers.

2. "J. N. McG." to Bolton Hall, Oct. 9, 1906, Bolton Hall letters, box 1, folder 3, Bolton Hall papers, New York Public Library.

3. *The Garden Magazine* was founded in 1905. *Farming* began in 1906 but ceased publication in 1907 and merged with the other magazine to become *The Garden Magazine and Farming*.

4. J. P. Mowbray, "Going Back to the Soil," *World's Work*, Jan. 1901, 267; Liberty Hyde Bailey, "Can I Make a Farm Pay?" *World's Work*, Mar. 1901, 548. Beginning at the

end of 1911, each issue for over a year featured reports on Page's study of conditions for going back to the land.

5. *The Country Life Press* (Garden City, NY: Doubleday, Page, 1919).

6. Truman DeWeese's books include *The Book on Advertising* (1907), *Keeping a Dollar at Work: Fifty Talks on Newspaper Advertising* (1914), and *Principles of Practical Publicity* (1906). A magazine notice mentioned his work for the Shredded Wheat Company (*The National Magazine*, Apr. 1913, 1114–15).

7. Truman A. DeWeese, *The Bend in the Road, and How a Man of the City Found It* (New York: Harper and Brothers, 1913), 74–75.

8. Christopher Wilson, *The Labor of Words: Literary Professionalism in the Progressive Era* (Athens: University of Georgia Press, 1985), 1–11. This scholarly and imaginative work explores the transformation of journalism into a grueling, competitive job in these years.

9. Suzanne Lighton to Hazel Deal, Feb. 9, 1968, series 2, subseries 1, box 8, folder 4, Lighton Family Papers, University of Arkansas Special Collections, Fayetteville, Arkansas.

10. William Lighton, *Happy Hollow Farm* (New York: Doran, 1914), 116.

11. William Lighton, "The Story of an Arkansas Farm—My Willamette Valley Postscript" (Portland: Oregon Electric Railway, 1913), 5.

12. Suzanne Lighton to Hazel Deal, Feb. 9, 1968, series 2, subseries 1, box 8, folder 4, Lighton Family Papers.

13. Pamphlets are in series 2, subseries 4, box 12, folder 2, Lighton Family Papers.

14. *Back to the Land* 1, nos. 1–2, 6, series 9, subseries 1, vol. 16, Lighton Family Papers.

15. Clipping, *Little Rock Daily Board of Trade Bulletin*, 1910, series 2, subseries 1, box 8, folder 11, Lighton Family Papers.

16. Clipping, *Omaha (NE) Daily News*, Sep. 30, 1906, series 2, subseries 1, box 8, folder 11, Lighton Family Papers.

17. Frederick S. Bigelow to William Lighton, Dec. 28, 1910, Dec. 8, 1911, series 2, subseries 1, box 8, folder 11, Lighton Family Papers.

18. Lighton, *Happy Hollow Farm*, 117.

19. Untitled printed leaflet dated "Fayetteville, Arkansas, February 1, 1910," series 2, subseries 1, box 8, folder 11, Lighton Family Papers.

20. Lighton admitted to only one real problem with farming in the Ozarks: it was hard to find skilled and motivated laborers among the hardscrabble hill farmers who were native to the place.

21. William Howard Kirkbridge, "One Acre Ranch: How to Make a Living from One Acre of Ground," *Century Magazine*, Mar. 1908, 752.

22. Lighton, *Happy Hollow Farm*, 29.

23. Harrison Whittingham, *That Farm: Recounting the Adventures of a Dry-Goods Merchant Who Went Back to the Land* (Garden City, NY: Doubleday, Page, 1914), 5. The $30,000 figure would have been a princely income for this "dry-goods merchant" and seems unlikely.

24. William Justin Harsha, "A Clergyman's Gamble with Uncle Sam," *Outlook*, Jan. 3, 1917, 24.

25. Lighton, *Happy Hollow Farm*, 9–10.

26. Ibid.

27. Florence Folsom to David Grayson, 1908, box 1, file 3, David Grayson papers (contained within the Ray Stannard Baker papers, but filed separately), Special Collections, Jones Library, Amherst, MA.

28. There are two intellectual biographies of Ray Stannard Baker: Robert C. Bannister, Jr., *Ray Stannard Baker: The Mind and Thought of a Progressive* (New Haven, CT: Yale University Press, 1966), and John E. Semonche, *Ray Stannard Baker: A Quest for Democracy in Modern America, 1870–1918* (Chapel Hill: University of North Carolina Press, 1969). Baker himself wrote a two-volume autobiography: *Native American: The Book of My Youth* (New York: Charles Scribner's Sons, 1941) and *American Chronicle: The Autobiography of Ray Stannard Baker* (New York: Charles Scribner's Sons, 1945).

29. Bannister analyzes Baker's relationship with Roosevelt in detail (*Ray Stannard Baker*, 102–7). Semonche considers the "muckraking" controversy and the press response in depth (*Ray Stannard Baker*, 150–52). Baker's own account is also revealing (*American Chronicle*, chap. 21, "I Try to Serve Theodore Roosevelt").

30. Baker, *American Chronicle*, 240.

31. The later books were *Adventures in Understanding* (1925), *Adventures in Solitude* (1931), *The Countryman's Year* (1936), and *Under My Elm: Country Discoveries and Reflections* (1942).

32. Baker, *American Chronicle*, 245.

33. Clipping, *Chicago News*, Dec. 23, 1907, David Grayson papers.

34. Clipping, *Springfield (MA) Republican*, Jan. 19, 1908, David Grayson papers.

35. David Grayson, *Adventures in Contentment* (Garden City, NY: Doubleday, Page, 1906), 3.

36. Frederick Rockwell, *The Key to the Land: What a City Man Did with a Small Farm* (New York: Harper and Brothers, 1912); Grace S. Richmond, *Strawberry Acres* (Garden City, NY: Doubleday, Page, 1911).

37. Grayson, *Adventures in Contentment*, 5.

38. Clipping, *Springfield (MA) Republican*, Jan. 19, 1908, David Grayson papers.

39. Grayson, *Adventures in Contentment*, 3–4.

40. Bannister, *Ray Stannard Baker*, 110.

41. Baker, *American Chronicle*, 115.

42. Most of Baker's papers are housed at the Library of Congress, but these letters are part of a separate David Grayson collection, held at the Jones Library in Baker's adopted home of Amherst, Massachusetts.

43. I counted 33 letters that inquired about David Grayson's "reality" out of 278 substantive letters (anything more than just "renew my subscription") between 1906 and 1912—just under 12 percent of correspondents.

44. Mary E. Knes (?) to David Grayson, 1907, box 1, file 2, David Grayson papers.

45. The "nature faker" controversy was in part a scientific debate over the relationship of the nonhuman world to the human. See Ralph H. Lutts, *The Nature Fakers: Wildlife, Science and Sentiment* (Charlottesville: University Press of Virginia, 1990).

46. For an insightful discussion of literary "fakery," see Wilson, *Labor of Words,* 35, 106, 128.

47. Back in 1864, *Ten Acres Enough* had sparked a similar debate in the pages of the *American Agriculturist.* See Loren C. Owings, *Quest for Walden: The "Country Book" in American Popular Literature* (Jefferson, NC: McFarland, 1997), 62.

48. Clipping, *Brooklyn (NY) Daily Eagle,* Jan. 25, 1908, David Grayson papers.

49. B. J. Hatmaker to David Grayson, 1907, box 1, file 2, David Grayson papers.

50. Ibid.

51. Ralph S. Howe to David Grayson, 1908, box 1, file 3, David Grayson papers.

52. Philip H. Kinsley to David Grayson, 1906, box 1, file 1, David Grayson papers.

53. Edward B. Leechow (?) to David Grayson, 1910, box 1, file 4, David Grayson papers.

54. I counted 41 letters in which the correspondents mentioned going back to the land themselves out of the 278 substantive letters received between 1906 and 1912. After 1912, almost no writers mention a return to the land—perhaps a response to the changing tone in the later books.

55. In an analysis of writers whose work was shaped by the early twentieth century's corporate transformation, Christopher Wilson writes, "If white collar fictions have a signature, it is the daydream" (*White Collar Fictions: Class and Social Representation in American Literature, 1885–1925* [Athens: University of Georgia Press, 1992], 18). In chapter 3, I argue that David Grayson's readers, and many would-be back-to-the-landers, were just such white-collar workers.

56. Mrs. Willie Mills to David Grayson, 1908, box 1, file 3, David Grayson papers.

57. Lena Walters to David Grayson, 1906, box 1, file 1, David Grayson papers.

58. John Van Breemen to David Grayson, 1907, box 1, file 2, David Grayson papers.

59. Henry Nelson to David Grayson, 1907, box 1, file 2, David Grayson papers.

60. Iva Whitman Robinson to David Grayson, 1908, box 1, file 3, David Grayson papers.

61. H. Waytum to David Grayson, 1906, box 1, file 1, David Grayson papers.

62. Unsigned to David Grayson, 1908, box 1, file 3, David Grayson papers.

63. This was not the only David Grayson imposter; they were numerous enough to warrant two large folders in the Jones Library's David Grayson collection (including requests for payment of hotel bills and notes from disappointed admirers).

64. Lilian M. Wilson to Ida M. Tarbell, Feb. 10, 1915, Imposters file, David Grayson papers.

65. Courtney Riley Cooper to Ray Stannard Baker, Imposters file, David Grayson papers.

66. Clipping, James R. Noland, "David Grayson Confesses He's Only Man from Wilds and Is Not Noted Author," *Denver Post,* Feb. 7, 1915, Imposters file, David Grayson papers.

67. The twist is even more bizarre: the man is now reportedly named "David Grayson-Ramsay," and is not only "one of the collaborators in the writing of the famous David Grayson stories," but also the "nephew of Sir William Ramsay, the noted English scientist." The story, complete with a photo of the bride, reports his marriage and details the "romance which had its inception at Grayson-Ramsay's American country place, Wide Ruins Trading Post, Arizona" ("'David Grayson' Will Wed Today," *Denver Post*, Feb. 21, 1915, Imposters file, David Grayson papers).

68. Della Thompson Lutes to John S. Phillips, Apr. 25, 1915, Imposters file, David Grayson papers.

69. David R. Grayson to Della Thompson Lutes, Apr. 12, 1915, Imposters file, David Grayson papers.

70. David R. Grayson to David Grayson, Nov. 9, 1914, Imposters file, David Grayson papers.

71. Lena Walters to David Grayson, 1906, box 1, file 1, David Grayson papers.

72. Madison Kuhn, *Michigan State: The First Hundred Years* (Lansing: Michigan State University Press, 1955).

73. Baker, *American Chronicle*, 229–31.

74. Ibid., 232. Both of Baker's biographers explore in some depth the role of the David Grayson writing as a fantasy escape for Baker. See Bannister, *Ray Stannard Baker*, especially x, 117–25; Semonche, *Ray Stannard Baker*, chap. 7.

75. Baker, *American Chronicle*, 183.

76. Baker, *Native American*, 286.

77. Baker, *American Chronicle*, 167.

78. Ibid., 185.

79. As Bannister puts it, as Grayson "Baker, in effect, debated with himself in public most of the issues that troubled his generation" (*Ray Stannard Baker*, x).

80. Grayson, *Adventures in Contentment*, 233.

81. Ibid., 38.

82. Ibid., 65.

83. Ibid., 136.

84. Ibid., 44.

85. Clipping, "Ik Marvel Afoot," *Chicago Evening Post*, Jan. 23, 1914, David Grayson papers.

86. Baker, *American Chronicle*, 516.

87. David Grayson, *Under My Elm: Country Discoveries and Reflections* (Garden City, NY: Doubleday, Doran, 1942), 125.

88. Ibid., 3–4.

Chapter 3. Who Wants a Farm?

1. "Does Anybody Really Want a Farm?" *World's Work*, Nov. 1911, 119. In this issue, too, as if to provide a model, Page's son Ralph W. Page wrote an article describing his decision to quit work as a lawyer and buy a farm in North Carolina.

2. "Do You Want a Farm?" *World's Work*, Dec. 1911, 235.

3. "A World's Work Farm Conference," *World's Work*, Apr. 1912, 614.

4. Conrad Taeuber and Irene B. Taeuber, *Changing Population of the United States* (New York: Social Science Research Council, 1958), 108.

5. George K. Holmes, "Movement from Cities and Towns to Farms," in *USDA 1914 Yearbook* (Washington, DC: Government Printing Office, 1914), 272.

6. William Lighton, "The Story of an Arkansas Farm—My Willamette Valley Postscript" (Portland, OR: Oregon Electric Railway, 1913), 5.

7. Of the forty-one correspondents who mentioned going back to the land—either that they wanted to do it or actually had done it—I was able to determine occupations for thirty-four.

8. Lewis G. Hosmer to David Grayson, 1912, box 1, file 7, David Grayson papers, Special Collections, Jones Library, Amherst, MA.

9. Theresa Jennings to David Grayson, 1912, box 1, file 7, David Grayson papers.

10. Edward Payson Powell, *How to Live in the Country* (New York: Outing Publishing, 1911), 256.

11. Mrs. R. J. McClintock, Washington Hotel, Fayetteville, to William Lighton, subseries 1, box 8, file 11, Lighton Family Papers, University of Arkansas Special Collections, Fayetteville, Arkansas.

12. Davis Parker Leach to David Grayson, 1907, box 1, file 2, David Grayson papers.

13. Pierce A. Chamberlain to David Grayson, 1907, box 1, file 2, David Grayson papers.

14. Horace Hendrick to David Grayson, 1907, box 1, file 2, David Grayson papers.

15. Rodney A. Elward to David Grayson, 1907, box 1, file 2, David Grayson papers.

16. George Adams to David Grayson, 1907, box 1, file 2, David Grayson papers.

17. N. T. Lauderbach Walker to David Grayson, 1907, box 1, file 2, David Grayson papers.

18. William James, "The Powers of Men," *American Magazine*, Oct. 1907, 57–65. One example is Freeman Tilden's story of a middle-aged professor: *Second Wind: The Plain Truth about Going Back to the Land* (New York: Huebsch, 1917).

19. Lena Walters to David Grayson, 1906, box 1, file 1, David Grayson papers.

20. Caroline Storrs to David Grayson, 1907, box 1, file 2, David Grayson papers.

21. Edward Payson Powell, *The Country Home* (New York: McClure, Phillips, 1904), 23–24.

22. "Does Anybody Want a Farm? The Answer," *World's Work*, Jan. 1912, 352.

23. Grayson, *Adventures in Contentment* (Garden City, NY: Doubleday, Page, 1906), 3.

24. Edward Payson Roe, *Driven Back to Eden* (New York: Dodd, Mead, 1885), 12.

25. E. R. Murphy to David Grayson, 1906, box 1, file 1, David Grayson papers.

26. Grayson, *Adventures in Contentment*, 6.

27. Matthew Lytle to David Grayson, 1907, box 1, file, 2, Grayson papers.

28. David Gray, "The Promised Land: Making a Country Home," *Collier's*, Mar. 13, 1909, 16. Perhaps this "David Gray" is a pseudonym intended to piggyback on the popularity of "David Grayson."

29. Mowbray, "Going Back to the Soil," *World's Work,* Jan. 1901, 268.

30. Because of the difficulty of comparing census occupational categories across time, these numbers are necessarily approximate. The original data comes from a published account (probably by founder William Ellsworth Smythe) listing 114 members' occupations in "The People of the Little Lands," *Little Landers in America,* Mar. 1916, 130. This list included 20 professionals, 16 clerical and sales workers, 38 skilled blue-collar workers, 8 retail or wholesale business owners, 2 service workers, and 28 people who had been farmers or gardeners before coming to the Little Lands. Before I located this source, I had searched census records using an earlier published list of members, finding 57 of them in the records. That smaller sample yielded an occupational profile very similar to this one. I determined to use the larger list from the published account after having compared it with my other source to check for biases.

31. The 1910 census taker in San Ysidro indicated which residents were part of the Little Landers' colony. Not all colonists were there by 1910, but I used those names, supplemented by other materials, to compile my list of occupations.

32. Ninety-five of the people who wrote to David Grayson between 1906 and 1912 made reference to an occupation (their own or that of the breadwinner of their household). I used the federal census to identify the occupations of another 65 writers, bringing the number of those with known occupations to 160. I looked first for the occupation of the person who wrote to David Grayson. If that person had no occupation, I counted the occupation of whoever was the breadwinner of the household. I never caught anyone lying to David Grayson about his or her occupation, so I assume that the letter writers were more or less honest.

33. This does not mean that blue-collar workers were not interested in returning to the farm or even that they did not read Grayson books. Baker later reported that he had communicated not only with accountants and clerks but also with railroad workers, police officers, and even factory workers about returning to the land (*Under My Elm: Country Discoveries and Reflections* [Garden City, NY: Doubleday, Doran, 1942], 116–25). Little Lands promotional writers also assumed that their readers knew David Grayson's works. (See, for example, Eleanor Pallette Eastman, "A New 'Adventure in Contentment,'" *Little Landers in America,* Mar. 1916, 94.) Moreover, the census occupational categories in these years were notoriously slippery. One 1910 article in the *Craftsman* featured the story of a Toledo printer named George Mueller. The census confirmed that Mueller was a printer. Charles Govier, the author of the story, was also in the census: he was described as a "foreman printer"—a blue-collar job—not "author." Govier's wife, however, was listed as a "magazine short story writer"—a professional.

34. Occupational categories are notoriously inaccurate, but "teacher" and "stenographer" are typically less slippery categories than "mechanic" or "manufacturer." I have followed the practice of the Minnesota Population Center at the University of Minnesota, which devised a means of comparing occupations over time for its Integrated Public Use Microdata Series by using the occupational categories of the 1950 census. I made one change: dividing the "professional" category in two. For a useful discussion of change in occupations over the twentieth century, see Ian D. Wyatt and Daniel E.

Hecker, "Occupational Changes in the Twentieth Century," *Monthly Labor Review* 129, no. 3 (2006): 35–57.

35. For example, these white-collar correspondents may have been responding disproportionately to the "dreamlike" quality of the Grayson fiction. My understanding of the impact of the transformation of white-collar occupations has been shaped by Christopher P. Wilson's *White Collar Fictions: Class and Social Representation in American Literature, 1885–1925* (Athens: University of Georgia Press, 1992), in which he asserts that "if white collar fictions have a signature, it is the daydream" (18).

36. The seventh was a waiter ("Does Anybody Want a Farm? The Answer," 354–55).

37. They might have written to the *Jewish Daily Forward* instead, as Abraham D. Lavender and Clarence B. Steinberg describe in *Jewish Farmers of the Catskills* (Gainesville: University Press of Florida, 1995), 23.

38. Robert Alan Goldberg reports that 29 percent were white-collar workers; this group probably included more store clerks and fewer teachers than the Grayson group, but the pattern is interesting (*Back to the Soil: The Jewish Farmers of Clarion, Utah, and Their World* [Salt Lake City: University of Utah Press, 1986], 31).

39. James Gilbert, *Work without Salvation: America's Intellectuals and Industrial Alienation, 1880–1910* (Baltimore, MD: Johns Hopkins University Press, 1977), xii.

40. These aggregate figures can reveal only a very general pattern, since different occupational categories were used in different decades.

41. Walter D. Moody, *Men Who Sell Things* (New York: McClure, 1907), qtd. in Timothy B. Spears, *100 Years on the Road: The Traveling Salesman* (New Haven, CT: Yale University Press, 1995), 196.

42. In 1900, the teaching workforce was three-quarters female, but barely 50 percent of high school teachers were women, and 95 percent of principals were men (John L. Rura, "Who Became Teachers? The Social Characteristics of Teachers in American History," in *American Teachers: Histories of a Profession at Work*, ed. Donald Warren [New York: Macmillan, 1988], 27).

43. Ray Stannard Baker, *American Chronicle* (New York: Charles Scribner's Sons, 1945), 52.

44. See Christopher Wilson, *The Labor of Words: Literary Professionalism in the Progressive Era* (Athens: University of Georgia Press, 1985), 149, on Phillips and Wilson, *White Collar Fictions*, 69, on Ferber.

45. Tilden, *Second Wind*, 131.

46. Gabriel Davidson, *Our Jewish Farmers and the Story of the Jewish Agricultural Society* (New York: L. B. Fischer, 1943), 67.

47. Jerome J. Bjelopera, *City of Clerks: Office and Sales Workers in Philadelphia, 1870–1920* (Urbana: University of Illinois Press, 2005), 17.

48. "Does Anybody Want a Farm? The Answer," 354–55.

49. "Who Became Teachers?" 28.

50. William W. Woodcock to David Grayson, 1909, box 1, file 4, David Grayson papers.

51. C. W. Govier, "How a Printer Bought a Five-Acre Farm with the Savings of His Salary," *Craftsman*, Apr. 1912, 99.

52. Truman A. DeWeese, *The Bend in the Road, and How a Man of the City Found It* (New York: Harper and Brothers, 1913), 207.

53. Mowbray, "Going Back to the Soil," 268.

54. *Historical Statistics of the United States, Colonial Times to 1970* (Washington, DC: Bureau of the Census, 1975), 175. These early statistics are often incomplete or based on faulty methods, but they provide a useful general basis for comparison.

55. Ibid., 165.

56. Scott Derks, ed., *The Value of a Dollar: Prices and Incomes in the United States, 1860–1998* (New York: Grey House, 1999), 52.

57. Qtd. in Goldberg, *Back to the Soil*, 31.

58. Lisa M. Fine, *The Souls of the Skyscraper: Female Clerical Workers in Chicago, 1870–1930* (Philadelphia: Temple University Press, 1990), 43; *Historical Statistics*, 168; *Value of a Dollar*, 52.

59. *Historical Statistics*, 321.

60. Ibid.

61. Bolton Hall, *A Little Land and a Living* (New York: Arcadia Press, 1908), 32–33.

62. Harrison Whittingham, *That Farm: Recounting the Adventures of a Dry-Goods Merchant Who Went Back to the Land* (Garden City, NY: Doubleday, Page, 1914), 228.

63. Grayson, *Adventures in Contentment*, 3.

64. Qtd. in "Does Anybody Want a Farm? The Answer," 352.

65. Will Carleton, *One Way Out: A Middle-Class New Englander Emigrates to America* (Boston: Small, Maynard, 1911), 42.

66. Liberty Hyde Bailey, "Can I Make a Farm Pay?" *World's Work*, Mar. 1901, 548.

67. Bjelopera, *City of Clerks*, 18.

68. Bailey, "Can I Make a Farm Pay?" 549.

69. Williams Ellsworth Smythe, *City Homes on Country Lanes: Philosophy and Practice of the Home-in-a-Garden* (New York: Macmillan, 1921), 70.

70. Bolton Hall, *The New Thrift* (New York: Huebsch, 1923), 108.

71. *New York Times*, May 13, 1908.

72. John R. Shook, ed., *Early Defenders of Pragmatism*, vol. 1 (Bristol, UK: Thoemmes Press, 2001), x n.2.

73. Powell, *Country Home*, 31.

74. William Justin Harsha, "A Clergyman's Gamble with Uncle Sam," *Outlook*, Jan. 3, 1917, 24.

75. "Reverend Doctor Harsha Departs," *New York Times*, Dec. 18, 1899.

76. Powell, *How to Live in the Country*, 254–55.

77. Arthur Markley Judy, "From the Study to the Farm: A Personal Experience," *Atlantic Monthly*, May 1915, 600.

78. DeWeese, *Bend in the Road*, 5.

79. Frederick Rockwell, *The Key to the Land: What a City Man Did with a Small Farm* (New York: Harper and Brothers, 1912), 65.

80. Ibid., 38.

81. Judy, "From the Study to the Farm," 611.

82. Ellen Cook, "Letter from a Farmer's Wife," *American Magazine*, Apr. 1909, 630.

83. William Lighton, "The Story of an Arkansas Farm," 8.

84. "Does Anybody Want a Farm? The Answer," 355.

85. Whittingham, *That Farm*, 17.

86. "Letter from Mrs. Caroline H. De Long of Kalamazoo, Michigan," *World's Work*, Apr. 1912, 619.

87. Robert C. Bannister discusses Grayson's women readers from another angle in "Adventures in Discontentment: David Grayson and Women Readers," in *Roots and Renewals*, ed. Mark Shackleton and Maarika Toivonen (Helsinki: University of Helsinki, Renvall Institute for Area and Cultural Studies, North American Studies Program, 2001), 127–37.

88. Elizabeth Haywood to David Grayson, 1910, box 1, file 5, David Grayson papers.

89. Bessie Alcott-Carret to David Grayson, 1911, box 1, file 6, David Grayson papers.

90. Mary Knes (?) to David Grayson, 1907, box 1, file 2, David Grayson papers.

91. Christopher Morley, *Parnassus on Wheels* (Garden City, NY: Doubleday, Page, 1917), n.p.

92. Persis Mather Cone to David Grayson, 1907, box 1, file 2, David Grayson papers.

93. James Harlean, "Cutting Loose from the City—III: How Two Women—A Mother and Daughter—Established a 'Department Farm' in Maryland and Made It Pay," *Country Life in America*, Dec. 1910, 158.

94. Gustav Stickley, "Women as Farmers," *Craftsman*, June 1912, 346–47.

95. Katherine Jellison argues that farm women in the early twentieth century did welcome new technological aids but that they rejected progressive propaganda that suggested that such technologies would "liberate" them from productive work and allow them to become full-time "home-makers" (*Entitled to Power: Farm Women and Technology, 1913–1963* [Chapel Hill: University of North Carolina Press, 1993], xx–xxii and throughout).

96. Hal Barron reports, for example, that about half the farm women surveyed in a rural northern community in the 1920s still baked all or most of their own bread, although store-bought bread was readily available. The women told the surveyors that their choice was not motivated primarily by a desire to save money (*Mixed Harvest: The Second Great Transformation in the Rural North, 1870–1930* [Chapel Hill: University of North Carolina Press, 1997], 237–38).

97. Powell, *Country Home*, 23–24.

98. Gustav Stickley, "A Country Home for the Business Man: A Second Visit to Craftsman Farms," *Craftsman*, Oct. 1910, 59.

99. That corresponds roughly with the pattern among letter writers in general: a little over half of the women who wrote to David Grayson were single, divorced, or widowed.

100. The story of Zoe M. Gilbert was pieced together by Mary Lou Pozzo, *Founding Sisters: Life Stories of Tujunga's Early Women Pioneers* (Tujunga, CA: Zinnia Press, 2005), 237.

101. On the Frish-Souto household and the Linaberry-Osgood household, see Pozzo, *Founding Sisters*, 233, 357, respectively; on Mabel Free Dean and Emma Kraft, see Pozzo, *Founding Sisters*, 213. I have supplied additional census information.

102. Alice Dinsmoor to David Grayson, 1909, box 1, file 4, David Grayson papers.

103. Florence Folsom to David Grayson, 1908, box 1, file 3, David Grayson papers.

104. Qtd. in *Founding Sisters*, 261. This account was first published in 1923 in the *Tujunga (CA) Record-Ledger* and reprinted in 1952 as *The Green Verdugo Hills* (Tujunga, CA: The Record-Ledger Press, 1952).

105. That they missed the boat suggests an interesting larger question. Most historians have been rather dismissive of back-to-the-landers and their producerist fellow travelers, viewing them as, among other things, defenders of antiquated notions of household patriarchy. One historian who did express sympathy, Christopher Lasch, did so as part of a sustained attack on the New Left's embrace of identity politics, sexual liberation, and especially feminism. (This position is articulated most clearly in *The True and Only Heaven: Progress and Its Critics*.) The story I am telling here suggests, however, that back-to-the-land enthusiasm was not necessarily at odds with feminism or individualism in general.

106. Smythe, *City Homes on Country Lanes*, 185–87.

107. Caroline Storrs to David Grayson, 1907, box 1, file 2, David Grayson papers.

108. Holmes, "Movement from Cities and Towns to Farms," 272.

109. Hal Tubbs to David Grayson, 1910, box 1, file 5, David Grayson papers.

110. W. H. Chamberlin to David Grayson, 1909, box 1, file 4, David Grayson papers.

111. Alice Dinsmoor to David Grayson, 1909, box 1, file 4, David Grayson papers. The next year, Dinsmoor wrote an article for the *Craftsman* detailing her experience as a truck farmer. Its clever title, "Three Acres and Chains," referred to the fact that she had not yet been able to achieve the profits promised by Bolton Hall in *Three Acres and Liberty* (*Craftsman*, Apr. 1910, 61–62).

112. Rodney Elward to David Grayson, 1907, box 1, file 2, David Grayson papers.

113. Matthew Lytle to David Grayson, 1907, box 1, file 2, David Grayson papers.

114. Matthew Lytle to David Grayson, 1910, box 1, file 5, David Grayson papers.

Chapter 4. From Little Lands to Suburban Farms

1. One writer reported a drop in publications on all agricultural subjects: "In 1917 there were 442 books published upon agriculture; in 1921, but 49" (David Stone Kelsey, *Kelsey's Rural Guide: A Practical Handbook* [Boston: Atlantic Monthly Press, 1925], vii).

2. Bolton Hall to "Dan," June 23, 1917, Bolton Hall letters, box 1, Bolton Hall papers, New York Public Library.

3. In the Bolton Hall papers, there is a reply from Eugene Debs to a letter Hall had written during his July 16, 1918, sedition trial; a letter from Samuel Gompers, thanking

Hall for his arguments against the Sedition Act, January 27, 1920; and a series of letters written by Hall during December 1920 protesting the presidential pardon of a German spy instead of Debs.

4. Clipping *New York World*, Mar. 14, 1926, box 2, Bolton Hall papers.

5. McMillen, the editor of *Farm and Fireside* at the time and later of *Country Home* and the *Farm Journal*, advocated the development of farm-produced chemical products for industry ("Wheeler McMillen, 99, a Pioneer in Industrial Use of Farm Crops," *New York Times*, Mar. 6, 1992).

6. Wheeler McMillen, *Farming Fever* (New York: Appleton, 1924), 9–10.

7. Richardson Wright, *Truly Rural: Adventures in Getting Back to the Earth* (Boston: Houghton Mifflin Company, 1922), 7.

8. David Grayson, *Adventures in Understanding* (Garden City, NY: Doubleday, Page, 1925), 1.

9. David Grayson, *Adventures in Contentment* (Garden City, NY: Doubleday, Page, 1906), 6.

10. Grayson, *Adventures in Understanding*, 7.

11. The annual average of migration from cities to farms in the 1920s was 1.3 million, as compared to an average of nearly 2 million from farms to cities (Frank Lorimer, *Statement on Farm Population Trends* [Washington, DC: Bureau of Agricultural Economics, 1940], 6).

12. See, for example, Elwood Mead, "Buying a Farm in the New Way: The Success of California's New Plan," *Ladies Home Journal*, June 1919, 36; Henry Irving Dodge, "Back to the Land for Soldiers: An Interview with Franklin K. Lane, Secretary of Interior," *Country Gentleman*, Feb. 15, 1919, 3–4, 43–47; and Elwood Mead, "Solution of the Land Question," *New Republic*, Apr. 29, 1916, 348–49.

13. David Vaught, *Cultivating California: Growers, Specialty Crops, and Labor, 1875–1920* (Baltimore, MD: Johns Hopkins University Press, 1999), 17–21.

14. Kevin Starr, *Inventing the Dream: California through the Progressive Era* (New York: Oxford University Press, 1985), 165, 46.

15. Warren E. Johnston and Alex F. McCalla, "A Stylized History of California Agriculture from 1769 to 2000," in *Whither California Agriculture: Up, Down, or Out? Some Thoughts about the Future*, Giannini Foundation of Agricultural Economics, Special Report series, June 1, 2004, http://repositories.cdlib.org/giannini/srs/SR041.

16. William Ellsworth Smythe, *The Conquest of Arid America* (New York: Harper and Brothers, 1899), 93.

17. Fresno developer Bernhard Marks, qtd. in Vaught, *Cultivating California*, 21–23.

18. David Vaught points out that California fruit growers were enthusiastic boosters for their way of life, portraying their work on small plots of land as the agrarian ideal, fostering both independence and professional expertise (*Cultivating California*, 3–14).

19. The story of the reclamation movement has been explored by several historians. Donald J. Pisani's studies provide a comprehensive and thoughtful analysis. Pisani argues that Smythe (as well as his colleague George H. Maxwell and to a lesser degree

Frederick H. Newell) was motivated by an "anachronistic homemaking ideal," rooted in a nineteenth-century "homestead ethic," which ultimately led to failure and to capitulation to the technocratic forces that came to control the irrigation projects (*Water and American Government: The Reclamation Bureau, National Water Policy, and the West, 1902–1935* [Berkeley: University of California Press, 2002], esp. chap. 1, "Saving Lost Lives: Irrigation and the Ideology of Homemaking"). In a related vein, Laura Lovett argues that for Smythe and particularly for Maxwell, irrigation and back-to-the-land projects were rooted in a nostalgic faith in the traditional patriarchal family. Lovett's analysis of Maxwell's career is part of a larger discussion of pronatalism in the United States (*Conceiving the Future: Pronatalism, Reproduction, and the Family in the United States, 1890–1938* [Chapel Hill: University of North Carolina Press, 2007], chapter 3, "Reclaiming the Home: George H. Maxwell and the Homecroft Movement").

20. George H. Maxwell was another important liaison between promoters of California agriculture, back-to-the-landers, and the reclamation movement. He was the principal propagandist for federal reclamation, operating as a lobbyist with the support of seven major railroads, which bankrolled his efforts and supported the National Irrigation Association he organized. He also edited (and apparently wrote) a magazine called *Maxwell's Talisman* and sponsored a series of suburban back-to-the-land communities outside several eastern cities. See Lovett, *Conceiving the Future*, chapter 3.

21. N. O. Nelson to Bolton Hall, Feb. 1, 1912, Bolton Hall letters, box 1, Bolton Hall papers. Nelson was a single-tax colleague; he was responding to a query from Hall, who had received a request for help from Smythe.

22. James R. Kluger, *Turning Water on with a Shovel: The Career of Elwood Mead* (Albuquerque: University of New Mexico Press, 1992), 24.

23. William Ellsworth Smythe, "For a Nation of Little Landers," in *Official Proceedings of the Nineteenth National Irrigation Congress*, ed. Arthur Hooker (Chicago: Donnelley and Sons, 1912), 178.

24. Ibid., 179–80.

25. William Ellsworth Smythe, *City Homes on Country Lanes: Philosophy and Practice of the Home-in-a-Garden* (New York: Macmillan, 1921), envoi.

26. The best account of San Ysidro is Lawrence B. Lee, "The Little Landers Colony of San Ysidro," *Journal of San Diego History* 21, no. 1 (1975): 26–48. A near-contemporary account is Henry S. Anderson, "The Little Landers' Land Colonies: A Unique Agricultural Experiment in California," *Agricultural History* 5, no. 4 (1931): 139–50.

27. A handwritten note in the margin of the census schedule for the township of Otay indicates the colony's limits.

28. William Ellsworth Smythe, "Quest of the Fortunate Life," *West Coast Magazine*, June 1913, 4.

29. John L. Cowan, "The Hope of the Little Landers: The Story of San Ysidro, California, Where Families Prosper on Two Acres and a Quarter," *World's Work*, Nov. 1911, 96–100; Olga Brennecke, "One Acre and Happiness: As Demonstrated by the Little Landers of San Ysidro Valley," *Craftsman*, Aug. 1912, 556–58.

30. William Ellsworth Smythe, *World's Fair Colony, 1915: Little Landers* (San Francisco: Society of the Little Lands, 1915).

31. Hartranft bought the land from the vast holdings of the Kern County Land Company and subdivided it for resale. The Wasco Historical Society's account is on the city's website (http://www.ci.wasco.ca.us/Public_Documents/WascoCA_WebDocs/wasco_history).

32. *Report of the Commission on Land Colonization and Rural Credits of the State of California* (Sacramento: California State Printing Office, 1916), 50. (Mead is not listed as the author, but he was the chair of the commission.)

33. Ibid., 79–80.

34. Smythe, "For a Nation of Little Landers," 180.

35. The ages are based on the census; San Ysidro residents were identified by the 1910 census itself; Los Terrenitos residents were identified from a membership list published in 1913 in *The Western Empire*, Bolton Hall scrapbook 1, Bolton Hall papers.

36. Smythe, *World's Fair Colony*, 10.

37. This was Peter Faber, a real estate developer who worked with Charles Weeks to establish the Palo Alto agricultural community called Runnymede (qtd. in Lee, "Little Landers Colony of San Ysidro," 44).

38. Smythe, "For a Nation of Little Landers," 177.

39. Smythe, *City Homes on Country Lanes*, 188–89.

40. The families selected to settle in Durham were required to possess at least $1,500 in savings, but the 110 families who were chosen possessed an average of $6,700—substantial start-up capital that probably could have been matched by only one or two of the Little Landers of San Ysidro or Los Terrenitos (Andrew Needham, "Qualified to Succeed: Elwood Mead and the Durham Agricultural Colony, 1915–1919," http://userwww.sfsu.edu/~epf/1996/mead.html).

41. Elwood Mead, *Helping Men Own Farms* (New York: Macmillan, 1920), 1.

42. Paul Conkin, *Tomorrow a New World* (Ithaca, NY: Cornell University Press, 1959), 7.

43. Bill G. Reid, "Agrarian Opposition to Franklin K. Lane's Proposal for Soldier Settlement, 1918–1921," *Agricultural History* 41, no. 2 (1967): 169.

44. The story is told in Kluger, *Turning Water on with a Shovel*, 99.

45. Charles Weeks, *Egg Farming in California* (n.p: n.p., n.d.), 21.

46. Ibid., 19.

47. Charles Weeks, *One Acre and Independence* (n.p: n.p., n.d.), 105–6.

48. David Watters first introduced me to the connection to Frost at a New England American Studies Association conference in 2006. Joseph Conforti describes Frost's egg farming in connection with his analysis of the imaginative reinvention of northern New England (*Imagining New England* [Chapel Hill: University of North Carolina Press, 2001], 267).

49. For a fascinating study of the Jewish chicken ranchers of Petaluma, see Kenneth L. Kann, *Comrades and Chicken Ranchers: The Story of a California Jewish Community* (Ithaca, NY: Cornell University Press, 1993), 41.

50. Milo Hastings, *Dollar Hen* (1909; repr., Blodgett, OR: Norton Creek Press, 2003), 23.

51. Weeks, *One Acre*, 90.

52. Smythe, *City Homes on Country Lanes*, envoi.

53. Kann, *Comrades and Chicken Ranchers*, 40–41.

54. Celeste Dameron, oral history interview, 1989, Oviatt Library Digital Archives, California State University at Northridge, http://digital-library.csun.edu/oh/dameronc.

55. Kann, *Comrades and Chicken Ranchers*, 222.

56. Anderson, "Little Landers' Land Colonies," 146.

57. William Ellsworth Smythe to George H. Maxwell, Dec. 31, 1915, Bureau of Reclamation records, RG 115, National Archives, Washington, D.C, qtd. in Lee, "The Little Landers Colony of San Ysidro," 45.

58. Ad, "Charles Weeks Poultry Colony," 1923, Charles Weeks Collection, Oviatt Library Digital Archives, http://digital-library.csun.edu/u?/SFVH,3342.jpg.

59. Marlene A. Hitt, *Sunland and Tujunga: From Village to City* (Charleston, SC: Arcadia Press, 2002), 46.

60. Samantha Basking, "The 'True' Story: *Life Magazine*, Horace Bristol, and John Steinbeck's *The Grapes of Wrath*," *Steinbeck Studies* 15, no. 2 (2004): 39–74.

61. Sarah Lombard, *Rancho Tujunga: A History of Sunland/Tujunga, California* (Sunland, CA: Sunland Woman's Club, 1990), 35.

62. Ibid., 35–39.

63. *Report of the Commission*, 78.

64. Matthew F. Bokovoy, "Inventing Agriculture in Southern California," *Journal of San Diego History* 45, no. 2 (Spring 1999): 66–85. Bokovoy writes, "It is difficult . . . to discern whether the model farm was a progressive experiment designed to rationalize intensive-farming, or whether it was a developer-led scheme (suburbanization)."

65. Bolton Hall, *Three Acres and Liberty* (New York: Grosset and Dunlap, 1907), 379.

66. Weeks, *One Acre*, 6.

67. Smythe argued, for example, that the David Grayson stories were as appealing as they were because they did not really describe rural life but provided instead a "luminous example" of a "rich and satisfying blend of city and country life" (*City Homes on Country Lanes*, 41, 60–61).

68. See Andrew Weise, *Places of Their Own: African American Suburbanization in the Twentieth Century* (Chicago: University of Chicago Press, 2004), and Richard Harris and Robert Lewis, "The Geography of North American Cities and Suburbs, 1900–1950: A New Synthesis," *Journal of Urban History* 27, no. 3 (2001): 262. See also Mary Corbin Sies, "North American Suburbs, 1880–1950: Cultural and Social Reconsiderations," *Journal of Urban History* 27, no. 3 (2001): 313–46, who notes that middle-class suburbanites, too, kept substantial gardens and raised animals for food.

69. Smythe, *World's Fair Colony*, 16.

70. Weise, *Places of Their Own*, 216.

71. Becky M. Nicolaides, *My Blue Heaven: Life and Politics in the Working-Class Suburbs of Los Angeles, 1920–1965* (Chicago: University of Chicago Press, 2002), 4.

72. Qtd. in Nicolaides, *My Blue Heaven*, 18. Nicolaides notes that the pitch here was similar to that used by Smythe.

73. Becky M. Nicolaides, "Where the Working Man Is Welcomed: Working-Class Suburbs in Los Angeles, 1900–1940," *Pacific Historical Review* 68, no. 4 (1999): 537.

74. The Los Angeles Suburban Home Company, which developed Owensmouth, is rather well known, but not for its chicken colonies. The company was one of the interlocking ventures through which Los Angeles high rollers William Mulholland, Harrison Gray Otis, and others grabbed control of the Owens River to create the aqueduct that ensured Los Angeles a water supply—a story told in the movie *Chinatown*.

75. Nicolaides discusses the racial, ethnic, and class categories of the residents of South Gate in *My Blue Heaven*, chap. 2, "Peopling the Suburbs."

76. Nicolaides, *My Blue Heaven*, 42.

77. There were a few exceptions at Los Terrenitos: one married couple came from Rumania and two women who lived together were from Portugal and Austria.

78. Smythe, *City Homes on Country Lanes*, 171.

79. Marshall Hartranft, "My Hand Made Home in the Hills," c. 1922, reprinted in Mary Lou Pozzo, *Founding Sisters: Life Stories of Tujunga's Early Women Pioneers* (Tujunga, CA: Zinnia Press, 2005), 133.

80. Weeks, *Egg Farming*, 94; Weeks, *One Acre*, 133.

81. *San Diego (CA) Union*, qtd. in Lee, "Little Landers Colony of San Ysidro," 46.

82. "The Big Question of Marketing," *Little Landers Library*, 1909, 9.

83. Nicolaides, *My Blue Heaven*, 19.

84. Robert Higgs, "Landless by Law: Japanese Immigrants in California Agriculture to 1941," *Journal of Economic History* 38, no. 1 (1978): 205–25.

85. Gustav Stickley, "Small Farms a Solution for the Evils of Overcrowded Cities and Unnatural Living," *Craftsman*, June 1911, 309.

86. Weeks, *One Acre*, 107.

87. Mead, *Helping Men Own Farms*, 5.

88. *Report of the Commission*, 59.

89. George H. Maxwell, *Secret of Nippon's Power* (n.p.: n.p., n.d.), 68.

90. George H. Maxwell, *Our National Defense: The Patriotism of Peace* (Washington, DC: Rural Settlements Association, 1915).

91. William Ellsworth Smythe, "For a Nation of Little Landers," *Official Proceedings of the Nineteenth National Irrigation Congress*, 178–79.

92. Mead, *Helping Men Own Farms*, 10.

93. Robert M. Fogelson describes the role of the chamber of commerce in *Fragmented Metropolis* (Cambridge, MA: Harvard University Press, 1967), 70.

94. Los Angeles Chamber of Commerce, "Facts About Industrial Los Angeles: Nature's Workshop" (Los Angeles: Chamber of Commerce, 1927), in *Suburb Reader*, ed. Becky M. Nicolaides and Andrew Wiese (New York: Routledge, 2006), 203.

95. Ross H. Gast, *Vegetables in the California Garden* (Los Angeles: Leland Stanford Junior University, 1933), iii.

96. Ross H. Gast, "The Lure of the 'Little Farm' in the Suburbs," *Los Angeles Times*, Mar. 27, 1921.

97. Ross H. Gast, "The Southland Garden and Small Farm Home," *Los Angeles Times*, July 15, 1928.

98. Gast, *Vegetables in the California Garden*, Victory Garden ed. (abridged) (Los Angeles: Ross H. Gast, 1943), 4.

99. Anthony Alofsin, "Broadacre City: The Reception of a Modernist Vision, 1932–1988," *Center: A Journal for Architecture in America* 5 (1989): 18.

100. Frank Lloyd Wright, *The Disappearing City* (New York: William Farquhar Payson, 1932), 4.

101. Joseph Dana Miller, ed., *Single Tax Year Book: The History, Principles and Application of the Single Tax Philosophy* (New York: Single Tax Review Publishing Co., 1917), 197; Wright, *Disappearing City*, 59.

102. Wright, *Disappearing City*, 44.

103. Ibid., 8–9.

104. Edward Payson Powell, *The Country Home* (New York: McClure, Phillips, 1904), 3–7.

105. Edgar Chambless, *Roadtown* (New York: Roadtown Press, 1910), 39. The *New York Times* reviewed the book rather favorably ("'Roadtown' a New Idea," Oct. 10. 1910). Chambless apparently committed suicide in 1936, after failing to interest New Dealers in his idea (Joseph L. Arnold, *The New Deal in the Suburbs: A History of the Greenbelt Town Program, 1935–1954* [Columbus: Ohio State University Press, 1971], 104).

106. Alexander V. Chayanov, *The Journey of My Brother Alexei to the Land of Peasant Utopia*, qtd. in Allan C. Carlson, *Third Ways* (Wilmington, DE: ISI Books, 2007), 66. Chayanov was an agricultural economist who supported the idea of preserving the best features of traditional peasant subsistence farming and improving them with new kinds of cooperation and greater access to education. He died in the gulag in 1939.

107. Howard P. Segal, *Recasting the Machine Age: Henry Ford's Village Industries* (Amherst: University of Massachusetts Press, 2005).

108. Wright, *Disappearing City*, 61.

109. Ibid., 44, 61.

110. Ibid., 63.

111. Ibid., 62.

112. Ibid., 44–45.

113. Qtd. in Alofsin, "Broadacre City," 25.

114. In a typical twenty-first century flowering of connections, Flores is also the co-creator of a website, a blog, and a permaculture advocacy group, Food Not Lawns, in Eugene, Oregon.

115. Sharon Astyk, *Depletion and Abundance: Life on the New Home Front* (Gabriola Island, BC: New Society, 2008).

116. Sharon Astyk and Aaron Newton, *Nation of Farmers: Defeating the Food Crisis on American Soil* (Gabriola Island, BC: New Society, 2009).

Chapter 5. Subsistence Homesteads

1. Clipping, Lemuel F. Parton, "Who's News Today: Veteran Single-Taxer Crusades against the Slums," *New York Sun*, July 22, 1935, Bolton Hall scrapbook 1, Bolton Hall papers, New York Public Library.

2. "Put Them on Farms," *Survey*, May 15, 1931, 198; "Relief Gardens Multiply," *Survey*, June 15, 1932, 278.

3. Howard P. Segal, *Recasting the Machine Age: Henry Ford's Village Industries* (Amherst: University of Massachusetts Press, 2005).

4. "Stirred Up by Henry Ford's Shotgun Gardens," *Literary Digest*, Sep. 12, 1931, 10.

5. The government appraisal of the subsistence homesteads edited by Russell Lord and Paul H. Johnstone reported that one bill before Congress was known as the "Macfadden bill" and judged Macfadden "probably more responsible than any other single individual outside of the Congress for the legislation that established a subsistence-homesteads program" (*A Place on Earth: A Critical Appraisal of Subsistence Homesteads* [Washington, DC: U.S. Department of Agriculture, Bureau of Agricultural Economics, 1942], 23–24).

6. Russell Lord, "Back to the Farm?" *Forum and Century*, Feb. 1933, 98.

7. Arthur Pound, "Land Ho!" *Atlantic Monthly*, June 1933, 714–15.

8. "From Ghetto to Farm," *Literary Digest*, Apr. 25, 1931, 25.

9. Charlie May Simon, "Retreat to the Land: An Experience in Poverty," *Scribner's*, May 1933, 309.

10. M. G. Kains, *Five Acres and Independence: A Practical Guide to the Selection and Management of the Small Farm* (New York: Greenberg, 1935), 4.

11. Eleanor de la Vergne Risley, *Abandoned Orchard* (Boston: Little, Brown, 1932), 5–6.

12. Charles Morrow Wilson, *Country Living Plus and Minus* (Brattleboro, VT: Stephen Daye Press, 1938), 51–52.

13. Gove Hambidge, *Enchanted Acre: Adventures in Backyard Farming* (New York: McGraw-Hill, 1935), 17–18.

14. Charles Allen Smart, *RFD* (New York: Norton, 1938), 57.

15. Ibid.

16. Henry Tetlow, *We Farm for a Hobby and Make It Pay* (New York: William Morrow, 1938), 38.

17. Risley, *Abandoned Orchard*, 5–6.

18. Wilson, *Country Living Plus and Minus*, 51–52.

19. Gertrude Pahlow, *Cabin in the Pines* (New York: Burt, 1934), 9–10.

20. Ralph Borsodi, *Flight from the City: An Experiment in Creative Living on the Land* (New York: Harpers, 1933), 105.

21. Wilson, *Country Living Plus and Minus*, 42.

22. William B. Duryee, *A Living from the Land* (New York: McGraw-Hill, 1934), 13.

23. Hambidge, *Enchanted Acre*, 14.

24. Elliott Merrick, *From This Hill Look Down* (Brattleboro, VT: Stephen Daye Press), 36.

25. Smart, *RFD*, 146.

26. Frederick F. Van De Water, *A Home in the Country* (New York: Reynal and Hitchcock, 1937), 2.

27. Smart, *RFD*, 146.

28. Hambidge, *Enchanted Acre*, 5–6.

29. Ralph Borsodi, "Subsistence Homesteads: President Roosevelt's New Land and Population Policy," *Survey and Graphic*, Jan. 1934, 11. The New Deal Network makes this article and a wide variety of Depression-era materials available at its website: http://newdeal.feri.org.

30. Franklin D. Roosevelt, "Address before the American Country Life Conference on the Better Distribution of Population Away from Cities," Aug. 19, 1931, in *The Public Papers and Addresses of Franklin D. Roosevelt*, 13 vols. (New York: Random House, 1938–50), 1:503.

31. Franklin D. Roosevelt, "Annual Message to the Legislature," Jan. 6, 1932, in *Public Papers and Addresses of Franklin D. Roosevelt*, 1:112–13.

32. Franklin D. Roosevelt, "Impromptu Talk to the Boys of Bowdoin Farm," Aug. 10, 1933, in *Public Papers and Addresses of Franklin D. Roosevelt*, 3:320.

33. William Ellsworth Smythe, "For a Nation of Little Landers," in *Official Proceedings of the Nineteenth National Irrigation Congress*, ed. Arthur Hooker (Chicago: Donnelley and Sons, 1912), 177.

34. Lord, "Back to the Farm?" 100.

35. Wolfgang Schivelbusch argues that New Deal programs shared many features, both practical and ideological, with fascist programs. He writes that for Roosevelt, as for many fascists and Nazis, "the soil was like a magic substance that would miraculously regenerate a world devastated by capitalism" (*Three New Deals: Reflections on Roosevelt's America, Mussolini's Italy, and Hitler's Germany, 1933–1939* [New York: Picador, 2006], 115).

36. *Time*, May 7, 1934.

37. Paul Conkin's *Tomorrow a New World: The New Deal Community Programs* (Ithaca, NY: Cornell University Press, 1959) remains the only complete account of the subsistence homesteads projects. It is based in part on Lord and Johnstone's government-sponsored progress report, *A Place on Earth*. More detailed studies of individual projects include Jacob H. Dorn, "Subsistence Homesteading in Dayton, Ohio, 1933–1935," *Ohio History* 78, no. 1 (1969): 75–93; Fred C. Smith, "The Tupelo Homesteads: New Deal Agrarian Experimentation," *Journal of Mississippi History* 68, no. 2 (2006): 85–112; Brian Q. Cannon, *Remaking the American Dream: New Deal Rural Resettlement in the Mountain West* (Albuquerque: University of New Mexico Press, 1996); and Joseph L. Arnold, *The New Deal in the Suburbs: A History of the Greenbelt Town Program, 1935–1954* (Columbus: Ohio State University Press, 1971).

38. Robert Gough, *Farming the Cutover: A Social History of Northern Wisconsin, 1900–1940* (Lawrence: University Press of Kansas, 1997); Richard White, "Poor Men on Poor Lands: The Back to the Land Movement of the Early Twentieth Century," *Pacific Historical Review*, 49, no. 1 (1980): 105–31; Susan O. Haswell and Arnold R. Alanen, "Colonizing the Cutover: Wisconsin's Progressive-Era Experiments in Rural Planning," *Landscape Journal* 14, no. 2 (1995): 171–87; Arnold R. Alanen, "Midwestern Colonists in the Matanuska Valley: Settling Rural Alaska during the Great Depression," in Sally McMurry and Annmarie Adams, eds., *People, Power, Places*, Perspectives in Vernacular Architecture 8 (Knoxville: University of Tennessee Press, 2000), 53–80.

39. Arnold, *New Deal in the Suburbs*, 25.

40. Ibid., 85.

41. Lord and Johnstone counted 33 Division of Subsistence Homestead projects, 34 FERA projects, and nearly 100 additional projects for full-time farmers (*A Place on Earth*, 3). Donald Holley reports that altogether, the FSA sponsored more than 150 rural resettlement projects ("The Negro in the New Deal Resettlement Program," *Agricultural History* 5, no. 3 [1971]: 184). The National New Deal Preservation Association lists 62 projects under the Division of Subsistence Homesteads, the Federal Emergency Relief Administration and the Resettlement Administration; see http://www.newdeallegacy.org/new_deal_towns.html.

42. Conkin, *Tomorrow a New World*, 86.

43. M. L. Wilson, "The Place of Subsistence Homesteads in our National Economy," *Journal of Farm Economics* 16, no. 1 (1934): 74.

44. Ralph Borsodi also used the word "homestead" in *This Ugly Civilization* (1929), discussed in the coda to this chapter.

45. Bill G. Reid, "Agrarian Opposition to Franklin K. Lane's Proposal for Soldier Settlement, 1918–1921," *Agricultural History* 41, no. 2 (1967): 167–78.

46. Hambidge, *Enchanted Acre*, 24–25.

47. Andrew Lytle, "The Small Farm Secures the State," in *Who Owns America? A New Declaration of Independence*, ed. Allen Tate and Herbert Agar (1936; repr., Washington, DC: University Press of America, 1983), 238.

48. Wilson, "The Place of Subsistence Homesteads," 76–77.

49. Paul K. Conkin, "The Vision of Elwood Mead," *Agricultural History* 34, no. 2 (1960): 96. Conkin argues that Mead's vision played a critical role in shaping the New Deal plans for agricultural colonies.

50. Becky M. Nicolaides, "Where the Working Man Is Welcomed: Working-Class Suburbs in Los Angeles, 1900–1940," *Pacific Historical Review* 68, no. 4 (1999): 517–59.

51. Charles C. Cohan, "Small Acreage Homes Here Beckon to Thousands," *Los Angeles Times*, Sep. 9, 1934.

52. Harold M. Finley, "Uncle Sam Points the Way Back to the Land," *Los Angeles Times*, Dec. 30, 1934.

53. "These Men, This Land: The Man Who Told the Truth about California," *Free America*, May 1940, 12.

54. Finley, "Uncle Sam Points the Way."

55. "Rural Home Head Quits," *Los Angeles Times*, Oct. 31, 1935.

56. See, for example, Ross Gast, "Small Farm Dwelling Plan Seen Permanent," *Los Angeles Times*, Nov. 10, 1935.

57. Lord and Johnstone, *Place on Earth*, 100–102.

58. "These Men, This Land," 12.

59. Lord and Johnstone, *Place on Earth*, 98.

60. Ibid., 99.

61. Ibid., 102.

62. "Rural Home Head Quits," *Los Angeles Times*, Oct. 31, 1935.

63. Robert Alan Goldberg explores the story of Brown and the Clarion community in *Back to the Soil: The Jewish Farmers of Clarion, Utah, and Their World* (Salt Lake City: University of Utah Press, 1986). For the meeting between Brown and Wilson, see Conkin, *Tomorrow a New World*, 261.

64. Paul Conkin writes, "Almost the total program of the Division of Subsistence Homesteads and the Resettlement Administration had been anticipated by the work of Jewish organizations in colonization, part-time farming, decentralization of industry, rehabilitation, and social engineering" (*Tomorrow a New World*, 256).

65. There were members of the radical Jewish labor union usually called the Bund, socialists, Zionists (who were also usually socialists), and anarchists (Goldberg, *Back to the Soil*, 49).

66. Pearl Seligman, "Notes for an Intellectual History of Jersey Homesteads (Roosevelt, New Jersey)—A Successful Experiment in Democracy and Creation of Community," http://pluto.njcc.com/~ret/Roosevelt/pearl.html.

67. Ellen Eisenberg, *Jewish Agricultural Colonies in New Jersey, 1882–1920* (Syracuse, NY: Syracuse University Press, 1995), chap. 6, "Dissolution of the Colonies."

68. Goldberg, *Back to the Soil*, 45.

69. "Member of the Hightstown Farm Group Says, 'Who Says Jews Can't Farm?'" Library of Congress American Memory project, http://memory.loc.gov/ammem/fsahtml.

70. Seligman, "Notes."

71. "Hightstown Homesteaders Live Millionaire's Life," *Newark (NJ) Sunday Call*, Aug. 2, 1936; "Costly Homesteads Blunders Left to Rot Tax Money Away," *Asbury Park (NJ) Press*, Feb. 22, 1938, 1–2; Ralph F. Armstrong, "Four Million Dollar Village," *Saturday Evening Post*, Feb. 5, 1938), 5–7, 36, 38, 39; "Einstein Likes Jersey Project: Scientist Is Amazed at Progress Achieved at Homesteads," *Asbury Park (NJ) Press*, Oct. 24, 1936.

72. Ralph H. Danhof, who wrote the report on Jersey homesteads in Lord and Johnstone's *A Place on Earth*, offers a bemused description of the conflict between government agents and the workers at Jersey Homesteads, highlighting the colonists' "cultural background" of "intense competition, personal striving, and shrewd bargaining and trading." "Jersey Homesteads," *A Place on Earth*, 155.

73. Federal Writers' Project, *Stories of New Jersey* (New York: M. Barrows, 1938), 209–15.

74. The mural can be viewed at http://www.njn.net/arts/shahn/mural.html.

75. Rutgers University Special Collections holds the papers of Jersey Homesteads. Its essay on the "History of Roosevelt, New Jersey" gives the most detailed overview of the colony, at http://www.libraries.rutgers.edu/rul/libs/scua/roosevelt/rstory.shtml.

76. Lord and Johnstone, *A Place on Earth*, 3.

77. Conkin, *Tomorrow a New World*, 213.

78. Recently historians have assessed the subsistence homestead projects not so much for cost overruns or poor management but for whether they helped those whom they were trying to help. Brian Q. Cannon, for example, takes issue with Conkin and other earlier historians who attributed the programs' failures to the participants' "culture of poverty" (*Remaking the Agrarian Dream: New Deal Rural Resettlement in the Mountain West* [Albuquerque: University of New Mexico Press, 1996]).

79. The community of Roosevelt began to take account of itself in an effort to defend itself from development. The entire municipality is now a registered historic district. Its story is available at the Fund for Roosevelt's website, http://pluto.njcc.com/~ret/ffr/. Similarly, for Arthurdale and Penderlea, see http://www.arthurdaleheritage.org and http://www.penderleahomesteadmuseum.org/.

80. The historian quoted is Steven Haid (http://www.arthurdaleheritage.org/history/a-cooperative-community).

81. Ann S. Cottle, *The Roots of Penderlea: A Memory of a New Deal Homestead Community* (Wilmington: University of North Carolina, Department of Creative Writing, 2008), 33.

82. Ibid., 42–43.

83. Seligman, "Notes."

84. The American Studies program at the University of Virginia maintains a website on the 1930s that includes a history of Aberdeen Gardens based on interviews with residents: "Aberdeen Gardens: Building a Community 'By Blacks, for Blacks,'" http://xroads.virginia.edu/~ug99/lane/introduction.html.

85. Resettlement Administration projects like these were not, strictly speaking, back-to-the-land projects, since they were geared toward landless tenant farmers already on the land. In my view they fit because they attempt to foster self-sufficiency and independence by offering people access to small plots of land.

86. Jess Gilbert and Spencer D. Wood, "Experiments in Land Reform and Racial Justice: The New Deal State and Local African-Americans Remake Civil Society in the Rural South, 1935–2004," paper delivered at the Rural Sociological Society Annual Meeting, Aug. 2004, Sacramento, CA, http://cgirs.ucsc.edu/conferences/whitefood/foodx/papers/gilbert.pdf.

87. Lord and Johnstone, *A Place on Earth*, 184.

88. Ralph Borsodi, *Flight from the City: An Experiment in Creative Living on the Land*, rev. ed. (Suffern, NY: School of Living, 1947), 64.

89. Ibid., 131–32.

90. Myrtle Mae Borsodi, "The New Woman Comes Home," *Scribner's*, Feb. 1937, 52–57; Dorothy Van Doren, "Breadwinner or Breadmaker?" *Scribner's*, May 1937, 33–34. See also Sara S. Moser and Myrtle Mae Borsodi, "Are Housewives Slaves: A Debate," *The Forum*, Sep. 1938, 114–19.

91. Jacob Dorn refers to the charitable organization as the Dayton Bureau of Community Service, but contemporary magazine accounts give the name as the Council of Social Agencies ("Subsistence Homesteading in Dayton, Ohio, 1933–1935," 77).

92. For the whole story, see Jacob Dorn, "Subsistence Homesteading in Dayton, Ohio." See also William H. Issel, "Ralph Borsodi and the Agrarian Response to Modern America," *Agricultural History* 41, no. 2 (1967): 155–66.

93. Issel, "Ralph Borsodi," 155.

94. Conkin, *Tomorrow a New World*, 122.

95. Borsodi, *Flight from the City*, rev. ed., xiii.

96. Borsodi, "Subsistence Homesteads," 11.

97. Borsodi, *Flight from the City*, 127.

98. Years later, Borsodi's second-in-command and chief administrator Mildred Loomis wrote that Borsodi had *always* counseled the Dayton project against accepting government money and that he had resolved from the beginning to quit the project if they accepted federal funds. Borsodi, however, recalled that he had been the one who went to Washington to solicit funds in the first place. See Mildred Loomis, "Ralph Borsodi's Principles for Homesteaders," *Land and Liberty* 75, no. 1015 (1978): 85–87, http://www.cooperativeindividualism.org/loomis_borsodi_bio.html, and "Dr. Ralph Borsodi: Legendary Back-to-the-Land Figure," *Mother Earth News*, Mar./Apr. 1974, 8.

Chapter 6. "I'll Take My Stand" (in Vermont)

1. Willard T. Davis and Malcolm Cowley, "How Far Back to the Land," *New Republic*, Aug. 9, 1933, 336.

2. Louis M. Hacker, "Plowing the Farmer Under," *Harper's*, June 1934, 69–74.

3. See William E. Leverette Jr. and David E. Shi, "Agrarianism for Commuters," *South Atlantic Quarterly* 79 (1980): 204–18, and "Herbert Agar and *Free America*: A Jeffersonian Alternative to the New Deal," *Journal of American Studies* 16, no. 2 (1982): 189–206.

4. The best-known English distributists were G. K. Chesterton and Hilaire Belloc, whom George Bernard Shaw referred to as the single entity "Chesterbelloc." Before World War I, distributist politics leaned toward labor politics, anti-imperialism, and Kropotkin-style anarchism, but after the war, many moved toward the right. Some supported Franco and Mussolini, some supported monarchy and the end of the British Parliament. See Jay P. Corrin, *G. K. Chesterton and Hilaire Belloc: The Battle against Modernity* (Athens: Ohio University Press, 1981).

5. Herbert Agar, "Free America," *Free America*, Jan. 1937, 1.

6. Agar, "Free America," 3. During the first year of publication, *Free America* writers referred to themselves as "distributists," but in 1938 they started calling themselves

"decentralists." They wanted to create a more inclusive term but also to distinguish their group from the more established U.S. distributist paper, the *American Review*, which was closely allied to the distributist movement in England. They dropped their ties to that magazine because of publisher Seward Collins's open support for fascism. See Leverette and Shi, "Agrarianism for Commuters," 215.

7. This account may be a little "Agar-centric," since he often spoke for the whole group. It somewhat understates the degree to which some *Free America* writers supported positions that look a lot like socialism and also somewhat underplays the vehemence with which others—Borsodi in particular—rejected collectivist solutions.

8. Herbert Agar and Allen Tate, eds., *Who Owns America?* (New York: Houghton Mifflin, 1936), vii–viii.

9. *Free America*, Jan. 1939, 2.

10. www.mutualist.org.

11. Ralph Borsodi, "Decentralization," *Free America*, Jan. 1938, 4.

12. On decentralism, see Edward S. Shapiro, "Decentralist Intellectuals and the New Deal," *Journal of American History* 58, no. 4 (1972): 938–57; Leverette and Shi, "Herbert Agar and *Free America*"; and Leverette and Shi, "Agrarianism for Commuters." See also Allan Carlson, *The New Agrarian Mind: The Movement toward Decentralist Thought in Twentieth-Century America* (New Brunswick, NJ: Transaction Publishers, 2000).

13. *New York Herald*, Jan. 24, 1938, qtd. in David Shi, *The Simple Life: Plain Living and High Thinking in American Culture* (New York: Oxford University Press, 1985), 240–41.

14. Ralph Borsodi, "Some Aspects of Homesteading," *Free America*, Jan. 1937, 11.

15. George Marion O'Donnell, "Looking Down the Cotton Row," in *Who Owns America?* 173.

16. *Free America*, Mar. 1937, 7.

17. Chard Powers Smith, "Something to Do Now," *Free America*, Jan. 1937, 6.

18. Andrew Nelson Lytle, "The Hind Tit," in *I'll Take My Stand: The South and the Agrarian Tradition* (Baton Rouge: Louisiana State University Press, 1977), 216–17.

19. Christian Gauss, "E Pluribus Unum," *Free America*, Sep. 1937, 16. Gauss was for many years dean of the college at Princeton. His daughter Katherine Gauss Jackson was an editor of *Free America*.

20. Over time, some reacted against the centralizing power of the New Deal, and others against the racially egalitarian potential in the projects. Political scientist Herman C. Nixon continued to support the New Deal's plans to extend farm tenancy programs and worked on behalf of the rural southern poor, including African Americans (Paul K. Conkin, *Southern Agrarians* [Knoxville: University of Tennessee, 1988], 100–102, 116).

21. One fifth of those who wrote to the *World's Work*—twenty—were looking for farms in New York or New Jersey. Eight aimed for New England; twelve were interested in Arkansas, Missouri, or Oklahoma; ten wanted to move to the Midwest; sixteen wanted Florida; twenty-four the south Atlantic states, and eleven the Pacific northwest (*World's Work*, Apr. 1912, 614).

22. Bernard DeVoto, "New England: There She Stands," *Harper's*, Mar. 1932, 405–15.

23. This is necessarily a subjective list, but the pattern is very clear. My list was compiled from a variety of sources, including the annotated bibliography in Loren Owings, *Quest for Walden: The "Country Book" in American Popular Literature* (Jefferson City, NC: McFarland, 1997). I have identified forty-two back-to-the-land and country life titles published between 1930 and 1946. Twenty-three are set in New England, five in other northeastern states, and five in the greater New York suburbs. One is set in the mountains of North Carolina, and three concern the Ozarks. I did not attempt to distinguish closely between country life titles and back-to-the-land books in this case because the categories overlapped to such a degree during the Depression.

24. Elswyth Thane, *Reluctant Farmer* (New York: Duell, Sloane and Pearce, 1950), 14.

25. "Ruth Mattie Cross," *The Handbook of Texas On-Line,* http://www.tshaonline.org/handbook/online/articles/CC/fcr46.html.

26. See, for example, Lucile Grebenc, *Under Green Apple Boughs* (Garden City, NY: Doubleday, Doran, 1933), 4.

27. My discussion of *Yankee Magazine* and Robert Frost follows the analysis of Joseph Conforti in *Imagining New England: Explorations of Regional Identity from the Pilgrims to the Mid-Twentieth Century* (Durham: University of North Carolina, 2001), chap. 6, "The North Country and Regional Identity: From Robert Frost to the Rise of *Yankee* Magazine, 1914–1940."

28. I counted twenty-three New England books published between 1930 and 1946. Ten were set in Vermont, seven in Connecticut, two in New Hampshire, three in Maine, and one in Massachusetts. (None were set in Rhode Island). Nearly all the books with a clear back-to-the-land agenda, as opposed to a playful or literary country life theme, were set in Vermont.

29. DeVoto, "New England: There She Stands," 410–11.

30. "Old Faithful," *New York Times,* Sep. 10, 1936. For some reason—perhaps having to do with *New York Times* editorial board vacationing practices—such jokes tended to be about Vermont rather than Maine.

31. Sara Gregg, "Can We Trust Uncle Sam? Vermont and the Submarginal Lands Project, 1934–1936," *Vermont History* 69, nos. 1/2 (2001): 201–21.

32. *Congressional Record,* 75th Cong., 3rd sess., 1938, Appendix, pt. 9:655.

33. Apparently that was not quite what he said. Mark A. Stoler sets the record straight in "What Did He Really Say? The 'Aiken Formula' for Vietnam Revisited," *Vermont History* 46, no. 2 (1978): 100–108.

34. Crane Brinton, review of *Speaking from Vermont* by George Aiken, *New England Quarterly* 12, no. 4 (1939): 172.

35. George Aiken, *Speaking from Vermont* (New York: Frederick Stokes, 1938), 159.

36. Aiken also made the shrewd point that what hurt the highland farms was not their inherent unsuitability for agriculture but market forces and changes in technology. The uplands had traditionally produced fine hay crops, but hay was no longer in much demand since horses had been replaced by automobiles. What market forces had destroyed, he implied, they might also resurrect in the future (ibid., 13–17, 21).

37. "These Men, This Land: The Man from Vermont," *Free America*, July 1940, 12–13.

38. Cooperative ventures were an important part of the decentralist agenda, since they substituted voluntary collective organization for government-run programs ("These Men, This Land," 14).

39. Qtd. in Conforti, *Imagining New England*, 291.

40. For example, frequent *Free America* contributor Vrest Orton wrote against the Green Mountain Parkway in *Yankee* in 1936, and *Free America* editor Chard Powers Smith wrote an article in *Yankee* in 1940 about the contributions of newcomers to the life of rural villages. But there appears to have been a significant difference in tone between the two magazines. As Joseph Conforti argues, *Yankee* was not an openly political magazine until New England "fell" to the Democrats in 1936. In 1937, the magazine came out of the closet: "Editorially and personally we are fed up with the New Deal. . . . We just can't take it any more." *Yankee* was not decentralist, however; it was "going Republican" (Conforti, *Imagining New England*, 303).

41. Dorothy Thompson, "Concerning Vermont," *Free America*, Oct. 1937, 4–5.

42. Some people who knew Orton assert that this was a completely serious proposal. One contends that "he never joked." Still, Orton's suggestion that Vermont "conquer New Hampshire outright and annex her as a colony, comparable to Siberia," strikes me as playful.

43. Vrest Orton, "Vermont—for Vermonters," *Driftwind*, July 1928, 26. Nicholas Clifford has discussed these essays in the contemporary secessionist journal *Vermont Commons* ("Take Back Vermont—in 1929: Vrest Orton and Green Mountain Independence," *Vermont Commons* 17 [2007], http://www.vtcommons.org/journal/2007/02/nicholas-clifford-take-back-vermont-1929-vrest-orton-and-green-mountain-ndependence).

44. Orton was wrong to imply that Vermont had no homegrown "factories belching smoke" ("How to Make Vermont Free," *Driftwind*, Jan. 1929, 145–46). The bitter strike at the Vermont Marble Company in the winter of 1935—the year when a child labor law was defeated in the Vermont Assembly by a vote of 229 to 6—is ample evidence that "crushing the workers and breaking their souls" was not something that could be attributed solely to outside influences.

45. Orton, "Vermont—for Vermonters," 27; Orton, "The White Elephant Road," *Yankee*, Feb. 1936, 37.

46. Orton, "Vermont—for Vermonters," 27.

47. Vrest Orton, "Country Industry," *Free America*, Aug. 1939, 10.

48. Vrest Orton, "Baby Yard and Bar Trays," *Free America*, July 1940, 17.

49. Crane Brinton, review of *Forays and Rebuttals* by Bernard DeVoto, *New England Quarterly* 10, no. 1 (1937): 172–73.

50. Richard Judd, *The New Deal in Vermont: Its Impact and Aftermath* (New York: Garland, 1979), 28.

51. Orton, "Country Industry," 9.

52. Elliott Merrick, "Sold Out to Bigness," *Free America*, Apr. 1937, 1–2, 16.

53. Vrest Orton, "A Village Experiment," *Free America*, June 1937, 9.

54. Chard Powers qtd. in Conforti, *Imagining New England*, 289.

55. It was a "cream puff," Katherine Gauss Jackson wrote, in comparison with Elliott Merrick's *From This Hill Look Down* or Muriel Follett's *New England Year* (*Free America*, Nov. 1940, 19).

56. Frederick F. Van de Water, *A Home in the Country* (New York: Reynal and Hitchcock, 1937), 1–2.

57. Ibid., 24.

58. Ibid.

59. Frederick F. Van de Water, *Reluctant Republic* (New York: John Day, 1941), 134.

60. Van de Water, *A Home in the Country*, 59–60, 70–71.

61. Ibid., 164.

62. Samuel Ogden, *This Country Life* (Rodale Press: Emmaus, Pennsylvania, 1973), 3.

63. Ibid., 14.

64. Samuel Ogden, *This Country Life* (New York: A. S. Barnes, 1946), 40.

65. Ibid., 6.

66. Samuel Ogden's gardening expertise became legendary. His first book, *How to Grow Food for Your Family* (1942), was reprinted twice in the 1970s. Ogden's grandson Shepherd Ogden later took up his mantle, becoming a highly regarded garden writer in the 1990s.

67. Ogden, *This Country Life*, 103.

68. Even his one Vermont book, *Country Living Plus and Minus*, declared his Arkansas roots. Wilson dedicated it to his mentor, Charles Finger, who was an Arkansas newspaperman, author, single-tax advocate, and comrade of Bolton Hall.

69. Charles Morrow Wilson, *Country Living Plus and Minus* (Brattleboro, VT: Stephen Daye Press, 1938), 39.

70. Ibid., 62.

71. Lytle, "The Hind Tit," 226–27.

72. Steinbeck, *The Grapes of Wrath* (New York: Penguin Books, 2002), 35–36.

73. Wilson, *Country Living Plus and Minus*, 38.

74. Ibid., 232.

75. Elliott Merrick, *From This Hill Look Down* (Brattleboro, VT: Stephen Daye Press, 1934), 22.

76. Merrick, "Sold Out to Bigness," 2.

77. Merrick, *From This Hill*, 29–30.

78. Walter Hard introduction, Merrick, *From This Hill*, 8.

79. Merrick, "Sold Out to Bigness," 16.

80. For Nearing's version, see Scott Nearing, *The Making of a Radical: A Political Autobiography* (New York: Harper and Row, 1972), and *Man's Search for the Good Life* (1954; repr., Harborside, ME: Social Science Institute, 1974). See also Stephen J. Whitfield, *Scott*

Nearing: Apostle of American Radicalism (New York: Columbia University Press, 1974), and John Saltmarsh, *Scott Nearing: The Making of a Homesteader* (Philadelphia: Temple University Press, 1991).

81. Helen Nearing tells her version of the story in *Loving and Leaving the Good Life* (White River Junction, VT: Chelsea Green Press, 1992). See also Margaret O. Killinger, *The Good Life of Helen K. Nearing* (Lebanon, NH: University Press of New England, 2007).

82. The story of the maple enterprise is told by Helen Nearing and Scott Nearing, *The Maple Sugar Book* (White River Junction, VT: Chelsea Green Press, 2000). This fiftieth anniversary edition includes a useful epilogue by Greg Joly exploring the publishing history of the book and the social context of the maple operation.

83. Helen Nearing and Scott Nearing, *Living the Good Life* (New York: Schocken, 1970), 4.

84. Nearing and Nearing, *Maple Sugar Book*, 214–15.

85. Nearing and Nearing, *Living the Good Life*, 16

86. Nearing and Nearing, *Maple Sugar Book*, 239.

87. Nearing and Nearing, *Living the Good Life*, 15.

88. Van de Water, *A Home in the Country*, 26.

89. In the 1940s, several members of Helen's family also moved to Vermont (Nearing, *Loving and Leaving*, 100; Killinger, *Good Life*, 46, 56–58).

90. Nearing and Nearing, *Maple Sugar Book*, 202.

91. Ibid., 246.

Chapter 7. Back to the Garden

1. Marguerite Lyon, *Take to the Hills: A Chronicle of the Ozarks* (New York: Grosset and Dunlap, 1941), introduction, n.p.

2. David Grayson, *Under My Elm* (Garden City, NY: Doubleday, Doran: 1942), 2–4.

3. Ibid., 116–18 (emphasis in original).

4. Among the titles that appeared were Don West, *Broadside to the Sun* (1946); Alfred and Helen Campbell, *Applejack for Breakfast* (1946); Haydn S. Pearson, *Success on the Small Farm* (1946) and *Successful Part-Time Farming* (1947); Eugene Hahnel, *Down to Earth: The Pleasures and Perils of Becoming a Farmer* (1947); Ladd Haystead, *The Squires Can Take It* (1948); Austin Jacobs, *We Chose the Country* (1948); and Gina Allen, *Rustic for Keeps* (1948). One might also mention the works of Louis Bromfield, a conservationist and advocate of sustainable farming who recounted his return to his family's Ohio farm in *Pleasant Valley* (1945). He followed *Pleasant Valley* with *Malabar Farm* (1948).

5. Farm populations grew rather than declined at just two points in the twentieth century: in the years 1932 to 1933 and in 1946. Joseph P. Ferrie, "Internal Migration," in chapter Ac of *Historical Statistics of the United States, Earliest Times to the Present: Millennial Edition*, edited by Susan B. Carter, Scott Sigmund Gartner, Michael R. Haines, Alan L. Olmstead, Richard Sutch, and Gavin Wright (New York: Cambridge University Press, 2006). http://dx.doi.org/10.1017/ISBN-9780511132971.Ac.ESS.01.

6. Available at Oldtime Radio Archives, http://otrarchive.blogspot.com/2009/04/granbys-green-acres.html.

7. I was able to identify only two other back-to-the-land books published in the 1950s, both at the very beginning of the decade: Herbert Jacobs, *A Practical Guide for the Beginning Farmer* (1951), and a reprint of M. G. Kains, *Five Acres and Independence* (1951), first published in 1935. "Country life" books did continue to be popular through the 1940s and 1950s and were often written by such well-regarded authors as Henry Beston, Hal Borland, Gladys Taber, and Louis Bromfield. After the Depression and the war were over, however, these books were easily distinguished from back-to-the-land books by their focus on the natural environment and a leisured country "lifestyle."

8. Greg Joly and Rebecca Lepkoff, *Almost Utopia: The Residents and Radicals of Pikes Falls, Vermont, 1950* (Barre: Vermont Historical Society, 2008). Lepkoff's 1950 photographs depict the community just before Cold War anticommunist pressure broke it apart.

9. The story of Melbourne Village is told in Richard C. Crepeau, *Melbourne Village: The First Twenty-Five Years, 1946–1971* (Orlando: University of Central Florida Press, 1988).

10. Ralph Borsodi, *Flight from the City: An Experiment in Creative Living on the Land*, rev. ed. (Suffern, NY: School for Living, 1947), xv.

11. Communes—sometimes but not always with a back-to-the-land component—appear to have peaked in numbers around 1970 (Hugh Gardner, *The Children of Prosperity: Thirteen Modern American Communes* [New York: St. Martin's Press, 1978]).

12. "News from Mother: Who Reads Mother Anyway?" *Mother Earth News*, Sep./Oct. 1977, 24.

13. Margaret O. Killinger, *The Good Life of Helen K. Nearing* (Lebanon, NH: University Press of New England, 2007), 76.

14. Mildred Loomis, introduction, John Seymour and Sally Seymour, *Farming for Self-Sufficiency: Independence on a Five-Acre Farm* (New York: Schocken, 1973), 2.

15. The performance at Big Sur is captured on YouTube: http://www.youtube.com/watch?v=PIDoxiQsE.

16. One obvious exception is the groundbreaking work of Jeffrey Jacob, *New Pioneers: The Back-to-the-Land Movement and the Search for a Sustainable Future* (University Park: Pennsylvania State University Press, 1997). Jacob's focus is on back-to-the-landers of the 1980s and 1990s, however.

17. Terry Allan Simmons gathered data from a small area in British Columbia—a hotbed of back-to-the-land activities in the 1970s. On the basis of those numbers, he calculated that there were around 15,000 back-to-the-landers in British Columbia and speculated that there might be as many as 1,343,750 back-to-the-landers in the United States and over one and a half million in North America ("But We Must Cultivate Our Garden: Twentieth-Century Pioneering in Rural British Columbia" [PhD diss., University of Minnesota, 1979], 189–94). Jacob refers to that last figure in *New Pioneers*, 3. Eleanor Agnew then cites Jacob's reference in her own study, *Back from the Land: How Young Americans Went to Nature in the 1970s and Why They Came Back* (Chicago: Ivan R. Dee, 2004), 5.

18. "Hobbling Back to Nature," *Nation*, Mar. 21, 1907, 259.

19. Gardner, *Children of Prosperity*, 10.

20. Helen Nearing and Scott Nearing, *Continuing the Good Life* (New York: Harper and Row, 1979), 360.

21. Jean Hay Bright, *Meanwhile, Next Door to the Good Life* (Dixmont, ME: Bright-Berry Press, 2003), 8.

22. Helen Nearing and Scott Nearing, *The Good Life: Helen and Scott Nearing's Sixty Years of Self-Sufficient Living* (New York: Schocken, 1989), 358–59.

23. Richardson Wright, *Truly Rural: Adventures in Getting Back to the Earth* (Boston: Houghton Mifflin, 1922), 1.

24. For example, Jerry Bledsoe, *You Can't Live on Radishes: Some Funny Things Happened on the Way Back to the Land* (Greensboro, NC: Grape Hill Press, 1976); Terry Silber, *A Small Farm in Maine* (New York: Doubleday, 1988); Agnew, *Back from the Land*; Tom Fels, *Farm Friends: From the Late Sixties to the West Seventies and Beyond* (North Bennington, VT: RSI Press, 2008); Bright, *Meanwhile, Next Door to the Good Life*; Wallace Kaufman, *Coming Out of the Woods: The Solitary Life of a Maverick Naturalist* (Cambridge, MA: Perseus Books, 2000).

25. Ray Mungo, *Famous Long Ago, My Life and Hard Times with Liberation News Service, at Total Loss Farm, and on the Dharma Trail* (New York: Citadel Press, 1990), 357.

26. Ibid., 191.

27. Gordy Stewart qtd. in Agnew, *Back from the Land*, 72.

28. Richard W. Langer, *Grow It! The Beginner's Complete in-Harmony-with-Nature Small Farm Guide* (New York: Avon Books, 1972), xi.

29. Linda Tatelbaum, *Carrying Water as a Way of Life: A Homesteader's History* (Appleton, ME: About Time Press, 1997), 46.

30. Agnew was dismayed by what she perceived as Eliot Coleman's flippant rejection of the need for insurance at a 1976 meeting of the Maine Organic Farmers' Association (Coleman was—and is now once again—an important figure in the back-to-the-land movement, in part because he was a protégé of the Nearings) (*Back from the Land*, 157).

31. "News from Mother: Who Reads Mother Anyway?" 24.

32. Jacob, *New Pioneers*, 48.

33. Jacob places the "readers" and "doers" he studies along a continuum, suggesting that going back to the land is not a single action but a process.

34. Richard Smith, "Homestead Ridge," *Mother Earth News*, July/Aug; 1979, 150.

35. Paul Edwards, "Report from Them That's Doin'," *Mother Earth News*, Mar./Apr. 1976, 76.

36. "Homesteading in the Kootenays," *Mother Earth News*, May/June 1970, 54.

37. Langer, *Grow It!* xi–xii.

38. Agnew argues that the rising cost of living and especially health care in the late 1970s and early 1980s undercut the ability of back-to-the-landers to make ends meet. While those economic difficulties might have encouraged more people to return to the land, she believes that they were also responsible for many failures (*Back from the Land*, 156–57).

39. John Vivian, *The Manual of Practical Homesteading* (Emmaus, PA: Rodale Press, 1975), 2.

40. Ibid., 1.

41. Joan Wells, *Downwind from Nobody* (Charlotte, VT: Garden Way Publishing, 1978), 4.

42. Dale Grant, "Visit to the Canadian Hog Farm," *Mother Earth News*, Mar./Apr. 1971, 54.

43. David Gumpter, "The New Pioneers," *Mother Earth News*, Sep./Oct. 1971, 38.

44. "How to Make It Your Way," *Mother Earth News*, Jan./Feb. 1970, 6.

45. Patricia Crawford, *Homesteading: A Practical Guide to Living off the Land* (New York: Macmillan, 1975), x.

46. Margaret Cheney, *Meanwhile Farm* (Millbrae, CA: Les Femmes Publishing, 1975), 177–78.

47. Ibid.

48. Jeanne Tetrault and Sherry Thomas, *Country Women: A Handbook for the New Farmer* (Garden City, NY: Doubleday, 1976). This is a compilation of articles from a journal of the same name.

49. Joyce Cheney, ed., *Lesbian Land* (Minneapolis, MN: Word Weavers, 1985). These publishers also brought out *Maize: A Lesbian Country Magazine*.

50. Wells, *Downwind from Nobody*, 223.

51. Jacob, *New Pioneers*, 144–45.

52. Mungo, *Famous Long Ago*, 214–15.

53. Cheney, *Meanwhile Farm*, 2–3, 133.

54. Langer, *Grow It!* xiii.

55. Mungo, *Famous Long Ago*, 215.

56. Ibid., 369.

57. John Shuttleworth, "The Plowboy Interview," *Mother Earth News*, Mar./Apr. 1975, 7.

58. Seymour and Seymour, *Farming for Self-Sufficiency*, 246.

59. Gove Hambidge, *Enchanted Acre: Adventures in Backyard Farming* (New York: McGraw-Hill, 1935), 5–6.

60. Langer, *Grow It!* 3.

61. John Shuttleworth, introduction to excerpt from Everett G. Reid, *The Good Acre*, *Mother Earth News*, July/Aug. 1973, 46.

62. David Robinson, *The Complete Homesteading Book: Proven Methods for Self-Sufficient Living* (Charlotte, VT: Garden Way Publishing, 1974), 13.

63. Paul Goodman, introduction, Helen Nearing and Scott Nearing, *Living the Good Life* (New York: Schocken, 1970), ix–x.

64. Robert Swann, "Peace, Civil Rights, and the Search for Community," chaps. 2 and 3, http://www.smallisbeautiful.org/about/biographies/swann_autobiography/swann_toc.html.

65. Decentralism was the philosophical backbone of Carl Oglesby's leadership of the Students for a Democratic Society. It also shaped the trajectory that moved arch-conservative Karl Hess—the speechwriter who gave the Goldwater campaign the immortal words "Extremism in the defense of liberty is no vice"—to oppose the war in Vietnam and ally himself with the left.

66. Vivian Ellen Rose offers a perceptive analysis of Mildred Jensen Loomis's role in creating a link between Borsodi's old-school decentralism and the new movements of the 1960s and 1970s ("Homesteading as Social Protest: Gender and Continuity in the Back to the Land Movement in the United States, 1890–1980" [PhD diss., State University of New York, Binghamton, 1997]).

67. Borsodi spent much of his time in India during the 1950s, collaborating with Indian political leader Jayaprakash Narayan on several projects.

68. "A Testimonial," *Green Revolution*, Dec. 1977, 6.

69. Shuttleworth, "Plowboy Interview," 9.

70. Ibid., 11.

71. John Shuttleworth, "Why the Magazine Was Founded, What It Has Accomplished during the First Ten Years, and What It Expects to Do during the Next Decade," *Mother Earth News*, Nov./Dec. 1979, 43. These were his last words on the subject. Shuttleworth, "an overworked genius suffering a well-deserved burnout," as a later chronicler recalled, sold the magazine to three of its employees (Sara Pacher, "The Story of Mother Earth News," *Mother Earth News*, Mar./Apr. 1990, 94–100).

72. Michael Gold, *Daily Worker*, qtd. in Scott Nearing, *The Making of a Radical* (Harborside, ME: Social Science Institute, 1972), 152.

73. "Living the Good Life with Helen and Scott Nearing," *Mother Earth News*, Mar./Apr. 1977, 40. The article is attributed to unnamed *Mother Earth News* editors but has the sound of Shuttleworth's writing.

74. Jean Hay, "The Personal Price of Free Speech—Scott Nearing: 1883–1983," Apr. 1997, at http://www.jeanhay.com/OTHER/SCOTT.HTM.

75. Rose argues that it was Helen who created the depoliticized image of Scott; I find her argument persuasive, but here it appears that Scott was following his own inclination ("Homesteading as Social Protest," 249).

76. John Shuttleworth, "Helen and Scott Nearing, Counterculture Authors, Speakers, and Farmers," *Mother Earth News*, Sep./Oct. 1971, 8.

77. Nearing and Nearing, *Living the Good Life*, 135.

78. Helen Nearing, *Loving and Leaving the Good Life* (White River Junction, VT: Chelsea Green, 1992), 96.

79. Nearing, and Nearing *Living the Good Life*, 135–36.

80. "The Wisdom of Helen and Scott," *Mother Earth News*, Mar./Apr. 1980, 56.

81. This assessment is based on a survey of *Mother Earth News* and 1970s books. *Green Revolution* did occasionally mention Henry George, Bolton Hall, and, once or twice, even Kropotkin in articles tracing the ideological evolution of decentralism. Scott Nearing described his experience at Arden in his biographical writing, which was read by far

fewer people than was *Living the Good Life* (*Man's Search for the Good Life* [1954; repr. Harborside, ME: Social Science Institute, 1974], 1–4).

82. Nearing and Nearing, *Living the Good Life*, xviii.

83. The most complete reassessment of the legacy of the Nearings is Jean Hay Bright's *Meanwhile, Next Door to the Good Life*. In addition to narrating her experiences living next door to the Nearings in Maine, Bright systematically dissects the undisclosed sources of the Nearings' income. Greg Joly provides a thoughtful assessment of the maple sugar business as an epilogue to *The Maple Sugar Book* (White River Junction, VT: Chelsea Green, 2000) that includes a careful account of the people (mostly unnamed in the Nearings' books) who worked the maple sugar operation with the Nearings. Killinger supplies important correctives to the official version of the story in *The Good Life of Helen K. Nearing*.

84. Agnew reports that most of her informants were too cash strapped to afford better plumbing and heating systems (*Back from the Land*, 26).

85. Ibid., 195–96.

86. Tatelbaum, *Carrying Water*, 2.

87. Ibid., 59.

88. Bright, *Meanwhile, Next Door to the Good Life*, 35.

89. Ibid., 198.

90. Tatelbaum, *Carrying Water*, 4.

91. Agnew, *Back from the Land*, 121.

92. Tatelbaum, *Carrying Water*, 4.

93. Ralph Borsodi, *This Ugly Civilization* (New York: Simon and Schuster, 1929), 231.

94. Terry Silber, *A Small Farm in Maine* (New York: Doubleday, 1988), 4–5.

95. Qtd. in Fels, *Farm Friends*, 55.

96. Among Jacob's informants, more people reported working with environmental activist organizations than rated as "important" or "very important" the essential back-to-the-land act of growing their own food (*New Pioneers*, 179–80).

97. For example, Jean Hay Bright found herself struggling against a proposed nuclear power plant (*Meanwhile, Next Door to the Good Life*, 161–68), and Linda Tatelbaum got involved in a project to limit subdivisions along her dirt road in inland Maine (*Carrying Water*, 40–62).

98. Agnew, *Back from the Land*, 112, and chaps. 5, 6, and 7.

Epilogue

1. Jeffrey Jacob, *New Pioneers: The Back to the Land Movement and the Search for a Sustainable Future* (University Park: Pennsylvania State University Press, 1997), 26.

2. William Ellsworth Smythe, *City Homes on Country Lanes: Philosophy and Practice of the Home-in-a-Garden* (New York: Macmillan, 1921), 59; Julie Flaherty, "Living by the Books; Vermont Publisher Succeeds with Guides for a Simpler Life," *New York Times*, June 19, 1999.

3. *USA Today* reported in 2009 that the seed company Burpee was expecting a growth of 25 percent in demand that spring and that other companies were experiencing increases from 5 percent to as much as 80 percent (Bruce Horovitz, "Recession Grows Interest in Seeds, Vegetable Gardening," *USA Today*, Feb. 20, 2009).

4. Verlyn Klinkenborg, "Sow Those Seeds!" *New York Times*, Feb. 14, 2009.

5. Natasha Metzler, "Michelle Obama Expands the White House Garden," *Christian Science Monitor*, Apr. 1, 2010.

6. http://www.meetup.com/Los-Angeles-Urban-Chicken-Enthusiasts.

7. Damien Cave, "In Recession, Americans Doing More, Buying Less," *New York Times*, Jan. 2, 2010.

8. Eric Schlosser, *Fast Food Nation* (New York: Penguin, 2002), 4–5.

9. Gene Logsdon, *The Contrary Farmer* (White River Junction, VT: Chelsea Green Press, 1994), xiii.

10. Sharon Astyk, *Independence Days: A Guide to Sustainable Food Storage and Preservation* (Gabriola Island, BC: New Society Publishers, 2009), 13.

11. Advertisement for Jerome D. Belanger's *The Complete Idiot's Guide to Self-Sufficient Living, Countryside and Small Stock Journal*, May/June 2010, 28.

12. Australian artist Tanya Curnow made the film, now widely available on a variety of websites and on YouTube.

13. Sharon Astyk, *Depletion and Abundance: Life on the New Home Front* (Gabriola Island, BC: New Society, 2008).

14. Matthew B. Crawford, *Shop Class as Soul Craft* (New York: Penguin, 2009), 47, 6.

15. Dwight Garner, "Real Men Don't Eat Quiche—They Ride Hogs Over It," *New York Times*, May 28, 2009.

16. Peggy Orenstein, "The Femivore's Dilemma," *New York Times*, Mar. 11, 2010.

17. Shannon Hayes, *Radical Homemaker: Reclaiming Domesticity from a Consumer Culture* (Richmondville, NY: Left to Write Press, 2009), 13.

18. McClaughry and Baldwin were both founders of the E. F. Schumacher Society, established in 1980 to build "strong local economies that link people, land, and community" (www.smallisbeautiful.org).

19. Frank Bryan and John McClaughry, *The Vermont Papers: Recreating Democracy on a Human Scale* (Chelsea, VT: Chelsea Green Press, 1989), 1.

20. Linda Tatelbaum, *Carrying Water as a Way of Life: A Homesteader's History* (Appleton, ME: About Time Press, 1997), 46.

21. Some areas have more options than others, of course. The map provided by Local Harvest, a web-based directory of "small farms, farmers markets, and other local food sources," shows many more CSAs and farmers' markets in the eastern states and on the west coast than in the desert and mountain states (www.localharvest.org).

22. Kim Severson, "Many Summer Internships Are Going Organic," *New York Times*, May 24, 2009.

23. Carla Emery, *The Encyclopedia of Country Living* (Seattle, WA: Sasquatch Books, 2008), v.

24. Bolton Hall, *A Little Land and a Living* (New York: Arcadia Press, 1908), 32–33.

25. Ben Ehrenreich, "How to Survive the Crisis (Organize!)," *Nation*, Aug. 2/9, 2010, 27–28.

Index

The Trashing of Margaret Mead: Anatomy of an Anthropological Controversy
Paul Shankman

*The Presidents We Imagine: Two Centuries of White House Fictions on the Page,
    on the Stage, Onscreen, and Online*
Jeff Smith

*Unsafe for Democracy: World War I and the U.S. Justice Department's Covert Campaign
    to Suppress Dissent*
William H. Thomas Jr.